ZAGATSURVEY®
25TH ANNIVERSARY

2004/05

PARIS RESTAURANTS

Local Editors: Alexander Lobrano, Mary Deschamps

Local Coordinator: Claire Fitzpatrick

Editor: Troy Segal

Published and distributed by
ZAGAT SURVEY, LLC
4 Columbus Circle
New York, New York 10019
Tel: 212 977 6000
E-mail: paris@zagat.com
Web site: www.zagat.com

Acknowledgments

We would like to thank the following people for their support: Erica Curtis, Amy Jeryl, Bruno Midavaine, Bibi Scuba, Steven Shukow and the Skoi family.

We also thank our staff, especially Michael Gitter and Robert Seixas, as well as Reni Chin, Schuyler Frazier, Jeff Freier, Katherine Harris, Natalie Lebert, Mike Liao, Dave Makulec, Jennifer Napuli, Rob Poole and Sharon Yates.

The reviews published in this guide are based on public opinion surveys, with numerical ratings reflecting the average scores given by all survey participants who voted on each establishment and text based on direct quotes from, or fair paraphrasings of, participants' comments. Phone numbers, addresses and other factual information were correct to the best of our knowledge when published in this guide; any subsequent changes may not be reflected.

© 2004 Zagat Survey, LLC
ISBN 1-57006-491-1
Printed in the United States of America

Contents

About This Survey	5
What's New	6
Ratings & Symbols	7
Most Popular	9

TOP RATINGS
- Food; Cuisines, Features, Arrondissements ... 10
- Decor; Outdoors, Romance, Rooms, Views ... 14
- Service 15
- Best Buys 16

RESTAURANT DIRECTORY
Names, Addresses, Phone Numbers,
Fax Numbers, Web Sites,
Ratings and Reviews 17

INDEXES
- **Cuisines** 194
- **Locations** 206
- **Special Features**
  - Breakfast 215
  - Brunch 215
  - Business Dining 216
  - Catering 217
  - Celebrity Chefs 217
  - Cheese Trays 218
  - Child-Friendly 219
  - Closed in August 220
  - Critic-Proof 222
  - Dancing 222
  - Dining Alone 222
  - Entertainment 223
  - Family-Style 224
  - Fireplaces 224
  - Historic Places 224
  - Holiday Meals 225
  - Hotel Dining 226
  - "In" Places 227
  - Jacket Required 227
  - Late Dining 227
  - Meet for a Drink 228
  - No Air-Conditioning 228
  - Nonsmoking Sections 230
  - Noteworthy Newcomers 234
  - Outdoor Dining 235
  - Parking 237
  - People-Watching 238
  - Power Scenes 239
  - Quick Bites 240
  - Quiet Conversation 240
  - Romantic Places 242

Singles Scenes	242
Sleepers	243
Sunday Dining	244
Tasting Menus	246
Teen Appeal	247
Theme Restaurants	248
Transporting Experiences	248
Views	249
Visitors on Expense Account	249
Waterside	250
Winning Wine Lists	250
Wine Chart	252

About This Survey

Here are the results of our *2004/05 Paris Restaurant Survey*, covering 950 restaurants as tested, and tasted, by over 4,300 avid restaurant-goers. This marks the 25th year that Zagat Survey has reported on the shared experiences of diners like you, on the scene or, in this case, on the Seine, since this survey was conducted in French as well as English. In fact, it was our own experience as young lawyers in Paris, from 1968 through 1970, that inspired all our surveys.

Those surveys formally started in 1979 in New York as a hobby involving 200 friends rating local restaurants. Today we have more than 250,000 surveyors and have branched out to cover entertaining, golf, hotels, movies, music, nightlife, resorts, shopping, spas and theater. Our restaurant *Surveys* are also available by subscription at **zagat.com**, where you can vote and shop as well.

By regularly surveying large numbers of avid customers, we hope to have achieved a uniquely current and reliable guide. A quarter-century of experience has verified this. This year's participants dined out an average of 3.3 times per week, meaning this *Survey* is based on roughly 738,000 meals. Of these surveyors, 38% are women, 62% men; the breakdown by age is 14% in their 20s; 24%, 30s; 22%, 40s; 24%, 50s; and 16%, 60s or above. Our editors have synopsized our surveyors' opinions, with their comments shown in quotation marks. We sincerely thank each of these surveyors; this book is really "theirs."

Of course, we are especially grateful to our editors, Alexander Lobrano, European correspondent for *Gourmet* and a food and travel writer based in Paris, and Mary Deschamps, a freelance writer in Paris. We would also like to thank *Le Figaro's* François Simon for his help and advice along the way, and our coordinator, Claire Fitzpatrick.

To help guide our readers to Paris' best meals and best buys, we have prepared a number of lists. See Most Popular (page 9), Top Ratings (pages 10–15) and Best Buys (page 16). In addition, we have provided 45 handy indexes and have tried to be concise. Also, for the first time, we have included Web addresses.

To join any of our upcoming *Surveys*, just register at zagat.com. Each participant will receive a free copy of the resulting guide when published. Your comments and even criticisms of this guide are also solicited. There is always room for improvement with your help. You can contact us at paris@zagat.com. We look forward to hearing from you.

New York, NY
April 5, 2004

Nina and Tim Zagat

get updates at zagat.com

What's New

If Parisians' appetite for new places seems insatiable, it could be because they spend so much time in restaurants. Our surveyors say they eat half their meals out each week, and over 30% report they venture forth more often than they did two years ago – even though the average meal price in Paris has increased 3.2% to 50.65 euros ($63.03), nearly double the cost of an NYC meal. Indeed, 74% of denizens declare they dig deeper into their pockets when dining out now, so it's understandable that they demand novelty when they nosh.

Small Gets Big: The biggest new toy is tiny tasting plates. Salon d'Hélène pioneered a tapas trend a few years ago, but now newcomers from Alain Dutournier, with his Basque table Pinxo, to the New French Café Lenôtre are offering sample-sized servings. The most high-profile place is Atelier de Joël Robuchon, the comeback chef's chic, sleek coffee shop–cum–sushi bar that has 'em lining up to sit at a counter and graze on the master's Haute Cuisine.

The Weight of the Eighth: Although various *quartiers* are showing signs of culinary life – La Famille has woken up Montmartre, for example, and the glittering Philippe Starck–designed Cristal Room has lent sparkle to the 16th – 44% of surveyors cite the 8th arrondissement as the city's best restaurant neighborhood. That's not surprising, since the area houses so many renowned establishments, from gastronomic temples like the Plaza-Athénée to grande dame tearooms like Ladurée. The 8th is also the preferred venue of many newcomers, such as Bocconi and Libre Sens, as well as noteworthies whose debuts were pending at press time, such as Alain Ducasse's double play (La Brasserie and Marcel) on the late Le Drugstore's site.

Fit to be Thai-ed: French institutions continue to dominate the Tops lists – Taillevent ranked No. 1 for Food for the fifth time – but the fact that the Japanese-Gallic Hiramatsu appears among the top 10 for the first time suggests a broadening of tastes here. In fact, over 50% of surveyors named some sort of Asian fare as their favorite – especially Thai, which bodes well not only for newcomer Banyan, but the diversity of the French culinary scene overall.

Bright Lights, Big City: The City of Lights continues to lure provincial chefs. Alsatian Antoine Westermann's Mon Vieil Ami does updates of Classic Bistro eats, while Michel Troisgros of the Rhône Valley is consulting at the Hôtel Lancaster's dining room. These arrivals offset some notable departures: the closing of Faugeron, as its eponymous chef-owner retires, and of Gualtiero Marchesi, the Milanese marvel. Throughout Paris, the gastronomic beat goes on, and the destinations have never been more diverse – or delicious.

Paris
April 5, 2004
Alexander Lobrano

Ratings & Symbols

Name, Address, Métro Stop, Phone* & Fax Numbers, & Web Site

Hours & Credit Cards

Zagat Ratings

F	D	S	€C
▽ 23	9	13	15

Tim & Nina's ◐ 🚫 ⌽

604, rue de Buci, 6ᵉ (Odéon), 01 23 45 54 32; fax 01 23 44 55 66; www.zagat.com

◪ *Jamais fermé*, this "crowded" 6th arrondissement cafe started the "Swedish-French craze" (e.g. herring and foie gras on tiny toasts with a choice of sauces); though it looks like a "garage" and T & N "never heard of credit cards or reservations" – yours in particular – the *très* "*merveilleuse* Stockholm-Lyonnaise cuisine" draws demented "debit-account" diners to this "deep dive."

Review, with surveyors' comments in quotes

Restaurants with the highest overall ratings and greatest popularity and importance are printed in CAPITAL LETTERS.

Before reviews a symbol indicates whether responses were uniform ■ or mixed ◪.

Hours: ◐ serves after 11 PM
🚫 closed on Sunday

Credit Cards: ⌽ no credit cards accepted

Ratings: Food, Decor and Service are rated on a scale of **0** to **30**. The Cost (€C) column reflects our surveyors' estimate of the price of dinner including one drink and tip, in euros.

F	Food	D	Decor	S	Service	€C	Cost
23		9		13		€15	

- **0–9**   poor to fair
- **10–15** fair to good
- **16–19** good to very good
- **20–25** very good to excellent
- **26–30** extraordinary to perfection
- ▽ low response/less reliable

For places listed without ratings or a numerical cost estimate, such as a newcomer or write-in, the price range is indicated by the following symbols.

| **I** | 25€ and below | **E** | 46€ to 75€ |
| **M** | 26€ to 45€ | **VE** | 76€ or more |

---

* When calling from outside France, dial international code +33, then omit the first zero of the number.

get updates at zagat.com

Most Popular

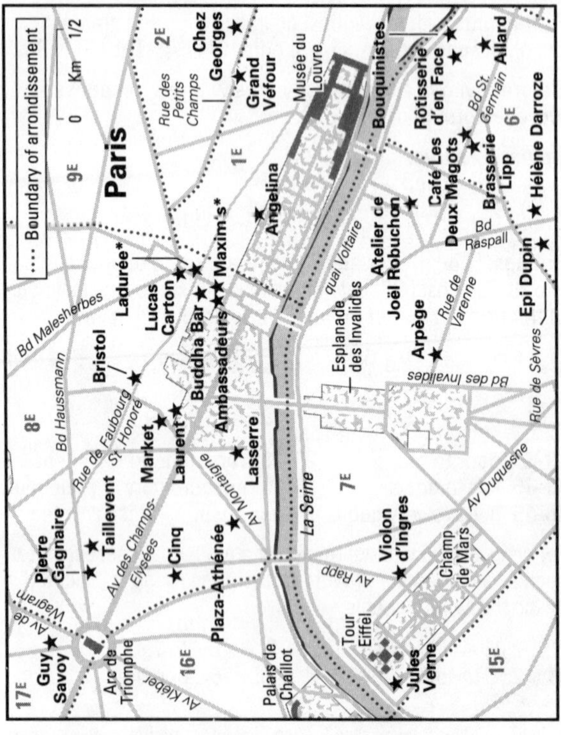

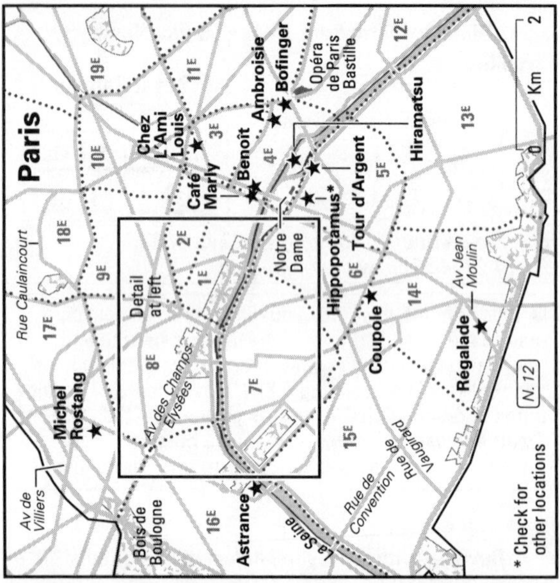

Most Popular

1. Taillevent
2. Tour d'Argent
3. Guy Savoy
4. Lucas Carton
5. Grand Véfour
6. Jules Verne
7. Bouquinistes
8. Cinq
9. Pierre Gagnaire
10. Arpège
11. Epi Dupin
12. Buddha Bar
13. Bofinger
14. Ladurée
15. Plaza-Athénée
16. Lasserre
17. Atelier Joël Robuchon
18. Benoît
19. Ambassadeurs
20. Ambroisie
21. Hélène Darroze
22. Bristol
23. Chez L'Ami Louis
24. Brasserie Lipp
25. Violon d'Ingres
26. Astrance
27. Michel Rostang
28. Chez Georges
29. Laurent
30. Market
31. Régalade
32. Rôtisserie d'en Face
33. Coupole
34. Hippopotamus
35. Hiramatsu
36. Café Les Deux Magots
37. Angelina
38. Café Marly
39. Allard
40. Maxim's*

It's obvious that many of the restaurants on the above list are among Paris' most expensive, but if popularity were calibrated to price, we suspect that a number of other restaurants would join the above ranks. Given the fact that both our surveyors and readers love to discover dining bargains, we have added a list of 80 Best Buys on page 16. These are restaurants that give real quality at extremely reasonable prices.

---

* Indicates a tie with restaurant above

get updates at zagat.com

Top Ratings

Top lists exclude restaurants with low voting.

Top 40 Food

28 Taillevent
Guy Savoy
Cinq
Pierre Gagnaire*
Grand Véfour
Hiramatsu
27 Michel Rostang
Bristol
Plaza-Athénée
Lucas Carton
Apicius
Gérard Besson
26 Ambroisie
Ambassadeurs
Chez L'Ami Louis
Astrance
Arpège
Lasserre
Relais Louis XIII
Elysées du Vernet
Magnolias
Pré Catelan
Atelier Joël Robuchon
Relais d'Auteuil/P. Pignol
25 Ledoyen
Sormani
Carré des Feuillants
Espadon
Tour d'Argent
Régalade
Jamin
Trois Marches
Jacques Cagna
Troquet*
Truffière*
Meurice
Duc
Grande Cascade
Moulin à Vent
24 Angle du Faubourg

By Cuisine (French)

Bistros (Contemporary)
26 Astrance
25 Troquet
24 Epi Dupin
23 Beurre Noisette
22 Ardoise

Bistros (Traditional)
26 Chez L'Ami Louis
25 Régalade
Moulin à Vent
23 Christine
Petit Marguery

Brasseries
21 Relais Plaza
20 Brasserie du Louvre
19 Brasserie/l'Ile St. Louis
18 Costes
Chien qui Fume

Classic
27 Villaret
Gérard Besson
26 Relais Louis XIII
25 Paul Chêne
Espadon

Contemporary
28 Hiramatsu
27 Michel Rostang
Bristol
Plaza-Athénée
Lucas Carton

Haute Cuisine
28 Taillevent
Guy Savoy
Cinq
Pierre Gagnaire*
Grand Véfour

Lyon
24 Bellecour
23 Benoît
22 Lyonnais
21 Moissonnier
20 Vieux Bistro

Other Regions
27 Bath's/*Auvergne*
21 Comte de Gascogne/*Gascony*
Pamphlet/*Basque*
20 Ambassade d'Auv./*Auvergne*
Bascou/*Basque*
Bistro d'Hubert*/*Basque*

10   subscribe to zagat.com

Top Food

Provence
- *22* Sept Quinze
- *21* Bastide Odéon
- Fish La Boissonerie
- Jardin
- Olivades

Seafood
- *25* Duc
- *24* Goumard
- Marée
- Cagouille
- Luna

Shellfish
- *22* Dôme
- Dessirier
- Marius*
- Maison Prunier
- *21* Marée de Versailles

Southwest
- *24* Trou Gascon
- Hélène Darroze
- *22* Ambassade du Sud-Ouest
- Maison Courtine*
- Baracane

Steakhouses
- *23* Relais de l'Entrecôte
- Boeuf Couronné
- *21* Gavroche
- Gourmets des Ternes
- *20* Relais de Venise

Wine Bars/Bistros
- *21* Bourguignon du Marais
- Vin sur Vin
- *19* Willi's Wine Bar
- *18* Cave de l'Os à Moëlle
- Caves Pétrissans*

By Cuisine (Other)

Chinese
- *22* Passy Mandarin
- *21* Chez Vong
- Tang
- Tong Yen*
- *20* Mirama

Eclectic
- *23* Ze Kitchen Galerie
- *22* Spoon, Food & Wine
- Market
- *21* Chamarré
- Relais Plaza

Greek/Mediterranean
- *20* Il Baccello
- Délices d'Aphrodite
- *19* Mavrommatis
- *16* 7ème Sud Grenelle
- *15* 16 Haussmann

Italian
- *25* Sormani
- *23* Ostéria
- Il Cortile
- *22* Chez Vincent
- *21* Romantica

Japanese
- *25* Isse
- *24* Isami
- *23* Benkay
- *22* Kinugawa
- *20* Yen

Middle Eastern
- *21* Byblos
- *20* Al Dar
- Al Diwan
- *19* Noura
- *16* Fakhr el Dine

North African
- *23* Timgad
- *22* Mansouria
- *21* Atlas
- 404
- El Mansour

Thai/Vietnamese
- *22* Thiou
- Tan Dinh
- *21* Lac-Hong
- Erawan
- *20* Blue Elephant

Wild Cards
- *24* Anahuacalli/*Mexican*
- *22* Caviar Kaspia/*Russian*
- *21* Copenhague/*Danish*
- *19* Anahï/*South American*
- *18* Flora Danica/*Danish*

get updates at zagat.com   11

Top Food

By Special Feature

Breakfast
- *22* Dôme
-     Dalloyau
- *21* Ladurée
-     Gavroche
-     Hédiard

Hotel Dining
- *28* Cinq
-     Four Seasons George V
-     Pierre Gagnaire*
-     Hôtel Balzac
- *27* Bristol
-     Hôtel Bristol
-     Plaza-Athénée
-     Hôtel Plaza-Athénée
- *26* Ambassadeurs
-     Hôtel de Crillon

"In" Places
- *28* Guy Savoy
- *26* Astrance
-     Atelier Joël Robuchon
- *25* Régalade
- *23* Ze Kitchen Galerie

Late Dining
- *22* Caviar Kaspia
- *21* Gavroche
-     Coupe-Chou
- *20* Al Diwan
- *19* Gamin de Paris

Newcomers/Rated
- *26* Atelier Joël Robuchon
- *19* Café Lenôtre
- *18* 1728
- *14* Kong
-     Suite

Newcomers/Unrated
-     Caïus
-     Cristal Room
-     Mesturet
-     Mon Vieil Ami
-     Pinxo

Sunday Dining
- *28* Cinq
-     Pierre Gagnaire*
- *27* Bristol
- *26* Ambassadeurs
-     Chez L'Ami Louis

Tea & Desserts
- *22* Dalloyau
- *21* Ladurée
- *19* Mariage Frères
- *18* Angelina
- *17* A Priori Thé

Wine Lists
- *28* Taillevent
-     Guy Savoy
-     Cinq
-     Pierre Gagnaire*
-     Grand Véfour

By Arrondissement

1st
- *28* Grand Véfour
- *27* Gérard Besson
- *25* Carré des Feuillants
-     Espadon
-     Meurice

2nd
- *25* Isse
- *23* Chez Georges
- *22* Lyonnais
-     Céladon
- *21* Gavroche

3rd
- *26* Chez L'Ami Louis
- *21* Pamphlet
-     404
- *20* Chez Janou
-     Ambassade d'Auvergne

4th
- *28* Hiramatsu
- *27* Ambroisie
- *24* Isami
- *23* Ostéria
-     Benoît

Top Food

5th
- *25* Tour d'Argent
  Truffière
  Moulin à Vent
- *24* Réminet
  Anahuacalli

6th
- *26* Relais Louis XIII
- *25* Jacques Cagna
- *24* Epi Dupin
  Hélène Darroze
- *23* Christine

7th
- *26* Arpège
  Atelier Joël Robuchon
- *24* Violon d'Ingres
  Bellecour
  Bourdonnais/Cantine

8th
- *28* Taillevent
  Cinq
  Pierre Gagnaire*
- *27* Bath's
  Bristol

9th
- *27* Muses
- *23* Chez Jean
  Table d'Anvers
- *21* Ladurée
- *20* Bistrot Papillon

10th
- *21* Chez Michel
  Deux Canards
- *18* Brasserie Julien
- *17* Brasserie Flo
  Terminus Nord

11th
- *27* Villaret
- *22* Mansouria
- *21* C'Amelot
  Astier
- *20* Blue Elephant

12th
- *24* Trou Gascon
- *21* Oulette
  Biche au Bois
- *17* Square Trousseau
  Train Bleu

13th
- *23* Petit Marguery
- *22* Avant Goût
- *21* Chez Paul
- *18* Terroir

14th
- *25* Régalade
  Duc
- *24* Cagouille
- *22* Dôme
  Maison Courtine

15th
- *25* Troquet
- *23* Os à Moëlle
  Beurre Noisette
  Benkay
- *22* Tire-Bouchon

16th
- *26* Astrance
  Pré Catelan
  Relais d'Auteuil/P. Pignol
- *25* Paul Chêne
  Jamin

17th
- *28* Guy Savoy
- *27* Michel Rostang
  Apicius
- *25* Sormani
- *24* Amphyclès

18th, 19th & 20th
- *23* Boeuf Couronné
  Beauvilliers
- *22* Chez Vincent
- *19* Zéphyr
- *16* Wepler

Outside Paris
- *26* Magnolias
- *25* Trois Marches
  Tastevin
- *22* Dalloyau
- *21* Comte de Gascogne

get updates at zagat.com

Top 40 Decor

28 Cinq
  Ambassadeurs
  Grand Véfour*
  Meurice
  Train Bleu
  Grande Cascade
  Tour d'Argent
27 Taillevent
  Espadon
  Pré Catelan
  Jules Verne
  Bristol
  Lasserre
  Ledoyen
26 Lucas Carton
  Lapérouse
  Beauvilliers
  Georges
  Plaza-Athénée
  Ambroisie
  Blue Elephant
  Laurent
25 China Club
  Bar Vendôme
  Costes
  Chalet des Iles
  Coupe-Chou*
  404
  Buddha Bar
  Guy Savoy
  Bon
  Pierre Gagnaire
  Fermette Marbeuf 1900
  Hiramatsu
24 Trois Marches
  Jacques Cagna
  Pershing
  Elysées du Vernet
  Brasserie Julien
  Jardin des Cygnes

Outdoors

Bristol
Café Lenôtre
Café Marly
Délices de Szechuen
Espadon
Georges
Jardins de Bagatelle
Laurent
Maison/l'Amérique Latine
Pavillon Montsouris
Pavillon Puebla
Pré Catelan
Rest. du Palais Royal
Tastevin

Romance

Allard
Ambassadeurs
Beauvilliers
Caviar Kaspia
Copenhague
Costes
Dôme
Espadon
Flora Danica
Grande Cascade
Grand Véfour
Jardins de Bagatelle
Jules Verne
Lapérouse
Lasserre
Ledoyen
Pré Catelan
Tour d'Argent

Rooms

Alcazar
Beauvilliers
Bon 2
Cristal Room
Gare
Kong
Ladurée (8e)
Maison Blanche

Views

Altitude 95
Copenhague
Georges
Jules Verne
Kong
Maison Blanche
R.
Rest. du Musée d'Orsay
Terrasse
Toupary

Top 40 Service

28 Taillevent
Cinq
Guy Savoy
27 Lasserre
Hiramatsu
Grand Véfour
Bristol
Espadon
Ambassadeurs
Pierre Gagnaire
26 Michel Rostang
Tour d'Argent
Plaza-Athénée
Meurice
Ambroisie
25 Lucas Carton
Grande Cascade
Relais d'Auteuil/P. Pignol
Apicius
Arpège

Bar Vendôme
Ledoyen*
Carré des Feuillants
24 Florimond
Elysées du Vernet
Obélisque*
Pré Catelan
Truffière
Laurent
Astrance
Gérard Besson
Jamin
Jacques Cagna
Relais Louis XIII
Ferme St-Simon
Jules Verne
23 Bellecour
Angle du Faubourg
Marée
Jardin des Cygnes

Best Buys

Top 40

1. Cosi
2. Crêperie de Josselin
3. Chartier
4. Lina's
5. BE Boulangépicier
6. Higuma
7. Angelina
8. A Priori Thé
9. Mariage Frères
10. Byblos
11. Zéphyr
12. Gourmet de l'Isle
13. P'tit Troquet
14. Ladurée
15. Café Charbon
16. Anahuacalli
17. Domaine de Lintillac
18. Polidor
19. Auberge/Champ de Mars
20. Dalloyau
21. Brasserie/l'Ile St. Louis
22. Bistrot du Peintre
23. Colette
24. Petit Rétro
25. Chez Paul (13e)
26. Florimond
27. Loir dans la Théière
28. Camille
29. Cave de l'Os à Moëlle
30. Beurre Noisette
31. Troquet
32. Chez Janou
33. Petit Prince de Paris
34. Brasserie du Louvre
35. Sept Quinze
36. Languedoc
37. Mirama
38. Tire-Bouchon
39. Bistrot d'Henri
40. Atlas

Other Good Values

Alivi
Astier
Aub. Pyrénées Cévennes
Avant Goût
Baan-Boran
Baracane
Biche au Bois
Café de Flore
Café de la Musique
Café du Commerce
Cafetière
C'Amelot
Chez Marianne
Chez Omar
Chez Paul (11e)
Chicago Pizza Pie
China Club
Christine
Coffee Parisien
Dame Tartine/Café Very
Délices d'Aphrodite
Deux Canards
Editeurs
Fish La Boissonnerie
Flore en l'Ile
Fumoir
Grand Louvre
Juvéniles
Matsuri
Monsieur Lapin
Nemrod
Pamphlet
Passy Mandarin
Petit Bofinger
404
Relais de l'Entrecôte
Rest./Musée d'Orsay
Scheffer
Villaret
Wadja

Restaurant Directory

				F	D	S	€C

Absinthe (L') ⓈⒷ   19 | 16 | 15 | 43
24, pl du Marché St-Honoré, 1er (Pyramides), 01 49 26 90 04; fax 01 49 26 08 64; www.michelrostang.com

■ "On Paris' seemingly only traffic-free square" (the Place du Marché-Saint Honoré), this "pleasantly situated bistro" offers "open-air delight" in summer and year-round "authentic" atmosphere, all agree; however, while devotees declare it "delivers" with often "innovative", "consistent Classic French food" at "quite reasonable" prices, doubters demur, saying "it's hard to believe it's owned by Michel Rostang"; "if only they could serve the real absinthe", maybe the disagreements would be dispelled.

A et M Le Bistrot Ⓢ   15 | 14 | 15 | 39
136, bd Murat, 16e (Porte de St-Cloud), 01 45 27 39 60; fax 01 45 27 69 71

■ "No miracles, but no disappointments" sums up this Contemporary Bistro, "an honest table with attentive service and justifiable prices" in the 16th arrondissement; though "inventive", the fish-heavy menu can be "a little boring", but "you can't do better in the Porte de Saint-Cloud area", especially when "lunching with executives of the TF1" TV station nearby.

Affiche (A l') Ⓢ   – | – | – | M
48, rue de Moscou, 8e (Rome), 01 45 22 02 20

In the up-and-coming Europe district, this year-old storefront bistro with a Contemporary French chalkboard menu is "a nice addition to a neighborhood that badly needed a decent, reasonably priced" place; most say it's made a "nice debut", even if a few find the namesake old "movie poster–themed" decor "an unnecessary gimmick."

Affriolé (L') Ⓢ   21 | 13 | 18 | 41
17, rue Malar, 7e (Ecole Militaire/Invalides), 01 44 18 31 33; fax 01 44 18 91 12

■ Chef Thierry Verola's table in a quiet corner of the 7th may be "noisy", but who cares when his "small but varied menu" of "inventive" Contemporary Bistro cooking is so "sublime" – an "exceptional value for the money"; and if many judge the "decor drab", the "charming service" helps "warm up" the room.

Aiguière (L') Ⓢ   – | – | – | E
37 bis, rue de Montreuil, 11e (Faidherbe-Chaligny), 01 43 72 42 32; fax 01 43 72 96 36; www.l-aiguiere.com

Maybe because it's tucked away in the 11th, not many know this "lovely, romantic" auberge with a "cozy atmosphere" created by exposed beams and a cheerful blue-and-yellow color scheme; "served with savoir faire" (the plates come covered with a dome), the "excellent" "albeit a bit pricey" Traditional French food is backed up with a 400-label wine list.

| F | D | S | €C |

Ailleurs ●🚭
| 11 | 13 | 13 | 38 |

26, rue Jean Mermoz, 8ᵉ (Franklin D. Roosevelt), 01 53 53 98 00; fax 01 53 53 98 01; www.ailleurs-fr.com

🗨 "You're not really someplace else [*ailleurs*], you're in the heart of the Champs-Elysées" smirk smarties about this Eclectic, a "fashion restaurant" that they claim is "fading away", its in-crowd clientele "like a flock of birds who've migrated to other places", due to the "uneven cuisine"; still, fans of this fusion fiesta find the "menu exotic" and the "staff nice", and the noise makes it "a good place to go when you really don't want to talk."

Aimant du Sud (L') ●🚭
| – | – | – | M |

40, bd Arago, 13ᵉ (Les Gobelins), 01 47 07 33 57

"A very-good, well-priced local" bistro is the sunny summary of this modest place in the 13th, whose Med menu features standards (as its name hints) for lovers of the south of France, plus a "nice Southwestern wine list"; in summer, "reservations are indispensable" if guests want to Basque on the "lovely terrace."

Al Caratello
| – | – | – | M |

5, rue Audran, 18ᵉ (Abbesses/Pigalle), 01 42 62 24 23

Though some might find this shop-front dining room off the rue Lepic over-lit and plain, the generously served Italian cooking has made the place a hit with trendy theater, TV and film-industry locals; friendly service and reasonably priced wines from The Boot add to the appeal, so be sure to reserve.

Alcazar ●
| 16 | 21 | 16 | 48 |

62, rue Mazarine, 6ᵉ (Odéon), 01 53 10 19 99; fax 01 53 10 23 23; www.alcazar.fr

🗨 Most admire the "soaring ceilings, ultramodern decor" and "exceptional open kitchen" that characterize Sir Terence Conran's "big" bi-level brasserie for the beautiful people, despite its un-Gallic air – kind of "like Santa Monica in the 6th arrondissement"; though it's "more a scene than a meal", the New French eats are, "if not inspired, consistent" (do try the "signature shellfish sampler"), and the hip types are "fun to watch", if hard to talk to (it's "a little noisy, even for a noisy place").

Al Dar ●
| 20 | 10 | 16 | 37 |

8, rue Frédéric Sauton, 5ᵉ (Maubert-Mutualité), 01 43 25 17 15
93, av Raymond Poincaré, 16ᵉ (Victor Hugo), 01 45 00 96 64;
fax 01 45 01 61 67

🗨 Falafel fans and meze mavens acclaim the "always-fresh", "super-good" food at these Lebanese tables in the 5th and the 16th – so it's a pita that the dining-room decor (think pastels and mirrors) is "a bit depressing" and the service slightly "stuffy"; of course one can always take advantage of the "absolutely amazing take-out section."

get updates at zagat.com

| | | | F | D | S | €C |

Al Diwan ●   20 | 14 | 16 | 42
30, av George V, 8ᵉ (Alma-Marceau/George V), 01 47 23 45 45; fax 01 47 23 60 98

◪ For a "little Beirut in Paris", fans flock to this "dining room with a modern Middle Eastern–style decor", which provides "possibly the most tasty Lebanese food in town" ("I even ate a goat's testicle, and it was delicious"); some feel the fare "in no way compensates" for the prices ("justified only by" the swanky Avenue George V address) or the "slow staff" – though it helps if you "wear black leather to fit in with the local" Arabic crowd.

Alivi (L') ●   19 | 16 | 19 | 36
27, rue du Roi de Sicile, 4ᵉ (Hôtel-de-Ville/St-Paul), 01 48 87 90 20; fax 01 48 87 20 60; www.restaurant-alivi.com

■ Perfect "for discovering Corsican cooking" ("don't miss the fish soup or the charcuterie plate") carol converts about this "intimate" island in the Marais; equally "fine" is the "friendly welcome" and "sweet service", all at tabs that are as easy to swallow as the native wines.

ALLARD ●🅂   22 | 17 | 19 | 52
41, rue St-André-des-Arts, 6ᵉ (Odéon), 01 43 26 48 23

■ Despite a few "too many Americans", this Saint-Germain stalwart "exudes" "a consummate old-time bistro" vibe, starting with its "delicious, hearty" Classic French food, especially "the best duck with olives on earth (who knew you could eat that many at once?)" and "superb wine list"; adding to the "authentic" ambiance are the "jam-packed tables" and "servers who can be crusty – but in a friendly way"; indeed, "it's thanks to restaurants like this that Paris will always be Paris."

Allobroges (Les) 🅂   – | – | – | M
71, rue des Grands Champs, 20ᵉ (Maraîchers/Nation), 01 43 73 40 00; fax 01 40 09 23 22

It's "in the boondocks, but that keeps prices relatively low for a genteel ambiance and well-prepared nouvelle-ish food" insist the intrepid who've journeyed to this "little jewel in the 20th"; the "welcome is warm" as you enter the wall-papered dining room to savor the New Bistro delights, preferably on one of the prix fixe options ("a real deal").

Al Mounia   19 | 22 | 19 | 44
16, rue de Magdebourg, 16ᵉ (Trocadéro), 01 47 27 57 28; fax 01 41 44 73 63; www.al-mounia.com

◪ A meal at this Moroccan near the Trocadéro is "almost as good as going to Marrakesh" since stylistically the "exotic" "decor is pure riad" (a North African villa); equally "respectful of tradition" is the "earnest food" and "caring service"; visual verisimilitude notwithstanding, however, some say that "the hammered brass tables are not the most comfortable to eat at" when seated on leather poufs.

| F | D | S | €C |

Alsace (L') ☽
16 | 15 | 14 | 44

39, av des Champs-Elysées, 8ᵉ (Franklin D. Roosevelt), 01 53 93 97 00; fax 01 53 93 97 09; www.restaurantalsace.com

◪ "It's brassy, noisy and filled with tourists", but "at 3 AM in the 8th", you're "always glad this place is around" note night-owls of this 24/7 "nonstop brasserie" that's generally "good" "for an Alsatian fix" of "delicious choucroute" or a "raw seafood platter on ice"; on the down side, often "the waiters act like you're invisible" and several say it strikes them as "pricey, due to its location" – an admittedly "grand" one "on the Champs-Elysées."

Alsaco (L') ⌧
18 | 10 | 17 | 38

10, rue Condorcet, 9ᵉ (Gare du Nord/Poissonnière), 01 45 26 44 31; fax 01 42 85 11 05; www.alsacoparis.com

■ "Excellent Alsatian cooking and a remarkable collection of eaux-de-vies" attract hearty eaters to this out-of-the-way" corner of the 9th (leaving no doubt this is a "bona fide *winstub*"); it's "ideal on a winter night", when you can expect "personal service from the chef" and get cozy over "wonderful choucroute" without spending a fortune.

Altitude 95
15 | 23 | 18 | 45

Tour Eiffel, Champs-de-Mars, 1st level, 7ᵉ (Bir-Hakeim/Champ-de-Mars), 01 45 55 20 04; fax 01 47 05 94 40

◪ The "fabulous" panorama of Paris is the chief lure of this Eiffel Tower eatery; but many "pleasantly surprised" surveyors say the place "has changed": if it once seemed "Paris' highest tourist trap", it now offers "decent" Classic French eats and, as a score rise attests, the service has gained altitude too; and if it still seems "overpriced" to several, remember you get "the best view in town at a fraction of the cost of the Jules Verne" (its sibling one flight up); P.S. "call 15 days in advance" for a window table.

Ambassade d'Auvergne
20 | 16 | 20 | 46

22, rue du Grenier St-Lazare, 3ᵉ (Rambuteau), 01 42 72 31 22; fax 01 42 78 85 47; www.ambassade-auvergne.com

■ If some "don't think of the Auvergne beyond Michelin tires and volcanoes", the "consistently excellent food" at "one of the best regional restaurants" in Paris will certainly put that province on the map; the "cordial welcome" and "attentive service" are almost as appetizing as the "hearty" fare that includes the must-have "aligot, that elastic mashed potato/cheese/garlic compound", and "chocolate mousse to die for"; it also offers "great value" in a "country-style" setting paradoxically "close to the Pompidou."

Ambassade du Sud-Ouest ⌧
22 | 12 | 20 | 48

46, av de La Bourdonnais, 7ᵉ (Ecole Militaire), 01 45 55 59 59; www.ambassade-sud-ouest.com

■ "Just blocks from the Eiffel Tower", the "foie gras palace of Paris" gets its ducks in a row with "basic, rustic but

get updates at zagat.com

good" Southwestern French cooking (you "toast your own bread at the table" to accompany the pâté); and if the "plain", stone-walled decor strikes some as "sad", others say it's "a trip to the country"; P.S. you can get it to go in the "great area up front."

AMBASSADEURS (LES) 26 | 28 | 27 | 129
Hôtel de Crillon, 10, pl de la Concorde, 8ᵉ (Concorde), 01 44 71 16 16; fax 01 44 71 15 02; www.crillon.com
■ The Food score may not reflect the post-*Survey* arrival of chef Jean-François Piège to this "marbled", "magnificent" room with a "million-dollar view of the Place de la Concorde"; but given his Plaza-Athénée pedigree, it's safe to say its renown for New French "delicious entrees and whimsical desserts" will continue – as does the "fawning" service ("never have there been so many to serve so few"); just "hold on to your wallet" because this "extraordinarily elegant" experience is "evisceratingly expensive."

AMBROISIE (L') ⍾ 26 | 26 | 26 | 156
9, pl des Vosges, 4ᵉ (Bastille/St-Paul), 01 42 78 51 45
■ Chef-owner Bernard Pacaud's "jewel box" of Haute Cuisine in the tony Place des Vosges is not only "one of the most beautiful in Paris", with a "spectacular" "Petit Versailles"–style decor, but the cooking, which runs to a "creative" riff on Classic French dishes, is "ambrosial" – "truly the food of the gods" "served by people determined to please you" (albeit with a sometimes "snooty" air); "little extras help lessen the blow of the bill", but "if you can get in", go no matter what the state of your savings ("what would your children learn in college anyway?").

Amici Mei ⍾⍾ – | – | – | M
53, bd Beaumarchais, 4ᵉ (Chemin Vert), 01 42 71 82 62
Parisian pie-heads say yes, it *is* worth "waiting in the street" until a table opens up ("they don't take reservations") at this hole-in-the-wall Marais Italian; "the pizza's excellent", so don't be put off by the "tiny", bright Formica-finished dining room and somewhat "lamentable" service.

Ami Pierre (A l') ⍾⍾ – | – | – | M
5, rue de la Main d'Or, 11ᵉ (Ledru-Rollin), 01 47 00 17 35
This "atmospheric" *bistrot à vins* near the Bastille is like being "propelled into France during the 1950s" with all the fixings: "friendly" atmosphere, "elbow-to-elbow" seating and "generous portions" of Southwestern–Classic Bistro "eats that are very Gallic" ("divine cheese plate"); don't forget to start out or "finish up at the zinc-clad bar."

Amognes (Les) ⍾ 19 | 10 | 15 | 44
243, rue du Faubourg St-Antoine, 11ᵉ (Faidherbe-Chaligny), 01 43 72 73 05
◪ For anyone who likes "wonderfully inventive" New Bistro cooking and "a really good buy", to boot, this "amazingly

creative little home near the Bastille is still waiting to be discovered"; a few doubters demur, citing a "lack of consistency", but most appreciate the "discreet service" that makes it "a good place for a tranquil discussion."

Ampère (L') 15 | 14 | 15 | 45
1, rue Ampère, 17ᵉ (Wagram), 01 47 63 72 05; fax 01 47 63 37 33
Near the Place Pereire, this "popular", "rather pleasant" neighborhood bistro wins praise for being "one of the rare places in Paris where children are always welcome"; otherwise, regulars rate the well-priced Classic French cooking as "reliable" and take a jab at the "spotty service."

Amphyclès 24 | 17 | 22 | 101
78, av des Ternes, 17ᵉ (Porte Maillot), 01 40 68 01 01; fax 01 40 68 91 88
■ "The cooking is just as inventive as ever" ("don't miss the sea crab specialty") at this New French in the 17th, which means you can expect a "delicious" meal in the company of a "chic crowd" in a pleasant, pale-hued dining room that's run by the chef's "very charming wife."

Amuse Bouche (L') ∇ 17 | 16 | 18 | 43
186, rue du Château, 14ᵉ (Gaîté/Mouton-Duvernet), 01 43 35 31 61; fax 01 45 38 96 60
In a quiet part of the 14th, this "amusing little" place "just buzzes, especially after 10 PM"; but while lovebirds chirp it's "ideal for a romantic night out", given the "good New French cuisine" and "charming staff", sourpusses pout it's gotten "overpriced" for the quality on hand.

Anacréon ∇ 17 | 12 | 16 | 38
53, bd St-Marcel, 13ᵉ (Les Gobelins), 01 43 31 71 18; fax 01 43 31 94 94
This "good neighborhood" establishment near the Place d'Italie is run by chef André Le Letty, ex Tour d'Argent, which explains why the Traditional French cooking is "intelligent, unusual" and "definitely not the kind of food you do at home"; the nonexistent decor gets nonexistent comments, but the fare is "served nicely" and the prices are especially gentle.

Anahï 19 | 14 | 17 | 48
49, rue Volta, 3ᵉ (Arts et Métiers/Temple), 01 48 87 88 24; fax 01 48 87 93 04
Ever since they took over an old-fashioned butcher's shop in the 3rd, sisters Carmen and Pilar (the chef) have been the "welcoming team" at this South American specializing in "succulent" Argentinean beef; however, whether they chose to pampa you or not seems to depend on your "beautiful-person" quotient, causing some to carp "your choice is simple: be a fashion victim or a victim of the manager"; many also moan that "the value-for-money ratio doesn't work here."

| F | D | S | €C |

Anahuacalli | 24 | 15 | 21 | 35 |
30, rue des Bernardins, 5ᵉ (Maubert-Mutualité), 01 43 26 10 20; fax 01 42 53 06 82
■ "It's not easy to find good Mexican food in Paris", which is why the hordes are so high on this 5th arrondissement "charmer", hailing its "original" "real cuisine" as a welcome antidote to "Tex-Mex rip-offs"; "killer margaritas" and "warm service" from the "adorable lady owners" add to the "convivial" ambiance of the yellow-painted dining room, and prices are pretty easy to swallow, too.

Androuët ⊠ | 20 | 14 | 20 | 50 |
51, rue de Verneuil, 7ᵉ (Rue du Bac), 01 45 48 51 98; fax 01 45 48 14 29; www.androuet.com
■ "A cheese-lover's paradise" awaits in the beamed Left Bank dining room near the Musée d'Orsay, where this venerable establishment now resides; while just about everything on the Classic French menu "centers on" the stuff, the various prix fixes and samplers offer a great opportunity to stop being mousy for lack of knowledge; "the waiters are wonderful" – not only do they "give great lessons in the geography of French *fromages*", they'll even "e-mail a picture of the tray" to curd cravers.

Andy Whaloo ●◐⊠ | – | – | – | I |
69, rue des Granvilliers, 3ᵉ (Arts et Métiers), 01 42 71 20 38; fax 01 42 74 03 41
Not many surveyors have noted this North African nibbles-and-drinks annex of the popular 404 in the 3rd; those who have hail the "super atmosphere" achieved by a '70s-funky, pop-Moroccan decor (stools made from old paint-drums, lots of bright colors) and "really nice service", even if the food's "a bit weak."

ANGELINA | 18 | 20 | 14 | 25 |
226, rue de Rivoli, 1ᵉʳ (Concorde/Tuileries), 01 42 60 82 00; fax 01 42 86 98 97
◪ Since 1903, this "old-world tea salon" across from the Tuileries has attracted sweet-toothed tourists for its "frighteningly decadent" hot chocolate, "so thick you almost have to scoop it", and "delectable" desserts; those au courant cavil the rest of the menu – salads, sandwiches, etc. – is "nothing special" and the "perennially stressed" staff seems often "on autopilot"; but if this "grande dame" is "past her prime" (and charging primo prices for pastries), she's still "a wonderful Parisian experience."

Angle du Faubourg (L') ⊠ | 24 | 19 | 23 | 67 |
195, rue du Faubourg St-Honoré, 8ᵉ (Charles de Gaulle-Etoile), 01 40 74 20 20; fax 01 40 74 74 20 21; www.cavestaillevent.com
■ "Fabulously" "fresh, inventive" New French cooking and an "excellent selection of lesser-known wines" have made this "classy" "young sister to the big champ" Taillevant

| F | D | S | €C |

("indeed located on the corner" of the Rue du Faubourg Saint-Honoré) "another success for M. Vrinat" (the owner); the terra cotta–colored "modern, sleek" decor strikes some as "sterile" – "I thought I was in a department store" – but the service, including the "delightful female sommelier", is generally "gracious"; it's "perfect for a business lunch", thanks to "a wonder of" a prix fixe.

Annapurna ●ᛉ | 18 | 16 | 18 | 48 |
32, rue de Berri, 8ᵉ (George V/St-Philippe-du-Roule), 01 45 85 63 91
⬛ "Good Indian cooking", "attentive service" and a "kitschy" decor "complete with a bearded sitar player" and "low tables" curry favor with fans of this 8th arrondissement Brahmin; but antagonists argue "for the price", everything "could be better", particularly the "portions (a bit small)."

Aoc (L') ᛉ | – | – | – | M |
14, rue des Fossés St-Bernard, 5ᵉ (Cardinal Lemoine/Jussieu), 01 43 54 22 52; fax 01 43 25 80 16; www.restoaoc.com
Specializing in pedigreed produce "as the name implies" (the prestigious AOC label denotes a "distinctive" food that meets strict government standards), this Latin Quarter bistro lives up to its name with "memorable" Classic French dishes, "graciously" and "generously served" (specifically recommended: "the rotisseried suckling pig, tender and crispy at the same time"); "prices are fair for such quality."

APICIUS ᛉ | 27 | 19 | 25 | 106 |
122, av de Villiers, 17ᵉ (Pereire), 01 43 80 19 66; fax 01 44 40 09 57
⬛ "Over the years" – about 20 – this 17th arrondissement "original has evolved into a classic" attest acolytes of chef-owner "Jean-Pierre Vigato's exquisite updated classics" (many "discovered the delight of pan-fried foie gras" here) that are "worth every euro"; accompanying the "grand finesse" in the Haute Cuisine kitchen is the "professional", "no-attitude" service out front; small surprise that some say it's "our favorite – regardless of the decor."

Apollo | ∇ 10 | 20 | 8 | 34 |
3, pl Denfert Rochereau, 14ᵉ (Denfert-Rochereau), 01 45 38 76 77; fax 01 43 22 02 15
⬛ Located in the street-level concourse of a métro station in the 14th, this "trendy" newcomer with groovy '70s retro decor wins kudos for its "superb terrace, in the middle of Paris but sheltered from traffic"; antogonists think it should apollo-gize for the "uninteresting" New French fare that seems "a little expensive" given its "disappointing" nature.

Appart' (L') ● | 14 | 18 | 14 | 46 |
9, rue du Colisée, 8ᵉ (Franklin D. Roosevelt), 01 53 75 42 00; fax 01 53 76 15 39; www.l-appart.com
⬛ Just off the Champs, this "fashionable" Classic French is "decorated to resemble a real Parisian apartment", hence

| F | D | S | €C |

the name; if most like the "warm" look and "amusing" concept, many add that's the "only memorable thing" about this place, since the food is "decent" but "nothing to write home about" and the service from an all-female staff seems "very slow."

Appennino (L') ⓢ — | — | — | M
61, rue de l'Amiral Mouchez, 13ᵉ (Cité Universitaire), 01 45 89 08 15
Maybe because it's hidden away in the 13th, few know this Northern Italian with a "modest setting", but those who do praise the "quality cooking", and note the "excellent wines at what may be the best prices to be found anywhere in Paris"; even if "the welcome's a little chilly", the "service is professional."

A Priori Thé ⓢ 17 | 18 | 15 | 25
35, Galerie Vivienne, 2ᵉ (Bourse/Palais Royal-Musée du Louvre), 01 42 97 48 75
■ With a "great location" in the "beautiful Galerie Vivienne", this "cozy" tearoom is nearly everyone's cuppa with crumble, "scones and pastries to die for", one of the "best cheesecakes in Paris" and "inventive homemade" "light meals"; the waiters are "sometimes overwhelmed" during the "abundant brunch" on weekends, "but the charm" of the place takes priority over any glitches.

Arbuci (L') ☻ 13 | 14 | 13 | 40
25, rue de Buci, 6ᵉ (Mabillon), 01 44 32 16 00; fax 01 44 32 16 09; www.arbuci.com
☒ They may serve "delicious" "all-you-can-eat oysters" at this Saint-Germain "bustling" brasserie that got a "*très* chic" but "too modern" makeover awhile back, but many mutter the rest of the "tradtional menu" seems "mediocre" and "disorganized service" doesn't help; still, they offer dancing to DJ-spun and live tunes toward the end of the week, leaving some to ponder "maybe the jazz is a better value than the food."

Ardoise (L') 22 | 12 | 17 | 38
28, rue du Mont Thabor, 1ᵉʳ (Concorde/Tuileries), 01 42 96 28 18
■ When you're "taking a break from the Louvre" nearby, this "tiny place with huge flavors" offers a weekly changing "appetizing chalkboard menu" of "hearty" New Bistro fare that has the crowds crowing over chef-owner Pierre Jay; despite its "being flooded with tourists", the "service is lightning fast"; and "at such affordable prices" (especially for the "overpriced 1st"), "it's easy to overlook" the near-"nonexistent" decor and "elbow-bumping" seating.

Argenteuil (L') 23 | 18 | 21 | 47
9, rue d'Argenteuil, 1ᵉʳ (Palais Royal-Musée du Louvre/ Pyramides), 01 42 60 56 22
■ "In a sort of lost corner of the 1st", this "intimate" New French delights devotees with "delicious" food, service

26   subscribe to zagat.com

that's "courteous without any irritating chumminess" and a "trim but handsome decor"; its "subtly exciting" charms are lost on some, but most find it "perfect if you're Louvre-d out."

Aristide ⊠ | – | – | – | M |

121, rue de Rome, 17ᵉ (Rome), 01 47 63 17 83; fax 01 47 54 97 55

With a gorgeous interior dating to 1893, this "good", moderately priced bistro in the 17th is "packed at noon" with a business crowd, but quiet in the evening – which makes it a fine "rendezvous for an intimate dinner" of "solid Classic" French dishes made with first-rate foodstuffs.

Armand au Palais Royal ⊠ | 21 | 21 | 23 | 48 |

4-6, rue du Beaujolais, 1ᵉʳ (Bourse/Palais Royal-Musée du Louvre), 01 42 60 05 11; fax 01 42 96 16 24

■ "Housed in the 17th century stables of the Palais Royal", this "agreeable" Classic French filly has a loyal following of local and foreign fans who "recommend" the "intimate ambiance" created by its "pretty" vaulted ceilings, "attentive and genuinely friendly service" and "marvelous" food (including a signature crêpe that contains "some of the best foie gras in Paris").

ARPÈGE (L') ⊠ | 26 | 23 | 25 | 176 |

84, rue de Varenne, 7ᵉ (Varenne), 01 45 51 47 33; fax 01 44 18 98 39; www.alain-passard.com

☑ "His creations express [food] the way God intended it to be tasted" acclaim acolytes of chef-owner Alain Passard, whose "exceptional" if "esoteric", vegetable-oriented Haute Cuisine is "styled like a haute couture designer's"; the decor at this "sophisticate" in the 7th is "sparse, but impressive", and the "staff is superb"; admittedly, the whole experience can be an "intellectual challenge", and "prices have soared out of control" – maybe that's why some would "be willing to work as a waiter to get the food free."

Asian | 14 | 21 | 13 | 45 |

30, av George V, 8ᵉ (Alma-Marceau/George V), 01 56 89 11 00; fax 01 56 89 11 01; www.asian.fr

☑ A "professional clientele" finds the glamorama decor – a sort of Disneyesque take on diverse decorative idioms of the Far East – "wonderful" at this "chic", "cavernous" Pan-Asian place off the Champs-Elysées; in fact, "you come here more for the pretty setting than the mediocre", "pricey" "theme cuisine" (though some "original" offerings have their advocates); all agree, however, that the staff "seems as if it's merely part of the decoration" – "beautiful" but "slow."

Assiette (L') | ∇ 26 | 16 | 16 | 74 |

181, rue du Château, 14ᵉ (Gaîté/Mouton-Duvernet), 01 43 22 64 86; fax 01 45 20 54 66

■ "Off the beaten path" in Montparnasse, this Traditional Bistro is sort of like "a private club with loyal, very-flush

| F | D | S | €C |

clients" (including the late President François Mitterrand) who love the "really good Southwestern cooking" of "Lulu Rousseau, the cigar-smoking chef"; "you get food from her heart and the pick of her region" in a simple dining room with tile floors, but an "astronomical price tag" as the price of admission.

Assiette Lyonnaise ● | 16 | 11 | 14 | 31 |
21, rue Marbeuf, 8ᵉ (Franklin D. Roosevelt), 01 47 20 94 80; fax 01 47 23 53 94

■ A roaring rise in the Food score makes this "charmer" of a regional bistro the Lyon king of Paris, given its "delicious", "honest" and "filling" fare that's "solid value for the money" and "for the area" (the 8th, where eating cheap isn't always easy); though the decor remains "unassuming", the atmosphere's "warm", thanks to "increased friendliness" on the staff's part.

Astier ⌧ | 21 | 12 | 17 | 35 |
44, rue J.P. Timbaud, 11ᵉ (Oberkampf/Parmentier), 01 43 57 16 35

■ It gets a little "hot, temperaturewise" and "it's not the place for quiet conversation", but this place "off the beaten (tourist) path" in the 11th packs 'em in with its "well prepared and pleasing" Traditional Bistro food "for a modest price", especially on the "extensive prix fixe" that includes a "mind-blowing cheese tray" that's "nearly the same size as the table"; though "precise", the servers speak "minimal English", but one's close, "friendly fellow customers are only too happy to guide the uninitiated."

Astor (L') | 22 | 21 | 21 | 90 |
Hôtel Astor, 11, rue d'Astorg, 8ᵉ (St-Augustin), 01 53 05 05 20; fax 01 53 05 05 30; www.hotel-astor.net

◪ "Under the guidance of Joël Robuchon" as culinary consultant, this Haute Cuisine hotel dining room in the 8th is favored by a business clientele for its "ambitious, delicious" New French cuisine, a "lunch menu that's a good buy" and the "elegant, art deco–style decor"; however, several say it seems "too expensive", especially since the "quality has become uneven" since a "chef change" last year, and the service, while "artful", bears "a touch of the scornful."

ASTRANCE (L') | 26 | 21 | 24 | 89 |
4, rue Beethoven, 16ᵉ (Passy), 01 40 50 84 40; fax 01 40 50 11 45

■ Provided you "book months ahead of time", "an exquisite experience" awaits at chef/co-owner Pascal Barbot's New French table "with a luminous gray decor" in a quiet street near the Trocadéro; his "food from out of a fantasy" has many "gasping in awe", with due appreciation for the "wonderful, accommodating staff", too; some suggest success has made it "self-important" (expecting their

| F | D | S | €C |

money "would buy me more fun than this"), but most say it's "still an extraordinary bargain for [this] level of cooking."

Astuce (L') ☒ — | — | — | M
138, rue de Vaugirard, 15ᵉ (Duroc/Falguière), 01 47 83 29 52; www.lastuce.fr
A large mirror dominates this snug Left Bank dining room where the creative New Bistro fare is starting to draw a stylish, young crowd as word gets around the *quartier*; friendly service and a warm atmosphere make it easy to linger on the banquettes here.

Atelier Berger (L') ●☒ 21 | 17 | 17 | 50
49, rue Berger, 1ᵉʳ (Louvre-Rivoli), 01 40 28 00 00; fax 01 40 28 10 65
◪ Dueling opinions duke it out about this "quiet" duplex dining room with "modern decor"; devotees declare Norwegian chef-owner Jean Christiansen's New French cuisine, a "carefully crafted" "combination of the inspired and the traditional", makes this "modern" place "among the best addresses in Les Halles"; but the "disappointed" deplore the "indifferent service" "and zero scene."

ATELIER DE JOËL ROBUCHON (L') ● 26 | 23 | 21 | 74
5, rue de Montalembert, 7ᵉ (Rue du Bac), 01 42 22 56 56
◪ From the day it opened in the 7th, chef Joël Robuchon's comeback has been a "real culinary hot spot"; within a "sleek", "black decor", diners "sit around a counter" "overlooking the kitchen" (think "glorified diner") to sample "tapaslike", "tasty morsels" ("plus some mains") of his "tongue-popping" Haute Cuisine; fans find it "fabulous", with the only "flat note" being that the "no-reservations policy" often causes a "long wait at the door" (which "doesn't open from the outside"); best advice: "eat early."

Atelier Gourmand ☒ — | — | — | M
20, rue de Tocqueville, 17ᵉ (Villiers), 01 42 27 03 71; fax 01 42 27 03 71
Though it's not very well known, this "fairly priced" New French in the 17th is "a neighborhood jewel" that's "always worthy of your confidence", even if its menu changes often; the owners, a "husband-wife team, provide good service", though the setting, decorated in a hybrid of Second Empire and artist's atelier styles, is "not *très* fun."

Atelier Maître Albert (L') ●☒ — | — | — | M
1, rue Maître Albert, 5ᵉ (St-Michel), 01 46 33 13 78; fax 01 53 10 83 23
Recently taken over by chef Guy Savoy, this "warm" and "very Latin Quarter" (read: noisy) bistro has gotten a dramatic revamp by his preferred decorator Jean-Michel Wilmotte since the last *Survey*; the new look is all exposed stone walls and cobalt-blue beams overhead, but the Maître's old pupils will be glad to hear that the large

get updates at zagat.com 29

| F | D | S | €C |

Renaissance fireplace and rotisserie have not been touched – in fact, the short menu stars roasted-on-a-spit fowl, fish and meats, served by a young staff.

Atlas (L') 21 | 16 | 18 | 36
12, bd St-Germain, 5ᵉ (Maubert-Mutualité), 01 46 33 86 98; fax 01 40 46 06 56
■ "Generous" helpings of "savory tagines" and other "classics", served by a "most welcoming and eager staff", keep the crowd coming to this long-running couscous casbah in the Latin Quarter; sure, it's "more expensive than the clip joints off the Boulevard Saint-Michel", but that's because you're paying for "atmospheric decor", "like something from an early James Bond film shot in Morocco."

Auberge Aveyronnaise – | – | – | M
40, rue Gabriel Lamé, 12ᵉ (Cour St-Emilion), 01 43 40 12 24; fax 01 43 40 12 15
"Good regional dishes" from the Aveyron district of the Auvergne acquire admirers to this "sweet bistro" in the 12th not far from Bercy; if the bill-of-fare runs to sturdy dishes like aligot (potatoes whipped with cheese curds), prices are light as a feather, making it a good choice for groups; all can enjoy the "jovial service."

Auberge Bressane (L') 21 | 16 | 19 | 43
16, av de La Motte-Picquet, 7ᵉ (Ecole Militaire/ La Tour-Maubourg), 01 47 05 98 37
■ "A great place to go to beat the Sunday-night blues" ("go in hungry, and come out ready to face the work week") attest those "addicted" to this "excellent auberge" in the 7th, which serves "hearty", "rustic" Classic French "quality cuisine" from Lyon and Burgundy; "almost-familial" service further "warms the heart and soul" of the well-heeled clientele here, which even smiles on the "outdated but charming" digs "decorated with heraldic emblems", wood paneling and wrought-iron light fixtures.

Auberge Dab (L') ● 16 | 14 | 16 | 52
161, av de Malakoff, 16ᵉ (Porte Maillot), 01 45 00 32 22; fax 01 45 00 58 50
☑ "The aroma of shellfish is heady" at this huge haven near the Porte Maillot, which offers a "classic brasserie experience" in that it's "always reliable for a seafood platter" and "people-watching by the window" in a "decor from a Jean Gabin film" of the '50s; but faultfinders feel it's a "factory"-like experience – from the food to the "pleasant, but often distracted" service – and a "relatively expensive" one to boot.

Auberge d'Autrefois (L) – | – | – | M
191, av de Versailles, 16ᵉ (Porte de St-Cloud), 01 42 24 49 28
With a change in ownership and the arrival of a talented new toque, Laurent Ternisien, this old-fashioned neighborhood

30 subscribe to zagat.com

| F | D | S | €C |

bistro has been reborn as a popular and stylish table not far from the Porte de Saint-Cloud, adorned with handsome butter-yellow-painted interior and Wenge wood chairs at white-linen-dressed tables; the chef puts a spin on Classic French dishes by varying their seasonings and garnishes, which pleases a business-y crowd at noon and well-heeled locals in the evening.

Auberge du Champ de Mars ⊠ | 19 | 17 | 18 | 32 |
18, rue de l'Exposition, 7ᵉ (Ecole Militaire), 01 45 51 78 08
■ Converts champion this "small, family-run" place, with a "romantic", "dark and mysterious setting", and a husband-wife team – "he's the chef, she's the hostess" – "who make you feel like guests in their home"; it's "great value for the money" in an expensive neighborhood near the Eiffel Tower, especially given such "good" Classic French cooking ("loved the duck").

Auberge du Clou (L') ◐⊅ | – | – | – | M |
30, av Trudaine, 9ᵉ (Anvers/Pigalle), 01 48 78 22 48; fax 01 48 78 30 08
At this fashionable table in the up-and-coming 9th, the "second floor with the fireplace is charming in winter" and the Eclectic–New French cooking is "interesting" and "original" year-round (though it's "too bad the menu doesn't change more" often, some sigh); "service is amiable", if "a little stuffy."

Auberge Etchégorry ⊠ | – | – | – | E |
41, rue Croulebarbe, 13ᵉ (Corvisart/Les Gobelins), 01 44 08 83 51; fax 01 44 08 83 69
Tucked away in the 13th, this vintage Basque isn't exactly basking in the attention of surveyors; but those who know insist it's "super" "for Southwestern cooking in Paris", even for "a spontaneous meal"; however, the folkloric, whitewashed decor strikes a "sort of miserable" note for several, especially given the expensive tabs.

Auberge Nicolas Flamel ⊠ | ▽ 16 | 16 | 14 | 44 |
51, rue de Montmorency, 3ᵉ (Etienne Marcel/Rambuteau), 01 42 71 77 78; fax 01 48 04 58 36; nicolasflamel.parisbistro.net
▣ "The decor alone is worth coming for" at this Marais mansion, purported to be "the oldest house in Paris", which offers a "warm welcome" to visitors; while folks feel cooler about the "so-so" Classic Bistro kitchen, they praise the "not-to-be-missed lamb that's slow-roasted for seven hours" and "a wonderful bargain-filled wine list."

Auberge Pyrénées Cévennes (L') ⊠ | 20 | 16 | 18 | 35 |
106, rue de la Folie-Méricourt, 11ᵉ (République), 01 43 57 33 78
■ "On a small street near the Place de la République" lies this "very-good country restaurant" serving "big portions" of "hearty", "old-fashioned" Southwestern dishes like

get updates at zagat.com

| **F** | **D** | **S** | **€C** |

"thick foie gras" and possibly "the best cassoulet ever"; a "happy staff" makes for "soigné service", and best of all, it offers "an enjoyable experience without having to take a second mortgage on the house."

Auvergne Gourmande (L') ⌀ _ | _ | _ | M

127, rue St-Dominique, 7ᵉ (Ecole Militaire), 01 47 05 60 79

This vest-pocket–size annex of the popular Fontaine du Mars a few doors down in the 7th is a "fun place", a *table d'hôte* usually populated with "friendly table partners" who can make for "a delightful evening"; everyone sits together on "high stools", dining on "delicious" Auvergnat edibles; it's "excellent value for the money", too.

Avant Goût (L') ⌀ 22 | 14 | 18 | 36

26, rue Bobillot, 13ᵉ (Place d'Italie), 01 53 80 24 00; fax 01 53 80 00 77

■ It's "quite a schlep" to the Butte-aux-Cailles quarter of "the far-flung 13th", but the crowds still come to this "deservedly popular" New French "neo-bistro" where chef-owner Christophe Beaufront, "a Guy Savoy protégé, offers excellent, creative cooking" for near-"bargain" prices (especially on the "frequently changing set menus"); since it's "hard to do better for the money" and the "welcome is warm", it's easy to overlook the "close tables"; just "book ahead" since it's "always full."

Avenue (L') ● 16 | 18 | 13 | 56

41, av Montaigne, 8ᵉ (Franklin D. Roosevelt), 01 40 70 14 91; fax 01 40 70 91 97

■ Kind of a "Paris version of a *Sex and the City* place", this "trendy" "hangout" on the Avenue Montaigne comes "courtesy of the Costes brothers" and bears all their "typical" features, from a "hip" decor by Jacques Garcia to "stylish" "servers who have a lot of room for improvement"; the "light" New French fare is "expensive for what you get", especially given the "tiny portions" geared for "young women to stay thin and still eat"; but "food is not the point here", and many find it all "fun" and "sexy . . . until you're put in a corner for not being sexy enough."

Azabu _ | _ | _ | M

3, rue André Mazet, 6ᵉ (Odéon), 01 46 33 72 05

Near the Odéon, this "excellent teppanyaki restaurant where the chef cooks your food in front of you" is such a reasonably priced crowd-pleaser that it's worth visitors "giving up a French meal for"; with specialties such as "okonomiyaki (fish and vegetable pancake) that's heaven", this may be "the best non-sushi Japanese in town"; be forewarned that service can be "slow", especially on weekends, but you can kill time checking out the "must-see Zen-style bathrooms."

| F | D | S | €C |

B*fly ◐   13 | 18 | 11 | 48
49-51, av George V, 8ᵉ (George V), 01 53 67 84 60; fax 01 53 67 84 67
◪ Populated by an "affluent" "twenty-to-fiftysomething" singles crowd, plus "wanna-be models" waiting for "pomaded Euros to buy them" "expensive" drinks, this restaurant-bar on the swank Avenue George V defines the label "has-been"; but it's admittedly more about the "great bartending" and people-watching than the Eclectic cuisine, and the service is about as helpful as a fly on the wall.

Baan-Boran ◐☒   20 | 14 | 19 | 35
43, rue de Montpensier, 1ᵉʳ (Palais Royal-Musée du Louvre), 01 40 15 90 45; fax 01 40 15 90 45
■ Across the street from the Palais Royal, this "intimate", "good-quality" Siamese is "one of the only restaurants in Paris that cooks to real Thai tastes, rather than toning it down for French palates" (though it's still "not spicy enough" for some); all agree "the presentation and service are colorful", though, and prices are tasty, too.

Babylone (Au) ☒≠   – | – | – | M
13, rue de Babylone, 7ᵉ (Sèvres-Babylone), 01 45 48 72 13
Only open during the day, this "wonderful" Classic Bistro near Sèvres-Babylone has the "atmosphere of a real old-fashioned hole-in-the-wall, plus succulent home cooking"; it's "good for a quick lunch after shopping at the Bon Marché" store, but come early because "just 40 minutes after opening, most of the *plats du jour* run out."

Bacchantes (Les) ◐☒   – | – | – | M
21, rue de Caumartin, 9ᵉ (Havre-Caumartin/Opéra), 01 42 65 25 35; fax 01 47 42 65 87
Near the Opéra Garnier and the big department stores, this "convivial", "debonair *bistrot à vins*" is "a good address for those who like Traditional French cooking at affordable prices" – not to mention a "menu that changes daily"; "be sure to book or come early, since it fills up quickly at noon."

Baie d'Ha Long (La) ☒   – | – | – | E
164, av de Versailles, 16ᵉ (Porte de St-Cloud), 01 45 24 60 62; fax 01 42 30 58 98; www.baiedhalong.com
Maybe it's because this "cozy, little" Southeast Asian is on the outer edges of the 16th that so few know it; those who traveled the long way praise the "high quality", if slightly "high-priced", "original specialties" (tip: "choose a dish that originates in the aquarium"), "efficiently" served by the *maîtresse de maison*, a veritable Vietnamese "princess."

Bains (Les) ☒   9 | 13 | 9 | 53
7, rue du Bourg l'Abbé, 3ᵉ (Etienne Marcel/Réaumur Sébastopol), 01 48 87 01 80; fax 01 48 87 13 70; www.lesbains-club.com
◪ "If you eat here, you get into the disco without braving the door policy" – the main reason citizens "suffer the club

get updates at zagat.com

| F | D | S | €C |

food" on a New French–Thai menu and the "pretentious personnel" at this venerable but still viable nightspot in the 3rd; otherwise, just "go for the bar" and the "jam-packed dance floor" with its "definite see-and-be-seen" scene; naturally, it's "overpriced, but by how much depends upon what wine one orders."

Ballon des Ternes (Le) ☾ | 15 | 15 | 15 | 43 |
103, av des Ternes, 17^e (Porte Maillot), 01 45 74 17 98; fax 01 45 72 18 84
■ "Well situated" near the Porte Maillot, this "find" of a "neighborhood brasserie" offers "especially good shellfish and fish", along with other traditional dishes like veal kidneys; its attractive ambiance stems equally from the "knowledgeable", "English-speaking", "unpretentious" waiters and the "beautiful" belle-epoque decor, complete with "a nice terrace" for the summer; it's "good value for the money", too.

Ballon et Coquillages | – | – | – | M |
71, bd Gouvion St-Cyr, 17^e (Porte Maillot), 01 45 74 17 98
Eight different varieties of bivalves star at this new shellfish-only annex of the nearby Ballon des Ternes, where customers sit at a stylish round bar (there are no tables, this is a real oyster bar) that promotes a certain degree of conviviality; with obliging service and an appealing decor enlivened by red stools, this Porte Maillot place is perfect to bear in mind for a quick, casual meal.

Bamboche (Le) ⌧ | 22 | 15 | 20 | 58 |
15, rue de Babylone, 7e (Sèvres-Babylone), 01 45 49 14 40; fax 01 45 49 14 44
■ Not only are chef-owner Claude Colliot and his wife "so charming", but the "audacious" New French cooking (an "oyster sorbet" that's "out of this world") is "first rate" at their Sèvres-Babylone site; "happy, caring service" and "calm", "minimalist decor" also explain why it's been "very discovered" despite "surprisingly expensive" prices.

Banyan ⌧ | – | – | – | M |
24, pl Etienne Pernet, 15e (Félix Faure), 01 40 60 09 31; fax 01 40 60 09 20
A former chef at the Blue Elephant and Asian goes out on his own with this pleasant little Thai in a quiet corner of the 15th; beautiful flower arrangements and soft lighting transform the storefront space into an appealing dining room that's instantly drawn locals for the quality of the authentic cooking and friendly service.

Baptiste ⌧ | – | – | – | M |
51, rue Jouffroy d'Abbans, 17^e (Malesherbes/Wagram), 01 42 27 20 18; fax 01 43 80 68 09
"All-around excellent" is the word from the few who know this Contemporary French near the Place Wagram; "clever"

| F | D | S | €C |

cooking from "a team that obviously cares about what it's doing", "cozy" vintage 1930s decor and prices that are moderate for this part of town make it ideal for "business or pleasure."

Baracane ●☒ 22 | 13 | 21 | 36
38, rue des Tournelles, 4ᵉ (Chemin Vert), 01 42 71 43 33
■ Lucky are those who "fall into" this "cheerful", little sibling of L'Oulette near the Place des Vosges, specializing in "lick-your-plate" traditional Southwestern dishes like "cassoulet" and "awesome house wine" at "terrific value"; given that there's "little room to exhale" in the tight but "homey" space, reservations are "highly recommended."

Bar à Huîtres (Le) ● 17 | 15 | 15 | 42
33, bd Beaumarchais, 3ᵉ (Bastille), 01 48 87 98 92; fax 01 48 87 04 42
33, rue St-Jacques, 5ᵉ (Maubert-Mutualité), 01 44 07 27 37; fax 01 43 26 71 62
112, bd du Montparnasse, 14ᵉ (Raspail/Vavin), 01 43 20 71 01; fax 01 43 20 52 04
www.lebarahuitres.com
☑ "It's all about the oysters" at this trio of strategically located seafooders with shell-themed interiors by decorator Jacques Garcia; while they are undeniable "tourist" havens, most praise the "remarkably fresh" shellfish and "reasonable prices", but "ignore the cooked offerings", which are "nothing special", and snarl about "rushed" service that can "take the pleasure out of a meal."

Bar des Théâtres ● 14 | 10 | 14 | 39
6, av Montaigne, 8ᵉ (Alma-Marceau), 01 47 23 34 63; fax 01 47 50 72 23
☑ For more than 50 years, Théâtre des Champs-Elysées patrons have found this "classic" on the Avenue Montaigne handy for "relaxing with friends" "after a show" (or before, given the "remarkably efficient service"); alas, "it's not what it used to be", now that the "entertainment- and model-crowd" is diluted by lesser-known faces, a remodeling has "diminished the atmosphere" and aside from one of "the best steak tartares" around, the Traditional French food's "without interest."

Baron Rouge (Le) ∇ 13 | 19 | 15 | 25
1, rue Théophile Roussel, 12ᵉ (Ledru-Rollin), 01 43 43 14 32
■ For a sip of "Old Paris", try this "superb *bar à vins* near one of the prettiest markets in the city" – the Marché d'Aligre in the 12th; join "regulars" gathered around "wine casks" or at the bar to "chat" and nibble "salty" charcuterie (and fresh oysters on Sunday mornings) and tipple "high quality" varietals that can be purchased to take home; a "warm welcome" and easy prices make it an ongoing hit.

get updates at zagat.com

			F	D	S	€C

Barramundi ●🚭
– | – | – | E

3, rue Taitbout, 9ᵉ (Richelieu-Drouot), 01 47 70 21 21; fax 01 47 70 21 20

"You come for the decor", which features elements from all over the world, including African masks, but "the loud music" can "make it hard to talk" at this "trendy" restaurant/club in the 9th; it's "fun for a night out with friends" of a wild stripe, assuming no one's really hungry since the "expensive" Eclectic menu incites minimal enthusiasm.

Barrio Latino ●
8 | 22 | 9 | 37

46-48, rue du Faubourg St-Antoine, 12ᵉ (Bastille), 01 55 78 84 75; fax 01 55 78 85 30

🔲 "Sexy" Latin atmosphere, "excellent music" and zingy mojitos rev up the "young" dance-ready crowd at this multilevel club/eatery near the Bastille; as for dining, most advise bypassing "the banal food", since even "supermarket guacamole is better" than its ilk here; a "rude door policy" doesn't whet appetites either.

Barroco
– | – | – | M

23, rue Mazarine, 6ᵉ (Odéon/St-Germain-des-Prés), 01 43 26 40 24

Not far from the Odéon, this Nuevo Latino taverna pulls in a stylish international crowd to sip good cocktails and Chilean wines and to sample a diverse menu that takes inspiration from Spain, Portugal and Latin America; "the pretty decor" reminiscent of a refined Brazilian home pleases, but service tends to be more "sexy than classy."

Bar Rouge 🚭
– | – | – | M

Galeries Lafayette Gourmet, 97, rue de Provence, 9ᵉ (Havre-Caumartin/Opéra), 01 40 23 52 59; fax 01 40 23 52 60

Tucked in the Galeries Lafayette in the 9th, this wine bar is now overseen by the Fogón Saint Julien team, so expect first-rate tapas and other Spanish nibbles in a contemporary setting; open only during store hours, it's very busy at lunchtime, sating local business types and "the shopping-weary" with a quick bite or a "coupe de champagne."

Bartolo ●🚭
17 | 9 | 11 | 39

7, rue des Canettes, 6ᵉ (St-Germain-des-Prés), 01 43 26 27 08

🔲 The word on this long-running Italian in Saint-Germain is decidedly mixed: most laud the "delicious pastas" and wood-oven fired pizzas but the "noisy", unremarkable room and the sullen service get the boot; P.S. "come with cash because they don't take credit cards."

Bar Vendôme
20 | 25 | 25 | 59

Hôtel Ritz, 15, pl Vendôme, 1ᵉʳ (Concorde/Opéra), 01 43 16 33 63; fax 01 43 16 33 75; www.ritzparis.com

⬛ "Feel like a character in an old Elizabeth Taylor movie" while taking tea or relishing apéritifs and "the best club sandwiches in Paris" at this "grand" bar in the Hôtel Ritz;

| F | D | S | €C |

expect "class, class, class" and "gracious" service; despite some comparatively ritzy prices, if you're looking to "indulge your desire for luxury while maintaining your budget" with a light meal, this is an "exquisite" option; P.S. enjoy the "enchanting terrace" in fair weather.

Bascou (Au) 🗷 | 20 | 14 | 16 | 42 |
38, rue Réaumur, 3ᵉ (Arts et Métiers), 01 42 72 69 25; fax 01 42 72 69 25
■ "A warm welcome and savory cooking" greet diners at this "exceptional" "Basque bistro" near the Place de la République; "interesting wines" are paired with the "rich", "distinctive" cuisine of the Southwest; add in a room that's "humanly scaled" and "sensible prices" and you get satisfied surveyors musing "what else can you ask for?"

Basilic (Le) | 13 | 15 | 12 | 43 |
2, rue Casimir Périer, 7ᵉ (Invalides/Solférino), 01 44 18 94 64; fax 01 47 53 77 96
◪ Like the "imposing Sainte-Clothilde church" nearby in the 7th, this Classic French upholds the bourgeois status quo with "simple" offerings, of which "the house special roast lamb" is the star; other than that, "the cooking's not terribly interesting", and "the service on par with that at a bar-tabac", but the "quiet terrace" always assuages.

Bastide Odéon (La) 🗷 | 21 | 18 | 19 | 45 |
7, rue Corneille, 6ᵉ (Odéon), 01 43 26 03 65; fax 01 44 07 28 93; www.bastide-odeon.com
◪ "Like a trip to Provence without the train ride" say contented armchair travelers of this "modern" bistro near the Luxembourg Gardens that turns out "original" but "not intimidating" southern-minded dishes in a "cheerful" yellow-and-red-accented bi-level space; a few suggest that it's "over-hyped" and "touristy" and have mixed feelings about the service, but all "appreciate the air-conditioning" and the relatively "reasonable" prices.

Bath's 🗷 | 27 | 21 | 24 | 90 |
9, rue de La Trémoille, 8ᵉ (Alma-Marceau), 01 40 70 01 09; fax 01 40 70 01 22; www.baths.fr
■ For such a *petit* "father-son operation", this Contemporary Bistro in the swank 8th is a startlingly "major address", "working wonders" with "excellent" Auvergnat cuisine that can be enjoyed à la carte or on a "remarkable" tasting menu; owner Jean-Yves Bath "greets all guests warmly", the room is "cozy with well-spaced tables" and service is "stellar", all of which makes the "steep" prices easier to swallow.

Bauta (La) 🗷 | – | – | – | E |
129, bd du Montparnasse, 6ᵉ (Vavin), 01 43 22 52 35; fax 01 43 22 10 99
"The cooking's very good" at this classic Venetian in Montparnasse, so "it's a shame that this place lacks a

certain charm" in its decor and service that would make a meal here more of an occasion; it's also unlikely to be a frequent pleasure, since it's "expensive" – although the two-course prix fixe isn't a bad deal.

Béatilles (Les) ⓈS   − − − E

11 bis, rue Villebois-Mareuil, 17ᵉ (Charles de Gaulle-Etoile/Ternes), 01 45 74 43 80; fax 01 45 74 43 81

It's worth sleuthing out this "lost corner" in the 17th, since chef Christian Bochaton's New French cooking is "a sure bet" and "notable for its clean, well-defined" flavors; his wife Catherine oversees the "attentive" staff in a modern dining room that unfortunately "lacks the zip" that's found on your plate.

Beato ⓈS   ∇ 15 | 15 | 18 | 52

8, rue Malar, 7ᵉ (Invalides), 01 47 05 94 27; fax 01 45 55 64 41

■ This well-heeled Italian in the 7th serves "very good" food ("taste the squid's ink pasta with langoustines") and is "popular with politicians at lunchtime" who rightly recognize that "the business prix fixe is a great deal" but are too busy to notice that "the decor could use an update"; P.S. "it's much more expensive in the evening."

Beaujolais d'Auteuil (Le)   17 | 11 | 13 | 39

99, bd de Montmorency, 16ᵉ (Porte d'Auteuil), 01 47 43 03 56; fax 01 46 51 27 81

■ You may be packed "tight like sardines" at this "red-check-tableclothed bistro" on the edge of the 16th, "but you always return for the good times" and "solid" "Classic" French dishes like "eggs poached in red wine and calf's liver", not to mention the "pretty terrace" in summer.

Beauvilliers ⓈS   23 | 26 | 23 | 101

52, rue Lamarck, 18ᵉ (Lamarck-Caulaincourt), 01 42 54 54 42; fax 01 42 62 70 30

■ Classic French foodies scale Montmartre to sample "historic dishes like a macaroni timbale that jibes perfectly with the Napoleon III decor" at "one of the most beautiful restaurants in Paris"; "filled with fresh blooms" and spilling onto a patio in summer, it's "an incredibly romantic place" (though "over-flowered" for less sentimental types); N.B. founding owner Edouard Carlier died in 2003, and the restaurant has been taken over by his sister.

BE Boulangépicier ⓈS   19 | 14 | 14 | 22

73, bd de Courcelles, 17ᵉ (Courcelles/Ternes), 01 46 22 20 20; fax 01 46 22 20 21; www.boulangepicier.com

■ "Alain Ducasse strikes again", in cahoots with master baker Eric Kayser, with this luxury bread and gourmet-food shop in the 17th; "it's chic and expensive but so good that you want to buy everything"; and while "it's not easy to have a meal on the spot" due to scant seating, you can pack the "creative" sandwiches for a "snob"-style picnic at nearby Parc Monceau.

Bel Canto 🚫 | 14 | 17 | 20 | 50 |

72, quai de l'Hôtel de Ville, 4ᵉ (Hôtel-de-Ville/Pont-Marie), 01 42 78 30 18; fax 01 42 78 30 28
88, rue de la Tombe-Issoire, 14ᵉ (Alésia), 01 43 22 96 15; fax 01 43 27 09 88

■ "Combine a show with dinner" – but not in the usual sense – at these Italians in the 4th and the 14th, where "young, energetic" students from the Opéra de Paris Conservatory "perform between taking orders"; while the kitchen garners no encores and not all servers can multitask so ably, "it's worth coming back" for the "jolly" ambiance and "charming" "musical program."

Bélier (Le) | – | – | – | M |

L'Hôtel, 13, rue des Beaux-Arts, 6ᵉ (St-Germain-des-Prés), 01 44 41 99 01; fax 01 43 25 64 81; www.l-hotel.com

Situated in the Saint-Germain hotel where Oscar Wilde passed away and chanteuse Mistinguett rested up, this "intimate" spot allows jet-setters to refuel on "well-presented", though slightly "pretentious", Classic French fare against a "*très* chic" and pleasurably louche backdrop designed by decorator Jacques Garcia; "accommodating" service rounds out the generally positive experience.

Bellecour (Le) 🚫 | 24 | 17 | 23 | 60 |

22, rue Surcouf, 7ᵉ (Invalides/La Tour-Maubourg), 01 45 51 46 93; fax 01 45 50 30 11

■ "Tables of friends and family" tuck into "exceptional" Lyonnais fare, like pike quenelles, at this "little gem" of a bistro not far from the Esplanade des Invalides in the 7th, where "outstanding service" helps diners to "relax" and feel like they're in "someone's living room"; though not cheap, most feel it's a fair "value."

Bellini 🚫 | 19 | 14 | 18 | 49 |

28, rue Lesueur, 16ᵉ (Argentine), 01 45 00 54 20; fax 01 45 00 11 74

■ "No pretense, just really nice food" say *amici* of this "neighborhoody" little Italian in the 16th that serves up "savory" "classic" dishes including "tagliatelle flambéed in a Parmesan wheel that's not to be missed"; all also appreciate the "attentive" reception and "good wine list."

Bellotta-Bellotta 🚫 | – | – | – | M |

18, rue Jean-Nicot, 7ᵉ (La Tour-Maubourg), 01 53 59 96 96; fax 01 53 59 70 44

■ "Authentic tapas" and "incredible" Iberian ham are the draws at this "cute, little" Spaniard in the heart of the 7th; but while moderately priced, several rounds of those tiny plates can end up being "pricey", so most use it as a place to "meet friends" for snacks over a glass of wine or sherry.

| F | D | S | €C |

Benkay
| 23 | 17 | 21 | 79 |

Hôtel Novotel Tour Eiffel, 61, quai de Grenelle, 15ᵉ (Bir-Hakeim/
Charles Michels), 01 40 58 21 26; fax 01 40 58 21 30;
www.novotel.com

◪ "Miracles on your plate and a fabulous view of the Seine" summarizes the scene at this Japanese in the 15th; "having a semi-private chef prepare [sushi and teppanyaki] in front of you is a dream", and polished service helps offset the "chilly decor"; "if you're looking for an inexpensive" meal, however, you won't find it here.

BENOÎT
| 23 | 20 | 22 | 72 |

20, rue St-Martin, 4ᵉ (Châtelet-Les Halles), 01 42 72 25 76;
fax 01 42 72 45 68

◪ One of the town's most popular and "just what a bistro should be" say cassoulet-cravers about this family-run homage to Lyon in the 4th that smacks of "Paris from the bygone days"; though seating may be "segregated" for natives "and foreigners" and the service, while filled "with gusto", can be "chilly", few quibble about the "fancy prices", deeming it all "worth it, in an old-time luxury way."

Berkeley (Le) ◐
| 10 | 15 | 10 | 42 |

7, av Matignon, 8ᵉ (Franklin D. Roosevelt/Miromesnil),
01 42 25 72 25; fax 01 45 63 30 06

◪ With its stripe-tent ceiling and slightly over-the-top decor, this "extremely chic" Costes Brothers Classic French–Eclectic hangout is a colorful locale for "drinks and dessert" or Sunday brunch on the "pretty terrace" after a stroll on the nearby Champs-Elysées; too bad service is more "snooty" "than the food quality merits" ("they treat us like tourists, even though we're not").

Bermuda Onion
| 13 | 19 | 15 | 46 |

16, rue Linois, 15ᵉ (Charles Michels), 01 45 75 11 11;
fax 01 40 59 92 94

◪ Sunday brunch can be a "sumptuous" affair at this Classic French in the 15th, but the rest of the time, the food is merely "mediocre"; if the decor recalls "a 1980s nightclub", optimists focus on "the great views of the Seine", especially from window tables or the patio; most turn their backs on service that needs refinement and prices that seem "high for what you get."

Beudant (Le) ⌧
| – | – | – | M |

97, rue des Dames, 17ᵉ (Rome/Villiers), 01 43 87 11 20;
fax 01 43 87 27 35

The "new owners really know what they're doing", so "follow their advice and you'll be happy" tip informants on this little-known Classic French near Villiers whose kitchen has a particular talent with fish; the lunch prix fixe is a particularly good value, and if the salmon-colored dining room's "a bit sad", this doesn't deter the local patrons.

			F	D	S	€C

Beurre Noisette (Le) ☒   23 | 15 | 19 | 35
68, rue Vasco de Gama, 15ᵉ (Lourmel/Porte de Versailles), 01 48 56 82 49; fax 01 48 56 82 49
■ This "excellent, little neighborhood" New Bistro "tries hard to make dining a pleasure", which explains why its reputation is growing despite a location "deep in the 15th"; the cooking is "outstanding" because the "chef is a true chef – no fooling around"; service is "personal", and "it's a great buy for the money" too.

Biche au Bois (A la) ☒   21 | 10 | 20 | 36
45, av Ledru-Rollin, 12ᵉ (Gare de Lyon), 01 43 43 34 38
■ Since 1925, this "clubby" bistro near the Gare de Lyon has fed generations of "regulars" "generous" portions of the "real thing": Classic French cooking highlighted by "seasonal game"; while no one swoons over the decor, everyone "loves the buzz" and "the jovial waiters", making it "always crowded" and reservations essential.

Bigorneau (Le)   – | – | – | E
71, av Paul Doumer, 16ᵉ (La Muette), 01 45 04 12 81; fax 01 45 04 64 50
Showcasing an upmarket sea-shack look that one might find featured in the French decorating magazine *Maisons Côté Ouest* – "so *comme-il-faut* for the 16th" – this fashionable "new" seafooder "from the owner of Marius et Jeanette" is winning over well-heeled locals with its high-quality "catch-of-the-day" menu, served by swift staffers.

Bistro 121 ◐   – | – | – | M
121, rue de la Convention, 15ᵉ (Boucicaut/Convention), 01 45 57 52 90; fax 01 45 57 14 69
A coterie of loyal "locals" appreciates the "simple" but "satisfying" "Traditional" Bistro cooking, "nice choice of wines" and "amiable" service at this 15th arrondissement stalwart; "the lights are bright for late-night dining" and the decor could use some sprucing up, but a "warm welcome" and fair prices compensate.

Bistro de Gala (Le) ☒   ▽ 18 | 15 | 17 | 42
45, rue du Faubourg Montmartre, 9ᵉ (Grands Boulevards/ Le Peletier), 01 40 22 90 50; fax 01 40 22 98 30
■ It "may not be one of the big guns yet, but it's not far off" say savvy scouts of this New Bistro in the slightly scruffy Faubourg Montmartre; as proof, they point to its "market-based" cooking, "appealing wine list" and "professional" service, all of which equals "excellent value for the money."

Bistro de l'Olivier   20 | 15 | 19 | 46
13, rue Quentin Bauchart, 8ᵉ (George V), 01 47 20 78 63; fax 01 47 20 74 58
■ For a "mini-vacation in the center of Paris", let this "cozy" Provençal-Mediterranean bistro transport you to

| F | D | S | €C |

the land of "lavender and thyme" via its fish-centric menu and "sunny" atmosphere; "the new management has done wonders", which explains why the crowd also chirps about "good cheer" from the staff and "bargain" bills for the pricey 8th.

Bistro des Deux Théâtres (Le) ◐ 16 | 13 | 16 | 35
18, rue Blanche, 9ᵉ (Trinité), 01 45 26 41 43; fax 01 48 74 08 92; www.bistro-et-cie.fr
◪ Popular with a business crowd at lunch, this purely prix fixe Classic French in the theater district in the 9th is "a handy place to dine after a show"; critics pan the food as "pedestrian" and the decor as even more so; but no one complains about getting "value for their euro", which is why it regularly plays to a full house.

Bistro d'Hubert (Le) 20 | 17 | 18 | 45
41, bd Pasteur, 15ᵉ (Pasteur), 01 47 34 15 50; fax 01 45 67 03 09; www.bistrodhubert.com
■ "Bridging the gap between bistro fare and inventive cooking" this "casual" address in the 15th specializes in "savory" Southwestern-inflected New French cuisine; diners can view the "open kitchen from most tables" or the bar in the "charming" blue-and-yellow room, making things "a little noisy" but nonetheless "fun."

Bistro du 17ème (Le) 16 | 15 | 15 | 34
108, av de Villiers, 17ᵉ (Pereire), 01 47 63 32 77; fax 01 42 27 67 66; www.bistro-et-cie.fr
■ "Bargain" hunters "line up" to "eat a lot for a little" at this Willy Dorr–owned Traditional Bistro that offers the "best prix fixe (including bottle of wine) in the 17th arrondissement"; such a winning formula also means that the room can be "hectic" and not a suitable place for "a quiet dinner."

Bistro Melrose ◐ – | – | – | M
5, pl Clichy, 17ᵉ (Place de Clichy), 01 42 93 61 34; fax 01 42 93 76 45; www.bistro-et-cie.fr
It may be "touristy" given its location on the edge of Montmartre overlooking the Place Clichy, but this Traditional Bistro belonging to Willy Dorr's prix fixe empire is both "lively" and a "good value", turning out serviceable food at a fast, efficient clip.

Bistrot à Vins Mélac ⌧ 16 | 15 | 14 | 39
42, rue Léon Frot, 11ᵉ (Charonne), 01 43 70 59 27; fax 01 43 70 73 10; www.melac.fr
■ Seated at "big wooden tables", groups of friends and a cast of "neighborhood characters" merrily sip wine "by the bottle or the glass" and partake of "simple" Aveyronnais eats at Jacques Mélac's "boisterous" *bistrot à vins* in the 11th; N.B. abstainers stay home, since (so a posted sign claims) the water is strictly reserved for cooking.

| F | D | S | €C |

Bistrot d'à Côté | 21 | 16 | 20 | 47 |
16, av de Villiers, 17ᵉ (Villiers), 01 47 63 25 61; fax 01 48 88 92 42 ⓈⒶ
10, rue Gustave Flaubert, 17ᵉ (Pereire/Ternes), 01 42 67 05 81; fax 01 47 63 82 75
4, rue Boutard, Neuilly (Pont-de-Neuilly), 01 47 45 34 55; fax 01 47 45 15 08 ⓈⒶ
www.michelrostang.com
■ Chef Michel Rostang's "mini-chain" purveys "hearty" bistro "classics" for those who "don't want to re-mortgage the house"; if they've become "too popular" for an "informal" meal, the "welcome" remains "warm" at all.

Bistrot d'Albert ⓈⒶ | – | – | – | M |
150, bd Pereire, 17ᵉ (Pereire/Porte de Champerret), 01 48 88 93 68; fax 01 48 88 93 68
Serial surveyors say this "cozy neighborhood" place near Place Pereire is "worth going back to" for "honest" if "far from exciting" Classic Bistro food at benign prices and "sweet" service that "makes up for" the "ordinary decor."

Bistrot d'Alex ⓈⒶ | 14 | 12 | 13 | 42 |
2, rue Clément, 6ᵉ (Mabillon/Odéon), 01 43 54 09 53; fax 01 43 25 77 66
☑ An "excellent location" across from the Marché Saint-Germain and its "quintessential bustling bistro" profile keep the "tourists" coming to this 30-year-old spot, despite what dissidents deem "dull" dishes, aging digs, "surly service" and "excessive" prices for the quality of the Classic French–Med meals and Provençal wines.

Bistrot d'André (Le) ⓈⒶ | ▽ 15 | 16 | 12 | 38 |
232, rue St-Charles, 15ᵉ (Balard), 01 45 57 89 14; fax 01 45 57 97 15
■ Inhabiting the former workers' canteen of the long-defunct Citroën plant in the 15th, this "typical" bistro is of "a type we'd like to find many more of in Paris": "good-value" Traditional French cooking and a backdrop that makes it "great for people-watching and a romantic drink."

Bistrot de Breteuil (Le) | 14 | 15 | 14 | 38 |
3, pl de Breteuil, 7ᵉ (Duroc), 01 45 67 07 27; fax 01 42 73 11 08; www.bistro-et-cie.fr
☑ "The lovely terrace" and "all-inclusive" formula by bargain-master Willy Dorr keep this epitomic "idea of a typical bistro" in the chic 7th "jam-packed"; not everyone is spellbound, citing "ordinary" Classic French food, a "limited wine selection" and brusque service, but they're overwhelmed by those who claim it a "stuff-your-face steal."

Bistrot de l'Etoile Lauriston ● | 20 | 14 | 18 | 53 |
19, rue Lauriston, 16ᵉ (Charles de Gaulle-Etoile/Kléber), 01 40 67 11 16; fax 01 45 00 99 87
☑ This "lively, attractive" spot near the Etoile in the 16th is a perpetual winner with both tourists and a "regular" crowd

get updates at zagat.com

thanks to "no-nonsense" but "elegant" Contemporary French food, "efficient" service and prix fixe formulas for lunch and on select nights; the only quibble here is that "you're squeezed in" at "tightly spaced tables."

Bistrot de l'Etoile Niel ●☒ | 21 | 15 | 17 | 49 |
75, av Niel, 17ᵉ (Pereire), 01 42 27 88 44; fax 01 42 27 32 12
☒ "A comfortable place to eat and linger", this New Bistro near the Etoile in the 17th chalks up its continued success to "very good products" and a "relaxed" vibe; some lament the "tightly spaced tables" and find it on the "expensive" side but concede that cooking is consistently "tasty."

Bistrot de l'Université ☒ | – | – | – | M |
40, rue de l'Université, 7ᵉ (Rue du Bac), 01 42 61 26 64; fax 01 42 61 26 64
Though it's decked with pretty stucco moldings and offers gentle prices, this "pleasant, neighborhood" Classic Bistro with a practical 7th arrondissement location remains little known; maybe it's "nothing special", but you can count on the "simple, old-fashioned dishes."

Bistrot de Marius (Le) ● | 17 | 12 | 15 | 46 |
6, av George V, 8ᵉ (Alma-Marceau), 01 40 70 11 76
☒ Given its situation in the "golden triangle" of the 8th, this "casual" but "animated" offshoot of Marius et Janette next door is judged a good catch for "high-quality" seafood at "a fraction of the cost" of the *maison mère*; if a few find it too "noisy", "cramped" and "touristy", more say it's "perfect for lunch" or "after a concert."

Bistrot de Paris (Le) | 17 | 15 | 16 | 43 |
33, rue de Lille, 7ᵉ (Rue du Bac/St-Germain-des-Prés), 01 42 61 16 83; fax 01 49 27 06 09
☒ Located near the Musée d'Orsay, this place embodies the "definition of a friendly, noisy" Classic Bistro; although it's "nothing spectacular", neighborhood types find it "reliable" "for hosting a spontaneous" dinner at fair prices.

Bistrot des Capucins ☒ | – | – | – | M |
27, av Gambetta, 20ᵉ (Père Lachaise), 01 46 36 74 75; fax 01 46 36 74 89
"Filled with personality and cheer", chef-owner Gérard Fouché's (ex Grand Véfour) Southwestern bistro is deemed "delightful" by denizens of the 20th; while the decor may "need some work", the "efficient" service and moderate prices are fine as they are.

Bistrot des Dames (Le) ● | – | – | – | I |
Hôtel El Dorado, 18, rue des Dames, 17ᵉ (Place de Clichy), 01 45 22 13 42; fax 01 43 87 25 97
The "laid-back" ambiance, and "great caipirinhas" get Batignolles "locals" "talking to the people at the next table" at this "neighborhood haunt" of a Classic Bistro; although

| F | D | S | €C |

it's not a gastronomic destination, service is "friendly", prices are low and there's a "private" little garden patio.

Bistrot des Vignes (Le) ▽ 17 | 18 | 20 | 43
1, rue Jean-de-Boulogne, 16ᵉ (La Muette/Passy), 01 45 27 76 64
■ "This is the kind of little restaurant that we like" – "unpretentious" atmosphere, "solid" Classic Bistro dishes (think blanquette de veau), "fast" service and an "excellent value for the money" proclaim patrons of this "lighthearted" locale in tranquil Passy.

Bistrot d'Henri (Le) 20 | 14 | 17 | 33
16, rue Princesse, 6ᵉ (Mabillon/St-Germain-des-Prés), 01 46 33 51 12
■ For "old-fashioned comfort food" like that served for "Sunday lunch in the country" (ah, the "mouthwatering" roasted-for-seven-hours lamb), you can hardly best this "tiny" Classic Bistro; it's "terribly popular", so prepare to be "short on elbow room" in exchange for "one of the best buys" in "jumping" Saint-Germain.

Bistrot du Cap (Le) – | – | – | M
30, rue Peclet, 15ᵉ (Convention/Vaugirard), 01 40 43 02 18; fax 01 40 43 02 18
"Bravo!" say the few who know this modestly priced Contemporary Bistro on a quiet pedestrian street in the 15th; the "great terrace" helps make it a "favorite casual spot" for summer fare of Provençal inspiration, such as "great fish soup" or "memorable tuna with tapenade."

Bistrot du Dôme (Le) 19 | 15 | 17 | 44
2, rue de la Bastille, 4ᵉ (Bastille), 01 48 04 88 44; fax 01 48 04 00 59
1, rue Delambre, 14ᵉ (Vavin), 01 43 35 32 00
◪ Spawned by Le Dôme, this seafood duo in the Bastille and Montparnasse features an "impressive" roster of "fab" "no-frills" gills at "unbeatable prices"; "prompt" service and a "value-laden wine list" are additional baits, but if some regret the "tight tables" and decor ready for an "upgrade", the fact that "they're jammed" says it all.

Bistrot du Peintre (Le) 15 | 20 | 14 | 29
116, av Ledru-Rollin, 11ᵉ (Bastille/Ledru-Rollin), 01 47 00 34 39; fax 01 47 00 34 39
■ The "old-fashioned" beauty of the art nouveau interior overshadows the kitchen's "solid" efforts at this "really cool" Classic Bistro near the Bastille; since the "setting is so romantic" and "it's a good value", most "would go back."

Bistrot du Sommelier 19 | 14 | 20 | 62
97, bd Haussmann, 8ᵉ (St-Augustin), 01 42 65 24 85; fax 01 53 75 23 23; www.bistrodusommelier.com
◪ Amateur sommeliers "have fun" letting the staff "match the wines to each course and then trying to guess" their

| F | D | S | €C |

provenance at "foremost expert" Philippe Faure-Brac's Classic Bistro in the 8th; a few sour grapes squirt that it's "expensive" and "pretentious", but they're outvoted by oenophiles thrilled to sample a range that includes some "little-known" vintages.

Bistrot La Catalogne ∇ 13 | 10 | 17 | 26
Maison de la Catalogne, 4-6-8, Cour-du-Commerce-St-André, 6ᵉ (Odéon), 01 55 42 16 19; fax 01 55 42 16 33

◪ Since it's run by the Catalan tourist office as a cultural and culinary showcase, perhaps reviewers expect more of this brightly lit Spaniard in a cobbled passageway just off the Odéon; if you're "in a hurry", they do "decent" if "not exceptional" tapas accompanied by "some very nice wines"; it's rather inexpensive for the neighborhood, but some still say "a bit overpriced for what one gets."

Bistrot Papillon (Le) 20 | 15 | 18 | 41
6, rue Papillon, 9ᵉ (Cadet/Poissonnière), 01 47 70 90 03; fax 01 48 24 05 59

◪ Bargain hunters flutter to this Traditional Bistro in a "hard-to-find" corner of the 9th that's named for the slightly "freaky butterfly collection on the wall"; for some, it's a "wonderful discovery", but others shrug it's "nothing special" and fly from the often "indifferent" service and "sad" decor.

Bistrot Paul Bert (Le) ∇ 19 | 16 | 17 | 56
18, rue Paul Bert, 11ᵉ (Faidherbe-Chaligny), 01 43 72 24 01; fax 01 43 72 24 66

■ "Be sure to have a meal" at this "unfussy" Classic Bistro in the 11th as the portions are "generous", the wine list over 300-labels strong and the owners "good folks"; the patina-ed decor might be "a bit shabby but what's on the plate more than makes up for it"; just remember to "reserve."

Bistrot St. Ferdinand ☾ ∇ 15 | 15 | 16 | 33
275, bd Pereire, 17ᵉ (Porte Maillot), 01 45 74 33 32; fax 01 45 74 33 12; www.bistro-et-cie.fr

■ Sure it's a bit of a "food factory", but this bistro that's "practical" for Palais des Congrès events is a "success" thanks to prix fixe pasha Willy Dorr's "well-priced" start-to-finish formula of a "consistent" Classic French meal that "includes wine."

Bistrot Vivienne 17 | 16 | 12 | 43
4, rue des Petits Champs, 1ᵉʳ (Bourse/Palais Royal-Musée du Louvre), 01 49 27 00 50; fax 01 49 27 00 40

◪ This Classic Bistro entices those "shopping in the Galerie Vivienne" who love "the feeling of being outdoors without the car exhaust"; maybe management "should make more of an effort", because the "cooking's neither here nor there" and service can be "indifferent" – but a "good spirit" survives, nonetheless.

| F | D | S | €C |

Blue Elephant ⓞ   20 | 26 | 18 | 53
43-45, rue de la Roquette, 11ᵉ (Bastille/Voltaire), 01 47 00 42 00; fax 01 47 00 45 44; www.blueelephant.com

■ Take a "fantasy trip" to the jungles of Thailand via this "superb" link in a global chain near the Bastille whose "over-the-top" interior is "lush" with "plants and exotic trappings"; "refined" dishes "adapted to a Western palate", plus "graceful" service, offer a welcome "break from French" cooking, but prices much higher than "in a Thai village" help re-orient you.

Bocconi (Trattoria) 🇿   - | - | - | M
10, rue d'Artois, 8ᵉ (St-Philippe-du-Roule), 01 53 76 44 44; fax 01 45 61 10 08

Elegant decor and generous portions of fresh, housemade pastas contribute to the appeal of this new trattoria that's popular with financial executives at lunchtime; in the evening it pulls in a stylish, young clientele that includes many Italian expats.

Boeuf Couronné (Au) ⓞ   23 | 20 | 21 | 58
188, av Jean Jaurès, 19ᵉ (Porte de Pantin), 01 42 39 44 44; fax 01 42 39 17 30

■ This king of beef "merits its crown (*couronne*)" and is "worth the trip" to the remote 19th for a knee-weakening côte de boeuf and other Classic French cuts; some come for the historic ties, as it "preserves" the "mythic aura of the slaughterhouses" (located here until 1974) and because it "bucks the tides of fashion and restaurant standardization."

Boeuf sur le Toit (Le) ⓞ   17 | 19 | 15 | 48
34, rue du Colisée, 8ᵉ (Franklin D. Roosevelt/ St-Philippe-du-Roule), 01 53 93 65 55; fax 01 53 96 02 32; www.flobrasseries.com

◪ This Flo Group-owned brasserie off the Champs-Elysées is "always enjoyable" thanks to its "consistent" classic menu and shellfish bar, "noisy", "theatrical" vibe and "historic clout" (it dates to 1870); if some snip it should be called "Le Touriste sur le Toit" and warn that the "corporate ownership is wearing thin", others detect "improvement over the past few years."

BOFINGER ⓞ   18 | 23 | 18 | 50
5, rue de la Bastille, 4ᵉ (Bastille), 01 42 72 87 82; fax 01 42 72 97 68

◪ Near the Bastille, this "old friend" is as "picturesque" and "Parisian" as brasseries come, with its "beautiful belle-epoque space" that's capped by a "spectacular" cupola ("don't forget to look up!"); the eye-popping "three-tiered shellfish platters" and "terrific choucroute" dazzle tourists and natives alike, and if sauer-pusses hiss its "setting surpasses the food and service", it remains a "classic experience."

| F | D | S | €C |

Bon ◐   15 | 25 | 16 | 62
25, rue de la Pompe, 16ᵉ (La Muette), 01 40 72 70 00; fax 01 40 72 68 30; www.bon.fr
☒ "You're not sure if you're in a restaurant or on a stage" at co-owner and decorator Philippe Starck's "radically" "austere" outpost in the 16th where "hipsters" go to "look at beautiful people, eat artistically arranged" vegetarian and Mediterranean-influenced fare and "put a dent in their checkbooks"; while the "kitchen's been making some progress" in overcoming "inconsistency", the staff remains "predictably cool."

Bon Accueil (Au) ☒   23 | 19 | 20 | 51
14, rue de Monttessuy, 7ᵉ (Alma-Marceau/Ecole Militaire), 01 47 05 46 11
■ Practically "in the shadow of the Eiffel Tower", this recently "remodeled" Classic French "lives up to its name" (which means 'warm welcome') thanks to the "hospitable" host and "helpful" if sometimes "overburdened" service that ministers to folks "jammed" into the "smallish" space and spilling out to sidewalk tables; the "fresh ingredients and imagination" go a long way here, as do your euros at bill time.

Bon 2 ◐   14 | 19 | 12 | 49
2, rue du Quatre Septembre, 2ᵉ (Bourse), 01 44 55 51 55; fax 01 44 55 00 77; www.bon.fr
☒ Co-owner and designer Philippe Starck's second act near the Bourse may be "visually stunning" with "private booths, chandeliers and contrasting colors", but the Contemporary French–Med "food does not live up" to the surrounds; at least "you can be served coming out of a show after 11 PM."

Bon Saint Pourçain (Le) ☒⊘   19 | 12 | 20 | 37
10 bis, rue Servandoni, 6ᵉ (Odéon/St-Sulpice), 01 43 54 93 63
■ Imagine you're "dining with a French family, except you get to choose what you eat" at this "little wonder" of a Classic French "tucked" in a wee street "behind Saint-Sulpice"; the "sign outside advertises bourgeois cuisine, and that's what we got in the best sense" say thankful patrons who also laud the "good-natured" staff, "old-fashioned" decor and "reasonable" cash-only tabs.

Bons Crus (Aux) ☒   – | – | – | M
7, rue des Petits-Champs, 1ᵉʳ (Bourse/Palais-Royal-Musée du Louvre), 01 42 60 06 45
The "atmosphere and satisfying" Lyonnais eats make this 1905 hole-in-the-wall wine bar a hit with the fashion and business people who traffic the Place des Victoires; "unpretentiously Parisian" and "a great lunch spot", it's also "a bargain" in a pricey part of town.

| F | D | S | €C |

Bouche à Oreille (De) 🖂   – | – | – | M

34, rue Gassendi, 14ᵉ (Denfert-Rochereau/Mouton-Duvernet), 01 43 27 73 14

The name means 'word of mouth', and that's exactly what's starting to build about this newcomer, set in a simple Montparnasse dining room; its talented young chef turns out inventive Contemporary Bistro dishes on a menu that follows the market.

Bouchons de   17 | 15 | 16 | 45
François Clerc (Les) 🖂

12, rue de l'Hôtel Colbert, 5ᵉ (Maubert-Mutualité), 01 43 54 15 34; fax 01 46 34 68 07
6, rue Arsène Houssaye, 8ᵉ (Charles de Gaulle-Etoile), 01 42 89 15 51; fax 01 42 89 28 67
7, rue du Boccador, 8ᵉ (Alma-Marceau), 01 47 23 57 80; fax 01 47 23 74 54
32, bd du Montparnasse, 15ᵉ (Montparnasse-Bienvenüe), 01 45 48 52 03; fax 01 45 48 52 17
22, rue de la Terrasse, 17ᵉ (Villiers), 01 42 27 31 51; fax 01 42 27 45 76
www.lesbouchonsdefrancoisclerc.com

◪ "The best wine value going" is the draw at this chain that provides varietals "at store prices"; foes fume "the remarkable list" "doesn't save the insipid dishes", which seem "expensive" for the quality; but friends, who find the New French fare "respectably creative", think of it as "paying for the wine, then the food is free"; "all the locations are different in decor", but the Latin Quarter branch located in a medieval "stone vaulted cellar" is "a favorite."

Bouillon Racine   13 | 22 | 13 | 35

3, rue Racine, 6ᵉ (Cluny-La-Sorbonne/Odéon), 01 44 32 15 60; fax 01 44 32 15 61

◪ "If only the food and service could live up to the decor" bemoan boosters of this Belgian "buried in the backstreets of the 6th"; its setting, "as if you're on a glittering art nouveau stage", remains "absolutely charming" and the Belgium-based beer selection "far out"; but it's a "better bet for a drink than a meal", as the cuisine, which has forsaken its Flemish roots in favor of Classic French fare, is "disappointing."

Boulangerie (La)   ∇ 15 | 19 | 18 | 25

15, rue des Panoyaux, 20ᵉ (Ménilmontant), 01 43 58 45 45; fax 01 43 58 45 46; www.restaulaboulangerie.com

■ It's "way off the beaten track in the 20th" and, aside from some nice mosaics by local artists, "the setting is simple"; but those who know this Classic Bistro praise its "homestyle cooking" at "a fraction of the cost" of the guidebook stars – a combination that makes it popular with trendy, arty, young Menilmontant types (think *La Bohème*) who create a "relaxed atmosphere."

| F | D | S | €C |

BOUQUINISTES (LES) ⓢ | 22 | 19 | 19 | 54 |
53, quai des Grands-Augustins, 6ᵉ (St-Michel), 01 43 25 45 94; fax 01 43 25 23 07; www.guysavoy.com

◪ "Delicious" market-fresh fare prepared under the auspices of owner Guy Savoy, plus "a fun modern decor" (think "New York in Paris") attract a "good mix of Parisians and tourists" to this New French with a "pretty view of the Seine" in Saint-Germain; some scold the service as "spotty", and penny-pinchers pout "you pay for [Savoy's] name rather than what's on your plate"; but most feel they're getting a good buy, given the "inventive" cooking.

Bourdonnais (Le)/ | 24 | 19 | 20 | 85 |
Cantine des Gourmets (La)
Hôtel de La Bourdonnais, 113, av de La Bourdonnais, 7ᵉ (Ecole Militaire), 01 47 05 16 54; fax 01 45 51 09 29; www.le-bourdonnais.com

◪ Life is "*luxe, calme et voluptué*" at this thirtysomething veteran in the 7th, which pulls a conservative gang of regulars thanks to the "considerable originality" displayed by new chef Dominique Gruel's "delicious" New French cooking, proffered by "good if distant service" in a "slightly faded" but still "elegant" room; a few carp that it's "too expensive and too old-fashioned" ("a retro experience for the blue-haired crowd"), but most find it "truly remarkable."

Bourguignon du Marais (Au) ⓢ | 21 | 17 | 19 | 42 |
52, rue François Miron, 4ᵉ (Pont-Marie/St-Paul), 01 48 87 15 40; fax 01 48 87 17 49

■ Maybe he's *un peu* "pushy", but "the owner really knows his Burgundies and is willing to share his knowledge with you" at this *bistrot à vins* that tops off a "small but excellent wine list" with "truly rustic", "great Classic Bistro food" in the Marais; the "modern decor is nice for a change", too.

B4 ◐ | – | – | – | E |
6-8, sq Ste-Croix de la Bretonnerie, 1ᵉʳ (Hôtel-de-Ville/ Rambuteau), 01 42 72 16 19; fax 01 42 72 16 19

As its punning name implies, this "animated", "upscale" Marais Mediterranean-Provençal is a pre-clubbing table par excellence; with "good foreign wines" and "pleasant fusion cooking", it pulls a young, "discreetly gay" crowd, though its "trendy but friendly" atmosphere welcomes all; b-ware – it can get "expensive, but then that's the price you pay for seeing and being seen."

Braisière (La) ⓢ | – | – | – | E |
54, rue Cardinet, 17ᵉ (Malesherbes), 01 47 63 40 37; fax 01 47 63 04 76

This "charming family-run" spot serves New French cooking with Gascon overtones, a "combination that's out-of-the-ordinary but not bizarre"; "a popular lunch place for people who work in the area" near the Parc Monceau,

F | D | S | €C

it's also "agreeable for a dinner with friends", since service is attentive and fresh flowers bedeck the wood-paneled dining room.

Brasserie Balzar ◐   18 | 19 | 18 | 40
49, rue des Ecoles, 5ᵉ (Cluny-La Sorbonne/St-Michel), 01 43 54 13 67; fax 01 44 07 14 91

■ "The Parisian brasserie par excellence", this "classy classic" across the street from the Sorbonne is popular with writers, university professors and "people who might be somebody"; most like the "old-fashioned decor", while the "professionalism" of the "seasoned, insouciant" servers is much appreciated ("our waiter didn't even flinch when my husband accidentally shot a snail across the dining room"); if some say "it's not as good as it always was, it's pretty close", and most would "go back in a heartbeat."

Brasserie de la Poste   14 | 14 | 15 | 40
54, rue de Longchamp, 16ᵉ (Trocadéro), 01 47 55 01 31; fax 01 47 55 01 31

◪ A "great hangout" near the Trocadéro, this "true neighborhood brasserie" boasts "cordial service" and "straightforward, standard fare"; malcontents mutter a "change in ownership has ruined the atmosphere", but for this expensive neighborhood, it's certainly a "sure value."

Brasserie de l'Ile St. Louis ◐   19 | 18 | 18 | 33
55, quai de Bourbon, 4ᵉ (Cité/Pont-Marie), 01 43 54 02 59; fax 01 46 33 18 47

■ "Not one of the chains", this "bustling", "authentic old brasserie" on the Ile Saint Louis "in the shadow of Notre Dame" not only has a "wonderful setting", but also Alsatian-oriented cooking that's "surprisingly good for such a touristy place" – and "at reasonable prices" as well; the "waiters are fun", too, and the wood-paneled decor "quaint."

Brasserie du Louvre ◐   20 | 21 | 20 | 39
Hôtel du Louvre, pl André Malraux, 1ᵉʳ (Palais Royal-Musée du Louvre), 01 42 96 27 98; fax 01 44 58 38 00; www.lutetia-Paris.com

■ The "great location" of this brasserie across the street from the Louvre makes it ideal "*après musée*" or "if you're pressed for time", since the service is "courteous, friendly and prompt"; the "lovely atmosphere", augmented by the "good traditional food", adds up to a fine "break from fancy places."

Brasserie Flo ◐   17 | 21 | 16 | 45
7, cour des Petites-Ecuries, 10ᵉ (Château d'Eau), 01 47 70 13 59; fax 01 42 47 00 80; www.flobrasseries.com

◪ "Buried in an alley in the 10th", this "lively" brasserie with an Au Printemps branch is "touristy" but tempting with an art nouveau "decor worth a detour" and "harried

F | D | S | €C

but professional waiters flying by with massive trays" of "fabulous shellfish"; some shrug "a chain is a chain is a chain"; but even if "the reputation is better than the food", it's still "more fun than just about any place else in Paris."

Brasserie Julien ●   18 | 24 | 17 | 50
16, rue du Faubourg St-Denis, 10ᵉ (Strasbourg-St-Denis), 01 47 70 12 06; fax 01 42 47 00 65; www.flobrasseries.com
■ "Get out your monocle, wax your moustache and pretend you're living in the Third Republic" when you come visit this "art nouveau gem" of a brasserie with "an exceptional decor" "hidden among the shish-kebab stands around the Porte Saint Martin"; "crowded" and "a bit noisy" it's "still pleasant" "for a quick business lunch", "romantic dinner" or a "late supper"; while the food plays second fiddle, it's definitely of a "decent level", particularly the profiteroles in "creamy hot-chocolate sauce."

BRASSERIE LIPP ●   17 | 20 | 15 | 46
151, bd St-Germain, 6ᵉ (St-Germain-des-Prés), 01 45 48 53 91; fax 01 45 44 33 20
■ "If you don't get sent to second-floor Siberia", but sit in the "art nouveau main dining room", this Saint-Germain brasserie can be "fun", with "waiters straight out of central casting" – e.g. "long aprons and big moustaches" – who manage to be "rude yet polite"; though "the food doesn't live up to the setting", it's still "solid" ("onion soup's so good you'd swim in it if it weren't so hot"); sure, it's "overpriced and touristy", but for "a thoroughly Parisian experience" à la Hemingway, you gotta "love the Lipp."

Brasserie Lorraine (La) ●   15 | 15 | 13 | 51
2-4, pl des Ternes, 8ᵉ (Ternes), 01 56 21 22 00; fax 01 56 21 22 09; www.brasserielalorraine.com
■ Nostalgists sigh this Frères Blanc–owned "classical brasserie" on the Place des Ternes "ain't like it used to be" – "aside from the shellfish", the "traditional dishes" are "inconsistent" and the "service, shall we say, leisurely"; but given the overall 1920s "charm", it's still "terrific on Sundays, for business lunches" or for dinner before or after a concert", especially on the "fun terrace from which to watch the world go by."

Brasserie Lutétia   15 | 16 | 17 | 49
Hôtel Lutétia, 23, rue de Sèvres, 6ᵉ (Sèvres-Babylone), 01 49 54 46 76; fax 01 49 54 46 00; www.lutetia-Paris.com
■ "Good and reliable" is how most brasserie buffs would sum up this "pleasant if not brilliant" example of the species with a "great location" just steps from the Bon Marché department store; the seafood platters "in particular are well done" and "breakfast is good", too, in this dining room designed by Sonia Rykiel in "chic" art deco style.

| F | D | S | €C |

Brasserie Mollard ◐ | 18 | 23 | 14 | 52 |
115, rue St-Lazare, 8ᵉ (Auber/St-Lazare), 01 43 87 50 22; fax 01 43 87 84 17

☑ It's the "beautifully preserved" "Ecole de Nancy mosaics" and other 1900 art nouveau decorations that make "this brasserie in front of the Gare Saint-Lazare a real institution"; though "a little expensive", the "humongous seafood platters" are "good" enough (in particular, the "lobster prix fixe is worth it") to "outweigh any shortcomings of the staff"; theatergoers also appreciate that "it's one of the [few] in the area open late."

Breakfast in America | – | – | – | I |
17, rue des Ecoles, 5ᵉ (Cardinal Lemoine/Jussieu), 01 43 54 50 28; www.breakfast-in-america.com

With a baseball-cap-wearing owner from Connecticut, this Latin Quarter diner with red vinyl banquettes and "a true diner feel" is "the only place in town to find a real American breakfast, with all the coffee you can drink"; but while the bottomless cup and the "friendly service" "transport the homesick back to the States", dissenters dis it as strictly a drive-by.

BRISTOL (LE) | 27 | 27 | 27 | 115 |
Hôtel Bristol, 112, rue du Faubourg St-Honoré, 8ᵉ (Miromesnil), 01 53 43 43 40; fax 01 53 43 43 01; www.hotel-bristol.com

■ "A wonderful restaurant in a wonderful hotel" is the prevailing opinion on the Bristol's Haute Cuisine table that hits the "irreproachable" "height of luxe"; served by a "cosseting staff", chef Eric Fréchon's New French cooking is "superb, refined, even artistic"; "the garden dining room is splendid" during the summer, while "the marvelous oval room" with oak paneling is one of the most "elegant" spaces in Paris; it all "makes for a delightful evening" or luncheon – expensive, oui, but "worth every penny."

BUDDHA BAR ◐ | 16 | 25 | 14 | 58 |
8, rue Boissy-d'Anglas, 8ᵉ (Concorde), 01 53 05 90 00; fax 01 53 05 90 09; www.buddha-bar.com

☑ "Amazing atmosphere" and "spectacular decor" that includes a "magnificent" gold-painted Buddha are the lures at this "trendy" Asian in the 8th; but even if it's "more scene than cuisine", "the food's actually pretty good", especially if you groove on the DJ's "awesome sounds" and overlook the often-"absent" service; some sniff that it's "not as 'in' as it once was" (witness the "tour operators and business groups"), but for most it's "a sexy, hip place for a romantic meal"; be a little Zen when the check comes, though.

Buffalo Grill | 7 | 8 | 10 | 24 |
15, pl de la République, 3ᵉ (République), 01 40 29 94 98
1, bd St-Germain, 5ᵉ (Jussieu), 01 56 24 34 49

(continued)

get updates at zagat.com

| F | D | S | €C |

(continued)
Buffalo Grill
3, pl Blanche, 9ᵉ (Blanche), 01 40 16 42 51
36, bd des Italiens, 9ᵉ (Opéra), 01 47 70 90 45
9, bd Denain, 10ᵉ (Gare du Nord), 01 40 16 47 81
2, rue Raymond Aron, 13ᵉ (Quai de la Gare), 01 45 86 76 71
117, av du Général-Leclerc, 14ᵉ (Porte d'Orléans),
01 45 40 09 72
154, rue St-Charles, 15ᵉ (Javel), 01 40 60 97 48;
fax 01 40 60 17 48
6, pl du Maréchal-Juin, 17ᵉ (Péreire), 01 40 54 73 75
29, av Corentin-Cariou, 19ᵉ (Porte de la Villette), 01 40 36 21 41;
fax 01 53 26 88 17
www.buffalo-grill.fr

■ Specializing in a "fast-food version of steak", these "cheap" "cafeterias for cowboys" are "ok for the kids" or when you "have to have some American food"; the "decor's very basic" and the service, though "fast", is somewhat lacking (they "couldn't keep beer cold during a heat wave"), but the health-conscious "appreciate seeing the chart, updated daily, that specifies the provenance of the meat."

Buisson Ardent (Au) ⓈЇ   – | – | – | M
25, rue Jussieu, 5ᵉ (Jussieu), 01 43 54 93 02; fax 01 46 33 34 77
It may not be very widely known, but this Contemporary Bistro in the 5th "near Jussieu" – "an area that doesn't have a lot of good eating" – gets raves from those who've found it; fans order "don't change a thing", since the food is "hearty and inventive", the "service nice" and the setting a pretty 1920s-style dining room that's "traditional and welcoming"; "it's a pleasure to sit down at the table here", especially since it's capped off by an easily digested check.

Butte Chaillot (La)   20 | 18 | 17 | 50
110 bis, av Kléber, 16ᵉ (Trocadéro), 01 47 27 88 88;
fax 01 47 27 41 46; www.guysavoy.com

■ "Convenient to the Trocadéro", this "Guy Savoy–owned bistro" boasts "sleek decor" and "a lively scene"; if "not grand gourmet", the menu offers a "good mix" of classics like the "incredible roast chicken and mashed potatoes" along with "more adventurous" New French dishes, served by a "friendly young staff"; and while this "neighborhoody, casual spot" is perhaps a bit "expensive for what it is", it remains "reliable", and a "safe bet for business luncheons."

Byblos Café   21 | 17 | 20 | 31
6, rue Guichard, 16ᵉ (La Muette), 01 42 30 99 99; fax 01 42 30 54 54

■ "Polite", "charming people" serving "delicious Middle Eastern specialties" "make this upscale Lebanese a must for aficionados"; the "modern decor" and "sure values" mean it's a "bustling lunch spot", though others appreciate that, compared to many establishments in the 16th, "they're open late, too."

	F	D	S	€C

Ca d'Oro ☒   ▽ 16 | 11 | 15 | 33
54, rue de l'Arbre-Sec, 1ᵉʳ (Louvre-Rivoli), 01 40 20 97 79
■ "Very good and very authentic", this "neighborhood Italian" near the Louvre serves "fine Venetian cooking"; though the "setting is simple", the "welcome is warm", and it's pretty "good value for the money."

Café Beaubourg ◐   14 | 19 | 12 | 35
100, rue St-Martin, 4ᵉ (Châtelet-Les Halles/Rambuteau), 01 48 87 63 96; fax 01 48 87 81 25
◪ "Wonderful people-watching" and a "great terrace" make this cafe with a "fun setting" in front of the Centre Pompidou a "pleasant stop" and "a perfect place to meet people since everyone knows where it is"; however, the "fashionable arty crowd" advises "stick to drinks", since, aside from "very good brunches", the Classic and New French "food is like what they serve" on airlines and the staff "slow and unfriendly."

Café Burq ◐   – | – | – | M
6, rue Burq, 18ᵉ (Abbesses), 01 42 52 81 27
Tucked away in a steep Montmartre street, this *bistrot à vins* is a "totally unpretentious place – but it works", thanks to "very good" New French Bistro fare and "some great quaffs", along with "wonderful atmosphere and music"; there's also a "good bar scene with a hip, young, slightly grungy crowd" of "locals avoiding the tourist" scene.

Café Charbon   14 | 24 | 14 | 30
109, rue Oberkampf, 11ᵉ (Oberkampf/Parmentier), 01 43 57 55 13; fax 01 43 57 57 41
◪ "You go to see and be seen" at this "cafe with a limited menu" in the 11th, whose "magnificent decor" and "cool crowd" make it an ideal "spot for afternoon lounging"; but those expecting more may be "disappointed", since the Traditional Bistro fare, many maintain, is merely "mediocre" and lacking the "spice of good service."

Café Constant ☒   – | – | – | I
139, rue St-Dominique, 7ᵉ (Ecole Militaire), 01 47 53 73 34
Low-budget eating doesn't have to be a letdown, as proven by this friendly corner cafe that's come to the cheerful precincts of the rue Saint Dominique; a hit for its daily changing menu of inexpensive but high-quality Traditional Bistro cooking, including a variety of comforting treats *à la grandmère*, it's owned by chef Christian Constant, whose more expensive Le Violon d'Ingres is just down the block.

Café d'Angel (Le) ☒   ▽ 18 | 11 | 15 | 40
16, rue Brey, 17ᵉ (Charles de Gaulle-Etoile/Ternes), 01 47 54 03 33; fax 01 47 54 03 33
■ Citing the "creative" Contemporary Bistro cuisine, converts carol this cozy, homey place with "a charming

get updates at zagat.com

| F | D | S | €C |

lady owner" deserves its halo; granted, the "tables are a little tight", but it's a pretty "great buy", so "bring your friends from out-of-town" to this "trendy" corner near the Etoile.

Café de Flore ⏺ 14 | 19 | 14 | 33
172, bd St-Germain, 6ᵉ (St-Germain-des-Prés), 01 45 48 55 26; fax 01 45 44 33 39; www.cafe-de-flore.com
◪ Even though "the only thing left of the Existentialists is their mention in the menu, it's still amusing to watch the crowd" (often "loaded with tourists") at this "Paris landmark cafe" with "a great location in the heart of Saint-Germain"; though "breakfast is good" and it's "a must for a drink", "no one really comes here for the brasserie food", which is "way overpriced" for what you get, fume foes who also find the waiters "tedious"; but despite all, this "mythic" place "still retains" "that je ne sais quoi."

Café de la Jatte ⏺ 15 | 19 | 14 | 43
60, bd Vital Bouhot, Neuilly (Pont-de-Levallois), 01 47 45 04 20; fax 01 47 45 19 32
◪ Find the "best view in Neuilly" at this Contemporary Bistro with a "fabulous setting complete with dinosaur skeleton" on the Ile de la Jatte; the "scene is beautiful", especially from "the tables overlooking the river", the "food decent" and the "service fast"; so even if "it's a little expensive for what you find on your plate", the "vibrant atmosphere" pulls a "business crowd at noon and fashion folks at night."

Café de la Musique ⏺ 14 | 17 | 12 | 29
213, av Jean Jaurès, 19ᵉ (Porte de Pantin), 01 48 03 15 91; fax 01 48 03 15 18
◪ The "stylish crowd", trendy soundtrack and "big terrace" strike a chord at this Villette-area cafe; a harsher note is sounded when it comes to the Brasserie cuisine, which seems "rather pricey" given its "ordinary" nature; still, most find it pleasant, especially "before a concert, or to people-watch on the weekend."

Café de la Paix ⏺ 17 | 22 | 17 | 52
Grand Hôtel Inter-Continental, 12, bd des Capucines, 9ᵉ (Auber/Opéra), 01 40 07 30 20; fax 01 40 07 35 29; www.paris.intercontinental.com
◪ At this reopened, perpetually "busy" address, "they've made some real efforts, especially in refurbishing the sublime 1882 decor" – and a Food score climb confirms they've "equally improved" the Classic French cuisine, to the extent that some quip "go for the people-watching, stay for the fare"; opponents opine it's "overpriced" and "living on its memories", but they're outvoted by those who say "it remains essential Paris", and "the perfect place for champagne after the Opéra" Garnier, across the street.

| F | D | S | €C |

Café de l'Esplanade (Le) ●   14 | 19 | 9 | 47
52, rue Fabert, 7ᵉ (Invalides/La Tour-Maubourg), 01 47 05 38 80; fax 01 47 05 23 75

☑ "The Costes brothers strike again with another of their triumphs of haute attitude over dining" is the general take on this table with an "elegant crowd, good-looking staff", "sophisticated" Jacques Garcia–designed decor and "great location across from Les Invalides"; it's the boys' "same old, same old menu" (a combo of Classic and Contemporary French cuisine), however, and "you need to be a movie star" or "to wear black" "to get any attention" from those comely servers; still, it's "not bad for a trendy."

Café de l'Industrie ●   ∇ 11 | 17 | 11 | 23
16-17, rue St-Sabin, 11ᵉ (Bastille/Bréguet-Sabin), 01 47 00 13 53; fax 01 47 00 92 33

☑ Near the Bastille (and hence very busy), this bar/eatery has "rather nice decor" and a "convivial", "authentic intellectual-cultural atmosphere" "reminiscent of post-war cafes"; most find the Traditional Bistro bites a bit "banal", but "on the other hand, the bill is light" on the wallet.

Café de Mars ●   ∇ 17 | 12 | 15 | 29
11, rue Augereau, 7ᵉ (Ecole Militaire), 01 47 05 05 91; fax 01 45 55 76 99; www.cafe-de-mars.com

■ "Great for a quick bite", this "always-smoky and crowded" cafe offers "sidewalk eating in the rue Cler area at its best"; the Traditional Bistro fare, augmented with a few innovations ("the Caesar salad is garnished with tandoori chicken"), is "good food for the price."

Café des Délices (Le) ●☒   21 | 14 | 17 | 43
87, rue d'Assas, 6ᵉ (Port-Royal/Vavin), 01 43 54 70 00; fax 01 43 26 42 05

■ Chef-owner Gilles Choukroun is a "rising star" with his increasingly popular address near the Luxembourg Gardens that serves a "short but delicious menu" of New "Bistro food with Middle Eastern" and other "influences from all over the world" (among the typical offerings, locals "love the langoustines with finely chopped pistachio nuts" and "the fantastic 'tomato in all its forms' appetizer"); a "warm welcome" and a "colorful setting" have *amis* advising "don't miss this gem."

Café des Lettres   – | – | – | M
53, rue de Verneuil, 7ᵉ (Rue du Bac/Solférino), 01 42 22 52 17; fax 01 45 44 70 02

"Located in a paved interior courtyard, a nice and quiet terrace" makes this "cozy" Scandinavian in the 7th "perfect for a summer meal with friends" before or after a visit to the Musée d'Orsay nearby; "discreet, efficient service" handles a clientele that's "very French with lots of locals" feasting on the "simple but good" cuisine.

get updates at zagat.com

| F | D | S | €C |

Café du Commerce (Le) ⓓ   10 | 18 | 11 | 28
51, rue du Commerce, 15ᵉ (Emile Zola), 01 45 75 03 27;
fax 01 45 75 27 40; www.lecafeducommerce.com
☎ "Edible, easy, unmemorable" summarizes the "standard Bistro food" at this "huge" 1920s brasserie in the 15th with "nice decor" ("especially during the summer when they open the roof") and "picture-perfect waiters" who can be "grumpy" but are "so Parisian"; true, it gets "noisy and overcrowded", but most find it "for all the hustle and bustle, fun" and "the prices right", making it ideal for "simple dinners with large groups of friends"; N.B. the scores may not fully reflect a recent change of ownership.

Café du Passage (Le) ⓓ   – | – | – | I
12, rue de Charonne, 11ᵉ (Bastille/Ledru-Rollin), 01 49 29 97 64;
fax 01 47 00 14 00
Not far from the Bastille, this *bistrot à vins* is "a hole-in-the-wall well worth finding" for its "excellent wine list" (380 different labels) and "very welcoming host"; the "ancient, cozy space", a former workshop in a mews, is animated with taped jazz and regulars devouring the house specialty of andouillette (tripe sausage), along with salads and grills for very affordable prices.

Café Faubourg   18 | 20 | 20 | 47
Sofitel Le Faubourg, 11 bis, rue Boissy-d'Anglas, 8ᵉ
(Concorde/Madeleine), 01 44 94 14 24; fax 01 44 94 14 28
■ Located in the Sofitel Le Faubourg, just off the Place de la Concorde, this Classic French serves "nice food" with a Southwestern accent in an "elegant", "airy" atrium dining room popular with a business crowd at noon and fashion execs at dinner; many appreciate the "refined", "serene atmosphere" created by the friendly, professional service and a pianist at night.

Café Flo   14 | 19 | 12 | 37
Au Printemps, 64, bd Haussmann, 9ᵉ (Auber/Havre-Caumartin),
01 42 82 58 84; fax 01 45 26 31 24; www.flobrasseries.com
■ "Strictly a shoppers' lunch spot" (though they do dinner on Thursday), this Flo Group–run restaurant on the top floor of the Au Printemps department store serves up a "good enough" Traditional French menu amid a "beautiful space" with "great views of Paris"; no surprise, "there are long waits during the height of the lunch hour", but it's fun to "go for a sundae just to see" the "exquisite glass ceiling."

Café Fusion ⓓ ⓩ   – | – | – | M
12, rue de la Butte aux Cailles, 13ᵉ (Place d'Italie),
01 45 80 12 02; fax 01 47 00 53 53
With a striking fluorescent-orange decor, aluminum-topped tables and tubular lighting fixtures, this new fusion food arrival in a trendy corner of the 13th has a decidedly '70s-retro look; the mixed, lively crowd loves the terrace out

| F | D | S | €C |

front for dining in good weather, as well as the moderately priced menu that skates all over the world with a variety of wok-cooked Eurasian dishes.

Café Lenôtre (Le) | 19 | 19 | 16 | 43 |
Pavillon Elysée, 10, av des Champs-Elysées, 8ᵉ (Champs-Elysées-Clémenceau), 01 42 65 85 10; fax 01 42 6576 23; www.lenotre.fr

■ Located in the Pavilion Elysée, a pretty wedding-cake of a building in the gardens of the Champs-Elysées, this "very trendy place" by the Lenôtre group has "a great terrace" for summer dining, but is also "fun indoors on a rainy autumn day"; the New French menu is "decent", but those in the know "go just for the divine desserts" brought by "charming servers"; P.S. there's also an "original" cookware boutique and cooking school offering daily lessons in French and English on the premises.

CAFÉ LES DEUX MAGOTS ● | 14 | 19 | 14 | 33 |
6, pl St-Germain-des-Prés, 6ᵉ (St-Germain-des-Prés), 01 45 48 55 25; fax 01 45 49 31 29

◪ "About as Left Bank as it gets", this Saint-Germain literary "landmark" remains the "quintessential cafe experience" and a "touristy must" – if only "to add 'been there' to your résumé", since the Classic French "food's not that great" ("breakfast is best"), the waiters are "typically rude" and for the quality, "prices are high"; still, even if "you pay to sit" and sip "something sinfully rich" on that "wonderful glassed-in terrace", "it's worth every penny", since it's "the perfect spot to contemplate the start of a new day in Paris."

Café M | 19 | 18 | 17 | 52 |
Hôtel Hyatt, 24, bd Malesherbes, 8ᵉ (Madeleine/St-Augustin), 01 55 27 12 34; fax 01 55 27 12 35; www.paris.madeleine.hyatt.com

■ Being located in the Hyatt near the Madeleine causes a "lack of Paris feeling" perhaps, but otherwise life is "surprisingly good" at this "simple, sleek" hotel dining room; the "fresh", fusion-y New French food is "even a little imaginative", and the effort of the staffers, who are often "interns, is sometimes tentative but always gracious"; the business-oriented believe it works well "for a low-key lunch with a client", especially if you snag a table in front of the fireplace.

CAFÉ MARLY ● | 15 | 23 | 14 | 43 |
93, rue de Rivoli, 1ᵉʳ (Palais Royal-Musée du Louvre), 01 49 26 06 60; fax 01 49 26 07 06

◪ "If it didn't have the best location and view in Paris, I'd give this place up" sigh surveyors about this "fashionable" Costes brothers' cafe overlooking the I.M. Pei pyramid entrance to the Louvre – and indeed, a "staff that's more stylish than helpful" and "mediocre" meals mar the experience for many; still, a gallery-full of fans finds the

Classic and New French fare "nice" enough, advising "the best thing is breakfast – you'll never taste a better omelette than the you-have-to-ask-for-it herb one they do here."

Café Max 🚭🚯   - | - | - | M
7, av de La Motte-Picquet, 7ᵉ (Ecole Militaire/La Tour-Maubourg), 01 47 05 57 66
Only a happy few know this Traditional Bistro with an endearing flea-market decor in the 7th, but they're not shy about vaunting its charms – it's not only "great fun" but "an honor to be invited to this convivial atmosphere" where the sweet grouch of a chef-owner "Max Gerchambeau does everything himself"; happily, "if he has character, so does the food", which includes many "decadent and hearty" Southwestern specialties.

Café Moderne 🚭   - | - | - | M
40, rue Notre-Dame-des-Victoires, 2ᵉ (Bourse), 01 53 40 84 10; fax 01 53 40 84 11
Just across the street from the old Bourse (Paris stock market), this slick newcomer with a long, narrow dining room overlooking an interior courtyard has a pleasant atmosphere that's at once hip and cozy; parquet floors, butter-colored walls and jewel-tone velvet upholstery create a modern urban backdrop for a stylish, young crowd to enjoy an Eclectic menu that finds inspiration everywhere from Spain to India before coming home to France.

Café Ruc ●   13 | 16 | 12 | 42
159, rue St-Honoré, 1ᵉʳ (Palais Royal-Musée du Louvre), 01 42 60 97 54; fax 01 42 60 94 81
✉ "Want to see a model? come here to look at the staff" advise the amorous about this "self-consciously trendy" "Costes brothers outpost" "in the center of everything" (well, "near the Louvre" and the Comédie Française, at least); skeptics sneer it's all "sizzle but no steak", citing "indifferent service and food" of the Classic and New Bistro variety, and all agree it's "too expensive", but at least there's "good people-watching", "sitting on the terrace."

Café Terminus   ▽ 19 | 13 | 17 | 39
Hôtel Concorde St-Lazare, 108, rue St-Lazare, 8ᵉ (St-Lazare), 01 40 08 43 30; fax 01 40 08 44 60; www.concordestlazare-paris.com
✉ This "surprising establishment in a location [Saint-Lazare] not known for cuisine" is "a solid hotel restaurant" that's a "nice little place to dine" on Brasserie cooking; the "dull transient atmosphere is as depressing as the food is good", but it's convenient before catching a train.

Cafetière (La) ●🚭   19 | 18 | 19 | 38
21, rue Mazarine, 6ᵉ (Odéon), 01 46 33 76 90; fax 01 43 25 76 90
✉ "Intimate and old-world", this "very cozy" Italian, "nicely decorated" with a signature collection of antique, enameled

| F | D | S | €C |

coffeepots, serves up "excellent food and desserts" "with a touch of [French-style] creativity" ("the foie gras lasagna is unbelievably delicious"); run by the "friendly" Giorgi brothers, its service is "delightful" and "efficient", prices are easy for Saint-Germain, and most judge it to be "worth every revisit."

Caffé Toscano   – | – | – | M

34, rue des Saints-Pères, 7ᵉ (St-Germain-des-Prés), 01 42 84 28 95; fax 01 42 84 26 36

Despite the fact that it's strategically located just off the Boulevard Saint-Germain, few seem to have found this "little piece of Italy in Paris"; but those who have say it's "a place we'd like to share", since "the owners receive you with real warmth" before you sit down to "simple and good", "authentic" eats with a Tuscan accent, "quickly served."

Cagouille (La)   24 | 14 | 18 | 49

10, pl Constantin Brancusi, 14ᵉ (Gaîté/Montparnasse-Bienvenüe), 01 43 22 09 01; fax 01 45 38 57 29; www.la-cagouille.fr

◪ "Fish heaven" profess fans of this Montparnasse mainstay that specializes in "simply" and "honestly prepared" seafood that's as "fresh as the ocean's" latest catch; the modern black-slate-and-wood decor may be just "average", but no one minds since a "warm", "casual atmosphere" pervades the room in winter, and there's "an agreeably tranquil terrace in the summer"; "service varies according to the team on duty", but most find it generally "pleasant and efficient."

Cailloux (Les) ⌧   – | – | – | I

58, rue des Cinq Diamants, 13ᵉ (Corvisart/Place d'Italie), 01 45 80 15 08; fax 01 45 65 67 09

Tucked away in the "charming and increasingly hip Butte-aux-Cailles neighborhood" of the 13th, this popular bit of The Boot with a "simple decor" sends out "generous plates" of pasta for low prices; a "sweet" "all-Italian staff and a relaxed atmosphere make it a local favorite."

Caïus ⌧   – | – | – | M

6, rue d'Armaillé, 17ᵉ (Argentine), 01 42 27 19 20; fax 01 40 55 00 93

Imaginative New French cooking has made this wood-paneled dining room with plaid upholstered banquettes in the 17th a huge hit; formerly at the late Le Troyon, chef Jean-Marc Notelet loves to surprise with an inventive but judicious use of spices, especially peppers of various different provenances; if his talent and modest prices attract businesspeople at noon, in the evening the crowd shifts to serious eaters from all over town in search of a good buy.

Caméléon (Le) ⌧   17 | 13 | 18 | 42

6, rue de Chevreuse, 6ᵉ (Vavin), 01 43 20 63 43; fax 01 43 27 97 91

■ Name aside, this "homey" spot is no chameleon, but rather "the real thing: a Parisian bistro" – one that after

get updates at zagat.com

| F | D | S | €C |

over 30 years on a "nice cozy" Montparnasse street remains "as good as ever", serving "solid, unpretentious Classic French food" that's "excellent for the price"; it's still "a sexy little nook", too, with an old-fashioned cracked-tile floor and offbeat floral wallpaper.

Camélia (Le)
▽ 23 | 19 | 23 | 53

7, quai Georges Clémenceau, Bougival (RER La Défense), 01 39 18 36 06; fax 01 39 18 00 25

■ "Fantastic food" that's "very inventive for the price" make many "wanting to go as often as possible" to this "peaceful bourgeois house on the banks of the Seine" in suburban Bougival; an "incomparable welcome", plus "just the right touch of New French cooking in the classic dishes" bring surveyors to full bloom, well watered by "a wine list the length of a bible."

C'Amelot (Le) ⓢ
21 | 11 | 18 | 35

50, rue Amelot, 11ᵉ (Chemin Vert), 01 43 55 54 04; fax 01 43 14 77 05

◪ For those seeking the best in "budget-priced gastronomy", the quest ends at this "quaint place" in the 11th, where "simple but sophisticated" New Bistro fare is served on a "designated menu of the day" ("you only choose dessert"); most have "no problem" with the "no-choice" *carte*, since it is "incredibly priced", and the "warm atmosphere" created by the "cheerful husband (chef) and wife (hostess)" overcomes the drawback of the "small, cramped space."

Camille ⓞ
19 | 18 | 21 | 36

24, rue des Francs-Bourgeois, 3ᵉ (St-Paul), 01 42 72 20 50; fax 01 40 27 07 99

■ "All the Bistro standards are well executed" at this "quaint" lace-curtain corner in the Marais, which may be "small and crowded" but is "worth a visit" for fans of "homestyle food at reasonable prices", served by "funny, endearing" staffers; but book ahead, since its "popularity with the locals" can make "weekends impossible if you don't have a reservation."

Canard ⓢ
– | – | – | M

36, rue Bayen, 17ᵉ (Péreire), 01 42 67 60 95; fax 01 42 67 60 95

"Eat the name" (it means 'duck') quacks the contented clientele of this Classic French near Péreire; not only is the fowl – along with the signature "foie gras terrine – delicious", but "the owner's lovely", offering a "warm welcome"; with a "nicely priced wine list" to boot, this place is "worth a visit."

Cantine Russe (La) ⓢ
▽ 15 | 15 | 15 | 26

26, av de New York, 16ᵉ (Alma-Marceau/Iéna), 01 47 20 65 17; fax 01 47 20 08 06; www.paris-moscou.com

■ "For a guaranteed getaway", come to this "really nice" Russian run by friendly Nicolas Novikoff near the Palais de Tokyo; not only does it have "a mad charm", decorated with

| F | D | S | €C |

musical instruments and artists' portraits, but prices for the pojarski and other Slavic specialties are low, attracting a "great mix of tourists and locals", including students.

Cap Seguin (Le) ⑤ ▽ | 16 | 18 | 11 | 39 |
face au 27, quai le Gallo, Boulogne (Pont-de-Sèvres), 01 46 05 06 07; fax 01 46 05 06 88; www.lecapseguin.com
◪ With a breezy Seine-side location in Boulogne, this wood-paneled barge is the place to come for "proof that the long business lunch still exists – a tradition that the escargotlike service does nothing to challenge"; it's "a pleasant place", though, with a nice "nautical atmosphere" and decor, and the Traditional French cooking seems to please the "chic" crowd, so rather than let the slow-paced meal get you down, "count to 10 and enjoy the view."

Cap Vernet (Le) ⑤ | 16 | 13 | 14 | 52 |
82, av Marceau, 8ᵉ (Charles de Gaulle-Etoile), 01 47 20 20 40; fax 01 47 20 95 36; www.guysavoy.com
◪ Owner Guy Savoy's split-level, seafood "updated brasserie" overlooking the Arc de Triomphe is an "efficient" place for a business meal, which makes it "very lively at lunch time"; but if the bait here is "good fish" (especially the "exceptional oysters"), there's some major crabbing about the New French menu, which seems "so-so" given the "high prices"; and "disappointed" designers believe the "boating decor could be renewed" too.

Carpaccio | – | – | – | E |
Hôtel Royal Monceau, 37, av Hoche, 8ᵉ (Charles de Gaulle-Etoile/Ternes), 01 42 99 98 90; fax 01 42 99 89 94; www.royalmonceau.com
Known to only a few reviewers, this "refined", "real" Italian in the flower-filled lobby of the Hôtel Royal Monceau wins raves for "the best risotto in Paris", among many other "inventive" and "authentic" dishes; the pastel decor is perhaps "impersonal", but the "service is impeccable."

Carpe Diem ⑤ | – | – | – | E |
10, rue de l'Eglise, Neuilly (Pont-de-Neuilly), 01 46 24 95 01; fax 01 46 40 15 61
What a difference a day makes if you have a meal at this "small", homey suburbanite in Neuilly; "memories of great magret de canard" and other solid, carefully prepared Classic Bistro dishes "always bring back" the customers, despite somewhat high prices.

CARRÉ DES FEUILLANTS ⑤ | 25 | 22 | 25 | 118 |
14, rue de Castiglione, 1ᵉʳ (Concorde/Tuileries), 01 42 86 82 82; fax 01 42 86 07 71; www.relaischateaux.com
◪ "Fantastic food and immaculate service – well mannered and effortless" – means a most "magnifique" meal at chef-owner Alain Dutournier's "superb Haute Cuisine" hangout in the 1st; though the "decor doesn't live up to" the rest,

| F | D | S | €C |

the new, sleek steel-gray setting is "a success" say most; of course, the usual minority of malcontents mutters about an "overrated reputation", but most happily hum along to this "song for the palate", "a place to visit often", provided you can swing an "excellent splurge."

Carr's — | — | — | M
1, rue du Mont Thabor, 1er (Tuileries), 01 42 60 60 26; fax 01 42 60 33 32
Those seeking "a sweet little corner of Ireland" can find it two steps from the Tuileries gardens, where lots of gab and Guinness make this Dublin denizen a friendly hangout; and even Gallic grumblers who grouse that Gaelic gastronomy "is not renowned" admit the grub's generally "very tasty", especially the "brunch on Sundays."

Cartes Postales (Les) ▽ 20 | 12 | 15 | 54
7, rue Gomboust, 1er (Opéra/Pyramides), 01 42 61 02 93; fax 01 42 61 02 93
Don't be misled "by the menu translated into Japanese and the numerous Nipponese tourists" – this sushi-sized spot in the 1st serves "excellent New French cuisine", albeit an Asian-fused version, since the chef-owner trained with Alain Dutournier after leaving his native land of the rising sun; regulars "really enjoy" "the opportunity to order half-size portions to sample a great variety of the wonderful dishes"; however, some stylists suggest "a little candlelight and flowers would improve the sterile decor."

Cartet — | — | — | E
62, rue de Malte, 11e (République), 01 48 05 17 65
"If your grandmother came from the country" around Lyon, "she'd cook like this", stuffing you with "heartwarming, hearty" "old-style Bistro fare"; situated behind the Place de la République, this "little place – and it is little", with 15 seats – is "heavy on flavor and on hospitality", as doled out by "a superb husband-and-wife team"; so, "come hungry" ("Madame won't let you stop at one dessert"), and early on weekdays, when the kitchen closes at 9 PM.

Casa Alcalde ▽ 16 | 14 | 13 | 39
117, bd de Grenelle, 15^e (La Motte-Picquet-Grenelle), 01 47 83 39 71
"Reservations are a must" if you want a table at this "always-full", "reliable address for paella" and other Spanish specialties; the Iberian eats and wines, served in an "intimate" innlike setting, create a "vacation atmosphere" in the midst of the 15th.

Casa Bini 20 | 12 | 17 | 41
36, rue Grégoire de Tours, 6e (Odéon), 01 46 34 05 60; fax 01 40 46 09 71
"Superb Tuscan cooking" and a "magnificent Italian wine list" pulls a chic crowd of Saint-Germain "habitués"

64 subscribe to zagat.com

| F | D | S | €C |

to this popular place; admittedly, the simple decor "could use some updating", so regulars recommend reserving a table in the upstairs dining room, which is "nicer" and less filled with "heavy smoke."

Casa Hidalgo

| – | – | – | I |

17, rue de la Forge Royale, 11ᵉ (Faidherbe-Chaligny/ Ledru-Rollin), 01 40 24 10 54
With its yellow-painted walls and tile floor, this new Spanish table brings a bit of southern sun to a neighborhood not far from the Bastille; owned by a friendly expat from Andalucia, the kitchen specializes in hot and cold tapas, paella and grills, and is attracting an enthusiastic neighborhood crowd with its cheerful decor and low prices.

Casa Olympe

| 19 | 12 | 16 | 50 |

48, rue St-Georges, 9ᵉ (St-Georges), 01 42 85 26 01; fax 01 45 26 49 33
☑ "Hidden" in the 9th near Saint-Georges, this "intimate" Med-Provençal bistro still wins medals from many for its "fresh", "inventive" cuisine that makes "reservations imperative"; however, some sterner judges have found the fare "disappointing lately", and even admirers critique the casa for its "too tightly spaced tables."

Casa Tina

| ∇ 12 | 16 | 13 | 34 |

18, rue Lauriston, 16ᵉ (Charles de Gaulle-Etoile/Kléber), 01 40 67 19 24; www.casatina.com
■ "Authentic atmosphere is guaranteed by Spanish-speaking waiters" at this "snug and noisy" outpost of Iberia in the 16th that's also "like Madrid" in its "copious tapas menu" (which some say are "better to order" than the mains), served late; though more inclined to Chanel than castanets, a young crowd finds it "great to go with a group to chat, drink and eat."

Casa Vigata

| – | – | – | M |

44, rue Léon Frot, 11ᵉ (Charonne), 01 43 56 38 66
"Pasta with all kinds of sauces and divine stuffed sardines" are among the homestyle Sicilian dishes that chef-owner Roberta Tringale ("she's charming and has real character") turns out at this little-known vest-pocket of a place in the 11th arrondissement; the "colored faïence" creates some warm Mediterranean atmosphere in the small space.

Caveau du Palais (Le)

| ∇ 21 | 15 | 18 | 41 |

17-19, pl Dauphine, 1ᵉʳ (Cité/Pont-Neuf), 01 43 26 04 28; fax 01 43 26 81 84
■ Anyone hoping to "hang out with a legal crowd" will testify to this Classic French near the Palais du Justice (hence the name) in "one of the prettiest squares in Paris"; but even if you care more about tarts than torts, it's still an "appealing" destination for a "lovely meal" that'll let you "travel back in time" until the bill comes.

get updates at zagat.com

	F	D	S	€C

Cave de l'Os à Moëlle   18 | 15 | 16 | 30
181, rue de Lourmel, 15ᵉ (Lourmel), 01 45 57 28 28; fax 01 45 47 40 10

■ "If you don't mind communal seating" and "helping yourself" from the dishes on tables and a stove, you'll probably love the "conviviality" of this wine-oriented bistro in the 15th; it "helps to speak *français*", since the stone-walled setting is packed with locals, but everyone enjoys the "high-quality" "Classic French food", including "succulent" all-you-can-eat terrines cooked at parent L'Os a Moëlle across the street, and "good selection of wines."

Cave Gourmande (La) -   ▽ 25 | 14 | 23 | 34
le Restaurant de Mark Singer
10, rue du Général Brunet, 19ᵉ (Botzaris), 01 40 40 03 30; fax 01 40 40 03 30

■ Though this "corner of the 19th isn't given to gastronomic highs", the New Bistro of Mark Singer, "an American who moved to Paris from Philadelphia at age seven and became an incredible chef", is "truly worth the métro ride"; as in any "inventive" kitchen, some ambitious dishes "can be confused", but overall the "attention given to detail" is "incredible"; Singer's French wife oversees the "welcoming staff", resulting in a "wonderful dining experience" that "offers spectacular value for the money."

Caves Legrand   – | – | – | M
Galerie Vivienne, 1, rue de la Banque, 2ᵉ (Bourse/Palais Royal), 01 42 60 07 12; fax 01 42 61 25 51; www.caves-legrand.com

"Isn't life great?" exclaims the small but happy crew who've discovered this "pleasant, efficient" wine bar in the Galerie Vivienne; sit under the glass-roofed terrace out front, or amid the "warm atmosphere" inside, and enjoy light eats – salads, sandwiches, cold meat and cheese – made with "first-rate ingredients" and accompanied by a 5,000-label strong selection of "inexpensive, good" labels.

Caves Pétrissans   18 | 17 | 18 | 48
30 bis, av Niel, 17ᵉ (Péreire/Ternes), 01 42 27 52 03; fax 01 40 54 87 56

■ "Crusty and dusty", this "old-style *bistrot/bar à vins*" in the 17th is a "tourist-free" "Parisian gem" "just the way we like 'em"; with the advice of "the owners who are more than willing to share a couple of glasses discussing wine and food", "the formula is that you buy a bottle from the [adjacent] shop and just pay a corkage fee" to accompany the "fine Traditional French cuisine" ("ah, the tête de veau").

Caviar Kaspia   22 | 17 | 22 | 98
17, pl de la Madeleine, 8ᵉ (Madeleine), 01 42 65 33 32; fax 01 42 65 09 55; www.kaspia.fr

■ "A luxurious trip to Russia" awaits when you "climb the stairs to caviar heaven" at this "elegant, expensive, decadent" dining room for a meal of "worldly treasures" and "a gorgeous view of the Madeleine across the street"; particularly perfect post-shopping or -theater, or just for a "special treat" of "a carafe of icy vodka, several hundred grams of sevruga, butter-splashed blini, smoked salmon and finally a tiny dish of wild strawberries"; it's "expensive", of course, but "what could be better?"

Cazaudehore La Forestière 18 | 21 | 18 | 54

1, av Kennedy, St-Germain-en-Laye (RER St-Germain-en-Laye), 01 30 61 64 64; fax 01 39 73 73 88; www.cazaudehore.fr

■ "Marvelous for an outdoor dinner during the summer" or "a romantic lunch", this "exclusive place in the middle of the Saint-Germain-en-Laye forest" "where Louis XIV used to hunt" serves up "very good" New and Classic French meals in a "cheerful and bright glass-paneled dining room"; a few find it "expensive relative to what you get", but to most, it's great for "a gallant moment in the greenery."

Céladon (Le) 22 | 22 | 21 | 81

Hôtel Westminster, 15, rue Daunou, 2ᵉ (Opéra), 01 47 03 40 42; fax 01 42 60 30 66; www.leceladon.com

■ A "sophisticated and gracious" experience awaits at this Classic French near the Place Vendôme; settled in a dining room with a slightly "crusty" restrained-pastel decor, the exigent extol not only the quality of the cooking ("the lobster special gave me a whole new appreciation of that marvelous food") but the "remarkable" value of the prix fixe menus; "a perfect spot for business lunches", it's also a charmer for "a special occasion or a special person."

182 Rive Droite ⊠ – | – | – | M

182, quai Louis-Bleriot, 16ᵉ (Mirabeau), 01 42 88 44 63; fax 01 42 88 79 17

The spacious, loftlike setting and "good, if not great" Mediterranean–New French cooking of this stylish newcomer more than compensates for its location "in the middle of nowhere" in the 16th; for the few who have found it, "it's a nice surprise" with "friendly service", relaxed atmosphere and easygoing prices.

Chai 33 13 | 17 | 15 | 40

33, cour St-Emilion, 12ᵉ (Cour St-Emilion), 01 53 44 01 01; fax 01 53 44 01 02; www.chai33.com

❷ Fans love "the incredible mix of old and new" – a historic stone-and-brick wine warehouse with an "original", "New Age-y" interior – that characterizes this sprawling wine bar/eatery in the popular Bercy district; oenophiles also "adore" "going down to the superb cave to choose their wine"; fewer corks pop over the "flavorless" Classic French fare, but smiling sippers outweigh sour grapers, even if you're paying "more for the place than for what's on your plate."

| F | D | S | €C |

Chalet des Iles (Le) | 13 | 25 | 13 | 52 |
Lac du Bois de Boulogne, 16ᵉ (Av Henri Martin/Rue de la Pompe), 01 42 88 04 69; fax 01 42 88 84 09; www.chaletdesiles.net
■ Maybe the Classic French "food's nothing special", but everyone loves escaping via a "brief but charming boat ride" to this "magical spot on an island in the Bois de Boulogne"; sure, it's a little "expensive" and the service can be "nonexistent" ("we had to call the main number by cell phone to ask them to come and take our order"), but "it's one of the most enchanting places around when the good weather comes"; make sure to get a terrace table, though, since if you sit "inside, the charm vanishes."

Chamarré (Le) ⍰ | 21 | 16 | 19 | 71 |
13, bd de la Tour-Maubourg, 7ᵉ (Invalides/La Tour-Maubourg), 01 47 05 50 18; fax 01 47 05 91 21
■ Arpège-trained Jérôme Bodereau collaborates with co-chef/co-owner Antoine Heerah of Mauritius to produce this "truly original" storefront in the 7th; supporters say "while not cheap", it's "Paris' best exotic" eatery, whose "harmony of Franco-Mauritian flavors" "absolutely must be tasted"; but to critics, a "cold" tropical-wood decor and somewhat "snooty staff" mean a meal here "isn't *très* fun."

Chantairelle ⍰ | – | – | – | E |
17, rue Laplace, 5ᵉ (Maubert-Mutualité), 01 46 33 18 59; fax 01 46 33 18 59; www.chantairelle.com
Hearty and "interesting food from an area not usually seen by tourists" – the rugged central Auvergne – pulls patrons to this "good-quality" table in the 5th; rare among regional restaurants, it cooks fresh, authentic dishes like pounti (pork, prunes and Swiss chard) without an overdose of kitschy decor – though the setting sweetly evokes this rural province with a well and a tape of birdsong; N.B. they also sell a nice selection of foodstuffs.

Chardenoux | ▽ 16 | 22 | 20 | 44 |
1, rue Jules Vallès, 11ᵉ (Charonne/Faidherbe-Chaligny), 01 43 71 49 52; fax 01 43 71 49 52
■ The location in the 11th may be "obscure", but most surveyors find it "a pleasure" to "travel in time to the [early] 1900s", when this bistro with a charming decor of etched glass and swirling stucco moldings opened; the kitchen surfs between Traditional and New French cooking that's "fresh and tasty" if "not inspired", but the "service more than makes up for this", so it's "well worth the trip"; N.B. a post-*Survey* chef change may outdate the Food score.

Charlot - Roi des Coquillages ☽ | 16 | 14 | 16 | 53 |
12, pl Clichy, 9ᵉ (Place de Clichy), 01 53 20 48 00; fax 01 53 20 48 09; www.charlot-paris.com
■ Overlooking the Place Clichy, this brasserie is known for its "fresh and filling fruits-de-mer" plates, "even in summer";

F | D | S | €C

some snap there's "not much else" on the Classic French menu, and "you need an archaeologist's eye to appreciate the kitschy '70s decor", but when it comes to "excellent seafood", the *roi* reigns on.

Charpentiers (Aux) ◐   16 | 16 | 19 | 38
10, rue Mabillon, 6ᵉ (Mabillon/St-Germain-des-Prés), 01 43 26 30 05; fax 01 46 33 07 98
■ Established in 1856 in the "old Carpenter's Guild hall" – hence the "charming architectural models" on display – this "classic" in Saint-Germain offers "Traditional Bistro fare" par excellence, "unpretentiously prepared with nothing nouvelle in sight"; it's "down-home cooking", so there's nothing "spectacular", but the staff appropriately acts "like you're one of the family."

Chartier   12 | 22 | 15 | 20
7, rue Faubourg-Montmartre, 9ᵉ (Cadet/Grands Boulevards), 01 47 70 86 29; fax 01 48 24 14 68; www.bouillon-chartier.com
◪ This "huge barn" of a Classic French "hasn't changed in 100 years", which explains the "unbeatable atmosphere" that has long made it "another check-the-box Paris experience"; ok, maybe "the food could be better", but it's very "cheap" and is served "fast" by "hurried" "waiters who scribble your order on the corner of the paper tablecloth", so "go for the history", if nothing else.

Chen Soleil d'Est 🖂   20 | 11 | 16 | 86
15, rue du Théâtre, 15ᵉ (Charles Michels), 01 45 79 34 34; fax 01 45 79 07 53
◪ Despite the demise of its namesake chef last year, friends find this 15th-arrondissement Asian "the best Chinese in Paris", praising its "refined", "sometimes startling" but "always delicious" dishes that contain pedigreed French produce; "the superiority of the cuisine more than makes up for the pushy service" and somewhat "soulless" setting in a Seine-side modern complex.

Cherche Midi (Le) ◐   18 | 14 | 16 | 41
22, rue du Cherche-Midi, 6ᵉ (Sèvres-Babylone/St-Sulpice), 01 45 48 27 44
◪ "Superb pastas" and a "nice-guy owner" have won "loyal clients" to this "local hangout for famous actors and politicians" in Saint-Germain that "hits the spot when you're looking for an easy Italian meal"; a niche of noodle naysayers note the "variable service" (perhaps "the regulars get more attention") and "squishy" seating, but most have fun, especially if they "get a table on the terrace."

Chez Albert 🖂   – | – | – | M
43, rue Mazarine, 6ᵉ (Odéon), 01 46 33 22 57
"Probably the best Portuguese in Paris", this long-running Lusitanian near the Odéon offers "a warm welcome and warming cooking", including myriad delicious takes on

get updates at zagat.com   **69**

cod; recently refreshed off-white decor is the backdrop for decorative bits of copper cookware, and the popularity of the place among Left Bank yuppies means it's often very "noisy"; be warned: "they put tourists in an upstairs Siberia."

Chez André ◐ 18 | 13 | 17 | 46
12, rue Marbeuf, 8ᵉ (Franklin D. Roosevelt), 01 47 20 59 57; fax 01 47 20 18 82

☒ The fact that it's one of those "increasingly rare" addresses for Traditional Bistro cooking ("as good a *gigot* as you can get anywhere") sells this stylishly "smoky", "humming" haven off the Champs; malcontents mutter the "menu is much more mundane" nowadays, and "you never know if the service will be great or terrible", but most are prepared to put up with ample "noise" and to "love thy neighbor" at thine elbow for a bona fide bistrot experience.

Chez Catherine ☒ 21 | 18 | 22 | 67
3, rue Berryer, 8ᵉ (George V/St-Philippe du Roule), 01 40 76 01 40; fax 01 40 76 03 96

☒ Surveyors are split on chef/co-owner Catherine Guerraz's relocation to a swank spot in the 8th, with some lamenting the "lost charm" of the old digs, and the "higher prices" that have come with "catering to an expense-account crowd"; but most maintain "the move is a major improvement", with a New French menu that "mixes well-prepared bistro classics with modern inspirations" (plus "wonderful wines"), "high-quality service" and elegant, dove-gray decor accented with orchids and antique silver.

Chez Clément ◐ 13 | 15 | 13 | 32
17, bd des Capucines, 2ᵉ (Opéra), 01 53 43 52 00; fax 01 53 43 82 09
21, bd Beaumarchais, 4ᵉ (Bastille/Chemin Vert), 01 40 29 17 00; fax 01 40 29 17 09
9, pl St-André-des-Arts, 6ᵉ (St-Michel), 01 56 81 32 00; fax 01 56 81 32 09
123, av des Champs Elysées, 8ᵉ (Charles de Gaulle-Etoile), 01 40 73 87 00; fax 01 40 73 87 09
19, rue Marbeuf, 8ᵉ (Franklin D. Roosevelt/George V), 01 53 23 90 00; fax 01 53 23 90 09
106, bd du Montparnasse, 14ᵉ (Vavin), 01 44 10 54 00; fax 01 44 10 54 09
407, rue de Vaugirard, 15ᵉ (Porte de Versailles), 01 53 68 94 00; fax 01 53 68 94 09
47, av de Wagram, 17ᵉ (Charles de Gaulle-Etoile/Ternes), 01 53 81 97 00; fax 01 53 81 97 09
99, bd Gouvion-St-Cyr, 17ᵉ (Porte Maillot), 01 45 72 93 00; fax 01 45 72 93 09
98, av Edouard Vaillant, Boulogne (Marcel Sembat), 01 41 22 90 00; fax 01 41 22 90 09
www.chezclement.com

☒ "Locals love to trash this chain", but since it pops up in "convenient locations", each invoking a "quaint" rusticity

| F | D | S | €C |

with copper pans, "silverware sculpture" and wood paneling, it's often "filled with budget-conscious eaters"; aside from the assorted "rotisseried meats", the "diverse", "no-frills" Classic French menu is "without culinary interest" and the "service seems tired" – but it's "consistent" ("ah, reliability") and "hey, for the price what do you expect?"

Chez Denise - La Tour de Montlhéry ●☒ 22 | 17 | 19 | 45

5, rue des Prouvaires, 1er (Châtelet-Les Halles), 01 42 36 21 82; fax 01 45 08 81 99

■ "Raffish, friendly" and "fun", this all-night Classic Bistro on the edge of Les Halles serves up "great traditional dishes that seem to fall off chicer menus: pot-au-feu, tripe stew", along with "superior" steaks and "the best frites on the planet"; "the waiters make a big difference with their sense of humor"; P.S. it's "the best of the real after-dark Paris", so be sure to book ahead.

Chez Diane ●☒ 19 | 15 | 21 | 43

25, rue Servandoni, 6e (St-Sulpice), 01 46 33 12 06; fax 01 43 25 96 55

◪ Before or "after a walk in the Luxembourg Gardens", many wander into this "wonderful, warm, welcoming place" in a pretty cobbled lane nearby; while some shrug over the "so-so" eats, the Classic Bistro cooking served by candlelight wins more friends than foes for its "delicious" flavors.

Chez Francis ● 15 | 17 | 15 | 52

7, pl de l'Alma, 8e (Alma-Marceau), 01 47 20 86 83; fax 01 47 20 43 26

◪ With a "beautiful location" at the Place de l'Alma providing a "fabulous view" of the Eiffel Tower, this "bright and flashy" brasserie offers a "romantic setting" in which to sample seafood and other "reliable" "comfort food" ("the oysters outclass the rest"); too bad that "rude service has apparently become a trademark here."

Chez Françoise ● 15 | 15 | 18 | 43

Aérogare des Invalides, 7e (Invalides), 01 47 05 49 03; fax 01 47 05 51 96 20; www.chezfrancoise.com

■ "Beyond the tides of fashion", this Classic French oddly located in the *aérogare* of Les Invalides is the clubby haunt of politicians from the nearby Assemblée Nationale and ministries, who endorse the "surprise-free, for-your-mother-in-law" cuisine and "attentive service"; all of it, including the "recently redone" decor, is somewhat "solemn", but then, "that's probably the image of the clientele too."

Chez Fred ☒ ▽ 18 | 10 | 15 | 43

190 bis, bd Péreire, 17e (Péreire/Porte Maillot), 01 45 74 20 48; fax 01 45 74 20 48

■ "A bouchon [bistro] like you find in Lyon" exclaim enthusiasts of the "good terrines and charcuterie" and

get updates at zagat.com

"wonderful steak" served at this traditional table ("not a hint of nouvelle cuisine") near the Porte Maillot; "the granite-topped tables and floors make for cold decor" but "nice service" warms things up a bit.

Chez Gégène ▽ 15 | 24 | 19 | 48

162 bis, quai de Polangis, Joinville (RER Joinville-le-Pont), 01 48 83 29 43; fax 01 48 83 72 62

■ In suburban Joinville, this barn on the Marne is "one of the rare surviving *guinguettes*" (restaurant/dance halls) that thrived in Paris circa 1900; "it's all about atmosphere" here, so come on weekends to dance and "dream", but "forget about" the Classic French food, which runs to mussels and fries served with cheap house wine.

CHEZ GEORGES 🖻 23 | 19 | 22 | 54

1, rue du Mail, 2ᵉ (Bourse), 01 42 60 07 11

■ "Such fun", this "venerable" "Parisian bistro par excellence" just off the Place des Victoires, with its "charming" waitresses serving a stylish crowd ("we saw Anna Wintour") that comes for "*oh-mon-Dieu*, what delicious" Classic French fare, from that "big ol' boat of béarnaise with the steak frites" to the "baba-au-rhum swimming in alcohol"; sure, the long, narrow dining room gets "a little crowded and noisy, but it's all part of the experience" where "authenticity reigns."

Chez Georges-Porte Maillot ❶ 18 | 13 | 15 | 49

273, bd Pereire, 17ᵉ (Porte Maillot), 01 45 74 31 00; fax 01 45 74 02 56; www.chez-georges.com

☑ It's "hard to be disappointed" by "old-fashioned" classics like "good roast lamb" and tête de veau, which is why this "traditional brasserie" ("any more so, and you'd die") near the Porte Maillot has become "an institution"; "the friendly service compensates for the rather lugubrious decor", if not completely for the "not-cheap" tabs.

Chez Gérard 🖻 ▽ 18 | 18 | 16 | 44

10, rue Montrosier, Neuilly (Porte Maillot), 01 46 24 86 37; fax 01 46 37 21 72

■ "Very fresh" fare that includes "many selections from the Auvergne" makes this "warm" Classic Bistro "a real find in Neuilly"; it's "lively at any time of day, with the most convivial waiters" and walls lined with "circus posters and framed cartoons."

Chez Gildo 🖻 ▽ 18 | 14 | 22 | 50

153, rue de Grenelle, 7ᵉ (La Tour-Maubourg), 01 45 51 54 12; fax 01 45 51 54 12

☑ Long "one of the best Italians in Paris", this "fashionable" place in the 7th offers *la dolce vita* on the Left Bank for the fans who say "from the pasta to the zabaglione, everything is good"; the outvoted parsimonious posit that perhaps "the portions could be more generous, in view of the prices."

| F | D | S | €C |

Chez Janou ◐   20 | 19 | 17 | 35 |
2, rue Roger Verlomme, 3ᵉ (Bastille/Chemin Vert), 01 42 72 28 41; fax 01 42 72 96 12

◪ "Just a stone's throw from the Place des Vosges", this Provençal bistro with a "decor of old movie posters" and "a young, hip, but not pretentious crowd" brings the taste of the Med to the Marais with "a stunning list of anise-flavored drinks" and "the best tapenade-smothered fish"; "one of the loveliest terraces" in Paris makes this an ideal summer address – "if you can get a place"; but year-round it's easy on the wallet with "excellent prices for the prix fixes and great carafe wines."

Chez Jean ⊠   23 | 17 | 21 | 47 |
8, rue St-Lazare, 9ᵉ (Notre-Dame-de-Lorette), 01 48 78 62 73; fax 01 48 78 66 04

■ "Under the management of Jean-Frédéric Guidoni, formerly maître d'hotel at Taillevent", "and his lovely wife, Delphine", this New French in the 9th has "lots of natural style"; the "creative", "limited menu is all about fresh and seasonal, and the chef, also a Taillevent alum, knows exactly what to do with it"; "the service is perfectly professional" and regulars say this young address "is continuously improving" – although it's already "really a bargain for what you get."

Chez Jenny ◐   18 | 19 | 18 | 40 |
39, bd du Temple, 3ᵉ (République), 01 44 54 39 00; fax 01 44 54 39 09; www.chez-jenny.com

■ Since the Alsacian decor has just been updated, the "very good choucroute" is no longer the only reason to make tracks for this sprawling "sturdy standby" of a brasserie just off the Place de la République; the spiffing-up didn't ruffle the "wonderful fish selections", "well chosen wines" from the region or the "welcoming" service, either.

Chez L'Ami Jean ⊠   16 | 9 | 14 | 38 |
27, rue Malar, 7ᵉ (Invalides/La Tour-Maubourg), 01 47 05 86 89

◪ Following the "much-publicized" arrival of "a new chef-owner" last year, the food is still Southwestern, but now it's "much more sophisticated" at this snug, rustic dining room with "tightly spaced tables" in the 7th; and if a few complain that "the atmosphere has evaporated due to the changes", the majority come to Basque in pleasure; P.S. "it's always packed", "so make sure to have a reservation."

CHEZ L'AMI LOUIS ◐   26 | 14 | 21 | 95 |
32, rue du Vert-Bois, 3ᵉ (Arts et Métiers), 01 48 87 77 48

■ "The best roast chicken, the best foie gras", "the best bistro in the world" are just some of the superlatives this "classic" harvests in the 3rd; geared for "trenchermen on high doses of cholesterol-lowering drugs", the "portions

get updates at zagat.com

| F | D | S | €C |

are immense", so do share (which, given the "outrageous prices", also "allows you to become a regular without being a Rockefeller"); "service is gruff but effective" and while it "looks like the decor hasn't changed since they opened 80 years ago", this is "a place to return to again and again."

Chez la Vieille ☒ | - | - | - | M |

1, rue Bailleul, 1ᵉʳ (Louvre-Rivoli), 01 42 60 15 78; fax 01 42 33 85 71

"Great homestyle food", occasionally with a Corsican accent, is the lure at this "little Classic Bistro" near Les Halles that's "saved its old-fashioned charm" but left its decor basically untouched since World War II; it's "no longer as fashionable as it was 10 years ago, but so much the better, since now it's easier to get a table" at this lunch locale that only serves dinner on Thursdays.

Chez Léon ☒ | - | - | - | M |

32, rue Legendre, 17ᵉ (Villiers), 01 42 27 06 82; fax 01 46 22 63 67

While it may be "hard to find", this Classic Bistro in the 17th arrondissement "near the Rue de Levis street market" is worth seeking out for the "reliably delicious regional cooking" at "reasonable prices"; some still miss the old owners, but most find the cozy room with a honeycomb-tile floor "professionally run."

Chez Livio | 12 | 11 | 13 | 34 |

6, rue de Longchamp, Neuilly (Pont de Neuilly), 01 46 24 81 32; fax 01 47 38 20 72

◪ "A warm welcome from Alfio and Vittorio Innocenti" keeps 'em coming back to this "noisy" Italian reputed for its pizzas and "reasonable prices"; for most of the regulars, however, the "convivial atmosphere" counts for as much as the "ordinary" kitchen – as well as the fact it's "one of the rare places open on Sunday in Neuilly."

Chez Maître Paul | 21 | 16 | 19 | 44 |

12, rue Monsieur-le-Prince, 6ᵉ (Odéon), 01 43 54 74 59

■ "A don't-miss" near the Odéon for its "delicious and fragrant cooking from the Jura" region (i.e. "wonderful chicken in a *vin jaune* sauce with morels"), fawn fans of this "quintessential neighborhood" bistro "of the old style"; it's still "cozy", "precious" and "not-so-touristy" (though visitors should "avoid the upstairs", also known as "the American ghetto").

Chez Marcel ☒ | - | - | - | M |

7, rue Stanislas, 6ᵉ (Notre-Dame-des-Champs), 01 45 48 29 94

"The owner's personality is everywhere" at this "somewhat undiscovered" Classic Bistro in Montparnasse, and that's good, since "he cares a great deal about his customers' experience"; "traditional-at-its-best" Lyonnais eats are dished up by "friendly service" amid "old-fashioned decor" with "just a handful of tables, so you feel like you're eating in someone's home."

Chez Marianne 15 | 10 | 12 | 25
2, rue des Hospitalières St-Gervais, 4ᵉ (St-Paul), 01 42 72 18 86

◪ "The decor is nothing to write home about" and "service is a little gruff", but that's "part of the charm" of the "old-fashioned, bare-bones" personality of this "cramped," "little slice of the Middle East in the middle of the Marais"; pedestrians find it "perfect after touring the area for a light meal", since "you can graze on the Jewish equivalent of tapas", i.e. pastrami, a variety of different salads and falafel sandwiches.

Chez Michel ●⌧ 21 | 13 | 18 | 45
10, rue de Belzunce, 10ᵉ (Gare du Nord/Poissonnière), 01 44 53 06 20; fax 01 44 53 51 31

◪ It may be "out of the way" in the 10th "near the Gare du Nord", but this doesn't deter "a clientele that's more concerned with food than frills" from trying chef Thierry Breton's "delicious" "reinventions of the dishes of his native Brittany", along with New French favorites; the digs are a little "cramped" and "cold, but the service isn't."

Chez Nénesse ⌧ – | – | – | M
17, rue de Saintonge, 3ᵉ (Filles-du-Calvaire/République), 01 42 78 46 49; fax 01 42 78 45 51

"Don't let the plastic-coated menus frighten you" – "this is the real thing" if you're looking for "a calm neighborhood" Classic Bistro in the Marais; few may have found it, but enthusiastic regulars "love this inimitable corner of old Paris" whose welcoming personnel "take you in."

Chez Ngo ● ▽ 19 | 17 | 13 | 42
70, rue de Longchamp, 16ᵉ (Trocadéro), 01 47 04 53 20; fax 01 47 27 81 06

■ It's "difficult to be disappointed" by this "authentic" Asian in the 16th, whose "refined Chinese cooking", along with some Thai delicacies, makes it more than a won-ton success; "come as a couple" for "the best Peking duck in Paris" while you relax in a cosseted, almost stereotypical decor of wood panels and calligraphic wall hangings.

Chez Omar ●≢ 20 | 12 | 14 | 31
47, rue de Bretagne, 3ᵉ (République/Temple), 01 42 72 36 26

■ Anyone who wonders why this North African not far from République is "always packed" with "trendy" types obviously hasn't sampled the "best couscous in Paris", which come in several different varieties, "even a vegetarian one"; "they don't take reservations", so prepare to stand at the bar for a while unless you "come before 8 PM or after 10 PM."

get updates at zagat.com 75

| F | D | S | €C |

Chez Paul ◐   20 | 17 | 18 | 36
13, rue de Charonne, 11ᵉ (Bastille/Ledru-Rollin), 01 47 00 34 57; fax 01 48 07 02 00

■ "A pretty postcard of why Paris will always be Paris", this "hip, lively" Traditional Bistro near the Bastille is "authentic right down to the swirling [cigarette] smoke and the two cognacs after lunch", with "a very impressive kitchen" and prices that "don't make you feel ripped off"; "it's always packed", so be sure to "call ahead" and prepare to stand your ground against service that can be "a little too speedy (to free up the table)."

Chez Paul ◐   21 | 17 | 21 | 37
22, rue Butte-aux-Cailles, 13ᵉ (Corvisart/Place d'Italie), 01 45 89 22 11; fax 01 45 80 26 53

■ "This is what Paris is all about" proclaim patrons who find this Classic Bistro in the "charming Butte-aux-Cailles neighborhood" "worth the detour from Downtown", given its "very-good regional cooking" and "high-quality service"; it's "ideal", whether you're a "middle-aged lady dining alone" or taking part in "a binge among buddies."

Chez Pauline ⌧   18 | 17 | 19 | 59
5, rue Villedo, 1ᵉʳ (Pyramides), 01 42 96 20 70; fax 01 49 27 99 89; www.chezpauline.com

◪ From the Classic cuisine to the "pleasant" red banquettes, "everything screams authentic French" at this "favorite" "on a quiet side street" near the Palais Royal; sure, it's "old-fashioned" and "overpriced for what you get", foes fume; but fans find it a "wonderful place to cocoon while dining on retro food" and enjoying service "that confounds stereotypes of unfriendly" staffers; P.S. make sure you "stay at ground level" to avoid sitting in the bland upstairs.

Chez Prune   14 | 16 | 11 | 31
36, rue Beaurepaire, 10ᵉ (Jacques Bonsergent/République), 01 42 41 30 47

◪ "It's pleasant to have a drink on the terrace overlooking the Canal Saint-Martin" at this "unpretentious" place in the 10th, "a part of town not known for great restaurants"; the scene "seems more about being trendy than about really good food" – e.g. the "weird sauces and mixes of sweet and sour" on the Eclectic menu – and "the service could be better", but none of that dismays the "noisy twenty- and thirtysomething crowd" that is revivifying this *quartier*.

Chez René ⌧   20 | 15 | 20 | 45
14, bd St-Germain, 5ᵉ (Maubert-Mutualité), 01 43 54 30 23; fax 01 43 26 43 92

■ This Saint-Germain "jewel" is "a step back in time" with "doting waiters", a "homey", lace-curtained atmosphere and "marvelous", "hearty Lyonnaise cooking" ("don't come if you're on a diet"), especially "the best boeuf

| F | D | S | €C |

bourguignon that tastes like they boiled a whole ox to make" "rich, thick dark syrup" of a sauce; with decor and "waiters that seemingly have been here since the Korean War", "it never changes" – "and that's a compliment."

Chez Savy

| – | – | – | M |

23, rue Bayard, 8ᵉ (Franklin D. Roosevelt), 01 47 23 46 98; fax 01 47 23 46 98

"Hiding in plain sight" for anyone who wants "great traditional cuisine and good-value wines" in the 8th, this "nice, quiet, little bistro" "specializes in super-fresh meat delivered directly from the Auvergne", "reasonably priced"; small wonder its 1923 interior often seems "reserved for the devoted regulars."

Chez Toutoune

| 20 | 18 | 17 | 46 |

5, rue Pontoise, 5ᵉ (Maubert-Mutualité), 01 43 26 56 81; fax 01 40 46 80 34

■ "Serving a menu that always begins with soup", this "cheerful Classic French–Mediterranean bistro" in the 5th arrondissement has won a loyal international following with "consistently delightful meals and friendly service"; perhaps the fare is rather "predictable", but for most the dining room decorated with "pretty Provençal" floral-print fabric is an enjoyable destination.

Chez Vincent

| 22 | 9 | 18 | 36 |

5, rue du Tunnel, 19ᵉ (Botzaris/Buttes-Chaumont), 01 42 02 22 45; fax 01 40 18 95 83

■ "When you really want to eat Italian you absolutely must come here" to this "super-convivial" corner in the 19th, where chef-owner Vincent Cozzoli, alias "the Picasso of antipasti", whips up an artful menu of "abundant and tasty food" and "occasionally breaks into an aria", to boot; though it seems to be "frequented only by regulars", "don't be afraid to step inside" the unpretentious digs.

Chez Vong ●⌀

| 21 | 20 | 19 | 64 |

10, rue de la Grande Truanderie, 1ᵉʳ (Etienne Marcel), 01 40 26 09 36; fax 01 42 33 38 15; www.chez-vong.com

◪ "Perhaps the most beautiful Chinese extant" – full of foliage, Buddhas, lacquered screens and low lights that create a "very different ambiance than the usual Paris restaurant" – this upmarket table in Les Halles promises "a delicious, exotic trip that doesn't disappoint" supporters say; however, doubters declare it goes vong when it comes to the cuisine ("routine and merely acceptable").

Chiberta

| 24 | 17 | 21 | 84 |

3, rue Arsène Houssaye, 8ᵉ (Charles de Gaulle-Etoile/ George V), 01 53 53 42 00; fax 01 45 62 85 08; www.lechiberta.com

◪ Some shiver the renovated "ultramodern decor" is "a bit cold", but the cuisine "quality has improved" at this

| **F** | **D** | **S** | **€C** |

"expensive" New French with "superior, innovative" and "refreshing" offerings in the 8th; augmented by "attention-to-detail" service, it's "a fine business-meal" destination with well-spaced "tables for discreet conversation"; those reviewers who find it "conducive to long romantic" evenings presumably aren't dining with the boss . . . or are they?

Chicago Pizza Pie Factory | 9 | 12 | 11 | 22 |
5, rue de Berri, 8ᵉ (George V), 01 45 62 50 23; fax 05 45 63 87 56

Just off the Champs, this "enjoyable" but "noisy" "American-style pizzeria" "decorated with Chicago street signs" is the "place to go if you need a deep-dish fix in Paris"; antagonists argue "you've got to be mighty desperate or homesick to pick this poor imitation of the vaunted" Chi pie, but "it's fun every once in a while" if you don't "expect a setting or service" (though the "dancing" "staff "will be happy to sing you a birthday song").

Chieng Mai ◐ | 18 | 8 | 13 | 31 |
12, rue Frédéric Sauton, 5ᵉ (Maubert-Mutualité), 01 43 25 45 45

"Authentic and spicy Thai" eats make this "nice local" Latin Quarter table "near Notre Dame" "a sure bet" for "good food at a good price" profess fans; but pessimists point to "small portions", "anonymous" "decor that's a bore" and service that's "pretty dire" unless you're "regular customers" as reasons to "go somewhere else."

Chien qui Fume (Au) ◐ | 18 | 19 | 16 | 43 |
33, rue du Pont-Neuf, 1ᵉʳ (Châtelet-Les Halles), 01 42 36 07 42; fax 01 42 36 36 85; www.au-chien-qui-fume.com

"Sit outside and watch the world of Les Halles unfold around you" or take a table in the dining room with a decorative motif of "dogs dressed as people" at this "good example of a brasserie"; "service can suffer from the crowds", but most are mollified by such "well-executed French classics" as a "delicious braised rabbit presented in a copper pot" or "outstanding onion soup."

China Club ◐ | 17 | 25 | 17 | 41 |
50, rue de Charenton, 12ᵉ (Bastille/Ledru-Rollin), 01 43 43 82 02; fax 01 43 43 79 85; www.chinaclub.cc

While it's "a little out of the way" in a quiet street near the Bastille, the "marvelous decor" reminiscent of "an old opium den" or "a brothel" and "a happening scene" make this Asian well worth seeking out; some clubbers cavil "it's best just for a drink in the cozy bar on the first floor", styled like an old-fashioned *fumoir*, or one of the weekend "jazz concerts in the basement" because the Chinese "cooking, although good, is not really interesting."

China Town Olympiades ◐ | – | – | – | I |
44, av d'Ivry, 13ᵉ (Porte d'Ivry), 01 45 84 72 21; fax 01 45 84 74 52

"The famous Peking duck carved before your eyes and the lazy Susans on the tables create some atmosphere" at this

F | D | S | €C

gigantic 300-seater, maybe "the best-known Chinese in the 13th"; but this Olympian's opponents opine it's become "a factory", with "mediocre food" and "slow service"; and while it remains cheap, its "run-down" decor really needs some work.

Christine (Le) ●🅢   23 | 23 | 23 | 47
1, rue Christine, 6ᵉ (Odéon/St-Michel), 01 40 51 71 64; fax 01 42 18 04 39

■ "They do quaint just right" at this "charming" Classic French with a "lovely" view over a courtyard garden; "the elegant decor matches the cuisine" ("simple", but "exquisitely prepared"), "the prix fixes are good value" and the young staff, often "art-history students who speak English", is "friendly"; though usually it's "only found by those in-the-know", it's well worth beating a path to this "wonderful place" in Saint-Germain.

CINQ (LE) 🅢   28 | 28 | 28 | 135
Four Seasons George V, 31, av George V, 8ᵉ (Alma-Marceau/ George V), 01 49 52 71 54; fax 01 49 52 71 81; www.fourseasons.com

■ "Exceptional from every point of view" aver acolytes of the George V's Haute Cuisine haven; start with the "original, fresh", "exquisite food" by Philippe Legendre (ex Taillevent) and a "splendid" wine list, add "majestic decor" (rated the *Survey*'s No. 1) "blooming with "beautiful flowers", finish with "impeccable" "yet not haughty service" and the total comes to a "very-special experience"; true, it "gives expensive a whole new meaning", but what wouldn't you pay for a place of utmost "class without pretension"?

59 Poincaré 🅢   21 | 22 | 21 | 81
Hôtel Le Parc, 59, av Raymond Poincaré, 16ᵉ (Boissière/ Trocadéro), 01 47 27 59 59

❏ "Steps from the Place Victor Hugo", this "stylish" duplex – the original location of Alain Ducasse, who still acts as consultant – sets a Contemporary French table that specializes in "high-quality" beef and lobster; but while the cooking is "tasty", critics call the cost "crazy" "for what it is", and sticklers think the service could be "better drilled"; however, the "beautiful courtyard dining" in summer mollifies many.

Cloche des Halles (La) 🅢⊄   _ | _ | _ | I
28, rue Coquillière, 1ᵉʳ (Les Halles/Louvre-Rivoli), 01 42 36 93 89

"There's no better Saturday lunch than sharing plates of charcuterie and cheese with a bottle of Chiroubles or Chénas" in this intimate, atmospheric wine bar, "one of the best in Paris"; named for the bell that used to ring the opening and closing hours of the old Les Halles market, it's a happy place and a "real bargain", to boot.

get updates at zagat.com

	F	D	S	€C

Clos des Gourmets (Le) 🚫   22 | 17 | 19 | 49
16, av Rapp, 7ᵉ (Alma-Marceau/Ecole Militaire), 01 45 51 75 61; fax 01 47 05 74 20

■ "One of the biggest little tables in Paris" rave reviewers of this New French run by a "charming husband-wife team"; though it's not bargain-priced, the "unbelievably creative" quality of the cuisine makes it "good value for this quarter" of the 7th, and despite "sardine-can seating", the room is "cozy and bright" and the "service warm" (though "one more *serveur* could increase efficiency").

Closerie des Lilas (La) ☾   17 | 22 | 17 | 58
171, bd du Montparnasse, 6ᵉ (Port Royal/Vavin), 01 40 51 34 50; fax 01 43 29 99 94

☒ This "mythic" Montparnasse table offers "two separate dining experiences: the brasserie for lunch and late-night and the restaurant for dinner"; while "both offer a chance to relive the Lost Generation life", it's the former, with its "famous steak tartare" and "piano-bar atmosphere", that fans favor, since otherwise the Classic French "food leaves a little to be desired"; but even if this "overpriced" place is "resting on its laurels", it remains "as romantic as all of Paris"; P.S. in summer, "the terrace is still the place to be."

Clos Morillons (Le) 🚫   ∇ 17 | 12 | 13 | 42
50, rue des Morillons, 15ᵉ (Porte de Vanves), 01 48 28 04 37; fax 01 48 28 70 77

■ With a renovated, sunny-yellow decor that's "simple, but bright and neat", this New French in the 15th now allows customers to concentrate on the "inventiveness" of such "succulent" dishes as kidneys in a juniper-berry *jus*; "moderate prices" are appreciated, too.

Clos Saint-Honoré (Le) ☾🚫   – | – | – | M
3, rue St-Hyacinthe, 1ᵉʳ (Tuileries), 01 40 15 09 36; fax 01 40 15 09 56; www.leclossainthonore.com

Despite a handy location near, or rather beneath, the Tuileries (the dining room is a 17th-century cellar that extends under the gardens), only a handful of surveyors have dug into the delights of this "quiet, romantic place that's perfect for a non-bank-breaking but delicious meal" of Classic French dishes, prepared by a buried "treasure" of a chef; the "attentive" service and modest prices are worth joining the underground movement for, too.

Clovis (Le)   ∇ 26 | 25 | 24 | 81
Sofitel Arc de Triomphe, 2, av Bertie Albrecht, 8ᵉ (Charles de Gaulle-Etoile/George V), 01 53 89 50 53; fax 01 53 89 50 51; www.accorhotels.com

■ It speaks volumes that this Contemporary French in the Sofitel Arc de Triomphe "doesn't feel like it's in a hotel, with its subdued and tasteful decor, creative and well-presented dishes and helpful staff", especially the "great sommelier" –

F | **D** | **S** | **€C**

all of which "make this an awesome experience", one that more folks "should discover"; it's "expensive", but "excellent for business lunches and dinners" or just "a real nice meal."

Clown Bar ●⌀   ▽ 17 | 23 | 16 | 28
114, rue Amelot, 11ᵉ (Filles-du-Calvaire), 01 43 55 87 35

🖃 The "wonderful antique decor" of landmarked circus-themed art nouveau tiles is more memorable than the fare at this *bar à vins* next to the Cirque d'Hiver in the 11th; still, it's a "comfortable, homey" place that's "fun for a light meal and drink" of comfort food like grilled andouillette; the major drawback is a staff that won't stop clowning around, necessitating that you "wave briskly for service."

Coco de Mer ⌀   – | – | – | M
34, bd St-Marcel, 5ᵉ (Les Gobelins/St-Marcel), 01 47 07 06 64; fax 01 47 07 41 88; www.pierre-frichot.com

🖃 "You'd think you were in the Seychelles (which might explain the indolent service)" at this address featuring the cuisine of the multicultural Indian Ocean islands; there's definitely a "vacation vibe", what with the "cocktails, colorful dishes and [having] your feet in the sand" that's sprinkled across the enclosed patio; while "attractive, the cooking lacks genius", but hey, a meal here will set you back a lot less than a plane ticket to Mahé.

Coconnas ⌀   17 | 18 | 19 | 50
2 bis, pl des Vosges, 4ᵉ (Bastille/St-Paul), 01 42 78 58 16; fax 01 42 78 16 28

🖃 Despite the valiant efforts of proprietor Claude Terrail of La Tour d'Argent, opinions on this Classic French with "a fabulous location in the Place des Vosges" cleave into two camps: converts crow "it's a real find" for "pleasant" bistro standards ("coq au vin to die for"), while critics carp "the cooking is, frankly, of no interest whatsoever"; all agree, however, that you should "go for the memories" of "eating outdoors" amid the arcades of "the most beautiful square in Paris."

Coffee Parisien ●   14 | 13 | 11 | 26
4, rue Princesse, 6ᵉ (Mabillon), 01 43 54 18 18; fax 01 43 54 94 96
7, rue Gustave-Courbet, 16ᵉ (Trocadéro), 01 45 53 17 17; fax 01 43 54 94 96
46, rue de Sablonville, Neuilly (Les Sablons), 01 46 37 13 13 ⌀

🖃 "You'd think you were in a little college town" in the U.S., but "it's actually the 16th", Saint-Germain or Neuilly, the locations of this trio of "noisy", "smoky" "coffee shops", "favorites of expats" and "a young crowd"; though lauded "for Sunday brunch, American-style", they frustrate foes who call the eats "just average" and slam the "slow", "irritating" service; still, they're "good if you're craving a

| F | D | S | €C |

burger, cheesecake" or other Yankee staples, though they're "not cheap considering the quality of the fare."

Coin de la Rue (Au) Ⓢ   — | — | — | E

10, rue Castellane, 8ᵉ (Madeleine), 01 44 71 06 12; fax 01 44 71 08 78

The "amusingly" "trendy decor" – walls covered in silver foil, plasma screens with stock prices and a triangular fireplace – provokes more comment than Contemporary French cooking that, though "nice", "lacks spark" at this self-consciously stylish spot near the Madeleine; while "efficient", the service seems "pretentious" at times too.

Coin des Gourmets (Au)   ▽ 24 | 10 | 19 | 30

5, rue Dante, 5ᵉ (Cluny-La Sorbonne/Maubert-Mutualité), 01 43 26 12 92

■ This tiny Latin Quarter corner is "one you shouldn't miss", because it's just the sort of place "you'd love to have just outside your door", with its "tasty, varied" Vietnamese vittles and "absolutely terrific" "Cambodian specialties"; it also offers "friendly" service and "great value – both hard to find in Paris" at times; "reserving is a must", since "it's always packed."

Colette Ⓢ   17 | 19 | 17 | 31

213, rue St-Honoré, 1ᵉʳ (Tuileries), 01 55 35 33 93; fax 01 55 35 33 99; www.colette.fr

◪ Located in the basement of Colette, Paris' perennially hot boutique, this "hip lunch hangout" has "healthy" New French–Italian "great salads and a water bar", with a choice of the wet stuff from all over the world ("a bit hasbeen" some sniff); it's "perfect for a quick stop while shopping", but as light meals go, damn if it isn't "expensive to be trendy."

Comédiens (Les) ●Ⓢ   — | — | — | M

7, rue Blanche, 9ᵉ (Trinité), 01 40 82 95 95; fax 01 40 82 96 96

Just after the curtain calls, this cozy place fills up with show-goers "coming out of the theaters of the 9th" and occasionally the namesake actors, giving the place sort of a Gallic Joe Allen buzz (as does the exposed-brick, self-styled 'NYC-like' decor); the New Bistro fare "is no better than good", "but the ambiance is lively and fun", "making you want to be one of the regulars who get kissed when they come in."

. . . Comme Cochon Ⓢ   — | — | — | E

135, rue de Charenton, 12ᵉ (Gare de Lyon/Reuilly-Diderot), 01 43 42 43 36

Devotees are "never disappointed by the ambiance or the cooking", "washed down" with a "smart selection of Languedoc wines" at this "appealing Classic Bistro" near the Viaduc des Arts in the 12th; with a simple decor of

| F | D | S | €C |

framed photographs and paintings, an arty, young crowd makes it "a fun place" where you're "always welcome."

Comptoir du Saumon – | – | – | M

60, rue François Miron, 4ᵉ (St-Paul), 01 42 77 23 08; fax 01 42 77 44 75
61, rue Pierre Charron, 8ᵉ (Franklin D. Roosevelt/George V), 01 45 61 25 14; fax 01 45 63 47 04
116, rue de la Convention, 15ᵉ (Boucicaut), 01 45 54 31 16; fax 01 45 54 49 68
3, av de Villiers, 17ᵉ (Villiers), 01 40 53 89 00; fax 01 40 53 89 89
www.saumon.com

This quartet of eat-in/take-out boutiques serves up a variety of hot and cold seafood plates that span the globe, from "very good Danish herring" to Scottish salmon to Iranian caviar; ambiancewise, they're "neither cozy nor warm" (the name doesn't mean 'salmon counter' for nothing), "but the food is very fresh, and your taste buds can't demand more than that."

Comptoir Paris-Marrakech ⏺ ▽ 15 | 21 | 12 | 37

37, rue Berger, 1ᵉʳ (Les Halles/Louvre-Rivoli), 01 40 26 26 66; fax 01 42 21 44 24

◪ Maybe "the Marrakesh branch is better than this Paris one – but it's a lot farther away", so most are happy to head for this Moroccan in Les Halles, and an atmospheric decor of "copper trays and leather hassocks" on which "a hip, young crowd" reclines; among the munchies, supporters single out the "very-good tagines" with "special mention for the fig, mint and ginger ice creams"; "too bad that prices have been creeping up lately", though.

Comte de Gascogne (Au) ⓈⒶ 21 | 20 | 20 | 80

89, av Jean-Baptiste Clément, Boulogne (Pont-de-St-Cloud), 01 46 03 47 27; fax 01 46 04 55 70

■ You can indeed dine like a count of Gascony on the "perfect foie gras" and other regional specialties at this swank spot in suburban Boulogne; its "original" greenhouse setting, a "pretty" courtyard with palm trees and fountains, makes a meal here "sort of like eating fantastic food in the middle of a tropical rainforest"; bear in mind, though, that while "very good", it's also "very expensive."

Congrès Maillot (Le) ⏺ 12 | 15 | 9 | 53

80, av de la Grande-Armée, 17ᵉ (Porte Maillot), 01 45 74 17 24; fax 01 45 72 39 80

◪ "Fresh shellfish" is the main reason to frequent this brasserie at the Porte Maillot; the '70s decor may be just on the verge of becoming vintage, but overall the place is "a far cry from what it used to be" all those opposed opine, complaining that "quantity has replaced quality" and the "service leaves a lot to be desired"; it's most useful "on Sundays or for events at the Palais des Congrès" close by.

get updates at zagat.com

	F	D	S	€C

Conti Ⓢ
19 | 15 | 18 | 70

72, rue Lauriston, 16ᵉ (Boissière), 01 47 27 74 67; fax 01 47 27 37 66

■ "Very-good cooking in a neighborhood that's not very lively" (the 16th) makes this refined Italian with a Venetian "theatrical decor" of Murano chandeliers a destination for locals in search of an "authentic" meal; it's "a bit expensive", and the service can be "a little slow", but ex–Orient Express chef Michel Ranvier's cooking is "innovative" and the clientele is mercifully quiet.

Contre-Allée (La) Ⓢ
∇ 18 | 18 | 20 | 48

83, av Denfert-Rochereau, 14ᵉ (Denfert-Rochereau), 01 43 54 99 86; fax 01 43 25 05 28; www.contre-allee.com

■ Located in a quieter part of the 14th, this "tranquil" table is popular for its "excellent" Bistro fare that's "neither too Classic, nor too world-food" trendy; the inside is "a nice environment", but the smart money "snags an outside table" when the weather permits.

Copenhague Ⓢ
21 | 18 | 19 | 60

142, av des Champs-Elysées, 8ᵉ (Charles de Gaulle-Etoile/George V), 01 44 13 86 26; fax 01 42 25 83 10; www.restaurantfloradanica.com

■ "It's really worth a detour" to discover this delightful Dane, especially since "it's amusing to watch people" through the picture windows of the "quiet" dining room with red-leather chairs and a large oil of the Queen of Denmark "just a few steps from the bustle of the Champs"; it's "expensive", but the "sublime" food ("best salmon and herring in France"), "a great selection of aquavit" and "pleasant service" "conquer" the crowd, especially during the summer when they serve on a greenery-filled terrace.

Cosi
20 | 10 | 13 | 14

54, rue de Seine, 6ᵉ (Mabillon/Odéon), 01 46 33 35 36

■ "As sandwiches go, they don't get much better than this" say supporters of this sandwicherie/wine bar, a "fantastic stop while shopping the 6th" that offers "wonderful ingredients stuffed into tasty focaccia" "to the sound of opera" "music playing in the background"; furthermore, all's quickly served up "at a price that makes you wish for a Cosi on every corner" – and ranks as the *Survey*'s No. 1 Best Buy among Paris restaurants.

Cosi (Le) ●Ⓢ⒵
– | – | – | M

9, rue Cujas, 5ᵉ (Cluny-La Sorbonne/Luxembourg), 01 43 29 20 20; fax 01 43 29 26 40

Not to be confused with the popular sandwich shop, this "very pleasant" place near the Panthéon offers a wonderful little "taste of Corsica in Paris" (think braised kid, sheep-cheese–filled ravioli and a variety of island wines), served in a relaxed high-ceilinged setting.

| F | D | S | €C |

Costes ❶   18 | 25 | 15 | 68
Hôtel Costes, 239, rue St-Honoré, 1ᵉʳ (Concorde/Tuileries), 01 42 44 50 25; fax 01 42 44 50 01

☑ "It's rare for a fashionable spot to become an institution", but after eight years, this brasserie near the Place Vendôme is "still perceived as one of the 'in' places to be"; decorator Jacques Garcia's "sumptuous", "seductive" *fin-de-siècle* interior attracts more acclaim than the Eclectic eats, which, while "surprisingly good", remain just "a distraction" from "the fashionistas strutting by" – a group that includes the staff, "perfectionists in the art of treating you like dirt."

Côté Coulisses 🅂   – | – | – | M
1, rue Monsigny, 2ᵉ (Quatre Septembre), 01 42 96 16 61; fax 01 42 97 40 97

Red, velvet curtains and upholstery, plus a disco soundtrack, are providing a second act to this theater-district locale in the 2nd, whose name roughly translates as 'backstage'; despite the nightclub vibe and contemporary decoration, the French cooking is impeccably Traditional, with prompt, professional service and reasonable prices.

Cottage Marcadet (Le) 🅂   ▽ 24 | 19 | 25 | 46
151 bis, rue Marcadet, 18ᵉ (Lamarck-Caulaincourt), 01 42 57 71 22

■ "A special dining experience" awaits those who make the effort of traveling to a remote, "charmless" corner of the 18th; "excellent value for the money" (especially on the 35-euro prix fixe, "which includes wine"), this "tiny" place "with a cozy atmosphere and very hospitable owner" wows and wins fans with New French "food to live for", such as red mullet in Balsamic vinegar in summer and raspberry *craquant* (a sugary 'sandwich' of the fruit and cookie discs).

Coude Fou (Le) ❶   16 | 12 | 16 | 36
12, rue du Bourg-Tibourg, 4ᵉ (Hôtel-de-Ville), 01 42 77 15 16; fax 01 48 04 08 98

■ Maybe depending on your neighbors, this Marais wine bar – reportedly the first one in Paris – is either cozy or "cramped", but most find the small room with stone walls a pleasant setting in which to enjoy "excellent" varietals and food that's "a cut above the usual" *bar à vins* including some "great duck dishes"; service is "friendly", prices are "middling" and "the crowd is mixed but respectable."

Cou de la Girafe (Le) ❶🅂   14 | 14 | 15 | 41
7, rue Paul Baudry, 8ᵉ (Franklin D. Roosevelt/St-Philippe-du-Roule), 01 43 59 47 28; fax 01 42 25 06 62

■ "Always nice" say surveyors about this Classic French "nestled behind the Champs"; "relaxed atmosphere" and a warm and fuzzy "welcome" make "a trendy, young crowd happy"; and if the "dishes are simple, they're successful" for the most part.

get updates at zagat.com

		F	D	S	€C

Couleurs de Vigne ⌧   ‒ | ‒ | ‒ | I
2, rue Marmontel, 15ᵉ (Convention/Vaugirard), 01 45 33 32 96; fax 01 45 33 32 96

This charming, little wine bar with olive-green walls, cork-colored floors and shelves stocked with an impressive array of vinous treasures also offers reasonably priced plates of charcuterie and cheeses that are easily enough for two; in addition to a range of inexpensive regional labels for on-premises consumption, patrons can select a bottle to take home.

Coupe-Chou (Le) ◐   21 | 25 | 21 | 49
9, rue de Lanneau, 5ᵉ (Maubert-Mutualité), 01 46 33 68 69; fax 01 43 25 94 15; www.lecoupechou.com

■ "A restaurant doesn't get any more romantic" than this Classic French situated "on one of the oldest streets" in the Latin Quarter; given the "marvelous decor" of candles, exposed stone walls, arched ceilings and a wood-burning fireplace, many "go more for the atmosphere than for the food", despite the many "mouthwatering" mains; still, its "consistent charm" makes this a bona fide "place to begin a seduction" – unless, of course, "there's a tour bus out front."

COUPOLE (LA) ◐   17 | 23 | 16 | 48
102, bd du Montparnasse, 14ᵉ (Vavin), 01 43 20 14 20; fax 01 43 35 46 14; www.flobrasseries.com

◪ "One of the eternal brasseries of Paris" resides in this "remarkable" Montparnasse "art deco beehive" that's "busy" until the wee hours with "efficient" if attitudinal "waiters traipsing through the huge", art-filled room, bearing platters of "superb" shellfish, steak frites and the like; admittedly, it's "noisy", something of "a tourist magnet" and many moan "the food is more fast than French"; but "it has tons of energy" and "a lot of history", and that "merits a visit" at least once.

Crêperie de Josselin (La) ◐⇗   19 | 14 | 16 | 20
67, rue du Montparnasse, 14ᵉ (Edgar Quinet/Montparnasse-Bienvenüe), 01 43 20 93 50

■ "Tasty crêpes" "so large they hang over the plate" have converts crowding into this bit of Brittany in Montparnasse; given that "one of those puppies would feed three hungry people", it's an "incredible bargain", and a "more efficient staff won't be found anywhere else in the City of Light"; the "smoky" digs fall flat for a few, but that doesn't deter those who "go straight for" "one of the foremost crêperies in Paris" ("and don't forget the cider").

Cristal Room ⌧   ‒ | ‒ | ‒ | E
Baccarat, 11, pl des Etats-Unis, 16ᵉ (Boissière/Iéna), 01 40 22 11 10; www.baccarat.fr

With chef Thierry Burlot running the kitchen, this intimate Philippe Starck–designed dining room in the new Baccarat

| F | D | S | €C |

showroom in the 16th has become one of the hottest (and hard-to-get-into) addresses in Paris; amid decor that plays off the grandeur of the former mansion of eccentric aristocrat Marie-Laure de Noailles, with big foppish plaster medallions and bare-brick walls in a sumptuous marble-accented salon, you can dine on New French dishes and drink from – what else? – Baccarat glasses.

Crus de Bourgogne (Aux)

–|–|–| M

3, rue Bachaumont, 2ᵉ (Les Halles/Sentier), 01 42 33 48 24; fax 01 40 28 66 41

◪ With red-checked tablecloths and red wine galore, this "old-style bistro" near Les Halles in the 2nd arrondissement is "a classic address"; some sigh the 72-year-old grandpa seems a tad "tired" – aside from a "spectacular lobster salad", the fare is rather "predictable" and the "service surly"; but if nostalgia is the best dish on the menu, at least it's moderately priced.

Dagorno ◐

–|–|–| M

190, av Jean Jaurès, 19ᵉ (Porte de Pantin), 01 40 40 09 39; fax 01 48 03 17 23

The handful of folks willing to head up to this meat-oriented veteran in La Villette in the 19th arrondissement, once the location of Paris' slaughterhouses, think it's more than worth the trip, since this "beautiful establishment" (the decor dates from the turn of the century) offers heartily "excellent" Traditional French feed, complemented by a variety of vintage Armagnacs.

Dalloyau

22| 16| 16| 32

5, bd Beaumarchais, 4ᵉ (Bastille), 01 48 87 89 88; fax 01 48 87 73 70
2, pl Edmond Rostand, 6ᵉ (Cluny-La Sorbonne/Odéon), 01 43 29 31 10; fax 01 43 26 25 72
63, rue de Grenelle, 7ᵉ (Rue du Bac), 01 45 49 95 30; fax 01 42 84 04 75
101, rue du Faubourg-St-Honoré, 8ᵉ (Miromesnil/St-Philippe-du-Roule), 01 42 99 90 00; fax 01 45 63 82 92
69, rue de la Convention, 15ᵉ (Boucicaut), 01 45 77 84 27; fax 01 45 75 27 99
65-67, av J.B. Clément, Boulogne (Boulogne-Jean Jaurès), 01 46 05 06 78; fax 01 46 03 90 30
www.dalloyau.fr

◪ "Celebrate Aunt Marie's birthday" at one of these well-bred, old-fashioned tearooms famous for their "decadent desserts" – especially "the most amazing macaroons in the world" – plus a "cornucopia of wonderful small dishes", "excellent cocoa" and "a good selection of brews"; the service is sometimes "inclined to be icy", and you can end up "paying a lot", but a stop here is "for pastry lovers, like going to heaven"; P.S. there's a "magnificent view of the Luxembourg Gardens" in the 6th.

get updates at zagat.com

| | | F | D | S | €C |

Dame Tartine/Café Very　　　| 11 | 11 | 9 | 22 |
Jardin des Tuileries, 1ᵉʳ (Concorde/Tuileries), 01 47 03 94 84;
fax 01 47 03 94 84
2, rue Brisemiche, 4ᵉ (Hôtel-de-Ville), 01 42 77 32 22;
fax 01 42 77 32 22

◼ Open-faced "sandwiches of every sort" star at these "simple" spots amid the Tuileries and "in the shadow of the Beaubourg"; "fast service" makes them popular with a "young, lively, noisy crowd"; and if some liken the experience to "eating in a cafeteria", it can be "fun" for a "light", "quick feed."

Da Mimmo ●⊠　　　| ▽ 19 | 9 | 12 | 35 |
39, bd de Magenta, 10ᵉ (Gare de l'Est/Jacques Bonsergent),
01 42 06 44 47

◼ Though it's located near the gritty Gare de l'Est, "a meal here is like going to Naples, with all that implies"; while advocates applaud the moderately priced "superb pizzas, the rest of the food is insolently expensive" – especially since the "often-absent servers" might fail to specify prices for "the daily specials" or mixed antipasti plates, "which can cause the bill to explode"; still, "if you're willing to spend" – as "a lot of people" are – "this is the place to go."

Daru (Le) ⊠　　　| – | – | – | E |
19, rue Daru, 8ᵉ (Courcelles/Ternes), 01 42 27 23 60;
fax 01 47 54 08 14

Given that it's been around since the Russian Revolution, it's surprising how few surveyors have been to this venerable Slav, "a precious address to know about" in the 8th; those who have herald the cuisine – smoked salmon, blini and caviar (both fish and eggplant) – as "great", even if the candlelit decor, with lots of framed bits and pieces on the wood-paneled walls, seems "a bit stuffy", and the prices could deplete a czar's treasury.

Dauphin (Le)　　　| 19 | 16 | 19 | 40 |
167, rue St-Honoré, 1ᵉʳ (Palais Royal-Musée du Louvre),
01 42 60 40 11; fax 01 42 60 01 18

◼ "Massive portions of fish", foie gras and other "simple" but "really solid" Southwestern eats "are served up in timely fashion" at this bistro from the team behind Biarritz's well-regarded Café de Paris; perhaps the vintage 1940 "interior is somewhat cold", but the "staff is friendly", and it offers "excellent value" "considering its location" across from the Comédie Française and "convenient to all the sights" in the 1st.

Davé ●　　　| 19 | 13 | 22 | 44 |
12, rue de Richelieu, 1ᵉʳ (Palais Royal-Musée du Louvre),
01 42 61 49 48

◼ "If you want to meet real stars and top models in the flesh, then come here" to this Asian near the Palais Royal,

subscribe to zagat.com

| F | D | S | €C |

where the "ever-present" owner Davé will "take the best care of you"; however, most visit more for the "beautiful-people" "atmosphere than the Chinese" and Vietnamese food – though "enjoyable", it's only "slightly better than the usual corner place" (and of course, "it costs more too").

D'Chez Eux ☒ | 21 | 17 | 20 | 61 |
2, av Lowendal, 7ᵉ (Ecole Militaire), 01 47 05 52 55; fax 01 45 55 60 74; www.chezeux.com
■ It's like being "in a time warp" to visit this "pleasant, casual neighborhood" place near Les Invalides, where "at tiny tables, enormous portions of Southwestern" and "Classic Bistro food is delivered" "nonstop" by "waiters in blue smocks" who "treat everyone like a long-lost friend" – or perhaps a valued hand ("from the size of the servings, you'd think they were feeding you to do a full day's work in the fields"); it's all "great fun", and "even though it's expensive, it's good value" the satiated insist.

Dédicace Café (Le) ☻ | - | - | - | M |
7, rue St-Benoît, 6ᵉ (Mabillon/St-Germain-des-Prés), 01 42 61 12 70; fax 01 42 61 22 04; www.dedicacecafe.com
In an area of the 6th infested with tourist traps, this casual, colorful cafe offers "quite good value" on a menu that features such New French specials as artichoke terrine, fillet of bass with fennel and roasted figs with crème fraîche; a "nice team" services the dining room where a mobile of manuscript pages hangs in homage to the numerous publishing houses nearby (the place's name, which means 'dedication', is a similar reference).

De Lagarde ☒ | - | - | - | M |
83, av de Ségur, 15ᵉ (Ségur), 01 40 65 99 10; fax 01 40 65 99 10
Occupying a "quiet corner" of the 15th, this Classic French in a former butcher's shop is "not to be missed", thanks to the "fantastic food" of chef-owner Yohann Marraccini (ex Arpège), who prognosticators promise is "going to become very well known"; perhaps the "courteous staff" is "a little slow", but you should still "go quickly" to this little dining room decorated with coffeepots, because in most ways it already is "a grand restaurant, except it lacks an astronomical check."

Délices d'Aphrodite (Les) ☻☒ | 20 | 12 | 15 | 33 |
4, rue de Candolle, 5ᵉ (Censier-Daubenton), 01 43 31 40 39; fax 01 43 36 13 08; www.mavrommatis.fr
■ The "same as [sibling] Mavrommatis, but cheaper" agree acolytes of this "typically Greek" goddess, tucked away in a quiet part of the Latin Quarter; it's become kind of "a Hellenic institution" for the "best moussaka in Paris" and other "inspired", "traditional" dishes, served in a somewhat "kitschy", "tightly spaced" taverna setting.

| F | D | S | €C |

Délices de Szechuen   18 | 12 | 17 | 38
40, av Duquesne, 7ᵉ (St-François-Xavier), 01 43 06 22 55
◪ Surveyors smile over the Szechuan servings, "freshly prepared with just the right [amount of] spice", at this Chinese "nestled in the heart of the 7th"; foes fret it's "kind of expensive" ("the fried dumplings should have been made of gold") compared to other Asians, and given the "gloomy" decor; however, a greenery-filled "good terrace in summer" compensates.

Dell Orto ☒   – | – | – | E
45, rue St-Georges, 9ᵉ (St-Georges), 01 48 78 40 30
"Only open in the evenings, alas", this corner shop-front near the Place Saint-Georges has won a loyal following among a stylish, young crowd for its "exceptional", "original Italian cooking", served with a sense of "privilege" in a traditional Tuscan-style room; if the pasta is perfect, it's "too bad the prices have gone up since it became successful" – now, it's "expensive."

Dessirier ◐   22 | 17 | 21 | 69
9, pl du Maréchal Juin, 17ᵉ (Péreire), 01 42 27 82 14; fax 01 47 66 82 07; www.pierrerostang.com
■ "You pay dearly, but there are few better for fresh seafood" than this "refined", "old-fashioned" house near the Place Péreire (case in point: the signature "sea bass cooked in a crust of salt, which shows how a complex preparation can result in simple perfection" in a dish); "unpretentious", solicitous service nets accolades too, along with "much-appreciated valet parking."

Deux Abeilles (Les) ☒   ▽ 14 | 12 | 15 | 26
189, rue de l'Université, 7ᵉ (Alma-Marceau), 01 45 55 64 04
◪ This well-mannered tearoom in the 7th is a place where "you run into attractive women who are watching their figures", as it's perfect for "a light lunch" of "specialty egg dishes" or an "original salad" – though then it tempts with "mouthwatering desserts"; the happy hum it's "worth a detour for the gracious service", even if the "unpretentious decor" "needs renovating."

Deux Canards (Aux) ☒   21 | 20 | 23 | 41
8, rue du Faubourg-Poissonnière, 10ᵉ (Bonne Nouvelle), 01 47 70 03 23; fax 01 47 70 18 85
■ "Exceptional" "owner Gérard Faesch is cordial and fun", "discoursing on his orange-based preparations" at this Traditional French where the emphasis is on "regional cooking made with fresh ingredients", which include the namesake fowl; if most "love the menu", one or deux critics quack over the costs ("it ain't a two-buck duck"); still, scores support those advocates who applaud this friendly, moderate "favorite."

| F | D | S | €C |

Devez (Le) ☻
| 12 | 11 | 13 | 45 |

5, pl de l'Alma, 8ᵉ (Alma-Marceau), 01 53 67 97 53; fax 01 47 23 09 48

☑ "An original approach to meat" – specifically, the featured Aubrac beef in the form of tapas, roasts or a 'MacD'Aubrac' hamburger – plus a "rich wine cellar" pleases carnivores at this "trendy steakhouse"; malcontents moo "you know there are service problems when your vino arrives after your dessert", but that doesn't "stop the 'in' crowd haunting the outside tables", possibly because this is "one of the few reasonably priced places" in the 8th.

Diamantaires (Les) ☻
| – | – | – | M |

60, rue La Fayette, 9ᵉ (Cadet/Le Peletier), 01 47 70 78 14; fax 01 44 83 02 73

Those who know this veteran in the 9th appreciate "the complete repertory" of dishes from Armenia "and nearby lands" on offer, including manti, "a seasoned ground lamb, chopped onion and parsley-filled pastry boat served with yogurt"; however, "you should avoid the nights they have live music if you want a tranquil" evening, when the joint jumps with members of Paris' large Armenian community.

Diep ☻
| 18 | 11 | 13 | 55 |

55, rue Pierre Charron, 8ᵉ (Franklin D. Roosevelt), 01 45 63 53 76; fax 01 42 56 46 56; www.diep.fr

☑ "One is never disappointed" is the Confucian judgment on this "quite good" Chinese-Vietnamese in a "bustling" "beautiful-people" corner of the 8th; however, you should be someone who "wouldn't have trouble enjoying Peking duck in a métro car at rush hour" as the place is "always packed" and the "service is so quick it's stressful"; some say wok on by, "there are better around for a lot less money", but for most this "upscale" table "merits its prices."

Divellec (Le) ☒
| 23 | 16 | 19 | 115 |

107, rue de l'Université, 7ᵉ (Invalides), 01 45 51 91 96; fax 01 45 51 31 75; www.ledivellec.com

☑ "Superb seafood" – "the menu even states if it's wild or farmed" – is the bait at this "old-fashioned" dining room overlooking Les Invalides, favored by politicians, expense-accounters and the occasional star "amenable to relaxed, unhurried dining"; however, even advocates admit "the fish is definitely fresher than the decor" and that "year after year, prices become more prohibitive and the service increasingly stuffy"; still, it's "one of the best" poisson palaces in Paris, and rank has its privileges.

1728 ☒
| 18 | 26 | 17 | 56 |

8, rue d'Anjou, 8ᵉ (Concorde/Madeleine), 01 40 17 04 77; fax 01 42 65 53 87; www.galerie-1728.com

☑ With a "surprising little jewel box" of a setting in an "exceptional 18th-century" townhouse in the 8th near Saint

|F|D|S|€C|

Augustin, this "beautifully decorated" place wins kudos from coo-ers for its Peking chef's "interesting cuisine", "a fusion of Japanese and New French trends"; "a must for romantic dinners", it's also "a pleasant place to meet for afternoon tea", though be forewarned that it's "expensive" – especially "for what it is" some naysayers note.

Dix Vins (Le) ●🖼⌿ ▽ 17 | 13 | 15 | 27
57, rue Falguière, 15ᵉ (Pasteur), 01 43 20 91 77
■ The "prices are good and the food is decent" at this Traditional Bistro in the 15th; though it can get "crowded and loud" with all its habitués ("I've been here 20 times in the last two years"), the owners have made "marvelous use of the small space", with "flowers always on the tables"; throw in the "cheap" list of wines, and you have an "incredible value", making this ideal "for an inexpensive night out with friends."

Djakarta Bali – | – | – | M
9, rue Vauvilliers, 1ᵉʳ (Châtelet/Louvre-Rivoli), 01 45 08 83 11
Along with the "interesting" Indonesian cooking, acolytes admire the "absolutely adorable" service from the brother-and-sister team that runs this small place near Les Halles; it may be "a little hard to find", but it's worth it to sample the often "outstanding" eats served in a traditional native setting; P.S. "the Friday-night dancing is highly entertaining."

Domaine de Lintillac 🖼 18 | 11 | 14 | 25
54, rue Blanche, 9ᵉ (Blanche/Trinité), 01 48 74 84 36; www.domainedelintillac-paris.com
■ "Simple but rich regional" "specialties from southwestern France", including "everything from the duck", make even the querulous quack with pleasure at this midsize table run by the Lintillac gourmet-food firm; not far from Pigalle, it's full of fun details like "a toaster on every table to ensure freshly crisped bread" and a reassuring "glow from the red lamp shades" to accompany the foie gras; virtually every visitor praises "the excellent value for the money" of the food and regional wine list.

Dôme (Le) ● 22 | 21 | 20 | 67
108, bd du Montparnasse, 14ᵉ (Vavin), 01 43 35 25 81; fax 01 42 79 01 19
◪ Suggestive of "something out of *A Moveable Feast*", this Montparnasse "grande dame" with "splendid decor" is "a pearl" serving up some of "the best oysters in the world", "other-worldly sole meunière" and other "fabulous seafood"; the crowd is a well-heeled mix of "regal, elegant, older" locals and tourists who appreciate that the "pro staffers" "don't rush you"; even admirers admit that it is "definitely too expensive", given the "careful rather than creative cuisine", but still, "it's a Paris institution."

| F | D | S | €C |

Dôme du Marais (Le) ◐🅾   18 | 21 | 18 | 46
53 bis, rue des Francs-Bourgeois, 4ᵉ (Hôtel-de-Ville/Rambuteau), 01 42 74 54 17; fax 01 42 77 78 17

🖃 Housed in a former church in the Marais, this "beautiful dining room with, of course, a dome above" "strikes an elegant balance, managing to be chic but not trendy", with a mix of "inventive" New and "Classic French food to match"; some find the scene a trifle "starchy", and snap the "personable service doesn't make up for the disappointing cuisine", but to most, it's ideal for "a romantic dinner" and offers one of the "rare good values in this quarter."

Dominique ◐🅾   – | – | – | E
19, rue Bréa, 6ᵉ (Vavin), 01 43 27 08 80; fax 01 43 27 03 76

Once a fixture of the White Russian community in Paris, this long-running (est. 1928) Montparnasse citizen soldiers on, offering "various vodkas" – they have some 80 different varieties – to kick back with such Slav specialties as beef stroganoff and salmon koulibiaka in an intimate dining room that conjures up the old country.

Doobie's ◐🅾   ▽ 11 | 9 | 16 | 46
2, rue Robert Estienne, 8ᵉ (Franklin D. Roosevelt), 01 53 76 10 76

■ Just off the Champs, this site with a "trendy" New French–Eclectic menu is *the* place to go for "the nicest brunch in Paris", since it "achieves an unusual balance: fashionable and kid friendly" at the same time; otherwise, the food's "the least of your worries when you come here to show off and be seen", and enjoy service that grooves to "lounge music"; a few find the new "velvet ropes up front" – designed to imply exclusivity – a bit charm-killing.

Dos de la Baleine (Le)   14 | 10 | 15 | 38
40, rue des Blancs-Manteaux, 4ᵉ (Hôtel-de-Ville/Rambuteau), 01 42 72 38 98; fax 01 42 71 40 59

■ Reservations are recommended at this "noisy but nice" Marais maven that has a sizable gay following, though "heterosexuals are warmly welcomed, too"; maybe the Traditional Bistro "food is average", but given the cozy ambiance and reasonable prices, it's a "good bargain."

Drouant 🅾   21 | 21 | 21 | 90
18, rue Gaillon, 2ᵉ (Opéra/Quatre Septembre), 01 42 65 15 16; fax 01 49 24 02 15

■ As the venue of the prestigious Prix Goncourt (France's highest annual prize for literature), this bastion of "refined elegance" in "a historic structure" near the Opéra "doesn't have to prove anything"; chef Louis Grondard's "fine" Classic French cooking may not "merit the Goncourt of the restaurant world" but it's "fashion-proof", particularly the "fresh fish", and overall, this "mythic" table, for "what it is", is "near perfect"; P.S. try eating in one of the "little salons" "for a hint of literary holiness."

get updates at zagat.com   93

| F | D | S | €C |

DUC (LE) 🈯   25 | 15 | 20 | 85
243, bd Raspail, 14ᵉ (Raspail), 01 43 20 96 30; fax 01 43 20 46 73

■ It may be in Montparnasse, but a meal at this "delightful, old standby" is "like a trip to Honfleur" because everything they serve is "sparkling fresh" as though it just landed on that docks of that Norman port; "the best sole meunière", "sublime oysters" and other "perfectly cooked (or uncooked) dishes" send seafood fans sailing toward rapture; sure, the porthole decor has "aged terribly", but the "genteel, accommodating service" and the cuisine's "quality make you forget all, even the exorbitant prices."

Durand Dupont ◐   9 | 15 | 11 | 46
14, pl du Marché, Neuilly (Les Sablons), 01 41 92 93 00; fax 01 46 37 56 79

■ "Definitely still on the 'in' list", this "chic (and so much-too expensive)" Neuilly bistro has "a great terrace for self-display"; this "sunny" outdoor perch is in fact the reason "you really come here", since most say the "nothing-special" Eclectic eats are quite "variable", qualitywise, and the "pretty waitresses' efficiency leaves a lot to be desired."

Ebauchoir (L') 🈯   – | – | – | M
43-45, rue de Citeaux, 12ᵉ (Faidherbe-Chaligny), 01 43 42 49 31

"Everyone is warmly welcomed at this bistro tucked away in the far reaches of the 12th", where the "delightfully unfussy" cuisine (Traditional French, with some "original" touches) and the company of an arty local crowd make "you jump back decades"; "the secret's out", however – "it's always packed" – so be sure to book.

Ecailler du Bistrot (L') ◐🈯   – | – | – | M
20-22, rue Paul-Bert, 11ᵉ (Faidherbe-Chaligny), 01 43 72 76 77; fax 01 43 37 24 66

Not many have navigated their way to this seafooder in a quiet corner of the 11th, but those who have rave about "superb fish and shellfish", especially the "excellent oysters" from Brittany; an attractive tiled-and-painted-wood decor and "friendly service puts the client at ease", as do the reasonably priced tabs.

Ecluse (L') ◐   14 | 13 | 14 | 35
34, pl du Marché St-Honoré, 1ᵉʳ (Pyramides/Tuileries), 01 42 96 10 18; fax 01 42 96 10 19
15, pl de la Madeleine, 8ᵉ (Madeleine), 01 42 65 34 69; fax 01 44 71 01 26
15, quai des Grands-Augustins, 8ᵉ (St-Michel), 01 46 33 58 74; fax 01 44 07 18 76
64, rue François 1er, 8ᵉ (George V), 01 47 20 77 09; fax 01 40 70 03 33
13, rue de la Roquette, 11ᵉ (Bastille), 01 48 05 19 12; fax 01 48 05 04 88

| F | D | S | €C |

(continued)
Ecluse (L')
1, rue d'Armaillé, 17ᵉ (Charles de Gaulle-Etoile), 01 47 63 88 29; fax 01 44 40 41 91
www.leclusebaravin.com

☑ "Still the poster child for wine bars everywhere", this mini-chain offers an "uneven" experience: there's a "vast choice of *vins*", especially "Bordeaux by the glass", and the "dark-wood, old-bar atmosphere" ("like a Gallic *Cheers*") offers "a place to relax"; but "the good grape doesn't excuse" a Classic French menu that's "serious but not really appealing" and service that swings from "professional" to "pretentious"; many say that valuewise, both the vino and the vittles seem "pricey" too.

Editeurs (Les) ● | 13 | 22 | 16 | 34 |
4, carrefour de l'Odéon, 6ᵉ (Odéon), 01 43 26 67 76; fax 01 46 34 58 30; www.lesediteurs.fr

☑ "It's charming to sit at a sidewalk table and watch the passers-by" at this site with a prime setting overlooking the Odéon – though the "comfortable", "library decor" (full of "warm colors, filled bookshelves" and "comfy nooks") is a best-seller too; alas, the "classic brasserie cuisine" "is just decent", but a "hip, young crowd" finds it "fine for a snack or drinks."

El Mansour ● | 21 | 21 | 17 | 55 |
7, rue de La Trémoille, 8ᵉ (Alma-Marceau), 01 47 23 88 18; fax 01 40 70 13 53

■ This "elegant" oasis off the Avenue George V serves "refined Moroccan cooking" to a business crowd at noon and Middle Eastern expats in the evening; a "traditional setting" – North African art, "spacious tables" and oak panels – contributes to the "quiet ambiance" of a room peopled by "efficient, serious" servers; just expect to pay princely prices for what's possibly Paris' "best tagine."

El Palenque ☒⌿ | ▽ 18 | 9 | 11 | 36 |
5, rue de la Mont. Ste-Geneviève, 5ᵉ (Maubert-Mutualité), 01 43 54 08 99

☑ "If you like meat", join the hungry gauchos who head for "one of the best Argentineans in Paris" near the Panthéon; but while all agree about the "impressively tender" beef and prices, the rest "is a mixed bag": the "unpretentious" decor offers rather "spartan comfort" and the "staff from all over the continent" ranges from "friendly" to "rude."

ELYSÉES DU VERNET (LES) | 26 | 24 | 24 | 109 |
Hôtel Vernet, 25, rue Vernet, 8ᵉ (Charles de Gaulle-Etoile/ George V), 01 44 31 98 98; fax 01 44 31 85 69; www.hotelvernet.com

■ After a year, chef Eric Briffard (ex Plaza Athénée) has emerged as a "winner" at this Haute Cuisine in the 8th;

get updates at zagat.com

amis adore his "delectable" earthy dishes ("if this is what heaven's like, I'll stop sinning now"), served by "staffers whose passion for food matches the chef's"; there's praise too for the "old-fashioned" dining room dominated by a "gorgeous stained-glass ceiling" "by Gustave Eiffel (yes, he did the tower)"; it's "terribly expensive", but "there aren't enough superlatives to describe dining here."

Elysées Hong Kong   _–_ _–_ _–_ M
80, rue Michel-Ange, 16e (Exelmans), 01 46 51 60 99
An established staple for "regulars" from "the residences and the offices nearby", this award-winning Chinese is also starting to become "a destination beyond its quarters" of the well-upholstered 16th; "savory cooking and warm service" hold sway in a room decorated in antiqued 19th-century Asian style.

Emporio Armani Caffé ⓈZ   19 16 15 49
149, bd St-Germain, 6e (St-Germain-des-Prés), 01 45 48 62 15; fax 01 45 48 53 17
❏ "Nice pastas and light entrees", accessorized with a bit of "people-watching", make this "hip hangout" atop the Emporio Armani boutique an ideal "place to stop when you're out shopping" around Saint-Germain; except for "the stupid lamps hanging down over the tables", most find the "modern decor appealing"; granted, it is "expensive for basic Italian" – but then, so are Giorgio's clothes.

Enoteca (L') ●   18 13 14 41
25, rue Charles V, 4^e (St-Paul/Sully Morland), 01 42 78 91 44; fax 01 44 59 31 72
■ "Nestled in a quiet corner of the Marais", this wine bar of The Boot is "a polished comfort zone" with pretty "Murano lamps" under the massive beams of an ancient stone house; "as the name suggests, it's a place to drink rather than eat" – "all of the major vineyards are represented" – but the kitchen sends out "rustic", "reasonably good" pastas as well; toss in a "cozy atmosphere" and some "very Italian staffers" and most agree "we need more of these places."

Entoto ⓈZ   _–_ _–_ _–_ M
143-145, rue L.M. Nordmann, 13e (Glacière), 01 45 87 08 51
Tucked away in the 13th, this "nice, little exotic Ethiopian" lets you "go back to basics by eating with your bare hands", scooping up the vegetables and meats with pieces of flatbread just like they do in the old country; the owners are "sweet and generous", and the tabs modest, so "maybe we shouldn't make a lot of noise about it" whisper worshipers.

Entracte (L') (Chez Sonia et Carlos)   _–_ _–_ _–_ M
44, rue d'Orsel, 18e (Abbesses/Anvers), 01 46 06 93 41
At the foot of the funicular that ascends to Sacré-Coeur lies this "tiny and pleasant little bistro" where all the homestyle Traditional French dishes, from rack of lamb to

veal kidneys, are cooked to order in a broom closet of a kitchen by chef-owner Gilles Chiriaux; decorated with Montmartre artists' work, it's ideal "when you're going to the Théâtre de l'Atelier" nearby, but you better book to snag one of the 20-odd seats.

Entredgeu (L') ⌧   _ | _ | _ | M

83, rue Laugier, 17e (Porte de Champerret), 01 40 54 97 24; fax 01 40 54 96 62

Young chef-owner Philippe Tredgeu learned how to set a successful table by "working with the Chez Michel" team; now he and his wife have gone out on their own with this Classic French bistro in the 17th, and while their "new, little" home is not yet widely known, devotees deem it "a good find" with a "delicious", daily changing menu served by a "pleasant, energetic staff"; moderate prices make it a "definite come-back-to place."

En Vue ●⌧   _ | _ | _ | M

39, rue Boissy d'Anglas, 8e (Concorde/Madeleine), 01 42 65 10 49; fax 01 40 17 09 28

"Well located in the rue Boissy d'Anglas", near Hermès, this posh spot boasts an "extremely original decor" of bird's-eye maple paneling, gray and rose hues, low lighting and "toilets worth a detour"; but despite "good cocktails", foes find the New French fare "frankly isn't very interesting", given the "desperately *petit* portions"; and while the service is "not unfriendly", overall the place is "trying to be too hip."

Epicure 108 ⌧   _ | _ | _ | M

108, rue Cardinet, 17^e (Malesherbes), 01 47 63 50 91

"Interesting Asian-French fusion food" (think wasabi-flavored veal kidneys), from a Japanese chef-owner who trained in Alsace, makes for memorable meals at this little-known address near the Square des Batignolles; the site is small, but suits who flock here for lunch attest that the fare is "wonderful"; clean-air advocates should know, however, that "cigar-smoking guests" are encouraged to light up.

Epi d'Or (L') ⌧   ▽ 21 | 18 | 20 | 47

25, rue Jean-Jacques Rousseau, 1er (Louvre-Rivoli), 01 42 36 38 12; fax 01 42 36 46 25; www.epidor.fr

■ "Classy yet *sans* attitude", this old-fashioned bistro in a quiet street near the Palais Royal offers a "friendly family ambiance" and "good value" for Classic French food, like a "lovely beef salad"; it's also a plus – and "a pleasant surprise" – that "you're eating with Parisians, not tourists."

EPI DUPIN (L') ⌧   24 | 15 | 18 | 45

11, rue Dupin, 6e (Sèvres-Babylone), 01 42 22 64 56; fax 01 42 22 30 42

◨ "There's a reason it's tough to get reservations" at this 6th-arrondissement "madhouse with only 45 seats" –

F | D | S | €C

namely, the "marvelously prepared updated French Bistro classics" served at "bargain" rates; critics carp the "creative" chow "is overshadowed by the elbow-to-elbow seating ("the closest tables in all Paris") and "friendly" but "frantic" service that "makes you feel rushed"; but if "you can stand the hectic pace", you may well join the worshipers who warble it's "one of our favorites."

Erawan ⌀ | 21 | 11 | 14 | 36

76, rue de la Fédération, 15ᵉ (La Motte-Picquet-Grenelle), 01 47 83 55 67; fax 01 47 34 85 98

◪ "One of the best Thais in Paris" offers "prices that defy comparison" sing savants about this Siamese veteran where "beautiful silk dresses on the waitresses" enliven an otherwise "dated" decor of plants and posters; its location may be off the beaten path, but the "peaceful" 15th is closer to get to than Bangkok.

Escargot Montorgueil (L') ⌀ | ▽ 18 | 22 | 18 | 47

38, rue Montorgueil, 1ᵉʳ (Les Halles), 01 42 36 83 51; fax 01 42 36 35 05

◾ In Les Halles, this Classic French bistro has always been "worth a detour for its decor", a "romantic", straight-out-of-a-Hollywood-set Second Empire scene; but after a few years of management by the Terrails of the Tour d'Argent, it's also on a roll for "creative dishes", including an "amazing escargot sampler" where the shelled slowpokes are cooked three different ways (the Roquefort version alone is "worth the flight across the pond"); it's a little "expensive" but worth it for the "lively location" and eats.

Espace Sud-Ouest/Chez Papa ● | 12 | 7 | 9 | 21

29, rue de l'Arcade, 8ᵉ (Madeleine/St-Lazare), 01 42 65 43 68
206, rue La Fayette, 10ᵉ (Louis Blanc), 01 42 09 53 87
6, rue Gassendi, 14ᵉ (Denfert-Rochereau/Raspail), 01 43 22 41 19
101, rue de la Croix Nivert, 15ᵉ (Commerce), 01 48 28 31 88

◪ "Cheap, copious" dishes from the Southwest make bargain hunters with big appetites happy at this "noisy", "smoky" chain perpetually packed with "a lot of students, who are part of the decor"; foes warn "fragile stomachs, abstain" (the fare "is all heavy, even the [giant] salads"), and dis the "deplorable service", but at least "you'll be stuffed for a small amount of euros."

Espadon (L') | 25 | 27 | 27 | 129

Hôtel Ritz, 15, pl Vendôme, 1ᵉʳ (Concorde/Opéra), 01 43 16 30 80; fax 01 43 16 33 75; www.ritz.com

◾ Life "is ritzy" in all respects at the Hôtel Ritz's main restaurant where a mini-"orchestra plays quietly" and "waiters seem to float across" the "sumptuous" "circular room with mirrored walls" and "gorgeous garden" in summer – both of which offer "unparalleled people-

| F | D | S | €C |

watching of new money, old wealth", "beautiful women and handsome men"; if a bit "staid", chef Michel Roth's Classic French menu is "beautifully executed"; so "if true love eludes you, come here for true romance at least."

Espadon Bleu (L') ⌧ | 21 | 19 | 17 | 44 |
25, rue des Grands-Augustins, 6ᵉ (Odéon/St-Michel), 01 46 33 00 85; fax 01 43 54 54 48; www.jacques-cagna.com
◨ "A good way of experiencing Jacques Cagna without paying Jacques Cagna prices" declare devotees of the celebrity chef-owner's Saint-Germain seafooder (facing his namesake establishment), which to them seems a "nice quiet place for a simple dinner" of "fresh, firm fish"; however, the less-happy harpoon "painfully slow" service and declare themselves "disappointed" in the fare.

Estaminet Gaya (L') ⌧ | – | – | – | E |
17, rue Duphot, 1ᵉʳ (Madeleine), 01 42 60 43 03; fax 01 42 60 69 35
"Hidden in a small street" near the Madeleine, this "simply excellent" seafooder reels 'em in with "really fresh fish" and "similarly scrumptious desserts"; the decor's "a bit like the métro stations, with nice mosaic tiles" and the service is "attentive"; it's "good for business lunches that don't have to be too fancy", and "although not horribly cheap" at night, it still qualifies as a "non-splurge dinner destination."

Etienne Marcel ● | ▽ 17 | 17 | 15 | 45 |
34, rue Etienne Marcel, 2ᵉ (Etienne Marcel), 01 45 08 01 03; fax 01 42 36 03 44
◨ Surveyors' views diverge on just about every facet of this establishment on the edge of Les Halles, from the '60s a-go-go decor ("nice" vs. "outdated after the first week") to the Eclectic cuisine ("quality" vs. "leaves a lot to be desired") to the prices ("affordable" vs. "excessively expensive"); suffice to say that, while it has its merits, it's "certainly not the best of the Costes brothers'" addresses; even "the staff seems less beautiful than those in their other restaurants."

Etoile (L') ● | 17 | 20 | 16 | 66 |
12, rue de Presbourg, 8ᵉ (Charles de Gaulle-Etoile), 01 45 00 78 70; fax 01 45 00 78 71
◨ "A spectacular view of the Arc de Triomphe", aka the namesake Etoile, is the star attraction of this "exorbitant" fashion plate; but most find the Classic French cuisine surprisingly "nice" for "a nightclub restaurant (there's a real chef in the kitchen!)"; of course, the unconvinced still grumble its main merit comes after the meal, "when you go downstairs to dance"; perhaps they're put off by the "rich-kid crowd" with "an average age of 18."

Etoile Marocaine (L') | ▽ 21 | 22 | 24 | 42 |
56, rue Galilée, 8ᵉ (George V), 01 47 20 44 43; fax 01 47 20 69 85
■ To be "treated like Moroccan royalty", head for this "small" place with a "really nice" North African–style decor

get updates at zagat.com

| F | D | S | €C |

off the Champs; the "authentic, interesting menu", which includes "excellent tagines and couscous", may be the "most succulent [of its kind] in Paris", and the "friendly staff" provides "efficient service"; all in all, a good deal for the dirham.

Excuse (L') ⌧ | 22 | 18 | 20 | 48 |
14, rue Charles V, 4ᵉ (St-Paul/Sully Morland), 01 42 77 98 97; fax 01 42 77 88 55

■ No excuses need be made by this "excellent find in the Marais" (and indeed, "it's worth going out of your way to find it"), since its "sophisticated and delicious" New French cooking is "presented with flair" by a staff that's "friendly to all" in "modern and romantic", albeit "snug", surroundings; "pricey but not outrageous", it has "an outstanding wine list", including some bottles from the "owner's winery in the Rhône Valley"; N.B. "the entire upstairs dining room is nonsmoking."

Fables de La Fontaine (Les) ⌧ | – | – | – | M |
131, rue St-Dominique, 7ᵉ (Ecole Militaire), 01 44 18 37 55

On a busy shopping street in the 7th, this "really small" seafooder, recently taken over by chef Christian Constant of Le Violon d'Ingres, is "great for fresh shellfish", served amid a nautical blue-and-black-tiled decor; perhaps the *poisson*'s "a bit pricey" in some cases, but you can console yourself with the "good" signature dessert, a cream-filled pastry commemorating a famous bicycle race between Paris and Brest.

Fakhr el Dine ☽ | 16 | 13 | 16 | 48 |
3, rue Quentin Bauchart, 8ᵉ (George V), 01 47 23 44 42; fax 01 53 70 01 81
30, rue de Longchamp, 16ᵉ (Trocadéro), 01 47 27 90 00; fax 01 53 70 01 81
www.fakhreldine.com

■ Offering an "upscale Lebanese" experience, these two addresses in the 8th and the 16th are admittedly "expensive", but you'll enjoy "inspired" creations in a "friendly atmosphere" with "accommodating" service; they're also "great for takeout."

Famille (La) ☽⌧ | – | – | – | M |
41, rue des Trois-Frères, 18ᵉ (Abbesses/Anvers), 01 42 52 11 12

A recent hit on the Paris culinary scene, this funky site on a cobbled Montmartre street features the "astonishing" Eclectic cooking of young Basque chef Inaki Aizpitarte, whose "fresh, different" menus reflect both his experience in Latin America and his interest in North Africa; the simple loftlike space with a large table d'hôte and bar is already always packed with an internationally diverse, but uniformly cool, crowd.

| F | D | S | €C |

Faucher 🗷 | 23 | 17 | 23 | 81 |
123, av de Wagram, 17ᵉ (Ternes/Wagram), 01 42 27 61 50; fax 01 46 22 25 72

■ "From the moment Madame [wife of the chef-owner] greets you, until your last taste of dessert, it's great to be in the hands of the Faucher family" fawn fans of this "minimalist" site in the 17th; not only is Monsieur's New French menu full of "original dishes", but the service is "remarkable" and it seems the "sommelier always has a surprise" for you too; true, the plates are pricey, but most find them "worthwhile" given this "calm" corner's caliber.

Fauchon 🗷 | – | – | – | M |
26, pl de la Madeleine, 8ᵉ (Concorde/Madeleine), 01 47 42 90 10; fax 01 47 42 90 30; www.fauchon.com

It may not have the same wow-factor that it did a century ago, but this grande dame of a luxury grocer overlooking the Place de la Madeleine remains a "must-stop" for its striped-fabric tea salon, "an oasis of civility [before or] after a tough day of shopping"; in addition to the "fabulous" delicacies and brews, "the lobster salad is memorable", and though it can get a bit "pricey" for pastry, "the ladies who lunch" insist "it's worth every euro."

Fellini | 21 | 14 | 20 | 43 |
47, rue de l'Arbre-Sec, 1ᵉʳ (Louvre-Rivoli), 01 42 60 90 66; fax 01 42 60 18 04
58, rue de la Croix Nivert, 15ᵉ (Commerce/Emile Zola), 01 45 77 40 77; fax 01 45 77 22 54

■ An "absolutely fantastic" cucina, including "excellent homemade pasta", has surveyors singing 'That's Amore' about this pair in the 1st and the 15th; "waiters who are always in a good mood (hard to find in Paris)" provide "a real Italian climate" along with "delightful, animated service"; this duo's usually "crowded with locals, so be sure to reserve."

Ferme (La) 🗷 | – | – | – | I |
55-57, rue St-Roch, 1ᵉʳ (Opéra/Pyramides), 01 40 20 12 12; fax 01 40 20 06 06

It's "a bit of heaven" to bite into the "light preparations" at this "high-quality sandwich"-and-salad eatery located in an organic food shop in the 1st; all the dishes are made with "super-fresh produce", and the "charming" setting makes eating here both "a treat for the palate and the eye"; while "perfect for a quick stop", it's an equally good place "to go and relax with a great cup of coffee."

Ferme des Mathurins (La) 🗷 | – | – | – | M |
17, rue Vignon, 8ᵉ (Havre-Caumartin/Madeleine), 01 42 66 46 39; fax 01 42 66 00 27

You come to this "dark, rustic" 1945-vintage traditional bistro in the 8th – a favorite of the mystery writer Simenon –

get updates at zagat.com

F | D | S | €C

out of "nostalgia" for "an almost-forgotten style of cooking: the classics of the peasant kitchen"; "don't expect anything artistic" advise regulars, but rest assured that if you "order the special", it'll "taste wonderful."

Ferme St-Simon (La) ☒   23 | 20 | 24 | 58
6, rue de St-Simon, 7ᵉ (Rue du Bac/Solférino), 01 45 48 35 74; fax 01 40 49 07 31

■ "When you want a Traditional French experience", consider this "plushy establishment" in the 7th that feeds "government bigwigs" and "a professional clientele" by day and the local bourgeoisie in the evening; it's highly "reliable for well prepared" fare – in particular, the housemade "desserts are tops" – and the "elegant service" is always "welcoming" ("even if you aren't from one of the surrounding ministries"); "each of the three dining rooms has a different style", but all offer "enjoyable atmosphere."

Fermette Marbeuf 1900 (La) ●   17 | 25 | 18 | 56
5, rue Marbeuf, 8ᵉ (Alma-Marceau/Franklin D. Roosevelt), 01 53 23 08 00; fax 01 53 23 08 09; www.fermettemarbeuf.com

▨ Just off the Champs-Elysées, tourists find the "turn-of-the-century flamboyance" of this Frères Blanc–owned Classic French – "not a place the locals frequent" – to be the best part of a meal here, especially since a "badly needed refurbishment of the cutlery is now done"; while it's "too bad the food and service don't come close" to the "superb" "art nouveau setting", the former is "dependable" and the latter "surprisingly friendly."

Fernandises (Les) ☒   – | – | – | M
19, rue de la Fontaine-au-Roi, 11ᵉ (Goncourt/République), 01 48 06 16 96

"Simple and appealing", this established table in the 11th arrondissement serves up hearty, homemade dishes from Normandy, such as roast skate with Camembert sauce and Calvados-flambéed crêpes; although some deem the decor downright "distressing" – a huge mural depicting the Paris Commune dominates the brightly lit room – the food's of "reliably good quality."

Feuilles Libres/Entrées Libres ☒   – | – | – | E
34, rue Perronet, Neuilly (Les Sablons), 01 46 24 41 41; fax 01 46 40 77 61
49, rue Madeleine Michelis, Neuilly (Les Sablons), 01 46 24 00 84; fax 01 46 40 77 61
www.feuilles-libres.com

Although few have found these New French enclaves helmed by a husband-and-wife team on a quiet Neuilly street, those who have know their "pleasant atmosphere" (especially on their linden-tree terraces in summer); the more "expensive" Feuilles restaurant where owner

| F | D | S | €C |

Emmanuel Laporte mans the stove is set up in a small house that sparkles with silver and colorful tablecloths; the brick bistro, run by Nathalie, serves up moderately priced seafood specialties in a more casual ambiance.

Findi ●
17 | 15 | 14 | 48

24, av George V, 8ᵉ (Alma-Marceau/George V), 01 47 20 14 78; fax 01 47 20 10 08; www.findi.net

◪ With a "great location across the street from the Hôtel George V", this slightly pricey, "lively" Italian boasts "a modish setting", remniscent of an updated Venetian palazzo; views vary about the food, ranging from "enjoyable" to "uninspired" and the same goes for the service; but that doesn't stop the place from being "packed with noisy thirtysomethings" and a few "famous faces and VIPs."

Fins Gourmets (Aux) 🖻🗲
16 | 14 | 14 | 33

213, bd St-Germain, 7ᵉ (Rue du Bac), 01 42 22 06 57

◪ Second-generation spots pervaded by a "real" "old-fashioned bistro" atmosphere are becoming rare, and so in the 7th, this specialist in Southwestern cooking "should be preserved"; but even loyalists lament that, aside from an "unequalled pipérade" (a mélange of cooked onions, eggs, peppers, tomatoes and garlic), the kitchen "seems to be tired" of late and the waiters "are phoning it in"; even if it's "not great", though, this vet remains "cozy and reliable" for "regional", reasonable meals.

Finzi ●
16 | 10 | 12 | 41

182, bd Haussmann, 8ᵉ (St-Philippe-du-Roule), 01 45 62 88 68; fax 01 45 61 41 05

◪ Popular with bankers and brokers by day and the bourgeois locals by night, this "good Italian" in the 8th serves up pretty "authentic" pastas and a nice "selection of wines" to boot; but negatives note it's "not necessarily worth the trip if you're not in the neighborhood", especially since "the brash service" "leaves something to be desired."

Fish La Boissonnerie
21 | 16 | 20 | 37

69, rue de Seine, 6ᵉ (Odéon), 01 43 54 34 69; fax 01 43 54 33 47

■ "Co-owned by an American, this funky, fresh and flavorful fish stop" is fine when you'd adore an "accessible (emotionally and geographically)" spot in Saint-Germain for an "informal" meal of "Mediterranean food and wine"; its "friendly, English-speaking staff" makes it "a favorite of expat" Yanks, and the fact that it's "fantastic value for the money" doesn't hurt either.

Flandrin (Le) ●
13 | 15 | 13 | 51

80, av Henri Martin, 16ᵉ (Rue de la Pompe), 01 45 04 34 69

■ A terrace that's "*the* place to be seen – provided you arrive in a Porsche" – is the main interest of this "snobby" brasserie "in an old train station"; while it's "a must for certain well-off inhabitants" of the 16th and show-biz folks,

get updates at zagat.com

| F | D | S | €C |

the more culinary-minded moan the "food is not more than ok", and it comes with a helping of "haughtiness" from the staff; as for the prices, let's just say they're geared to the type of folks "that don't mind overpaying."

Flora ☒ 23 | 18 | 21 | 69
36, av George V, 8ᵉ (George V), 01 40 70 10 49; fax 01 47 20 52 87

■ "She is just so good" swoon supporters of chef-owner Flora Mikula, the namesake force behind this "small" but "sophisticated" address on the Avenue George V; her "imaginative", "internationally flavored New French menu" is "smartly presented" by "attentive servers" in a dining room that manages to be "elegant and informal at the same time"; here, for once, is a place that's "no flash, all substance", so "run", don't walk, to its "civilized" site.

Flora Danica 18 | 18 | 16 | 50
142, av des Champs-Elysées, 8ᵉ (Charles de Gaulle-Etoile/ George V), 01 44 13 86 26; fax 01 44 13 89 44; www.restaurantfloradanica.com

■ "An unexpected oasis in the wildness of the Champs-Elysées", this Classic French–Dane "keeps drawing you back for an unrivaled selection of salmon", "tasty herrings" and "aquavit, *vite!*"; more casual than cousin Copenhague upstairs, this Viking is vaunted also for a "Scandinavian decor that's clean-lined and tidy" (kind of "like a designer furniture store") and service that's friendly, if "a trifle slow"; P.S. bear in mind the backyard's "stunning terrace for hot summer days" and nights.

Flore en l'Ile (Le) ☻ 17 | 20 | 17 | 36
42, quai d'Orléans, 4ᵉ (Hôtel-de-Ville/Pont-Marie), 01 43 29 88 27; fax 01 43 29 73 54

■ When you long for "that Ile Saint-Louis look", this "good neighborhood place" is "one of the most beautifully situated in Paris", with a spectacular "view of the back of Notre Dame" "whether you're sitting indoors or out"; "always crowded", it's "a favorite spot for a quintessential breakfast" *français* ("the flakiest croissants"), "afternoon tea", or "lovely" "late-night dessert"; less recommended are the Classic French dinners, but it's unbeatable for a "Berthillon ice cream with flying buttresses out the window."

Florimond (Le) ☒ 22 | 16 | 24 | 39
19, av de La Motte-Picquet, 7ᵉ (Ecole Militaire), 01 45 55 40 38; fax 01 45 55 40 38

■ In the 7th, this "tiny" eatery is a "well-kept secret that deserves attention", thanks to a "courteous, kind chef/co-owner" and "service that goes the extra kilometer" with such Classic French comestibles as "delicious stuffed cabbage" and "ooh-la-la, puff-pastry dishes – Napoleons or langoustines"; "it's a funky setting, but most friendly."

| | | F | D | S | €C |

Fogón Saint Julien ◐ ▽ 23 | 14 | 19 | 47
10, rue St-Julien-le-Pauvre, 5ᵉ (Maubert-Mutualité/St-Michel), 01 43 54 31 33; fax 01 43 54 07 00
■ "The best Spanish in Paris, no contest" contend converts who charge to this "quaint" and "cozy place" in the 5th; the menu stars "wonderful paella", which fans find unsurpassed "not only in this country but in Europe", along with "amazing tapas", "original wines" and "desserts that are as good as the rest"; prices may be a little "high", but this "is a must for Iberian cuisine lovers."

Fontaine d'Auteuil (La) ⊠ – | – | – | M
35 bis, rue La Fontaine, 16ᵉ (Jasmin), 01 42 88 04 47; fax 01 42 88 95 12
"A hidden treasure" maintain mavens of this small, "pleasant and easygoing" Contemporary French buried in an area (Auteil) bereft of good tables; "the ambiance leaves a little to be desired, but you quickly forget that when you eat the food", which "is always fabulous", especially the "exceptionally mouthwatering fish"; "the service is equally good."

Fontaine de Mars (La) 19 | 18 | 20 | 44
129, rue St-Dominique, 7ᵉ (Ecole Militaire), 01 47 05 46 44; fax 01 47 05 11 13
■ In the "chic 7th", this "bustling little bistro" offers a "great experience" for fans of "consistently" "authentic", "hearty" Gascon-Southwestern cooking served in a dining room with "retro red-checked tablecloths" (though in good weather, "it's wonderful to sit outside next to the fountain"); creating an atmosphere that's "at once relaxed and sophisticated", "the service is so professional", especially "the warm welcome" from the proprietor; in short, it's "everything a meal in Paris should be."

Fontaine Gaillon (La) ◐⊠ 17 | 17 | 18 | 56
1, rue de la Michodière, 2ᵉ (Opéra/Quatre Septembre), 01 42 65 87 04
■ The ratings may not fully reflect the regime of a new pair of *propriétaires* – actors Gérard Depardieu and Carole Bouquet – who have lovingly rejuvenated this "old favorite" near the Opéra Garnier; the chief coup was hiring chef Laurent Audiot (ex Marius et Janette), whose knack for Classic French cuisine is especially evident in seafood; "bursting with atmosphere", it's a "great place to take visitors, as it looks and tastes like their expectations" of a Gallic eatery.

Fontaines (Les) ⊠ 20 | 9 | 16 | 35
9, rue Soufflot, 5ᵉ (Cardinal Lemoine/Luxembourg), 01 43 26 42 80; fax 01 44 07 03 49
◪ "Copious – maybe too copious" quantities of "Traditional Bistro food" make this Latin Quarter table "an oasis in a

culinary desert"; certainly, the worn '70s "decor could be nicer" and "the service can be a little slow", but that doesn't daunt the "intellectual", "very French clientele", including the wife of Paris' former mayor, that creates a "bustling", "lively" scene.

Fontanarosa ▽ 21 | 13 | 18 | 41
28, bd Garibaldi, 15ᵉ (Cambronne/Ségur), 01 45 66 97 84; fax 01 47 83 96 30

■ "Vive Sardinia!" shout supporters of this red-and-ochre-colored Italian in the 15th, which re-creates the cucina of the chef and owner's native land – much of it featured on a "great serve-yourself antipasti table"; it's also renowned for its "nice little terrace" "gorged with sunshine" and potted olive trees that "keeps you returning with pleasure."

Foujita 16 | 6 | 11 | 39
41, rue St-Roch, 1ᵉʳ (Pyramides), 01 42 61 42 93
7, rue 29 Juillet, 1ᵉʳ (Tuileries), 01 49 26 07 70

◪ When it comes to these veteran Japanese in the 1st, sushi-lovers roll into two different camps; loyalists find the fish "good" for a "quick", "exhausted-executive lunch"; but adversaries argue that "although the prices are still reasonable, this place used to be so much better" – a sentiment supported by a lower Food score; a universally disliked, "depressing decor" doesn't help either.

Fouquet's (Le) ● 16 | 19 | 15 | 62
99, av des Champs-Elysées, 8ᵉ (George V), 01 47 23 50 00; fax 01 47 23 50 55; www.lucienbarriere.com

◪ Love it or hate it, this grande dame of a Classic French on the Champs is "still going strong" after 105 years; indeed the emotions are extreme, with foes fuming "Fouquet about it" – it's the "epitome of tourist joints", with "lackadaisical service" and "ordinary" eats, and friends finding the cuisine "getting better" since the arrival of a new chef and lauding the "classic" decor; all agree that "prices are scandalous", so maybe it's best to "just come for a drink" and "nice people-watching" along Paris' "main drag."

Fous d'en Face (Les) ●⌧ ▽ 12 | 13 | 12 | 32
3, rue du Bourg Tibourg, 4ᵉ (Hôtel-de-Ville), 01 48 87 03 75; fax 01 42 78 38 03

■ With "a nice terrace and an appealing selection of wines", this *bistrot à vins* "not far from the Hôtel de Ville" is a "good spot" for "simple" Classic Bistro "cooking using very fresh produce"; fans find it's fun "to discover a variety of [varietals] by the glass" amid a "pleasant atmosphere."

Fumoir (Le) ● 15 | 20 | 15 | 35
6, rue de l'Amiral de Coligny, 1ᵉʳ (Louvre-Rivoli), 01 42 92 00 24; fax 01 42 92 05 05; www.lefumoir.com

◪ "Facing the Louvre (you can't get more central than that)", this Eclectic eatery attracts an "interesting crowd"

F | D | S | €C

of cognoscenti who "expressly ask to be seated in the calm, cozy library room" – with actual books! – in back; staffed by servers "who aren't great, but are at least alert", it's "famous mainly for" its "delightfully complete Sunday brunch" – at other meals, "drinks and starters are best"; just bear in mind that as it heats up, the scene gets "smoky (as its name implies)."

Gallopin ◐ 🗷   15 | 20 | 16 | 46

40, rue Notre-Dame-des-Victoires, 2ᵉ (Bourse/ Grands Boulevards), 01 42 36 45 38; fax 01 42 36 10 32; www.brasseriegallopin.com

☑ "You feel as if you've stepped back in time" (1876 to be precise) at this antique "across the street from the old Bourse [stock market]" that boasts a "classic brasserie atmosphere with a large wooden bar and lots of mirrors"; like a blue-chip investment, the "traditional food is reliable rather than original", but at least it's a "constant" – unlike, alas, the "irregular service"; still, the "superb decor" remains a sure thing.

Gamin de Paris (Au) ◐   19 | 16 | 16 | 36

51, rue Vieille du Temple, 4ᵉ (Hôtel-de-Ville/St-Paul), 01 42 78 97 24

☑ "Always packed and noisy", this candlelit "bistro-type restaurant with a neighborhood feel" in the Marais is "an old-time favorite that never disappoints" for those who like its "funky and fun" atmosphere and typical but "tasty" Southwestern cuisine; some find the staff "competently rough" (or should we say 'roughly competent'?), and sometimes "you have to wait", but "the food delivers", and that "makes the queuing worthwhile."

Gare (La) ◐   13 | 19 | 12 | 41

19, chaussée de la Muette, 16ᵉ (La Muette), 01 42 15 15 31; fax 01 42 15 15 23; www.restaurantlagare.com

☑ The "cool location of an old train station" and a "fantastic terrace" are among the reasons that a "trendy, young crowd" stops by this "large space" in the 16th; maybe "this railroad won't bring you to gastronomic paradise", since the Traditional French "food is just average", with a "few simple things (e.g. the mashed potatoes) well done", and the service is "relatively inefficient"; but that doesn't derail its "popularity with an interesting late-night crowd, for whom going home with somebody else might be the dessert."

Garnier ◐   18 | 15 | 15 | 67

111, rue St-Lazare, 8ᵉ (St-Lazare), 01 43 87 50 40; fax 01 40 08 06 93

■ Just across the street from the Gare Saint-Lazare, this venerable brasserie is something of "a neighborhood secret" for its "superb shellfish stand" of "fresh, fresh fruits de mer"; blending Lalique lamps, '70s stylings and

get updates at zagat.com   107

| F | D | S | €C |

modern furnishings, the "setting lacks real character" some sigh; but the "service is courteous", and the overall experience, while expensive, is "well worth every euro."

Gastroquet (Le) 🇿 — | — | — | M
10, rue Desnouettes, 15ᵉ (Convention/Porte de Versailles), 01 48 28 60 91; fax 01 45 33 23 70

The "friendly chef-owner" "comes to the table and explains the menu" at this "good example of a neighborhood restaurant catering to locals" of the 15th; the Traditional French cuisine is "solid, if not stellar" (though there are some "fantastic desserts"), and that, combined with the "pleasant" service, "provides a sense of well-being."

Gauloise (La)   17 | 17 | 19 | 38
59, av de La Motte-Picquet, 15ᵉ (La Motte-Picquet-Grenelle), 01 47 34 11 64; fax 01 40 61 09 70

■ For a "nice no-surprises meal" and a "typical" Second Empire decor, disciples doff their berets to this Traditional Bistro "near the Ecole Militaire and the Eiffel Tower"; amid an atmosphere that's "as smoky as its name" suggests, "you can meet members of Parliament" (the late President Mitterrand was a regular); "friendly service" and "a pretty little terrace" are additional pluses.

Gavroche (Le) ●🇿 21 | 17 | 17 | 43
19, rue St-Marc, 2ᵉ (Bourse/Richelieu-Drouot), 01 42 96 89 70

◪ "Calling all meat eaters" to this "vibrant" "institution" in the 2nd, which carries "the charm of the Classic Bistros of yesteryear"; there's a "good selection of Beaujolais" to wash down that "good beef", and while it gets "a bit crowded" with all the "close tables", it remains "perfect" for those seeking that "Parisian atmosphere."

Gaya Rive Gauche 🇿   22 | 17 | 21 | 61
44, rue du Bac, 7ᵉ (Rue du Bac), 01 45 44 73 73; fax 01 45 44 73 73

■ In the rue du Bac, this "bastion for the chic and sleek" offers "absolutely superb seafood" in a blond-wood bi-level dining room (it's "Americans upstairs and French downstairs") with a "somber, elegant modern decor"; a "staff that knows when to arrive promptly and when to stay away" serves a clientele of "publishing people" and the occasional celebrity; not surprisingly, the "marvelously fresh fish" is "expensive", and you'll need to "book ahead."

Georges ●   17 | 26 | 15 | 53
Centre Georges Pompidou, 19, rue Beaubourg, 4ᵉ (Hôtel-de-Ville/Rambuteau), 01 44 78 47 99; fax 01 44 78 16 80

◪ It's all about the "amazing" "360-degree" view atop the Pompidou Center ("dining on the Paris rooftops, wow") at this "wildly chic" creation, since the servers, seemingly "hired for their catwalk struts", "take haughty to new heights" and the "Eclectic food interpretations", while "good, are definitely second to the buzzing atmosphere generated by the 'in'-crowd (and "overpriced" too); up to you to decide if the "high-tech" "panorama of the city makes up for an arrogant staff and [barely] above-par cuisine."

GÉRARD BESSON | 27 | 22 | 24 | 100 |

5, rue Coq Héron, 1er (Louvre-Rivoli/Palais Royal-Musée du Louvre), 01 42 33 14 74; fax 01 42 33 85 71

■ "Simply extraordinary but not overly precious" is how fans describe chef-owner Gérard Besson's "old-school Classic French with an updated twist" near Les Halles; "great detail in the preparation" of the "delicious fare", including "superb game dishes" and a "fabulous" seasonal truffle menu, make most happy in a "mirrored" dining room that's been renovated to "lovely" effect; despite "congenial service", however, a few find the prices "hard to swallow."

Gitane (La) | ▽ 18 | 13 | 18 | 35 |

53 bis, av de La Motte-Picquet, 15^e (La Motte-Picquet-Grenelle), 01 47 34 62 92; fax 01 40 65 94 01

■ "Unpretentious" but "prime Southwestern"–Classic French fare, administered by "really nice service", ensures this bistro in the 15th is "always full" with a "mixed crowd of graying heads and hipsters"; "generous portions" for modest prices attract urban gypsies (*gitanes*) of all varieties.

Giulio Rebellato | 20 | 14 | 20 | 53 |

136, rue de la Pompe, 16^e (Victor Hugo), 01 47 27 50 26

■ "You'd think you were in Italy", except that the "properly spiced", "fresh dishes aren't as wonderful" there say fans of this "small" "well-kept secret" in the 16th; a "chic", "jet-setty" crowd and "good service" make "it always a treat to dine" here – and make "reservations necessary" too.

Glénan (Les) | ▽ 25 | 19 | 25 | 46 |

54, rue de Bourgogne, 7e (Varenne), 01 45 51 61 09; fax 01 45 51 27 34

■ Maybe "it could do with a bit more warmth in the decor", but fin fans say this "always-welcoming" "hidden gem" with "impeccable service" is "fun, fun, fun" for "super-fresh and delicious fish", done in the best Brittany style; many judge chef/co-owner Emmanuel Jerz (ex Guy Savoy) to be a rising star, so "go now so that you can say you knew him when."

Gli Angeli | 17 | 12 | 10 | 30 |

5, rue St-Gilles, 3^e (Chemin Vert/St-Paul), 01 42 71 05 80

■ Near the Place des Vosges, this "neighborhood Italian" gets mixed notices; certainly it's "always full" ("reservations are essential") with those who find the pasta and seafood "very nice"; but opponents argue "it's lost it", particularly when it comes to the "the nasty staffers – not a big draw."

get updates at zagat.com

| F | D | S | €C |

Goumard
24 | 23 | 22 | 81

9, rue Duphot, 1ᵉʳ (Madeleine), 01 42 60 36 07; fax 01 42 60 04 54; www.goumard.fr

◪ Following a "change in owners" and chefs, this elegant, established seafooder near the Madeleine reels in a range of opinions; if scores side with fans who fawn over the "fish fantasy" of a menu served in a "beautiful Lalique-insets room" by "choreographed" waiters, a sizable school of sharks are "disappointed" by "dishes that strive for more than they attain" and the "pompous service"; perhaps the problem is that while everything's technically "excellent", "at these prices you want to be thrilled."

Gourmand (Au) ⌧
– | – | – | M

22, rue de Vaugirard, 6ᵉ (Odéon), 01 43 26 26 45

Located in a simple yellow dining room just across the street from the Senat in Saint-Germain, this newcomer features talented young chef Christophe Courgeau (ex Arpège and Les Ambassadeurs), who is pulling in a well-heeled crowd of politicians and publishing types enamored with his market-fresh New French Bistro cooking, offered on a brief, daily changing menu.

Gourmet de l'Isle
23 | 16 | 24 | 35

42, rue St-Louis-en-l'Ile, 4ᵉ (Pont-Marie), 01 43 26 79 27; fax 01 43 26 79 27

■ "For price-to-quality ratio, you can't beat this cozy neighborhood spot", especially if you indulge in the prix fixe, which offers "interesting takes on old Classic French favorites", served by "cordial waiters" in a "quaint" beamed, vaulted 17th-century cellar; small wonder supporters swoon it's the "best bargain on the Ile Saint-Louis" – and it's not bad for the rest of Paris, either.

Gourmets des Ternes (Les) ⌧
21 | 12 | 12 | 43

87, bd de Courcelles, 8ᵉ (Ternes), 01 42 27 43 04

■ Near the Place des Ternes, "one of the last real bistros in Paris" is "the real McCoy" when it comes to some of "the best meat in town", followed by heavenly "homemade baba au rhum"; it's usually "crowded" with a bawdy bunch, kept in line by "surly servers", but most find it worth putting up with the macho atmosphere for "the intense pleasure of really good chow."

Graindorge ⌧
∇ 21 | 16 | 21 | 49

15, rue de l'Arc-de-Triomphe, 17ᵉ (Charles de Gaulle-Etoile), 01 47 54 00 28; fax 01 47 54 00 28

■ "Extraordinary" enthuse fans of this Northern French in a slightly "isolated" location in the 17th; the "tasty" Belgian "cooking is careful and refined", and "you have to try" their selection of Flemish beers and genièvre, a regional version of gin; if the "tables are a bit tightly spaced", it doesn't deter the "great service."

---

110   subscribe to zagat.com

| F | D | S | €C |

Grand Café (Le) ⓥ   16 | 20 | 15 | 44
4, bd des Capucines, 9ᵉ (Opéra), 01 43 12 19 00; fax 01 43 12 19 09
☑ Yet "another belle-epoque brasserie" owned by the Frères Blanc, this "grande dame" near the Opéra Garnier boasts "beautiful" decor – now, "if only the food matched" sigh stalwarts ("nothing wrong", but "nothing outstanding either"); its sidewalk cafe offers "great people-watching", though, and "you can have a hot meal any time of the day", even if "uneven service" makes its delivery uncertain.

Grand Colbert (Le) ⓥ   16 | 23 | 16 | 45
2, rue Vivienne, 2ᵉ (Bourse/Palais Royal-Musée du Louvre), 01 42 86 87 88; fax 01 42 86 82 65
☑ A bit "hard to find" in the Passage Vivienne arcade, this "classic of the 2nd" "defines brasserie", with "superb" "movie-set" decor of mosaic floors, "potted palms, lots of mirrors, high ceilings, booths and waiters bustling about"; although the "traditional" food seems "standard" to savants, this remains a "great place to take visitors" if you think they'd like "to sample 'scary' French cuisine like escargots and frogs' legs" amid an "appealing" ambiance.

Grande Armée (La) ⓥ   12 | 15 | 13 | 47
3, av de la Grande-Armée, 16ᵉ (Charles de Gaulle-Etoile), 01 45 00 24 77; fax 01 45 00 95 50
☑ On "the wrong side of the Arc de Triomphe", this "little foodie boudoir" (the Napoleon III decor is by ubiquitous decorator Jacques Garcia) is an address where "young Eurotrash and old aristocrats mingle" with "neighborhood locals" of the 16th; "cuisinewise, it's the worst of the Costes brothers'" establishments cavil critics "uninspired" by the Classic French fare and the "pretentious service"; but advocates "appreciate that they serve quite late", which works well for an "informal", "naughty dinner for two."

GRANDE CASCADE (LA)   25 | 28 | 25 | 112
Bois de Boulogne, allée de Longchamp, 16ᵉ (Porte Maillot), 01 45 27 33 51; fax 01 42 88 99 06; www.lagrandecascade.fr
■ With a "spectacular setting" – "Napoleon III's former hunting lodge in the Bois de Boulogne" – this Haute Cuisine table is a "romantic dream", whether you dine "outdoors in summer or in the round room in winter"; though "outshone" by the locale, chef Richard Mebkhout's "original yet not ostentatious" cooking is certainly "nothing to complain about", and the same goes for the "stupendous wine list" and "impeccable" staff; so when that "special occasion" calls for "true luxury", this is the trail to follow.

Grande Rue (La) ⌧   – | – | – | M
117, rue de Vaugirard, 15ᵉ (Falguière), 01 47 34 96 12; fax 01 47 34 96 12
In a vintage 1900 setting decorated with flea-market finds, this tiny, off-the-beaten-track bistro is "a terrific discovery"

	F	D	S	€C

in the 15th; those who have tracked it down delight in the contemporary twists that young chef-owner Emmanuel Billaud, who worked with Alain Ducasse and Joël Robuchon, gives to Classic French dishes (roast rabbit with green anise, monkfish poached with coriander); "try the lemon tart" if it's available.

Grandes Marches (Les) ●   17 | 17 | 14 | 51

6, pl de la Bastille, 12ᵉ (Bastille), 01 43 42 90 32; fax 01 43 44 80 02; www.flobrasseries.com

■ "Right next door to the Opéra Bastille", this "modern" brasserie equipped with "sleek decor" by architects Christian and Elizabeth de Portzamparc is "a good place to stop into" before or after a performance; otherwise, the "not-very-original" cooking and "maddeningly slow service" inhibit very many standing ovations from surveyors for this "expensive" locale.

Grand Louvre (Le)   16 | 18 | 17 | 36

Musée du Louvre, under the Pyramide, 1ᵉʳ (Palais Royal-Musée du Louvre), 01 40 20 53 41; fax 01 42 86 04 63

■ For "a quiet respite from the museum crowds", culture vultures perch at this Classic French with "elegant decor" by Jean-Michel Wilmotte; but while admirers argue it'd be "a place to dine even if you weren't visiting the Louvre", the "not-so-impressed" paint a different picture, saying it's mainly "a time-out when you're tired of looking at art"; for most, though, this is "the only place to re-energize between Mona Lisa and Marie de Medici."

GRAND VÉFOUR (LE)   28 | 28 | 27 | 146

Palais Royal, 17, rue de Beaujolais, 1ᵉʳ (Palais Royal-Musée du Louvre), 01 42 96 56 27; fax 01 42 86 80 71; www.relaischateaux.com

■ At this "sans pareil" Haute Cuisine in the Palais Royal, the "divine" Directoire decor ("Napoleon and Josephine ate here") is "so sublimely transforming that the food plays at slighted suitor" – not that he's neglected long, since "the gods don't eat any better" than they would at chef Guy Martin's "mind-boggling" meals; many "expect to be intimidated by the staff, but they are kind and helpful"; in short, "everything is extraordinary, including the bill" ("to avoid a third mortgage, go for the prix fixe lunch").

Grand Venise (Le)   ▽ 24 | 17 | 24 | 72

171, rue de la Convention, 15ᵉ (Convention), 01 45 32 49 71; fax 01 45 32 07 49

■ "Don't eat for two days before going" to this Italian in the 15th, since the "gargantuan" portions are enough to fill a gondola – a plentitude that is reflected on the bill; still, it's "a truly wonderful experience", since "the family [of owners] makes you feel right at home" as does the "wonderful staff, including mama."

| F | D | S | €C |

Grille (La) ⓈB   – | – | – | M
80, rue du Faubourg-Poissonnière, 10ᵉ (Poissonnière), 01 47 70 89 73

Few know this "charming" bistro in the 10th, but those who do find it "just right for the price and a typical Paris experience"; expect a "tiny space" (30 seats) with friendly staffers, flea-market decor of antique lace, bric-a-brac and "very-noisy" caged birds, along with an "admirable" Traditional French menu that never swerves from classics such as grilled turbot and profiteroles.

Grille St-Germain (La) ●   16 | 15 | 17 | 36
14, rue Mabillon, 6ᵉ (Mabillon), 01 43 54 16 87; fax 01 43 54 52 88

◪ While this "comforting and conventional" corner in Saint-German recently changed hands, all its aspects remain untouched, from the "interesting" decor of Studio Harcourt black-and-white photos and '30s "old movie posters" to the "old-fashioned" Classic Bistro cuisine and "straightforward service"; a "low-key" party vibe prevails, reflecting its popularity with a Parisian nightcrawling crowd.

Guinguette de Neuilly (La)   ▽ 12 | 15 | 14 | 39
12, bd Georges Seurat, Neuilly (Pont de Levallois), 01 46 24 25 04; fax 01 47 38 20 49

◪ Foreigners find "this is what being French is all about" when it comes to the jolly sepia-tinted atmosphere of this 1920s veteran on the Ile de la Jatte; some scold the Classic French cooking as "bad, bad", but this remains an ideal place to "let yourself go on the edge of the Seine" like something straight out of Seurat (painterly homages to whom hang on the walls).

Guirlande de Julie (La)   ▽ 14 | 17 | 15 | 44
25, pl des Vosges, 4ᵉ (Bastille/St-Paul), 01 48 87 94 07; fax 01 48 87 01 22

◪ It may be "nicely located on the Place de Vosges" but doubters are "disappointed" by this table owned by the Terrails of Tour d'Argent, since, aside from the "delicious pot au feu", the Classic French cuisine is "pedestrian at best"; still, it's "relatively inexpensive" and "the pleasure of sitting outdoors on the Place" remains unparalleled.

GUY SAVOY, RESTAURANT ⓈB   28 | 25 | 28 | 144
18, rue Troyon, 17ᵉ (Charles de Gaulle-Etoile/Ternes), 01 43 80 40 61; fax 01 46 22 43 09; www.guysavoy.com

■ For a "true Haute Cuisine experience" – "terrific, not terrifying" – the knowledgeable kneel in homage to Guy Savoy's table in the 17th; the "innovative" fare, including a "heaven-sent artichoke-truffle soup", "keeps getting better" ("the chef-owner is usually here, unlike some other places"); and it's served by a "flawless", "surprisingly unstuffy" staff amid a "California"-like "modern decor";

even the "cost-conscious" confess this is "worth the splurge" for "a Beethoven symphony of taste and smell."

Hangar (Le) ●🆔⌀ ▽ 21 | 8 | 16 | 36

12, impasse Berthaud, 3ᵉ (Rambuteau), 01 42 74 55 44

■ In a dead-end passage near the Pompidou Center, this "laid-back", "little hole-in-the-wall" is "full of culinary surprises" in its Classic French "dishes that are simple" but done with "delicacy", such as the "seared foie gras" or "perfect poached salmon"; the room's rather "boring", and the "cash-only [policy] is a drag, too" – but that's the price you pay for "one of the best values to be had in Paris."

Hédiard 🆔 21 | 18 | 16 | 40

21, pl de la Madeleine, 8ᵉ (Madeleine), 01 43 12 88 99; fax 01 43 12 88 98; www.hediard.fr

■ Situated within the luxury grocer on the Place de la Madeleine, this Contemporary French with a vaguely Colonial atmosphere (parquet floors, wooden shutters) offers "fantastic" fare that "you'll love" assuming that "you can get served" by the staff; even so, it's certainly "several cuts above a walk-in cafe", and of course there's "wonderful shopping in the store" afterwards.

HÉLÈNE DARROZE 🆔 24 | 22 | 20 | 96

4, rue d'Assas, 6ᵉ (Rennes/Sèvres-Babylone), 01 42 22 00 11; fax 01 42 22 25 40; www.relaischateaux.com

☑ It may be "rare for a female chef to reach this level of excellence in French restaurants", but Hélène Darroze has made the ascent, serving up "cutting-edge" New French–Southwestern "food from heaven" at her dining room with "warm contemporary decor" in the 6th; a few pessimists pout the place is "seriously pretentious", especially the "erratic servers" who swing from "oblivious" to "professional"; but most agree that if "it's not the best, it's certainly in the running."

Higuma 16 | 6 | 10 | 15

32 bis, rue Ste-Anne, 1ᵉʳ (Pyramides), 01 47 03 38 59; fax 01 47 03 38 52

☑ "Don't be put off by the rather dingy decor" at this Nipponese near the Opéra Garnier – just concentrate on the feed, which includes "finger-licking-good" gyozas and "true Japanese curry"; it's "perfect for a quick lunch" or a dinner, provided you "don't expect friendly service (they're turning the tables over too fast to care)."

HIPPOPOTAMUS ● 10 | 10 | 10 | 25

29, rue Berger, 1ᵉʳ (Les Halles), 01 45 08 00 29; fax 01 40 41 98 63
1, bd des Capucines, 2ᵉ (Opéra), 01 47 42 75 70; fax 01 42 65 23 08
1, bd Beaumarchais, 4ᵉ (Bastille), 01 44 61 90 40; fax 01 48 87 84 67

| F | D | S | €C |

(continued)
HIPPOPOTAMUS
9, rue Lagrange, 5ᵉ (Maubert-Mutualité), 01 43 54 13 99; fax 01 44 07 18 20
119, bd du Montparnasse, 6ᵉ (Vavin), 01 43 20 37 04; fax 01 43 22 68 95
42, av des Champs-Elysées, 8ᵉ (Franklin D. Roosevelt), 01 53 83 94 50; fax 01 53 83 94 51
20, rue Quentin Bauchart, 8ᵉ (George V), 01 47 20 30 14; fax 01 47 20 95 31
8, bd St-Denis, 10ᵉ (Strasbourg-St-Denis), 01 53 38 80 28; fax 01 53 38 80 26
68, bd du Montparnasse, 14ᵉ (Montparnasse-Bienvenüe), 01 40 64 14 94; fax 01 43 21 46 10
CNIT, 2, pl de la Défense, Puteaux (La Défense-Grande Arche), 01 46 92 13 75; fax 01 46 92 13 69
www.hippopotamus.fr
Additional locations throughout Paris

◪ "Pretty mediocre" is the prevailing opinion about this omnipresent steakhouse chain, whose branches are suffused by the "smell of grill smoke" and service that is at best "absent-minded"; but those undeterred note "in an expensive city, it's cheap and reliable", and works well as a "place to take the kids" or "for late at night."

HIRAMATSU ⓩ | 28 | 25 | 27 | 128 |
7, quai Bourbon, 4ᵉ (Pont-Marie), 01 56 81 08 80; fax 01 56 81 08 81; www.hiramatsu.co.jp

■ At this "minimalist but exquisite" 18-seater on the Ile Saint-Louis, "rising star" Hiroyuki Hiramatsu does an "insanely creative", "intelligent interpretation of Haute Cuisine" in which "French and Japanese cuisines meld seamlessly" and are brought to table by "energetic young servers" who are "attentive but not intrusive"; "prices are terribly high", and "it's hard to get into", but for a "romantic splurge" most say it's "worth every euro."

Huîtrier (L') | ∇ 18 | 9 | 15 | 46 |
16, rue Saussier-Leroy, 17ᵉ (Ternes), 01 40 54 83 44; fax 01 40 54 83 86

■ It may be "off the beaten track" and the decor is dull, but mavens maintain this seafood bar in the 17th is worth it for "the mountains of" "marvelous oysters", along with a nice menu of "the freshest fish"; if a little expensive, it's "always dependable", which explains why "it can be crowded."

I Golosi ⓞⓩ | 18 | 12 | 16 | 46 |
6, rue de la Grange-Batelière, 9ᵉ (Richelieu-Drouot), 01 48 24 18 63

◪ The "short but well designed menu" and "good selection of wines by the glass" have won this Italian with a "'70s decor" a solid following among the arts-and-antiques crowd who frequent the nearby Drouot auction rooms; however,

get updates at zagat.com

while the fare is "inventive", its quality can be "irregular", and "rather distant service" doesn't "compensate."

Il Baccello 20 | 18 | 22 | 46
33, rue Cardinet, 17^e (Monceau/Wagram), 01 43 80 63 60; www.ilbaccello.com
■ "You won't find any pizza or pasta bolognaise" at this "well-hidden Italian-Med jewel" in the 17th, since young chef Raphael Bembaron proposes a "refined" and "highly original" menu that reflects his training at Joia, the famed Milanese meat-free restaurant; it's sometimes "smoky" in the small dining room with a "surprisingly Japanese-looking decor", but the "personal attention" from the staff creates a "highly agreeable atmosphere", and prices are "reasonable" for such "excellent" food.

Il Barone 19 | 5 | 13 | 38
5, rue Léopold Robert, 14e (Raspail/Vavin), 01 43 20 87 14; fax 01 43 20 87 14
■ If you're after a "genuine trattoria in Paris", come to Montparnasse, where this *famiglia*-style place offers a "really good antipasti buffet" and "puntarella salad like you only find in Rome"; no one minds the "too-tight" digs, especially when the service is so "*bel canto*"; but "to be hip, make sure you sit in the back room" and not in the crowded one up front.

Il Cortile 23 | 21 | 20 | 70
Hôtel Castille, 37, rue Cambon, 1er (Concorde/Madeleine), 01 44 58 45 67; fax 01 44 58 45 69; www.accor.com
◪ Few know it, but the "excellent French interpretation of Italian cuisine" you'll find at this 1st arrondissement address is actually the work of a talented Dutchman, Tjaco Van Eijken, who trained at the Louis XV in Monte Carlo; the "lovely courtyard" garden with a fountain and faience tiles is a midsummer's night dream, but views vary about the staff, which is generally "gracious" but sometimes "young and clumsy"; a few fuss it's "overrated", but to happier hearts, this hotel eatery is "heaven."

Ile (L') 15 | 19 | 11 | 44
170, quai de Stalingrad, Parc de l'Ile St-Germain, Issy-les-Moulineaux (RER Issy-Val de Seine), 01 41 09 99 99; fax 01 41 09 99 19
■ With a waterside location in Issy-les-Moulineaux ("the country only minutes from Paris"), this "trendy TV and show-biz place" is a "pretty factory", perfect for "out-of-towners or to celebrate a birthday" ("every five minutes, another cake is brought out"); it's "not very interesting from a culinary point of view", but the combo of Classic and Contemporary French dishes offers "something for every taste"; "disorganized service" is a problem though – "even in a fashion restaurant, you need professional service."

| F | D | S | €C |

Il Etait une Oie dans le Sud-Ouest ⑤
▽ 15 | 8 | 14 | 35

8, rue Gustave Flaubert, 17ᵉ (Ternes/Wagram), 01 43 80 18 30; fax 01 43 80 99 50

◪ "One of the best deals" in solid Southwestern specialties is at this "pleasant" place near the Place des Ternes; perhaps "they could make a little [more] effort" when it comes to decor and service, but at "these prices, you don't hesitate", especially when the foie gras is so "succulent."

Il Viccolo ⑤
17 | 13 | 17 | 44

34, rue Mazarine, 6ᵉ (Odéon), 01 43 25 01 11

◪ In Saint-Germain, this "affable, trendy Italian" serves up "modern", "original" fare that most "enjoy immeasurably", even if some shrug it's sometimes "so-so"; with glassed-in sidewalk seating, the site may be "decorated like an airport hotel bar", but the "welcoming atmosphere" is definitely "first class", even if you're flying "solo."

Impatient (L') ⑤
– | – | – | M

14, passage Geffroy Didelot, 17ᵉ (Rome/Villiers), 01 43 87 28 10; fax 01 43 87 28 10

"Hidden in a romantic spot" on a pedestrians' passageway in the 17th, this little-known neighborhood place is worth discovering for the "imaginative" New French cooking in a funky setting (e.g. the bathtubs–turned–flower beds along the terrace); though "smiling", the servers are laid-back, which means "don't come if you're in a hurry" or you may end up becoming impatient yourself; still, "good things are worth waiting for", especially at these "sweet prices."

Inagiku ⑤
▽ 17 | 11 | 15 | 53

14, rue de Pontoise, 5ᵉ (Maubert-Mutualité), 01 43 54 70 07; fax 01 40 51 74 44

◼ The seafood is "irreproachably fresh" at this quiet, "reliable Japanese" in the Latin Quarter, where it's "fun to watch the chef griddle and sizzle your shrimp", scallops and "other delicacies" "under your nose" "on a heated table"; "though it is, alas, expensive", it's "a good option on the Left Bank, where relatively few" teppanyaki places exist.

Indiana Café ●
8 | 8 | 9 | 23

7, bd des Capucines, 2ᵉ (Opéra), 01 42 68 02 22
1, pl de la République, 3ᵉ (République), 01 48 87 82 35
130, bd St-Germain, 6ᵉ (Odéon), 01 46 34 66 31
235-237, rue du Faubourg St-Honoré, 8ᵉ (Ternes), 01 44 09 80 00
79, bd de Clichy, 9ᵉ (Place de Clichy), 01 48 74 42 61
14, pl de la Bastille, 11ᵉ (Bastille), 01 44 75 79 80
72, bd du Montparnasse, 14ᵉ (Montparnasse-Bienvenüe), 01 43 35 36 28; fax 01 43 35 07 25
www.indiana-cafe.com

◪ Yup, "Paris has it all – even" a "parody of American food" sneer cynics about this "touristy" chain serving "bad

| F | D | S | €C |

burgers" and a "sorry excuse for Tex-Mex food" ("Tex-Mess would be more like it"); fans find it "practical for a rapid", "reasonable" snack washed down with "specialty drinks", but more folks urge "avoid" the "poor service" and "dark", "strange Americana-style decor" that's so "generic you might as well be in Indianapolis" – though come to think of it, "why would you call a Tex-Mex place Indiana?"

Indra ⌧ ▽ 21 | 18 | 18 | 49
10, rue du Commandant Rivière, 8ᵉ (St-Philippe-du-Roule), 01 43 59 46 40; fax 01 42 25 00 32
■ Equipped with an "amusing theatrical decor", this thirtysomething has been "one of the best Indians in Paris" for nearly 40 years; though some speculate that "the cooking's been toned down for French tastes", most recommend you come here when you're in a hurry for curry, even if it is "a bit expensive" (after all, "they have to pay for their site" in the high-rent 8th).

Isami 24 | 12 | 16 | 52
4, quai d'Orléans, 4ᵉ (Pont-Marie), 01 40 46 06 97
◪ This vest-pocket Japanese on the Ile Saint-Louis is "incontestably the best place in Paris for sushi and sashimi prepared by a real master" – which means, "dammit, it's always full when you want to go"; those who persevere proclaim the service and "atmosphere a little cold" and warn that while "prices are low" on the "limited menu", "the desire to eat more and more creates a big bill"; still, "the technique and exceptional quality of the fish" make it all worthwhile.

Isse ⌧ 25 | 19 | 20 | 58
56, rue Ste-Anne, 2ᵉ (Pyramides/Quatre Septembre), 01 42 96 67 76; fax 01 42 96 82 63
■ A stylish crowd swoons over the "subtlety" of the recipes at this time-honored address in the 2nd, which offers "delicious", "super-fresh" sushi and sashimi that's "among the finest in town"; "but unless you're a Rockefeller, you can't afford to eat here often", since this is not only "one of the best Japanese in Paris", it's one of "the most expensive" as well; P.S. the Decor score may not reflect a post-*Survey* re-do of the Asian "minimalist" digs.

JACQUES CAGNA ⌧ 25 | 24 | 24 | 89
14, rue des Grands-Augustins, 6ᵉ (Odéon/St-Michel), 01 43 26 49 39; fax 01 43 54 54 48; www.jacquescagna.com
■ "It's always a treat to dine with Jacques" declare devotees of this "special-occasion" veteran, which for nearly 40 years has been serving traditional, "rich" Haute Cuisine "as if nouvelle had never been invented"; it's an "elegant" "old-world" experience here throughout, from the "charming" 16th-century environs, adorned "with beautiful oil paintings", to the service that's "a little stuffy"

but "pleasantly" "attentive"; "dated" or not, "this is one of the [last] truly romantic spots left."

JAMIN 🖂   25 | 20 | 24 | 103
32, rue de Longchamp, 16ᵉ (Boissière/Trocadéro), 01 45 53 00 07; fax 01 45 53 00 15

■ "It's no longer the temple of Joël Robuchon", but his protégé chef Benoît Guichard still insures "sumptuous", "creative" Haute Cuisine dining at this "small, discreet spot" in the 16th; sometimes the "service is initially cool, but it warms up" fast in the pastel-colored "pretty room"; so most visitors "can't wait to go back" to experience the "enormous charm" once more; P.S. "lunch is a great value if you order the prix fixe."

Jardin (Le) 🖂   21 | 23 | 21 | 88
Hôtel Royal Monceau, 37, av Hoche, 8ᵉ (Charles de Gaulle-Etoile), 01 42 99 98 70; fax 01 42 99 89 90; www.royalmonceau.com

■ "One of the nicest settings in Paris" – a dining room "covered by a glass dome, in a garden" – imparts a "sense of calm" to this address near the Etoile; it's a "good place to slow down" and sample "nice Med" and New French specialties and a southern regional wine list, all the while being waited upon by "refined servers."

Jardin des Cygnes   20 | 24 | 23 | 92
Hôtel Prince de Galles, 33, av George V, 8ᵉ (George V), 01 53 23 78 50; fax 01 53 23 78 82; www.luxurycollection.com

■ "The garden is absolute heaven on a nice night" say surveyors about this "oasis of calm" "located in the Hôtel Prince de Galles"; "attentive servers" proffer "a variety of pleasing dishes" in the Classic French mode three times a day; and while some joke "it only costs two arms and legs", the "prix fixes are great deals", especially on the "very good breakfast buffet."

Jardins de Bagatelle (Les)   18 | 22 | 15 | 67
Parc de Bagatelle, Route de Sèvres, 16ᵉ (Pont-de-Neuilly), 01 40 67 98 29; fax 01 40 67 93 04; www.restaurantbagatelle.com

☑ This large Classic French is, "in the summer, a great place to have lunch" "or a romantic dinner", thanks to its "beautiful setting" in the Bois de Boulogne (they've even managed "to get rid of the mosquitoes"); pessimists posit it's "rather pricey" for the "middling quality" of the cuisine, but a "walk through the Bagatelle Gardens" before or after "makes it all worthwhile."

Jean-Paul Hévin 🖂   ▽ 22 | 20 | 19 | 26
231, rue St-Honoré, 1ᵉʳ (Madeleine/Tuileries), 01 55 35 35 96; fax 01 55 35 35 95; www.jphevin.com

■ Bet you didn't know the 1st arrondissement branch of the "earth's best chocolatier" also possessed a tearoom on the second floor; those who did find its snacklike savories such as quiches and salads "quite easy on the taste buds" – though of course, others just "go for the pastries" and the "most sumptuous gateaux in the world"; with its cocoa-colored decor, some even believe it "a blessing for a [light] business lunch", presumably with a sweet-toothed client.

Je Thé ... Me ∇ 21 | 22 | 20 | 38
4, rue d'Alleray, 15ᵉ (Convention/Vaugirard), 01 48 42 48 30; fax 01 48 42 70 66

In the 15th arrondissement, this tearoom suits many to a 'T' indeed, since the "extremely hospitable", "bilingual" "family that runs this place inspires joy and happiness"; served in a fin-de-siècle setting "with cachet", the light "simple plates" "will not let you down"; "you eat well and the owner has a sense of humor, so what else do you want?"

Joe Allen 16 | 15 | 18 | 38
30, rue Pierre Lescot, 1ᵉʳ (Etienne Marcel), 01 42 36 70 13; fax 01 42 36 90 80; www.joeallenparis.com

"A little corner of America" in Les Halles, this "low-key" branch of the NY theater district restaurant offers "*très bon* T-bones, a burger worthy of the name and cheesecake" in "large portions (American-style)"; some scold "why bother when you're in Paris, for God's sake", especially since to them this joint is "past its prime"; but expats parry that "it's a nice haven when you need a little break from the whole Europe thing."

Jo Goldenberg 13 | 10 | 12 | 31
7, rue des Rosiers, 4ᵉ (St-Paul), 01 48 87 20 16; fax 01 48 87 64 08; www.restaurantgoldenberg.com

"The nostalgia is almost as heavy as the chopped liver" at this 1920 delicatessen "in the heart of the Marais" (Paris' historic Hebrew quarter) that's "a standard" for the Jewish "specialties"; but "don't expect grandma's cooking" carp critics "disappointed" in the "overpriced", "tasteless" fare and staff that acts "as if they were doing you a service to allow you in"; "if you need a deli fix, this is the place"; otherwise, "don't bother."

Joséphine "Chez Dumonet" 19 | 16 | 17 | 53
117, rue du Cherche-Midi, 6ᵉ (Duroc/Falguière), 01 45 48 52 40; fax 01 42 84 06 83

Voilà, here's a "bistro-lover's bistro" on the Left Bank, "authentic" in everything from the "old-fashioned atmosphere" and "1900-style decor" to the "Traditional French food and service" (Grand Marnier soufflé, anyone?); one pleasantly modern touch: "you choose the size of your portions" – full-serving or "small-plate", the latter "a nice option for grazing."

| F | D | S | €C |

JULES VERNE
| 24 | 27 | 24 | 107 |

Tour Eiffel, 2nd level, 7ᵉ (Bir-Hakeim), 01 45 55 61 44; fax 01 47 05 29 41; www.tour-eiffel.fr

■ The Classic French cooking may be "*magnifique*" but it's the "magical setting" atop the Eiffel Tower "that makes this place worthwhile", since you dine with all Paris at your feet; not surprisingly, it's "chock-full of tourists", which may be why the maitre d' displays "a little too much attitude with the altitude", though the rest of the staff is "attentive and polished" as they negotiate the '70s-disco, "black-clad interior"; tabs, of course, are sky-high, but this is the "No. 1 impress-your-date place in town."

Jumeaux (Les) 🖂
| - | - | - | M |

73, rue Amelot, 11ᵉ (Chemin Vert), 01 43 14 27 00; fax 01 43 14 27 00

Near the Cirque d'Hiver in the 11th, this small site run by "eponymous twins who are the maitre d' and the cook" is "just delightful" with "good service" and "amazing" food that offers an "imaginative" mixture of "Asian flavors and New French cuisine" on a "menu that changes all the time"; decorated with modern art, the "unpretentious" dining room has a "certain New York feel to it."

Juvéniles 🖂
| 16 | 12 | 18 | 32 |

47, rue de Richelieu, 1ᵉʳ (Bourse/Palais Royal-Musée du Louvre), 01 42 97 46 49; fax 01 42 60 31 52

◪ "Known for its amazing selection" of varietals, this *bar à vins* near the Palais Royal is "an inspired, wacky, friendly joint with a funky staff" led by owner "Tim Johnston, the irrepressible Scotsman", who some say is its "key selling point"; an Eclectic array of "well prepared, wine-friendly food" – this has got to be Paris' "only place with haggis regularly on the menu" – is on hand; only the "noisy", "unkempt" surroundings seem a bit juvenile.

Kaïten ●🖂
| - | - | - | M |

63, rue Pierre Charron, 8ᵉ (Franklin D. Roosevelt), 01 43 59 78 78; fax 01 43 59 71 51

At this "amusing", moderately priced Japanese just off the Champs, the "conveyor belt could make you fear the worst, but the sushi, sashimi and maki [revolving on it] are really very good"; regulars might follow them up with a hot dish or two, then finished off with some "green-tea ice cream that alone is worth elbowing up to the bar for."

Kambodgia 🖂
| ▽ 20 | 20 | 19 | 45 |

15, rue de Bassano, 16ᵉ (Charles de Gaulle-Etoile/George V), 01 47 23 31 80; fax 01 47 20 41 22

■ "Don't be put off by the walk down to the basement" room of this Asian in the 16th, since the bamboo-and-tropical-woods interior is "exceptional", "the service is irreproachable" and the Cambodian and Vietnamese

get updates at zagat.com 121

| F | D | S | €C |

cuisine is "amazingly authentic"; all in all, it's a "refined" experience that "transports you" to Southeast Asia.

Khun Akorn ▽ 18 | 18 | 15 | 35
8, av de Taillebourg, 11ᵉ (Nation), 01 43 56 20 03; fax 01 40 09 18 44
■ Even if you have to guide your elephant to an outlying part of the 11th, it's worth it, since this "creative" Thai table, though "one of the lesser-known in Paris, offers the best bang for the buck" followers find; the regulars also rave about the "beautiful" "rooftop terrace", which come summer offers a "bucolic view" "for a lovers' dinner."

Kim Anh ▽ 23 | 16 | 23 | 42
51, av Emile Zola, 15ᵉ (Charles Michels), 01 45 79 40 96; fax 01 40 59 49 78
■ You "absolutely have to discover" this compact corner in the 15th for "the best Vietnamese food outside of Saigon"; Viet vets vaunt the "immensely subtle cooking", including "perfect brochettes de boeuf with lemongrass", "nems stuffed with more crab than you'd think they could fit in the tiny kitchen" and "great sweet-corn pudding", dished out by "helpful, charming servers"; small wonder the adoring aver they've "been here at least 100 times and never been disappointed."

Kinugawa ☒ 22 | 14 | 18 | 65
9, rue du Mont Thabor, 1ᵉʳ (Tuileries), 01 42 60 65 07; fax 01 42 60 57 36
4, rue St-Philippe-du-Roule, 8ᵉ (St-Philippe-du-Roule), 01 45 63 08 07
◪ "Beautiful, delicate sushi" and Kyoto-style delicacies rule at this duo in the 1st and 8th, "classic, consistent" contenders for "the best Japanese in town"; but many mutter their traditional decor falls "far from reaching the cuisine's heights", and nearly all agree the pair's "outrageously overpriced", with tabs that practically "justify a trip to Japan" instead.

Kiosque (Le) 17 | 16 | 15 | 44
1, pl de Mexico, 16ᵉ (Trocadéro), 01 47 27 96 98; fax 01 45 53 89 79
◪ At this "lively" Classic French overlooking "a pretty square" in the 16th, "a different region stars on the menu every week – an amusing concept even if the cooking is uneven"; as its name suggests, "the inventive decor has a journalistic theme" ("they distribute a local newspaper" with the meal), and while the "service is slow", "the place is always busy" with well-heeled crowds craving "comfort food in a relaxed atmosphere."

Kong ● 14 | 24 | 14 | 45
Pont Neuf Bldg., 1, rue du Pont Neuf, 1ᵉʳ (Pont-Neuf), 01 40 39 09 00; fax 01 40 39 09 10
■ This new, "cool place" offers "spectacular views" from the top floor of the Pont Neuf building, "enticing music"

| F | D | S | €C |

and "a nice bar area"; but while enthusiasts find the Eclectic "cuisine full of imagination", critics cry "Kong is the king of rip-offs": "entirely too expensive", and its "servers nowhere to be found"; at least Philippe Starck's Asiatique "renovation of the old Samaritaine building is superb" – though some wonder "how long do you want to see geisha holograms on the back of your chair?"

Lac-Hong

| 21 | 12 | 15 | 49 |

67, rue Lauriston, 16ᵉ (Boissière/Victor Hugo), 01 47 55 87 17

■ "Worth finding on the streets of the 16th", this midsize site serves some of "the best Asian food in Paris" "short of Hanoi"; though the "waiters are helpful", many deem the decor kind of "kitschy" and sigh about "sky-rocketing prices", "but if you like genuine Vietnamese food" you'll be happy "even after seeing the bill."

LADURÉE

| 21 | 23 | 16 | 34 |

21, rue Bonaparte, 6ᵉ (St-Sulpice), 01 44 07 64 87; fax 01 44 07 64 93
75, av des Champs-Elysées, 8ᵉ (George V), 01 40 75 08 75; fax 01 40 75 06 75
16, rue Royale, 8ᵉ (Concorde/Madeleine), 01 42 60 21 79; fax 01 49 27 01 95
Printemps, 64, bd Haussmann, 9ᵉ (Havre-Caumartin), 01 42 82 40 10; fax 01 42 82 62 00
www.laduree.fr

■ Others "may be more trendsetting, but this remains the classic patisserie" say the sweet-toothed about these "upscale tea salons" known for their "plush atmosphere" (especially the Champs address, with its "Napoleon III–style delirious decor"); "they can be noisy" and the "zippy" staff "impolite", but they're still "places to frequent from morning till night": "a must for breakfast", "lunch when shopping" or "wonderful teas"; no matter which meal, the "world-famous macaroons" "are not to be missed."

Languedoc (Le)

| 17 | 13 | 18 | 31 |

64, bd de Port-Royal, 5ᵉ (Les Gobelins/Port Royal), 01 47 07 24 47

☑ Time seems to have stopped at this long-running, "homey" "old-style bistro with mimeographed menus that never change" in the 5th; it serves "consistently good" Classic French food that "offers a glimpse of the flavorful region" of Languedoc; prices are "inexpensive", but there are a couple of complaints about "skimpy portions."

Lao Siam

| – | – | – | M |

49, rue de Belleville, 19ᵉ (Belleville/Pyrénées), 01 40 40 09 68; fax 01 42 03 14 26

It may be a bit of a trudge up to Belleville in the 19th, but most don't mind when there's this "excellent Thai" table at the end of the slog; both the service and "the decor are

get updates at zagat.com 123

neutral", but that "lets you concentrate on the essential" – the "fresh dishes" on the "enormous, original menu"; "prices are a lot lower than at other places with the same level of quality."

Lao Tseu ▽ 16 | 12 | 17 | 34
209, bd St-Germain, 7ᵉ (Rue du Bac), 01 45 48 30 06; fax 01 45 50 36 38

■ The worldly, well-heeled citizenry of the 7th come into (or take out from) this "good neighborhood Chinese" whose dishes are savored for their "subtle flavors", though malcontents mutter "even dishes classified as spicy are really not"; "the staff is terribly nice", which makes it easy to overlook the nonexistent decor.

Lapérouse ⑤ 21 | 26 | 22 | 91
51, quai des Grands-Augustins, 6ᵉ (Pont-Neuf/St-Michel), 01 43 26 90 14; fax 01 43 26 99 39

■ "Spreading through several elegant rooms" "overlooking the Seine" and decorated with "18th-century antiques", this "institution" in the 6th is "one of Paris' most romantic restaurants", ideal "if you like to kiss between courses" or as a "place to propose" (legend has it that the scratched-up mirrors reflect ladies testing the diamonds before saying yes or no); happily, chef Alain Hacquard has "rejuvenated" the Haute Cuisine, which now is "lovely", if "traditional" – as are the "discreet, unhurried waiters."

LASSERRE ⑤ 26 | 27 | 27 | 121
17, av Franklin D. Roosevelt, 8ᵉ (Franklin D. Roosevelt), 01 43 59 02 13; fax 01 45 63 72 23

■ A meal at this "magical place" in the 8th is "more like attending an elegant dinner party than a restaurant", though it'd have to be one fabulous fete to offer the Haute Cuisine "in the traditional manner" of chef Jean-Louis Nomicos; "a dream for food and wine, if a nightmare for your wallet", this "very-romantic" "reminder of days gone by" is also memorable for "service that's impeccable without being stuffy" and the famous "ceiling that opens up" on summer nights; "it doesn't get better than this."

LAURENT ⑤ 24 | 26 | 24 | 123
41, av Gabriel, 8ᵉ (Champs-Elysées-Clémenceau), 01 42 25 00 39; fax 01 45 62 45 21; www.le-laurent.com

■ Come to this "elegant", "extremely expensive" belle-epoque pavilion in the Champs-Elysées gardens "to meet the crème de la crème of French politics (there's always a minister or two in the dining room") or just for the "sublime" Haute Cuisine, the "team of attentive waiters" and the "great garden patio for romantic summer dining"; "snipers" snip that the "classic" food needs "a restorative kick toward modernity" to "justify the outrageous prices", but most insist on the pleasure of this "fabulous piece of Paris theater."

| F | D | S | €C |

Lavinia
| 15 | 17 | 15 | 39 |

3-5, bd de la Madeleine, 8ᵉ (Madeleine), 01 42 97 20 20; fax 01 42 97 54 50

■ "A great address for a business lunch" (they don't serve in the evening), the dining room at this shop with reportedly "the largest selection of wines" in Paris – "any of which you can try with your meal" "at retail prices" – is a "sleeper" with "good", "intelligently conceived" Classic French dishes; and if it gets "a little noisy sometimes", most are too happy swirling the contents of their Reidel glasses to notice.

LEDOYEN
| 25 | 27 | 25 | 135 |

1, av Dutuit, 8ᵉ (Champs-Elysées-Clémenceau/Concorde), 01 53 05 10 01; fax 01 47 42 55 01

■ "Perched above the trees overlooking the Champs-Elysées" gardens, the "elegantly refurbished decor" of this pretty Second Empire pavilion makes it "a fabulous place to have a special meal", aided by chef Christian Le Squer's "creative yet classical" Haute Cuisine and an "attentive" staff; pessimists find the "formality" of the food and service "somewhat impersonal", but scores support those who say it's "superb in every way" – even if you'll pay "atmospheric prices."

Lei
| – | – | – | M |

17, av de la Motte-Picquet, 7ᵉ (Ecole Militaire/La Tour-Maubourg), 01 47 05 07 37

Yes, this "newcomer" is "another Italian", from the owners of the popular Les Cailloux and Sasso – and given that pedigree, "it's sure to be a hit with the young fashion crowd of the 7th"; though "not vast, its menu" offers eats from all over The Boot, served in minimalist decor of cement floors, bare walls and unadorned "windows everywhere"; and if the jaded jeer it's "neither better nor worse than all the others", kinder hearts "hope it keeps going."

Léna et Mimile
| ∇ 16 | 20 | 19 | 36 |

32, rue Tournefort, 5ᵉ (Censier-Daubenton/Place Monge), 01 47 07 72 47; fax 01 45 35 41 94

■ "The setting is lovely and the service is sincere" at this 1937-vintage bistro with a "pretty" perched terrace "in between the Panthéon" and "the busy Rue Mouffetard"; maybe the food, "a mix of original and Traditional" French dishes, "is not that special, but who cares" when you've got such a "heavenly" location that it "doesn't even feel like you're in Paris"?

Léon de Bruxelles
| 13 | 9 | 13 | 25 |

120, rue Rambuteau, 1ᵉʳ (Les Halles), 01 42 36 18 50; fax 01 42 36 27 50 ●
3, bd Beaumarchais, 4ᵉ (Bastille), 01 42 71 75 55; fax 01 42 71 75 56 ●

(continued)

| F | D | S | €C |

(continued)
Léon de Bruxelles
131, bd St-Germain, 6ᵉ (Mabillon/Odéon), 01 43 26 45 95;
fax 01 43 26 47 02 ●
63, av des Champs-Elysées, 8ᵉ (Franklin D. Roosevelt/
George V), 01 42 25 96 16; fax 01 42 25 95 42 ●
1-3, pl Pigalle, 9ᵉ (Pigalle), 01 42 80 28 33; fax 01 42 80 27 72 ●
8, pl de la République, 11ᵉ (République), 01 43 38 28 69;
fax 01 43 38 33 41 ●
64, av des Gobelins, 13ᵉ (Les Gobelins/Place d'Italie),
01 47 07 51 07; fax 01 47 07 89 04 ●
82 bis, bd du Montparnasse, 14ᵉ (Edgar Quinet/Montparnasse-
Bienvenüe), 01 43 21 66 62; fax 01 43 21 66 76
349, rue de Vaugirard, 15ᵉ (Convention), 01 55 76 99 72;
fax 01 55 76 99 71 ●
95, bd Gouvion-St-Cyr, 17ᵉ (Porte Maillot), 01 55 37 95 30;
fax 01 55 37 95 35 ●
www.leon-de-bruxelles.fr
Additional locations throughout Paris

◪ "Featuring huge bowls of moules" ("prepared a gazillion ways"), "plates of frites and cold Belgian beer", "the McDonald's of mussels" "hits the spot when you want a quick, cheap meal"; you have to deal with "nondescript chain-restaurant decor", and the "overly busy staff can make obtaining service a challenge", but it's a more-or-less "safe bet anytime of the day" (most serve until 1 AM), if "nothing to get excited about."

Lescure ⌧ | 13 | 12 | 14 | 29 |
7, rue de Mondovi, 1ᵉʳ (Concorde), 01 42 60 18 91

◪ "They really cram the diners in", but that's actually part of the "enormously convivial" "charm" of this "boisterous" bistro "at the end of a small alley" in the 1st; the "old-fashioned Traditional" fare is no better than "standard", but there's "a lot of it for the money", and that's proved a working formula for this family-run "favorite" since 1919.

Libre Sens | – | – | – | M |
33, rue Marbeuf, 8ᵉ (Franklin D. Roosevelt), 01 53 96 00 72
Occupying the space that housed the late Korova, this new spot off the Champs is attracting a young crowd that likes the prompt, attentive service, the low-lit dining room that feels like a nightclub and the diverse menu, which includes sandwiches and salads, along with more elaborate New French dishes.

Lina's | 13 | 10 | 10 | 15 |
50, rue Etienne Marcel, 2ᵉ (Bourse/Etienne Marcel),
01 42 21 16 14; fax 01 42 33 78 03 ⌧
47, rue des Francs-Bourgeois, 4ᵉ (Hôtel-de-Ville),
01 44 78 95 00; fax 01 44 78 95 01
22, rue des Saints-Pères, 7ᵉ (St-Germain-des-Prés),
01 40 20 42 78; fax 01 40 20 42 79 ⌧

Lina's
(continued)
105, rue du Faubourg-St-Honoré, 8ᵉ (Miromesnil),
01 42 56 42 57; fax 01 42 89 93 01 🖼
8, rue Marbeuf, 8ᵉ (Alma-Marceau), 01 46 23 04 63;
fax 01 47 23 93 09 🖼
30, bd des Italiens, 9ᵉ (Opéra/Richelieu-Drouot),
01 42 46 02 06; fax 01 42 46 02 40
2, rue Henri Desgrange, 12ᵉ (Bercy), 01 43 40 42 42;
fax 01 43 40 65 11 🖼
23, av de Wagram, 17ᵉ (Charles de Gaulle-Etoile/Ternes),
01 45 74 76 76; fax 01 45 74 76 77 🖼
156, av Charles de Gaulle, Neuilly (Pont-de-Neuilly),
01 47 45 60 60; fax 01 47 45 34 68 ●🖼
www.linascafe.com

"Handy" for "healthy, dependable" "sandwiches on various breads, soups, salads and cookies", this string of shops with seating is ideal for "anyone who doesn't have time for a long lunch with red wine"; on the downside, the "disorganization and long lines" are a bore, the "decor's nothing special" and many lament it's "a little expensive for what it is (only sandwiches, after all)."

Loir dans la Théière (Le) | 12 | 15 | 14 | 25 |
3, rue des Rosiers, 4ᵉ (St-Paul), 01 42 72 90 61

The "*très* cool" atmosphere, "funky flea-market decor and communal seating" are part of the charm of this *salon de thé* in the Marais, patronized by "an interesting mix of people"; however, there's a general feeling that "it's gone downhill a bit" if you're hungry for anything more than one of their "excellent cakes", which gives it "less appeal to adults" than to twentysomethings.

Lô Sushi ● | 17 | 19 | 13 | 38 |
Pont Neuf Bldg., 1, rue du Pont Neuf, 1ᵉʳ (Pont-Neuf),
01 42 33 09 09; fax 01 42 33 09 20
8, rue de Berri, 8ᵉ (Franklin D. Roosevelt/George V),
01 45 62 01 00; fax 01 45 62 01 10
www.losushi.com

At the new Pont Neuf branch of this "sophisticated" self-serve spot, it's "fun to play on the Internet stations" at every seat, while the original in the 8th is "a perfect stop before heading out to the bars"; both feature a "pretty cool" "conveyor-belt system of presenting" the "fresh" fish; and while fin fans deem the fare just "decent", most enjoy the "sushi-a-go-go" at "a steal of a price" – until "you realize how many plates you've chosen."

Louchebem (Le) ●🖼 | ∇ 17 | 13 | 13 | 31 |
31, rue Berger, 1ᵉʳ (Châtelet), 01 42 33 12 99; fax 01 40 28 45 50;
www.le-louchebem.fr

Steak lovers swear "some of the best meat in Paris" is served at "one of the few remaining originals in Les Halles";

it's "rather noisy" and the service can be "cold", but why beef when there are such good buys as an "an all-you-can-eat rotisserie plate" that's "a must on a winter night."

Lozère (La) ☒ ▽ | 21 | 11 | 17 | 30 |
4, rue Hautefeuille, 6ᵉ (St-Michel), 01 43 54 26 64; fax 01 44 07 00 43; www.lozere-a-paris.com
■ Tucked away in a tiny street in the 6th, this funky place is one of the longer-running regionals in Paris, specializing in the "tasty" "homestyle cooking" of Lozère; "reservations are essential" on Thursdays, aka 'aligot night', when special menus feature the cheesy whipped potato dish served with sausage, tripe or steak; "service is pleasant", too.

LUCAS CARTON ☒ | 27 | 26 | 25 | 163 |
9, pl de la Madeleine, 8ᵉ (Concorde/Madeleine), 01 42 65 22 90; fax 01 42 65 06 23; www.lucascarton.com
■ Those who are "Haute to trot" set a course for this "bit of French heaven" appropriately "right by the Madeleine"; its "magnificent art nouveau decor" is the backdrop to "cutting-edge" "dishes you will taste in your dreams", especially if you do the *dégustation* menu, which pairs "a suitable glass of wine" with each course brought by "approachable staffers who never hover"; prices are enough to make "a mogul blanch", but you can always "go for the prix fixe lunch if you don't want to hock all your limbs."

Luna (La) ☒ | 24 | 16 | 18 | 63 |
69, rue du Rocher, 8ᵉ (Villiers), 01 42 93 77 61; fax 01 40 08 02 44
■ The "exceptionally talented" kitchen team at this New French seafooder stirs up culinary excitement in an otherwise "ho-hum" locale behind the Gare Saint-Lazare; some venture it's "one of the best fish restaurants in Paris", making it a hot table for a deep-pocketed lunchtime crowd as well as a smart bet for a dinner "date."

Lyonnais (Aux) ☒ | 22 | 20 | 20 | 51 |
32, rue St-Marc, 2ᵉ (Bourse/Richelieu-Drouot), 01 42 96 65 04; fax 01 42 97 42 95
■ "What a difference a new owner can make" – especially one named Alain Ducasse – say those who've noticed a "quantum leap" in the Lyonnais fare (the "quenelles melt in your mouth!") as well as a stylish "tidying up" of the vintage-bistro decor at this Bourse oldie; while the change (undertaken with Thierry de la Brosse, of Chez L'Ami Louis) has made this table a "tough ticket", devotees dig the newfound "buzz in the room" and "pleasant" staff, calling prices "reasonable" "considering the quality of the cuisine."

Ma Bourgogne ◐⊄ | 17 | 16 | 16 | 39 |
19, pl des Vosges, 4ᵉ (Bastille/St-Paul), 01 42 78 44 64; fax 01 42 78 19 37
◪ It's the "privilege of dining on the Place des Vosges" that makes this "highly trafficked" cash-only bistro worth its

| F | D | S | €C |

salt, especially when fair weather permits "alfresco" seating; though the "decor and service have worn a little thin", the "quintessential" classics, like "steak tartare", "eggs poached in red wine" and "gigantic salads", plus an "appealing" wine list, offer fitting compensation.

Macéo ⓢ   19 | 20 | 20 | 54
15, rue des Petits-Champs, 1ᵉʳ (Bourse/Palais Royal-Musée du Louvre), 01 42 97 53 85; fax 01 47 03 36 99; www.maceorestaurant.com

◪ Take a "wine suggestion from the skilled staff" and you're off to a flying start at oenophile Mark Williamson's (owner of nearby Willi's Wine Bar) eatery behind the Palais Royal; while some are more enthusiastic about the *vins,* "spacious" belle-époque room and "casual vibe" than the New and Classic French food, others "delight" in what's on their plate and are thankful that there's always a "very good vegetarian option."

MAGNOLIAS (LES) ⓢ   26 | 19 | 23 | 64
48, av de Bry, Perreux-sur-Marne (RER Nogent-le-Perreux), 01 48 72 47 43; fax 01 48 72 22 28; www.lesmagnolias.com

■ "Well-informed gastronomes" happily board the RER train to the eastern suburb of Perreux-sur-Marne to visit chef-owner Jean Chauvel's New French that's "wonderful in every way"; from the "highly innovative blends of flavors" woven into his edible "works of art" to the room overseen by Mme C. to the "astonishing bargain" at bill time, diners are in for a "incomparably" favorable experience.

Maharajah (Le) ◐   ▽ 15 | 8 | 13 | 34
72, bd St-Germain, 5ᵉ (Maubert-Mutualité/St-Michel), 01 43 54 26 07; fax 01 40 46 08 18

◪ While the room might be a little "chilly" and in need of a decorative jump-start, the "spices will warm your blood" at this Saint-Michel Indian that's one of the oldest of its ilk in town; the staff is "friendly", the prices suit the Latin Quarter collegiate crowd and vegetarian options abound.

Main d'Or (La) ◐ⓢ   – | – | – | M
133, rue du Faubourg St-Antoine, 11ᵉ (Faidherbe-Chaligny/Ledru-Rollin), 01 44 68 04 68; fax 01 44 68 04 68

"Terrific traditional Corsican food" ("the roast kid is a true delight") and wine "is worth the trek" out to this bastion near Bastille, where "the service is friendly, if a bit slow"; while the millstone-and-wrought-iron "setting is simple", a recent renovation "has improved the place somewhat with the addition of ventilation to chase away the cigarette smoke."

Maison Blanche   20 | 24 | 17 | 85
15, av Montaigne, 8ᵉ (Alma-Marceau), 01 47 23 55 99; fax 01 47 20 09 56; www.maison-blanche.fr

◪ No one disputes the "sumptuous view" of "Paris rooftops" from a "movie set"–like "all-white" room ("don't spill your

| F | D | S | €C |

wine!") at this *atelier* atop the Théâtre des Champs-Elysées; but while some find the Haute French cuisine "creative", more counter it "doesn't live up to expectations", given that the Pourcel twins (from Montpellier's acclaimed Jardin des Sens) are consultants; many also fault the "amateurish" service and "high prices", but it nonetheless remains a "chic" place to "see and be seen."

Maison Courtine (La) ⊠   22 | 15 | 19 | 49

157, av du Maine, 14ᵉ (Mouton-Duvernet), 01 45 48 08 04; fax 01 45 45 91 35

◪ "Like eating in the provinces" profess fans of this Southwestern in Montparnasse who'd rather keep quiet "so it's still possible to get a table"; the modern dining room with "decorative birds" isn't everyone's bag, but the "diverse wine list" and "bargain" tabs are universally pleasing.

Maison de l'Amérique Latine ⊠   ▽ 14 | 24 | 13 | 57

217, bd St-Germain, 7ᵉ (Rue du Bac/Solférino), 01 49 54 75 10; fax 01 40 49 03 94

◪ In summer, the "divine" garden terrace of this Latin-American cultural center housed in an elegant 18th-century mansion in Saint-Germain's diplomatic quarter is a "splendid" backdrop for a "peaceful" lunch or dinner, particularly when one "anticipates a proposal"; alas, the Classic French food can't quite compete with the surrounds, and prices are scaled to an expense-account clientele.

Maison du Caviar (La) ◐   19 | 12 | 21 | 95

21, rue Quentin Bauchart, 8ᵉ (George V), 01 47 23 53 43; fax 01 47 22 21 76

■ The "name says it all", as this longtime haunt for "caviar lovers and socialites" aptly situated in the push 8th is *the* place for "flawlessly" fresh fish eggs, plus salmon, the "best borsch" and, of course, Russian vodka; while time hasn't been kind to the decor, the "great" service and "animated" atmosphere remain, making this splurge "ideal for a quick lunch or a late supper after the movies or theater."

Maison du Jardin (La) ⊠   ▽ 24 | 17 | 22 | 43

27, rue de Vaugirard, 6ᵉ (Rennes/St-Placide), 01 45 48 22 31

■ From the owners of La Ferme St-Simon, this "charming" Left Bank bistro across the street from the Luxembourg Gardens is still a bit confidential, but those who've been say "the kitchen works with care" to arrive at "delicious" New French results; a room that's like a "civilized jewel box for grown-ups" and a "good value" prix fixe help make it a "favorite" "find."

Maison Prunier ⊠   22 | 25 | 22 | 70

16, av Victor Hugo, 16ᵉ (Charles de Gaulle-Etoile), 01 44 17 35 85; fax 01 44 17 90 10

■ The "gorgeous, admirably restored art deco interior" featuring mosaics of sea creatures mirrors the caviar and shellfish served at this 16th-arrondissement seafooder owned by Pierre Bergé, co-founder of Yves Saint Laurent; though not the temple of Haute gastronomy it was in its previous life, it remains a "magnificent", and "pricey", reminder of "les Années Folles."

Maison Rouge (La) ● | 12 | 19 | 13 | 45 |
13, rue des Archives, 4ᵉ (Hôtel-de-Ville), 01 42 71 69 69; fax 01 42 71 04 08

☑ The seductively "modern", almost-all-white dining room – don't let the 'red' in the name fool you – at this Marais youngster sets the perfect stage for a good-looking crowd intent on "being seen"; with respect to the Contemporary French cooking, however, this house is in need of some serious repair, as most politely describe their meal as "unmemorable", adding that the staff could renovate its "attitude" as well.

Mandalay (Le) ☒ | – | – | – | M |
35, rue Carnot, Levallois (Anatole France/Louise Michel), 01 45 57 68 69

Chef Guy Guenego, formerly at L'Orénoc, goes out on his own with this tremendously popular suburbanite in Levallois-Perret whose Eclectic menu visits all points of the compass, from Brittany to Japan, along with stops in Africa, India and the Seychelles; the small dining room is dominated by brown and mauve tones and furnished with metal chairs and miscellaneous ethnic art, and the service is well-informed – a good thing, since dishes like shellfish ravioli 'blanquette style' need explanation.

Mandarin de Neuilly ☒ | – | – | – | M |
148, av Charles de Gaulle, Neuilly (Pont-de-Neuilly), 01 46 24 11 80

"This little Chinese in Neuilly has a good reputation" for serving "consistently" "high-quality" Szechuan dishes, including "excellent chef specials", at "prices that are reasonable for the neighborhood"; true, the decor's drab, but it's "comfortable" and come summer, the outdoor deck is fit for a mandarin's repose.

Man Ray | 15 | 23 | 13 | 59 |
34, rue Marbeuf, 8ᵉ (Franklin D. Roosevelt), 01 56 88 36 36; fax 01 42 25 36 36; www.manray.info

☑ "Go for a drink to see what the hoopla is about" – i.e. the "impressive" transporting decor and people-watching potential that keep this celebrity-backed club/restaurant off the Champs perennially on the radar; critics kvetch that the "glitz can't hide" that the Eclectic fare is "nothing special", not to mention "overpriced" for what it is, and service "shaky"; yet, it's a "scene" – albeit a "touristy" one now – particularly once the "DJ pumps" up some very loud house music.

| F | D | S | €C |

Mansouria ⌧ | 22 | 17 | 18 | 41 |
11, rue Faidherbe, 11ᵉ (Faidherbe-Chaligny), 01 43 71 00 16; fax 01 40 24 21 97

■ It's "always a treat" to "feast" on the "extremely large portions" of "flavorful" couscous and "excellent tagines" at this "tastefully" decorated Moroccan; near Place de la Nation, it's "worth the detour if you like to travel" without loading up your caravan for the Dark Continent.

Manufacture (La) ⌧   ▽ | 23 | 21 | 16 | 38 |
20, esplanade de la Manufacture, Issy-les-Moulineaux (Corentin-Celton/Porte de Versailles), 01 40 93 08 98; fax 01 40 93 57 22; www.restaurantmanufacture.com

■ The "exceptional setting" of this "trendy" retrofitted tobacco factory in Issy-les-Moulineaux makes it popular with an aesthetically sensitive clientele, who likewise appreciate the "lusty" New Bistro cooking off "a menu that changes with the seasons" – and for which, given its quality, "you'd pay twice as much for in Paris" itself.

Maoh Noodles Bar ⌧   ▽ | 13 | 20 | 12 | 28 |
6, rue du Cdt-Pilot, Neuilly (Les Sablons), 01 47 47 19 94; fax 01 47 38 60 49

◪ Some say the "sophisticated, cool interior" of this large noodle bar seems "incongruous", given its location in staid "suburban Neuilly", but the concept is "unique" and welcomed by the locals, who commend the "fresh" ingredients and "large choice of teas", even if the fare seems "more like trendy stir-fry" than authentic Asian.

Marée (La) ⌧ | 24 | 17 | 23 | 95 |
1, rue Daru, 8ᵉ (Ternes), 01 43 80 20 00; fax 01 48 88 04 04

■ This "impeccably in-the-swim" Traditional French *poissonerie* near the Place des Ternes serves "spectacular and titanic fish" accompanied by a "great wine list"; although prices could send you scrambling for a lifeboat, most among the heavily local crowd feel it's "worth" it for such a "pleasant dining experience" that's nurtured by "heartwarming management and staff."

Marée de Versailles ⌧ | 21 | 21 | 19 | 46 |
22, rue au Pain, Versailles (RER Versailles-Rive Droite), 01 30 21 73 73; fax 01 39 49 98 29

■ Versailles may be landlocked, but this midsize seafood specialist reels in fish fans with luxury specimens, including lots of lobster; the nautical decor helps set the mood, and there's a "delightful terrace" for deck-inclined diners.

Mariage Frères | 19 | 20 | 19 | 30 |
30, rue du Bourg-Tibourg, 4ᵉ (Hôtel-de-Ville), 01 42 72 28 11; fax 01 42 74 51 68
13, rue des Grands-Augustins, 6ᵉ (St-Michel), 01 40 51 82 50; fax 01 44 07 07 52

| F | D | S | €C |

(continued)
Mariage Frères
260, rue du Faubourg St-Honoré, 8ᵉ (Ternes), 01 46 22 18 54; fax 01 42 67 18 54
www.mariagefreres.com

■ "Forget London – the best afternoon tea" some swear is served at this chainlet of "posh" importers/salons with an "overwhelming" selection of blends as well as "sublime" pastries, "inventive sandwiches and salads"; "waiters clad in linen suits" contribute to the "elegant" "Colonial" atmosphere, as they impart their knowledge on the basics of brewing; P.S. try to "go early" for weekend brunch, lest the queues cause you to steep your "golden leaves" at home.

Marius
22 | 15 | 17 | 53

82, bd Murat, 16ᵉ (Porte de St-Cloud), 01 46 51 67 80; fax 01 47 43 10 24

■ In the 16th, this "handsome" oceanic address is "never empty because the fish are prepared to perfection", with some finding their way into a justly famous bouillabaisse; most concede it's a "solid value" relative to the first-rate catch, and the "attentive" service ensures smooth sailing.

Marius et Janette
21 | 17 | 18 | 75

4, av George V, 8ᵉ (Alma-Marceau), 01 47 23 84 36; fax 01 47 23 84 36

☑ This Neptunian lair by the Seine in the 8th has built a reputation on "delicious seafood" and "personality"-sightings amid a "goofy" nautical decor of portholes and knotty-pine paneling; mutineers claim "it's overrated", citing "perfunctory" service and elevated prices, and with "high noise and table density", it's not a place for intimate conversation; but such energy, along with a side of "wonderful oysters", is sure to "raise your spirits."

MARKET
22 | 23 | 19 | 70

15, av Matignon, 8ᵉ (Champs-Elysées-Clemenceau), 01 56 43 40 90; fax 01 63 59 10 87; www.jean-georges.com

☑ Housed in the Christie's building in the 8th, "his majesty Jean-Georges Vongerichten's" first eatery in his homeland channels "NYC-cool" via its "sleek", "minimalist" decor and "imaginative", "Asian-influenced" Eclectic eats that allow diners to "discover new flavors"; as at his stateside restaurants, the clientele counts many "cool dudes and beautiful chicks" who turn a blind eye toward "inconsistent" bumps in the kitchen and blips in the service, heralding it as a "hip" place that's also handy "for Sundays."

Marlotte (La)
17 | 15 | 17 | 40

55, rue du Cherche-Midi, 6ᵉ (Sèvres-Babylone/St-Placide), 01 45 48 86 79; fax 01 45 44 34 80; www.lamarlotte.com

■ "Quintessentially Parisian" and ever "reliable", this Classic French near the Bon Marché is a "busy place"

F | **D** | **S** | **€C**

thanks to its "high-quality" cooking (including "excellent lamb"), "appealingly rustic" decor and the "charming family that runs it"; though you may hear "more English than French" at the tables on some days, the prices are decent in any language.

Martel (Le) ◐ — | — | — | M
3, rue Martel, 10ᵉ (Château d'Eau), 01 47 70 67 56
"Owner Mehdi Gana" maintains the "sweet ambiance" at this "trendy", if buzzingly "noisy", low-lit spot in the increasingly hip 10th that specializes in "copious portions" of "simple" North African dishes like couscous, tagines and grilled meats, plus some Classic French offerings, at gentle prices.

Marty ◐ 17 | 19 | 15 | 46
20, av des Gobelins, 5ᵉ (Les Gobelins), 01 43 31 39 51; fax 01 43 37 63 70; www.marty-restaurant.com
◧ The "beautiful" art deco decor is the "best part of the experience" at this circa-1913 and still independently owned brasserie at Les Gobelins; but while the "shellfish stand outside is inviting" and there are some "old classics" to be had, most lament that the food is merely "fair" with service that's equally "lackluster."

Mascotte (La) ⌧ — | — | — | E
270, rue du Faubourg St-Honoré, 8ᵉ (Ternes), 01 42 27 75 26; fax 01 40 31 15 06
Regulars tick off several "reasons why it's increasingly difficult to find a table" at this "reliable old bistro" in a "nice area" near the Place des Ternes: "well-prepared Classic French food" (based on "great meat"), "good wine and friendly service" overseen by a "professional boss."

Mascotte (La) ◐ — | — | — | M
52, rue des Abbesses, 18ᵉ (Abbesses/Blanche), 01 46 06 28 15; fax 01 42 23 93 83
"Decorating is not a concept that crossed the door" here, but that doesn't deter Montmartre denizens from seeking "a refuge against the increasing trendiness of the *quartier*" at this Auvergnat brasserie that traffics in "great, little wines by the glass" and "solid, authentic traditional food from the Massif Central"; it also boasts "the only shellfish stand" on the Rue des Abbesses.

Mathusalem (Le) ⌧ 18 | 12 | 15 | 41
5 bis, bd Exelmans, 16ᵉ (Exelmans), 01 42 88 10 73; fax 01 45 25 81 07; www.mathusalem.fr
■ Situated "in a lost corner of the 16th", this "amiable" bistro is a "typical" "neighborhood place", dishing up consistently "solid" Classic French fare like a "tempting tête de veau" from time to time; a "friendly owner who greets everyone" and "correct prices for what you get" make it the kind of place you "return to with pleasure."

	F	D	S	€C

Matsuri   15 | 16 | 13 | 31
36, rue de Richelieu, 1ᵉʳ (Pyramides), 01 42 61 05 73; fax 01 42 33 10 38 🗵
2, rue de Passy, 16ᵉ (Passy), 01 42 24 96 85; fax 01 42 24 14 54 ☽
◪ The "recently redone dark-wood-and-mauve decor" has gentrified this pair of sushi sisters in the 1st and the 16th that converts call standbys for "good, basic meals" of maki; but malcontents mutter that the little morsels' emergence on an "automatic conveyor belt", while "entertaining", "perfectly represents their industrial taste."

Maupertu (Le)   19 | 14 | 22 | 42
94, bd de La Tour-Maubourg, 7ᵉ (Ecole Militaire/ La Tour-Maubourg), 01 45 51 37 96; fax 01 45 50 26 70; www.restaurant-maupertu-paris.com
■ "Delightful owners" Sophie and Alain de Guest offer "good-humored" "personal service" at their "quiet place" known for its highly "tasty" "Traditional French cuisine at reasonable prices"; the interior itself "isn't much to look at", but it does boast "a lovely view of the dome of Les Invalides", especially when "reflecting the rays of the setting sun"; so most praise their "pleasant" time here as "worth every penny."

Mauzac (Le) 🗵   ▽ 15 | 11 | 12 | 30
7, rue de l'Abbé de l'Epée, 5ᵉ (Luxembourg), 01 46 33 75 22; fax 01 46 33 25 46
◪ A recent change in ownership has many regulars railing that this wine bar/bistro near the Luxembourg Gardens has "lost its charm" and now serves "only average" "Traditional French cuisine"; but more short-memoried supporters find the combination of "private labels" and "generous portions" a recipe for "total relaxation."

Mavrommatis   19 | 14 | 16 | 42
42, rue Daubenton, 5ᵉ (Censier-Daubenton), 01 43 31 17 17; fax 01 43 36 13 08; www.mavrommatis.fr
■ The "authentic old-world charm" of this Greek in the Latin Quarter comes from its "understated decor of crocheted curtains, ficus trees" and sepia photos, plus some "superb" cooking that "updates the classics with real verve" ("you have to try the zucchini and eggplant moussaka"); "owned by a well-known Cypriot caterer", it's "a little expensive", but "probably the best [of its ilk] in town."

MAXIM'S 🗵   20 | 22 | 21 | 84
3, rue Royale, 8ᵉ (Concorde/Madeleine), 01 42 65 27 94; fax 01 42 65 30 26
Aérogare Orly Ouest, Orly (Orly Ouest par liaison OrlyVal), 01 49 75 16 78; fax 01 46 87 05 39
◪ Even if she's "past her prime" – after all, she is 112 – this "famous" grande dame off the Place de la Concorde (with an outpost at Orly) remains "a special place", not just "for

get updates at zagat.com

F D S €C

nostalgia" but also for "surprisingly" "quite good" Classic French fare fans find; the irreverent retort "everything here seems worn, even the friendly service" and the "art nouveau decor, lovely" as it may be; still, it remains "a must, at least once" – perhaps on "Friday nights, when it transforms into an exotic club" frequented by *le tout* Paris.

Méditerranée (La)   20 | 20 | 19 | 63
2, pl de l'Odéon, 6ᵉ (Odéon), 01 43 26 02 30; fax 01 43 26 18 44; www.la-mediterranee.com
■ "The light Cocteau-esque decor" ("Cocteau actually designed the tableware and menus") lends a *la-vie-en-rose* atmosphere to this "specialist in fish dishes" "overlooking the Place de l'Odéon"; while "it's worth it for the refreshingly elegant decor" alone, the cuisine "has improved in the last few years" and is now "very nice", especially the signature "superb bouillabaisse" proffered by a "proud staff."

Mesturet (Le) ⌧   – | – | – | M
77, rue de Richelieu, 2ᵉ (Bourse), 01 42 97 40 68; fax 01 42 97 40 68
Located in the heart of town not far from the Bourse, the old Paris stock exchange, and featuring modest prices on Traditional French dishes, this cafe/bistro has quickly become a hit with bankers and brokers at noon, and locals seeking supper at night; despite lots of hustle and bustle, the service is good-natured and the atmosphere friendly.

MEURICE (LE)   25 | 28 | 26 | 108
Hôtel Meurice, 228, rue de Rivoli, 1ᵉʳ (Concorde/Tuileries), 01 44 58 10 55; fax 01 44 58 10 76; www.meuricehotel.com
■ This "regal" Right Bank dining room, with a mélange of mirrors, marble, crystal chandeliers, painted ceilings and ormolu ("could this be Versailles?"), "comes very close to perfection"; the arrival of chef Yannick Alléno (ex Les Muses) has made this Haute Cuisine table "a must-try for foodies" as he dazzles with dishes that display culinary "creativity" in "picture-perfect presentations"; "impeccable service" "puts everyone at ease here", and if the tabs are "eye-popping", they're "worth every euro."

MICHEL ROSTANG ⌧   27 | 23 | 26 | 139
20, rue Rennequin, 17ᵉ (Pereire/Ternes), 01 47 63 40 77; fax 01 47 63 82 75; www.michelrostang.com
■ "A first-class experience from start to finish" carol converts about Michel Rostang's New French in the 17th, where "big flavors and complex sauces" – "especially fine when game [or truffles] are in season" – reign in a "luxurious setting" of paneling, porcelains and paintings; the servers are all "polished professionals", especially the "superb sommeliers", who act "friendly even if you're not a regular" – though it's certainly worth becoming one, "if you can afford it."

| F | D | S | €C |

Mirama
| 20 | 5 | 11 | 23 |

17, rue St-Jacques, 5ᵉ (Maubert-Mutualité/St-Michel), 01 43 54 71 77; fax 01 43 25 37 63

◪ Ok, "the decor is nonexistent" and the "waiters surly, but just try and get a table" at this "old and known" Latin Quarter Chinese; the secret is in the "amazing food" "that's not like anywhere else – it's better" – and at bargain-basement prices too; just remember, if the service seems "pressed", it's to "clear spaces for those in the long line", "drooling outside the window."

Moissonnier ⌧
| 21 | 15 | 20 | 42 |

28, rue des Fossés St-Bernard, 5ᵉ (Cardinal Lemoine/Jussieu), 01 43 29 87 65; fax 01 43 29 87 65

■ "Year after year, the menu remains true to" "hearty Lyonnais cooking" – "oeufs en meurette (poached eggs in red-wine-and-bacon sauce)", "real quenelles" and a whole heaping table of "traditional hors d'oeuvres" – which explains the enduring popularity of this "old standard" bistro in the 5th; its "simple decor makes you feel like you're in the provinces" circa 1962 (as does the "smoky atmosphere"), and with its moderate prices, it's perfect for those craving a "culinary cocooning" in "heavy cream and sauces."

Monsieur Lapin
| 21 | 20 | 20 | 40 |

11, rue Raymond Losserand, 14ᵉ (Gaîté/Pernety), 01 43 20 21 39; fax 01 43 21 84 86

■ "There are bunnies everywhere" decorating the walls and the plates at this veteran Traditional French "jewel in Montparnasse"; happy hares hop over for the "charming service" and the "delectable food, even for non-rabbit eaters", topped off by "very reasonable prices."

Montalembert (Le)
| 15 | 21 | 18 | 54 |

Hôtel Montalembert, 3, rue de Montalembert, 7ᵉ (Rue du Bac), 01 45 49 68 03; fax 01 45 49 69 49; www.montalembert.com

◪ Mainstay of Saint-Germain's publishers, antique dealers and fashionistas, this "chic but expensive" ground-floor dining room is known for providing an "excellent hotel lunch" of French fare with an innovative touch; but while most appreciate the "minimalist charm" of Christian Liaigre's decor (and the "pretty patio"), malcontents mutter the designer's "magic no longer works" to overcome only "ok food."

Mont Liban (Le)
| – | – | – | I |

42, bd des Batignolles, 17ᵉ (Rome), 01 45 22 35 01; fax 01 43 87 04 59

In a bustling part of the 17th, this ethnic watering hole is "a real steal for great Lebanese food" ("the falafel sandwich is so inexpensive they practically give it away") and native wines, served in a smiling, familial atmosphere; the deals are so good, devotees disregard the nondescript digs.

get updates at zagat.com

| F | D | S | €C |

Montparnasse 25 (Le) ⓈΔ ▽ 23 | 21 | 23 | 67
Le Méridien-Montparnasse, 19, rue du Cdt. René Mouchotte, 14ᵉ (Montparnasse-Bienvenüe), 01 44 36 44 25; fax 01 44 36 49 03; www.lemeridien-montparnasse.com
■ For a "luxurious experience", sink "into the comfort of deep chairs and the silence of well-spaced tables" that characterize the Méridien-Montparnasse's second-floor, '20s-style (hence the name) dining room; the Haute Cuisine hits some as "a little expensive", but everyone raves about the "memorable cheese platter", accompanied by "a surprisingly rich commentary."

Mon Vieil Ami – | – | – | M
69, rue St-Louis-en-l'Ile, 4ᵉ (Hôtel-de-Ville/St-Michel), 01 40 46 01 35; fax 01 40 46 01 36
In a handsome setting of glass-paneled walls trimmed with black mock timbering – a stylized reference to the construction of this ancient Ile Saint-Louis home – this Contemporary Bistro is off to a hot start, helmed by a young chef who was second-in-command to owner Antoine Westermann, chef of Strasbourg's acclaimed Buerehiesel; under a beamed ceiling, diners can choose to sit at either a long ebony-stained *table d'hôte* or at regular tables to feast on follow-the-market prix fixes and plats du jour.

MOULIN À VENT 25 | 17 | 22 | 51
"CHEZ HENRI" (AU) ⓈΔ
20, rue des Fossés St-Bernard, 5ᵉ (Cardinal Lemoine/Jussieu), 01 43 54 99 37; fax 01 40 46 92 23
■ The "decor hasn't changed in decades – and it shouldn't" in this "oh-so-French" vet that offers "everything you want in a Classic Bistro" (including a typical "Parisian staff"); "always reserve ahead", because it's "filled with meat-eating locals" of the arty 5th, devouring "the best entrecôte in town."

Moulin de la Galette (Le) – | – | – | M
83, rue Lepic, 18ᵉ (Abbesses/Lamarck-Caulaincourt), 01 46 06 84 77; fax 01 46 06 84 78
With a "great location at the top of Montmartre", this Classic French has undergone "a renaissance", thanks to a revamp last summer; the combination of a new modern interior and "nice garden patio" in the shadow of a landmarked mill makes for "stunning atmosphere"; it's an ideal place for a "reasonably priced" "romantic dinner" or a "pleasurable Sunday brunch."

Murat (Le) ☉ 13 | 16 | 13 | 52
1, bd Murat, 16ᵉ (Porte d'Auteuil), 01 46 51 33 17; fax 01 53 17 88 54
◪ Yes, this is "one more Costes place [geared] for small appetites and showing off", but still its "kitschy" digs are "always filled" with the "air-kissing" "16th arrondissement 'in'-crowd", which claims the Classic French cuisine (with

| F | D | S | €C |

some Asian touches) is "good despite the malicious gossip"; the unmollified mutter over the "mediocre food" and "itchy service", but on the plus side, it's "kid-tolerant" and for those "who have no problem forking out the euros, valet parking is available."

Muscade – | – | – | M

36, rue Montpensier, 1er (Palais Royal-Musée du Louvre/Pyramides), 01 42 97 51 36; fax 01 42 97 51 36
The wonderful setting at the Palais Royal makes this "cozy" eatery/tearoom definitely "worth the trek"; its Classic Bistro fare, "well-prepared seafood" and "big salads" can easily make it a "lunch staple in the summertime" especially if you can "score a table outside" amid the historical gardens where the writer Colette lived for many years.

Muses (Les) ⌕ 27 | 16 | 23 | 96

Hôtel Scribe, 1, rue Scribe, 9e (Opéra), 01 44 71 24 26; fax 01 44 71 24 64; www.sofitel.com
◪ Despite a "basement location" that's "a little oppressive", this "quiet, high-quality" "restaurant in the Hôtel Scribe" near the Opéra Garnier "does not disappoint", thanks to its "enchanting", "creative" Haute Cuisine and "wonderful staff", including an "outstanding sommelier"; it's "a bit expensive", though connoisseurs commend the (relative) "bargain four-course lunch."

Natacha ●⌕ 17 | 15 | 17 | 53

17 bis, rue Campagne-Première, 14e (Raspail), 01 43 20 79 27; fax 01 43 22 93 97
◪ Even though namesake-owner Natacha is no longer there, this dual-level Montparnasse hangout "with a history as a celebrity hot spot" continues to exhibit "more attitude than a drag queen with a broken heel"; but while devotees dig the "deep, dark and sexy" decor and "typical Classic French cuisine", the jaded jeer "oh, how the trendy have fallen": these days, it's all "average food" and "people looking at people looking for stars."

Natachef ⌕ 16 | 14 | 13 | 45

9, rue Duban, 16e (La Muette), 01 42 88 10 15; fax 01 45 25 74 71
■ In a residential quarter, this "tiny" establishment offers "a short menu" of "original", market-fresh–oriented Classic French fare, served at "often-changing", "inventive table settings" overseen by the "smiling owner" Nathalie Vigato ("wife of the Apicius chef"); although the tab "has gone up", it's still "reasonably priced", and "the new mommies of the 16th" appreciate that "you can take cooking lessons."

Nemrod (Le) ⌕ 15 | 9 | 14 | 26

51, rue du Cherche-Midi, 6e (Sèvres-Babylone/St-Placide), 01 45 48 17 05; fax 01 45 48 17 83; www.lenemrod.com
◪ "Great for lunch when shopping" around the Bon Marché store, this "fun" "neighborhood favorite" offers "lots of

F	D	S	€C

choice" to "refill you", from "good Auvergnat products" like "gigantic steaks" to "copious salads", all at "cheap" prices and slung by "friendly servers"; just "stay away if you're hard of hearing" 'cuz it gets "very crowded and noisy" at noontime.

New Jawad ● ▽ 17 | 13 | 18 | 38

12, av Rapp, 7ᵉ (Alma-Marceau), 01 47 05 91 37;
fax 01 45 50 31 27

☑ Perhaps the decor's a bit bland, but don't worry – the place is "better than it looks" promise patrons of this Pakistani-Indian in the 7th that serves "surprisingly good" food "365 days a year"; the "staff's very friendly" and the check's "extremely reasonable", so go ahead and shoot the ja-wad on the "authentic" eats.

New Nioullaville ● ▽ 17 | 8 | 11 | 31

32-34, rue de l'Orillon, 11ᵉ (Belleville), 01 40 21 96 18;
fax 01 40 21 96 58

☑ With "trolleys of dim sum rolling around the tables", this "huge", funky Belleville space is "one of the most authentic" "carnivals of Chinese cuisine" (plus some Thai and Vietnamese) in Paris; some dis the digs, claiming it's "better to block out the decor", but most find that "for the price, this is a welcome, exotic outing."

Noces de Jeannette (Les) – | – | – | M

14, rue Favart, 2ᵉ (Richelieu-Drouot), 01 42 96 36 89;
fax 01 47 03 97 31; www.lesnocesdejeannette.com

"Tourists come by the busload" to this century-old standby, since it's situated conveniently near 2nd-arrondissement theaters and its several "pleasant" salons are decorated in different florid styles; featuring well-priced classics like duck à l'orange, the Classic Bistro cuisine is quite "correct, if nothing more."

No Stress Café – | – | – | E

2, pl Gustave Toudouze, 9ᵉ (St-Georges), 01 48 78 00 27

A touch of Tangiers in the 9th's theater district, this latenight watering hole (bar closes 2 AM) also serves "nice" Eclectic fare earlier in the eve – from Chinese stir-fries to burgers, "delicious salads" to Traditional French dishes – in a Moroccan-inspired setting; stressed-out surveyors who sigh it's "way overpriced" can relax with an in-house, inchair shiatsu massage and tarot-card readings (several times a week), or get fresh air on the large terrace.

Noura 19 | 13 | 15 | 34

29, bd des Italiens, 2ᵉ (Opéra/Richelieu-Drouot),
01 53 43 00 53
121, bd du Montparnasse, 6ᵉ (Vavin), 01 43 20 19 19;
fax 01 43 20 05 40 ●
21, av Marceau, 16ᵉ (Alma-Marceau/George V), 01 47 20 33 33;
fax 01 47 20 60 31 ●

| F | D | S | €C |

(continued)
Noura
27, av Marceau, 16ᵉ (Alma-Marceau/George V), 01 47 03 02 20; www.noura.fr

◪ "Some of the best Lebanese fare in Paris" is the buzz about these "authentic" Middle Eastern enclaves issuing "exquisite" eats to an often "packed" and "noisy" crowd (leaving the "servers to do what they can"); the more "upscale" experience at the 21 Avenue Marceau original (Noura Pavillon) "comes at a higher price" than at its informal offshoots; P.S. "great takeout, too."

Nouveau Village Tao-Tao ◐ ▽ 18 | 12 | 15 | 39
159, bd Vincent Auriol, 13ᵉ (Nationale), 01 45 86 40 08; fax 01 45 86 46 21

◪ Tucked deep in the 13th, this Thai-tinged Chinese offers a "wide choice" of "agreeable" dishes; satisfied villagers Tao-t the "cheaply priced Peking duck" and choose "not to be put off" by the "rather unsophisticated" digs.

O à la Bouche (L') ⌧ | 18 | 12 | 12 | 43 |
124, bd du Montparnasse, 14ᵉ (Vavin), 01 56 54 01 55; fax 01 43 21 07 87

◪ "As neighborhood bistros go, this is wonderful" vow voters who make "the long trek" down Montparnasse's eponymous boulevard for chef Franck Paquier's "creative" New French cooking that's a "very good value"; on the down side, word of mouth is that service is so-so and decor "remains a little sad."

Obélisque (L') | 23 | 20 | 24 | 71 |
Hôtel de Crillon, 10, pl de la Concorde, 8ᵉ (Concorde), 01 44 71 15 15; fax 01 44 71 15 02; www.crillon.com

■ "An excellent alternative to its stratospherically priced peers", this "elegant" but "comfortable setting" located "discreetly" within the posh Hôtel de Crillon offers "a first-class meal" in the Classic French style; the "superb, warm service" adds to the "luxuriously Parisian" experience, so much so that "it's hard to leave."

Oeillade (L') ⌧ | 16 | 12 | 14 | 43 |
10, rue de St-Simon, 7ᵉ (Rue du Bac/Solférino), 01 42 22 01 60

◪ Though "low on decor", this "friendly neighborhood" Classic Bistro is a pleasant "place to unwind" according to followers who favor its fresh flower arrangements and "authentic, old-fashioned" cuisine; sure, it may be a bit "boring", but being a bona fide "bang for the buck" makes it "a place worth going back to."

Oenothèque (L') ⌧ | – | – | – | M |
20, rue St-Lazare, 9ᵉ (Notre-Dame-de-Lorette), 01 48 78 08 76; fax 01 40 16 10 27; www.oenotheque.fr

Eager oenophiles enjoy this small wine bar near the Saint-Lazare train station, where the "chatty owner" showcases his sensibly priced sipping selections (available by the bottle or glass) with Traditional French food considered "ok but nothing special"; while some have been "disappointed" recently by "iffy service", more-wine and less-whine types insist "don't miss the place."

Oïshi ◐ — | — | — | M
106, rue de Richelieu, 2ᵉ (Richelieu-Drouot), 01 42 96 45 94; fax 01 42 96 43 58
"Oïshi means delicious in Japanese", and though the "basic" bites at this bento box near the Grands Boulevards may "not be the best" translation, at least the fare – from sushi to sukiyaki – is "fresh"; what's more, the rather "sedate" setting is offset by "comfortable seating" and a "pleasant staff."

Olivades (Les) ⌧ 21 | 15 | 17 | 48
41, av de Ségur, 7ᵉ (Ségur/St-François-Xavier), 01 47 83 70 09; fax 01 42 73 04 75
■ "Still stellar despite the departure" of chef Flora Mikula, this "tiny" Traditional French presents tempting "tastes of Provence" in a "posh residential neighborhood" near the Ecole Militaire; the "accommodating" staff tends the "well-heeled Americans" and "chic" locals who happily squeeze into "tight tables" for a "truly delightful" experience.

Opportun (L') ◐⌧ — | — | — | M
64, bd Edgar Quinet, 14ᵉ (Edgar Quinet), 01 43 20 26 89; fax 01 43 21 61 88
"Authentic cooking" and "fresh products" characterize this small, wallet-friendly Lyonnais bistro just behind the Tour Montparnasse, which serves regional specialties like sweetbreads fricassee and Royan ravioli; all in all, an "excellent" address for "Beaujolais, meat, cognac and a cigar with pals."

Orangerie (L') ◐ 22 | 23 | 22 | 84
28, rue St-Louis-en-l'Ile, 4ᵉ (Pont-Marie), 01 46 33 93 98
◪ A "great find" in the "quaint neighborhood" of the Ile Saint-Louis, this once "very in", "old-style" Classic French has lost some of its star sizzle (now actor-owner Jean-Claude Brialy only hosts "film people from time to time"); but it remains "one of the most romantic restaurants in Paris", complete with "gorgeous flowers", "wonderful" food and "personal" service; claustrophobic critics caution that the "cozy" space is really "too cramped": "I wanted a tête-à-tête with my husband, not the guy at the next table."

Orenoc (L') 21 | 22 | 18 | 57
Le Méridien Etoile, 81, bd Gouvion St-Cyr, 17ᵉ (Porte Maillot), 01 40 68 30 40; fax 01 40 68 30 81; www.lemeridien-etoile.com
■ On the ground floor of the refurbished Méridien Etoile near the Porte Maillot, this "beautiful" dining room serves "incredible" Classic French cuisine with "innovative"

| F | D | S | €C |

international influences in a "lovely" room crafted in "exotic wood"; all told, it's a "pleasant surprise" and an ideal place for a "business lunch" – especially if you can write it off.

Orient-Extrême ●⊠ | 19 | 16 | 15 | 48 |
4, rue Bernard Palissy, 6ᵉ (St-Germain-des-Prés), 01 45 48 92 27; fax 01 45 48 20 94

◪ This "hip" Japanese in the center of Saint-Germain-des-Prés is often filled with "show-biz stars" who come for "refined", "fresh fish" dishes and "very good sushi" that's "better than most" admirers insist; however, those oriented toward negativity say the "rather expensive" tabs are too extrême for what they maintain is "mediocre" fare.

Ormes (Les) ⊠ | – | – | – | M |
8, rue Chapu, 16ᵉ (Exelmans), 01 46 47 83 98; fax 01 46 47 83 98

There's a "chef to watch" at this "real discovery" in the "outermost reaches" of the 16th: "shy but extremely gifted" Stéphane Molé (ex Jamin), who creates "superb" contemporary Haute Cuisine that's presented by a "warm, hospitable" staff; if the "provincial-looking dining room" is just "too tiny", it's a small sacrifice for "top-drawer" food at reasonable rates.

Os à Moëlle (L') ⊠ | 23 | 13 | 19 | 44 |
3, rue Vasco de Gama, 15ᵉ (Lourmel), 01 45 57 27 27; fax 01 45 57 28 00

■ This "diamond in the rough" (aka "hole-in-the-wall") is "always packed" with "lots of buzz from the many locals" who trek deep into the distant 15th for chef-owner Thierry Faucher's "fabulous" Traditional French fare that's "on the inventive side" thanks to a daily changing menu; ok, it's "out of the way" and "tables are tight", but the "service makes you feel like a regular" and gentle prices translate to "one of the greatest bangs for the buck in Paris."

Ostéria (L') ⊠ | 23 | 12 | 17 | 49 |
10, rue de Sévigné, 4ᵉ (St-Paul), 01 42 71 37 08; fax 01 48 06 27 71

◪ "Don't be discouraged by the decor or the wait" when you march to the Marais for this Italian "treasure", considered one of the "best-kept secrets in Paris"; the staff can be "aloof", but the "fresh and delicious" food (the "daily risotto is a must") is ever-present.

Osteria Ascolani ●⊟ | – | – | – | I |
98, rue des Martyrs, 18ᵉ (Abbesses/Pigalle), 01 42 62 43 94

This simply decorated new Italian on a fashionable street in increasingly trendy Montmartre draws an arty, young crowd that appreciates the value prices; while the menu does not provide any choices, what leisurely comes to the table usually appeals to a wide array of appetites; book

get updates at zagat.com 143

early to avoid the smoky atmosphere that develops as the night goes on.

Oulette (L') ⓈУ   21 | 16 | 20 | 48
15, pl Lachambeaudie, 12ᵉ (Cour St-Emilion/Dugommier), 01 40 02 02 12; fax 01 40 02 04 77; www.l-oulette.com
■ A "fantastic" find turning out "tasty" Southwestern specialties at "reasonable prices", this "snug little place" is "worth the trip off the beaten path" to the increasingly trendy 12th; the owners' "warm welcome" adds a personal touch that offsets the sometimes "slow service."

Oum el Banine Ⓢ   – | – | – | E
16 bis, rue Dufrenoy, 16ᵉ (Porte Dauphine/Rue de la Pompe), 01 45 04 91 22; fax 01 45 03 46 26
Creating "colorful zest" in the 16th, this "authentic" Moroccan is known for its "cozy" space, "friendly welcome" from the owner and "delicious cuisine", including couscous *mechoui* (roasted lamb) and classic tagines; P.S. if you feel like staying at home, "you can even have it delivered" (if it's a large order) – something that's not run of the mill in the City of Lights.

Palanquin (Le) Ⓢ   ▽ 13 | 14 | 16 | 32
12, rue Princesse, 6ᵉ (Mabillon/St-Germain-des-Prés), 01 43 29 77 66; www.lepalanquin.com
◪ "For something completely different" amid the bustle of Saint-Germain, try this "oasis of calm" that offers "authentic Vietnamese" victuals at "reasonable prices", though also in "paltry portions"; "gracious servers" add to the relaxing experience.

Pamphlet (Le) ●Ⓢ   21 | 18 | 20 | 42
38, rue Debelleyme, 3ᵉ (Filles-du-Calvaire), 01 42 72 39 24
■ The innlike "dining room's attractive and the service good, but the star is the food" at this "savory" Basque in the trendy Marais; it "gets much press" for its "novel takes on traditional Southwestern dishes", and folks are also willing "to write home about" the fact that "the price is right."

Paolo Petrini Ⓢ   20 | 6 | 15 | 60
6, rue du Débarcadère, 17ᵉ (Argentine/Porte Maillot), 01 45 74 25 95; fax 01 45 74 12 95
◪ Behind the Porte Maillot, this "calm, classy" vintage Italian is one of "the best on the Right Bank", offering "terrific" eats ("don't miss the truffle menu at the end of the year") and "attentive" service, which alleviates the "expensive" tab; an "old-fashioned", "depressing decor" is the main drawback (a redo was due at press time).

Papinou   – | – | – | M
26, rue du Château, Neuilly (Pont de Neuilly), 01 55 24 90 40
Recently taken over by Christian Constant (Le Violon d'Ingres), this Neuilly outpost is now a "super address for

good, down-to-earth" Classic Bistro cuisine, served in a "typical Gallic ambiance" – either on the ground floor decorated with wooden beams and a bar, or in the darker wine cellar where you can pick among a "large choice of reasonably priced" labels; whichever you choose, the "endearing service" "warrants a return visit."

Paradis Thai | – | – | – | M |
132, rue de Tolbiac, 13ᵉ (Tolbiac), 01 45 83 22 26
This two-story Thai temple, equipped with golden Buddhas and native decorations, serves up "spicy" Siamese savories near Chinatown; as a "reliable" source for something "different", certainly "it's a good idea for the area", even if, some sniff, the cuisine itself is "not very distinctive."

Parc aux Cerfs (Le) | ▽ 15 | 13 | 17 | 42 |
50, rue Vavin, 6ᵉ (Notre-Dame-des-Champs/Vavin),
01 43 54 87 83; fax 01 43 26 42 86
■ Behind the Luxembourg gardens, this Montparnasse "favorite" is a "good choice for a well-prepared", if "rather Traditional" French "neighborhood meal"; "service that is always friendly" ensures a "pleasant, relaxed" atmosphere, especially if in summer you "get a table in the back" – the "little patio is a haven of peace."

Paris (Le) ☒ | – | – | – | E |
Hôtel Lutétia, 23, rue de Sèvres, 6ᵉ (Sèvres-Babylone),
01 49 54 46 90; fax 01 49 54 46 00; www.lutetia-paris.com
"First-rate in all respects" proclaim passengers of this "uncrowded" Haute Cuisine haven with an "understated" ocean-liner decor by designer Sonia Rykiel for the very chic Hotel Lutétia; the "solid", classically oriented food and "realistically priced, well-chosen wine list" is offered by "service that is attentive, without hovering or rushing", resulting in a "calm, luxurious" atmosphere that is "worth every penny."

Paris Seize (Le) ☒ | 15 | 11 | 14 | 37 |
18, rue des Belles Feuilles, 16ᵉ (Trocadéro), 01 47 04 56 33
■ Run by the Dumant brothers, Jérôme and Stéphane, this "easygoing", easy-on-the-wallet bistro near the Place Victor Hugo offers "solid" Italian fare "without pretension" in a sports-themed setting; survey seize the ambiance is "lively", thanks to a "young crowd" that doesn't mind cramming into the "tight, smoky" quarters.

Park (Le) ☒ | – | – | – | VE |
Hyatt Paris Vendôme, 4, rue des Capucines, 2ᵉ (Opéra),
01 58 71 12 34; fax 01 58 71 10 32
Dynamo decorator Ed Tuttle's modern, open-kitchen design – a refreshingly "unusual environment for a hotel restaurant" – serves as a dramatic backdrop to globe-trotting chef Christophe David's Classic French grills menu; a "convivial staff" ensures a "very pleasant and attentive

| F | D | S | €C |

meal", but beware of prices as stunning as the nearby Place Vendôme shops.

Passiflore ☒ | 24 | 20 | 20 | 66 |
33, rue de Longchamp, 16ᵉ (Boissière/Trocadéro), 01 47 04 96 81; fax 01 47 04 32 27

■ A "real find" on a residential street in the 16th, this Classic French with "exotic" Asian accents is the passion of the "inventive" Roland Durand (ex Pré Catelan), a "friendly" chef who blossoms as he "works the room"; service is "attentive" and the dining room "pleasant and spacious", so even if "prices have crawled up recently", it's an "excellent address."

Passy Mandarin | 22 | 19 | 22 | 42 |
6, rue Bois-le-Vent, 16ᵉ (La Muette), 01 42 88 12 18; fax 01 45 24 58 54

■ This "well-hidden" Asian in Passy serves consistently "superb" cuisine ("the Peking duck is incredible") in a "beautifully wood-carved" space complemented by "accommodating, efficient" service; tightwads wonder "why prices are so high", but still appreciate it as "one of the better Chinese" choices around; N.B. the popular Opéra location has closed, alas.

Patrick Goldenberg | – | – | – | M |
69, av de Wagram, 17ᵉ (Ternes), 01 42 27 34 79

Ask your "Ashkenazi grandmother" where to go for "hearty portions of traditional Eastern European food" or a pastrami sandwich, and she'll likely laud this Jewish standby near the Place des Ternes serving "good, cheap" noshes; if a bit low on decor, it's as close as you'll get to a deli around here – and it's even open Saturdays.

Paul Chêne ☒ | 25 | 16 | 26 | 57 |
123, rue Lauriston, 16ᵉ (Trocadéro/Victor Hugo), 01 47 27 63 17; fax 01 47 27 53 18

■ Sending you back to Paris of the 1950s, this old-school Traditional French offering "excellent" eats with "super service" is a "great neighborhood spot" in the 16th; perhaps the "intimate" setting's a tad "reminiscent of an old-world bordello", but most call it a "favorite" that, while not cheap, is less expensive "than those more famous, fancy" establishments.

Paul, Restaurant | ▽ 15 | 15 | 18 | 40 |
15, pl Dauphine, 1ᵉʳ (Pont-Neuf), 01 43 54 21 48; fax 01 56 24 94 09

■ It's a "treat to settle down" at the sidewalk tables of this "Classic" French old-timer (circa 1900) on the Ile de la Cité for views of the Seine and "men playing boule under the trees"; the proximity to the Palais de Justice lures lawyer types who advocate its "reliable food and friendly service", and the verdict is: "it's still nice after all these years."

| F | D | S | €C |

Pavillon Montsouris | 20 | 24 | 18 | 54 |
20, rue Gazan, 14ᵉ (Porte d'Orleans), 01 43 13 29 00; fax 01 45 88 63 40; www.pavillon-montsouris.fr

■ "An ideal spot in summer" thanks to an "unbelievable setting" overlooking the Parc Montsouris ("you feel like you're in the country"), this "charming" belle-epoque "greenhouse" with a new Colonial interior is also "quite nice in winter"; the Classic French menu offers "good quality" for the price, and service is almost up to the scenic snuff, too.

Pavillon Puebla ⑤ | – | – | – | E |
Parc des Buttes-Chaumont, 19ᵉ (Buttes-Chaumont/Pyrénées), 01 42 08 92 62; fax 01 42 39 83 16

"Fantastically situated" in the well-groomed grounds of the beautiful Buttes-Chaumont park in the 19th, this "imaginative" Classic French with Catalan influences serves specialties, like duck with figs, in a Napoleon III conservatory; on a beautiful summer day, the large outdoor terrace is "perfect."

Père Claude (Le) | – | – | – | M |
51, av de La Motte-Picquet, 15ᵉ (La Motte-Picquet-Grenelle), 01 47 34 03 05; fax 01 40 56 97 84

This family-run Classic French rotisserie near the Ecole Militaire is a steady standby offering "adequate bistro food" and "good grilled meat" in modern surroundings; patrons particularly appreciate when Papa Claude Perraudin, the eponymous owner, is around to add a parental touch.

Pergolèse (Le) ⑤ | ▽ 22 | 16 | 21 | 85 |
40, rue Pergolèse, 16ᵉ (Porte Dauphine/Porte Maillot), 01 45 00 21 40; fax 01 45 00 81 31

■ Porte Maillot locals have uncovered a "neighborhood jewel" in this "small" Traditional French with an "innovative" menu (think langoustine ravioli and lamb carpaccio) that's "ideal for a business dinner or an intimate celebration."

Perraudin ⑤ | – | – | – | M |
157, rue St-Jacques, 5ᵉ (Cluny-La Sorbonne/Luxembourg), 01 46 33 15 75

Just behind the Panthéon "is the real deal" for a Traditional French meal: "homey, warm, simple, good food" at unbeatable prices in a mirror-and-tile decorated room that's typical turn-of-the-century Latin Quarter (1903, to be exact); it's quite popular, so "don't go without a reservation", and once there be sure to check out "the classic Turkish toilet", a "rare survivor."

Perron (Le) ⑤ | ▽ 21 | 14 | 18 | 56 |
6, rue Perronet, 7ᵉ (St-Germain-des-Prés), 01 45 44 71 51

■ "A pleasant welcome" always awaits pasta aficionados at this "very good Italian" whose "aromas titillate the taste

| F | D | S | €C |

buds" (but whose bills burn wallets a bit); the place is generally "hopping at lunch" with a "local crowd" of Saint-Germain dwellers, and more "quiet at dinner", creating the "ideal ambiance for romance."

Pershing, Restaurant ◐ | 12 | 24 | 11 | 65 |
Hotel Pershing Hall, 49, rue Pierre Charron, 8e (Charles de Gaulle-Etoile), 01 58 36 58 36; fax 01 58 36 38 01

◪ It's "all in the looks" at this "smart" hotel eatery near the Champs-Elysées with "very modern" decor by Andrée Putman and an "impressive vertical garden" covering one wall of an "agreeable patio"; however, neither the setting nor the "well-proportioned" (but "badly trained") waitresses can make up for the food, "uninteresting" Asian-inspired Eclectic–Contemporary French cuisine "out of sync with the pretentious prices."

Petit Bofinger ◐ | 16 | 15 | 18 | 34 |
6, rue de la Bastille, 4e (Bastille), 01 42 72 05 23; fax 01 42 72 04 94
20, bd Montmartre, 9e (Richelieu-Drouot), 01 47 70 91 35; fax 01 42 47 08 99
46, bd du Montparnasse, 14e (Montparnasse-Bienvenüe), 01 45 48 49 16; fax 01 45 44 92 05
10, pl Maréchal Juin, 17e (Péreire), 01 56 79 56 20; fax 01 56 79 56 21

◪ While "nothing outstanding", this Flo Group chain of Traditional Bistros is "good in a franchise sort of way" – i.e. handy "post-opera or if you're alone" for a "quick snack" of "honestly prepared", though sometimes "uneven" eats; alas, they have "none of the charm of the original Bofinger", but at least the service is reassuringly "crisp."

Petit Colombier (Le) ⌧ | ∇ 22 | 17 | 21 | 83 |
42, rue des Acacias, 17e (Argentine/Charles de Gaulle-Etoile), 01 43 80 28 54; fax 01 44 40 04 29

■ Loyalists of this Classic French in the Etoile area are happy to announce that its new owner extends an "excellent welcome" at the door, and that once *à table*, the "cooking merits special consideration", in particular the "game" offerings; be sure to "pay attention to the wine list", which features some "good bottles" at moderate prices.

Petit Colombier Côté Mer ⌧ | – | – | – | M |
40, rue des Acacias, 17e (Argentine/Charles de Gaulle-Etoile), 01 40 55 06 63; fax 01 44 40 04 29

In the 17th, this new annex of the neighboring Petit Colombier has a seafood vocation, as seen in its appealingly varied and modestly priced catch-of-the-day menu, which specializes in shellfish; cozy, friendly and open daily, it's immediately become popular with oyster-loving locals, especially since prices are moderate compared to other belly-up-to-the-counter bivalve veterans in Paris.

| F | D | S | €C |

Petite Chaise (A la)   17 | 15 | 17 | 39
36, rue de Grenelle, 7ᵉ (Rue du Bac), 01 42 22 13 35; fax 01 42 22 33 84

▰ For "old-fashioned" "Country French" fare in a "cozy setting", locals and tourists ("too many", some add) "rely" on this circa-1680 address in the 7th; though its pint-size digs have some dining on their "neighbor's lap" and exacerbates the "noise", the staff is ever "accommodating" and the price *toujours* a "bargain."

Petite Cour (La) ◐   20 | 18 | 19 | 49
8, rue Mabillon, 6ᵉ (Mabillon/St-Germain-des-Prés), 01 43 26 52 26; fax 01 44 07 11 53; www.la-petitecour.com

■ An "international clientele" lauds the "very good" Classic Bistro offerings, "helpful service" and "intimate setting" at this Mabillon site whose "lovely terrace" permits a "peaceful" meal in fair weather; factor in the "good-value prix fixe" and "interesting" wines and you have a "favorite."

Petite Sirène de Copenhague (La) ⌧   ▽ 23 | 16 | 23 | 46
47, rue Notre-Dame-de-Lorette, 9ᵉ (St-Georges), 01 45 26 66 66

■ Sea-starved sirens sing nothing but praises for this "Danish delight" in the 9th, where pedigreed chef-owner Peter Thulstrup (ex Crillon and Tour d'Argent) and staff "warmly greet" guests and serve "refined" fish-centric cuisine based on "high-quality ingredients" in a "laid-back" atmosphere; although it's "not cheap", all concede it's "one of the best tables in the neighborhood."

Petite Tour (La)   – | – | – | E
11, rue de la Tour, 16ᵉ (Passy), 01 45 20 09 31; fax 01 45 20 09 31

It has a new owner, but this Passy "classic" "nestled in the upscale 16th" still takes its cue from the local crowd ("no trendy types here") that appreciates the "Traditional French cuisine" and "attentive" service in a recently refreshed, "restful" environment; while it can be costly, some note more "reasonable prices" of late.

Petit Laurent (Le) ⌧   ▽ 21 | 18 | 22 | 55
38, rue de Varenne, 7ᵉ (Rue du Bac), 01 45 48 79 64; fax 01 45 44 15 95

■ A "favorite" among politicos seeking a "tranquil" respite from ministerial machinations in the 7th, this "friendly" "neighborhood" Classic French may be "unexciting" but it also "never disappoints" with "quality" fare, "classy" ambiance and "unpretentious" service.

Petit Lutétia (Au)   ▽ 14 | 17 | 18 | 36
107, rue de Sèvres, 6ᵉ (Vaneau), 01 45 48 33 53; fax 01 45 48 74 59

▰ "Step back into old Paris" at this circa-1915 brasserie that lures loads of "American tourists" and Rue de Sèvres shoppers with its "romantic" air and "not special, but solid"

| F | D | S | €C |

traditional offerings at "reasonable" prices; however, some scoff that it's "not worth the detour."

Petit Marché (Le) ⬤   _|_|_| I
9, rue de Béarn, 3ᵉ (Bastille/Chemin Vert), 01 42 72 06 67
"Hip" in a very "Parisian" way, this New French just a "stone's throw from the Place des Vosges" is an "excellent place to lunch with the locals", who agree the "good food" and "friendly" service makes this quite a "decent value."

Petit Marguery (Le) ☒   23 | 18 | 22 | 47
9, bd de Port-Royal, 13ᵉ (Les Gobelins), 01 43 31 58 59; fax 01 43 36 73 34
■ Though this Port Royal mainstay is under new ownership, the "superb" "menu and quality remain" report delighted devotees of "bistro classics" ("if you like cèpes and game, this is your place"); in addition, "veteran" waiters still attend to your needs and the decor is forever "old-fashioned"; some words of advice: order the dessert soufflé or "you'll regret it to the end of your days."

Petit Marguery (Le)   ∇ 20 | 16 | 18 | 38
81, rue la Fontaine, 16ᵉ (Michel Ange-Auteuil), 01 42 88 00 86
■ While nostalgists miss the "old iconoclastic Petit Marguery", this Franco-Italian current incarnation entices "budget-conscious students" and office workers at lunch and Porte d'Auteuil locals in the evening with its "pretty darn good" food, including a "delicious pizza."

Petit Niçois (Le)   ∇ 16 | 12 | 15 | 38
10, rue Amélie, 7ᵉ (La Tour-Maubourg), 01 45 51 83 65; fax 01 47 05 77 46; www.lepetitnicois.com
■ This "lively" bistro in the residential 7th trawls the waters of Nice to present an "authentic bouillabaisse" and other Southern-style dishes that match the "Provençal decor"; it's a "simple place", but "pleasant" enough for a Sunday supper.

Petit Pergolèse (Le) ☒   _|_|_| M
38, rue Pergolèse, 16ᵉ (Argentine/Porte Maillot), 01 45 00 23 66; fax 01 45 00 44 03
Imbued with "the advantages of the mother ship next door", this young Porte Maillot adjunct of Le Pergolèse offers a "rather original" New French menu "without the prices" of its parent (but "with more noise", alas); though the "decor is simple", most remember it as a "pretty little" address.

Petit Pontoise (Le) ☒   _|_|_| M
9 rue de Pontoise, 8ᵉ (Maubert-Mutualité), 01 43 29 25 20
"Close to the Seine on the Left Bank", this "tiny" "joint" is "not fancy" – you order from "blackboards [scattered] all around" the environs – but it's a "great place to indulge in

good" Classic Bistro cooking, served by a "helpful, efficient staff"; relaxed prices ensure that those who've discovered it "will definitely go back."

Petit Poucet (Le) | 17 | 19 | 15 | 43 |
4, rd-pt Claude Monet, Levallois (Anatole France), 01 47 38 61 85; fax 01 47 38 20 49; www.le-petitpoucet.net
■ Owing to an "exceptional setting" on the Ile de la Jatte, this multilevel Contemporary French is "still trendy" – ergo "always packed" – especially "when it's warm enough to sit on the terrace" "overlooking the Seine"; because "the cuisine is simple", technically moderate tabs can seem "a little expensive", but it's a really "fun place to go, plus you can get your car washed (and parked) while you eat."

Petit Prince de Paris (Le) ⏺ | 21 | 19 | 22 | 39 |
12, rue de Lanneau, 5ᵉ (Maubert-Mutualité), 01 43 54 77 26
■ "All are welcome" – "gay, straight", "English-speaking" – at this "slightly campy establishment" in the 5th that's a "must for *The Little Prince* lovers" and "smoochy couples" everywhere; certainly the "old-school" French menu is "delicious", but to many the "attractive", "entertaining staff is the reason to keep coming back."

Petit Rétro (Le) ⊠ | 20 | 20 | 20 | 37 |
5, rue Mesnil, 16ᵉ (Victor Hugo), 01 44 05 06 05; fax 01 44 05 06 05
■ "What we imagine a Parisian bistro to be" sigh *amants* of this "gem" off the Place Victor Hugo; the "Classic" dishes can be "delicious", service is usually "gracious" and the glazed art nouveau tile walls and an old bar are "charming"; plus, the *prix* are "reasonable" for the neighborhood; P.S. it's also a hospitable place to dine alone "with a book."

Petit Riche (Au) ⏺⊠ | 15 | 20 | 15 | 46 |
25, rue Le Peletier, 9ᵉ (Le Peletier/Richelieu-Drouot), 01 47 70 68 68; fax 01 48 24 10 79; www.aupetitriche.com
■ At this "old-style brasserie" in the 9th, "nothing seems to have changed for years", starting with the "satisfactory" "post-war"–era Classic French menu and the "lovely" turn-of-the-century decor featuring mirrors and banquettes – all of which make it a smart bet "to bring foreigners to"; an Opéra Garnier and "theater crowd" pops in late at night when perchance you can spy "a well-known face."

Petits Marseillais (Les) ⏺ | ▽ 15 | 15 | 17 | 38 |
72, rue Vieille-du-Temple, 3ᵉ (Hôtel-de-Ville), 01 42 78 91 59; fax 01 42 78 91 59; www.lespetitsmarseillais.com
◪ This tiny Provençal enclave in the Marais tries to make things "comfy" with an "intimate space and subdued lighting"; but while its defenders find the fare "decent", Marseilles expats are sometimes "disappointed" by a lack of care in the kitchen.

F	D	S	€C

Petit St. Benoît (Le) ⊄   16 | 12 | 17 | 37
4, rue St-Benoît, 6ᵉ (St-Germain-des-Prés), 01 42 60 27 92

☑ "Everyone is packed in tight" at this "fun", "noisy" "student canteen" behind the Saint-Germain-des-Prés church, whose authentic 1901-bistro decor draws many retro-oriented tourists (even though "you can't make a reservation"); the Traditional French menu is "passable", but critics claim that, despite its "cheap prices", it's not necessarily "a good value."

Petit Victor Hugo (Le) ◐ ⌀   14 | 14 | 14 | 41
143, av Victor Hugo, 16ᵉ (Victor Hugo), 01 45 53 02 68; fax 01 44 05 13 46

☑ This Traditional French in the 16th is popular with "classy locals" who receive a "golden welcome" when they slip in for a "fairly priced", "honest" meal of "salad, frites and a glass of wine"; unknowns, however, tell a different story, citing "cranky" service and inconsistency in the kitchen.

Petit Zinc (Le) ◐   16 | 20 | 16 | 49
11, rue St-Benoît, 6ᵉ (St-Germain-des-Prés), 01 42 86 61 00; fax 01 42 86 61 09; www.petitzinc.com

☑ While the "wonderful belle-epoque interior" is the main asset of this venerable Saint-Germain brasserie, it doesn't prevent the Frères Blanc property from exuding a "franchise feel" – not that this deters the multitudes of "touristy" types, who stick to such "simple" choices as "a shellfish platter that's a treat"; still, a vocal handful huffs that, given the "wandering service", this "old standby" is "better for people-watching than for eating."

Petrossian ⌀   24 | 18 | 20 | 85
18, bd de la Tour-Maubourg, 7ᵉ (La Tour-Maubourg/Invalides), 01 44 11 32 32; fax 01 44 11 32 35; www.petrossian.fr

■ If "luscious smoked salmon" and "caviar is your pleasure, this is the spot" say seduced surveyors of this *de luxe* seafooder/shop in the 7th; it's a top "address to invite a client" to as the "adventurous mixes" and "magnificent desserts" "always get people talking", even if the "chic gray decor" leaves warm-water species feeling a trifle "cold"; while a "full wallet" is indeed a prerequisite, the prix fixe lunch is a tantalizing lure.

Pharamond ⌀   15 | 23 | 15 | 60
24, rue de la Grande Truanderie, 1ᵉʳ (Etienne Marcel/Les Halles), 01 40 28 45 18; fax 01 40 28 45 87; www.le-pharamond.com

■ Exhaling a whiff of the bygone Les Halles market, this "splendid old standby" of the 1st seems the "last of an era", with its "beautiful" belle-epoque decor; "if you're in the mood for tripes" and other Classic Bistro favorites, this is "an offal place" (and we mean that nicely).

| F | D | S | €C |

Pichet de Paris (Le) ☒ ▽ 18 | 13 | 17 | 62
68, rue Pierre Charron, 8ᵉ (Franklin D. Roosevelt), 01 43 59 50 34
▣ The "fresh" "seafood classics" are "sole good" at this "typical brasserie" in the 8th; however, some say that "unless you're a regular" (as was the late President Mitterrand) "the service is on the cooler side"; but whether you lean left or right, your oysters come straight from the "shellfish shucker" stationed out front.

Pied de Chameau (Au) ☻ ▽ 15 | 18 | 12 | 35
20, rue Quincampoix, 4ᵉ (Hôtel-de-Ville), 01 42 78 35 00; fax 01 42 78 00 50; www.aupieddechameau.fr
▣ For "fun with a group of friends", those missing Morocco head toward this North African address behind the Centre Beaubourg that's best known for its "kitschy", fantasy decor and nightly "entertainment"; though it's of "good quality", the fare "lacks pep" foes fume; perhaps they should just fixate on the "delights of the belly dancer" or snake charmer.

Pied de Cochon (Au) ☻ 17 | 18 | 16 | 45
6, rue Coquillière, 1ᵉʳ (Châtelet-Les Halles), 01 40 13 77 00; fax 01 40 13 77 09; www.pieddecochon.com
▣ "For onion soup at the break of dawn", revelers trot down to this 24/7 "touristy", "lively" "leftover from the Les Halles market glory days" in the 1st; some say the balance of the brasserie standards is "disappointingly" "ordinary", but the namesake pig's feet, accompanied by a chilled Brouilly from the Beaujolais-heavy wine list, hits a weak spot for happy hogs who dream of "gnawing on the bone till they roll me out."

Pierre au Palais Royal ☻☒ 16 | 13 | 15 | 61
10, rue Richelieu, 1ᵉʳ (Palais Royal-Musée du Louvre), 01 42 96 09 17; fax 01 42 96 26 40
▣ Now under new ownership, this Traditional French has been "enlarged" and "renovated" along ancient lines after a fire (which may not be reflected in the Decor score); it's a "good place for lunch" if you're breezing through the Palais Royal supporters say, even if a rebellious contingent finds it "too fussy" and the loss of the charming flower shop in front "a pity."

PIERRE GAGNAIRE 28 | 25 | 27 | 171
Hôtel Balzac, 6, rue Balzac, 8ᵉ (Charles de Gaulle-Etoile/George V), 01 58 36 12 50; fax 01 58 36 12 51; www.pierre-gagnaire.com
■ A hands-down "must-try for any real foodie", this Haute Cuisine "extravaganza" near the Etoile portends an "unforgettable" experience that "blows away" diners with a "dazzling", "endless parade" of "edible art", "exquisitely served" in an "elegant" sycamore setting; admittedly,

get updates at zagat.com

| | | | F | D | S | €C |

some of the "strange combinations" are "not for the faint of heart – or wallet", but to those up for a multi-hour meal, chef-owner Pierre Gagnaire, aka the "Picasso of the palate", "is worthy of a special trip to Paris."

Pinxo ◐ — | — | — | M
9, rue d'Alger, 1er (Tuileries), 01 40 20 72 00
'Pinxo' means 'to pinch' in Basque, and the concept at this handsome newcomer near the Place Vendôme is to pinch whatever tasty morsels or little plates you fancy from the updated Southwestern and New French menu; then you watch them being assembled in the open kitchen by a staff trained by chef Alain Dutournier of Carré des Feuillants and Thierry de la Brosse, owner of Chez L'Ami Louis.

Pitchi Poï — | — | — | M
7, rue Caron, 4e (St-Paul), 01 42 77 46 15; fax 01 42 77 75 49; www.pitchipoi.com
In the Marais, this "cute" Eastern European enclave serves kosher food with a Polish flair in a "pleasantly" classic setting brightened by mosaics and an endearing terrace; the "large choice of vodkas" is perfect for washing down the homemade salmon blini or the signature apple strudel.

Planet Hollywood ◐ 8 | 12 | 10 | 31
78, av des Champs-Elysées, 8e (Franklin D. Roosevelt/George V), 01 53 83 78 27; fax 01 45 63 02 84; www.planethollywood.com
▰ As an ambassador of "Yankee" cuisine, this "noise" "factory" serves "industrial" "chain" fare on the Champs-Elysées that has Americans fretting over "what the Europeans think of us"; it's "fun with the kids" or "if you're homesick for burgers and fries"; otherwise, "you're better off with a candy bar."

PLAZA-ATHÉNÉE, RESTAURANT ⌧ 27 | 26 | 26 | 164
Hôtel Plaza-Athénée, 25, av Montaigne, 8e (Alma-Marceau/Franklin D. Roosevelt), 01 53 67 65 00; fax 01 53 67 65 12; www.alain-ducasse.com
■ Chef "Alain Ducasse is king", but it's the diners who get "treated like royalty" gush guests of his Plaza-Athénée outpost where "sumptuous", "imaginative" Haute Cuisine is presented at the "pinnacle of elegance" by "service so discreet you won't realize when your roll is replenished"; the room's "draped crystal chandeliers and bold design make a grand", if "stark", impression and prices are pretty "stunning" as well; "but "if you're able to get a reservation", this is a ticket to "true happiness."

Polidor ⌀ 14 | 14 | 14 | 24
41, rue Monsieur-le-Prince, 6e (Luxembourg/Odéon), 01 43 26 95 34; fax 01 43 26 22 79
▰ "Everyone should go" once to this 150-plus-year-old "authentic bistro" near the Luxembourg Gardens, if only to

| F | D | S | €C |

"step back in time" to Vieux Paris and experience the "communal tables" that have tourists sitting cheek-by-jowl with "Sorbonne students" and local "characters"; yes, the Classic French cuisine "is pretty basic" and the service "hasty", but at least the prices "leave you with lots of pocket change."

Pomponette (A la) ◐ 🗷 — | — | — | M
42, rue Lepic, 18ᵉ (Abbesses/Blanche), 01 46 06 08 36; fax 01 42 52 95 44
Those trolling for a "typical" Classic Bistro experience won't be disappointed by this "friendly" Montmartre locale run by the same family since 1909; serving well-prepared standards and "affordable wines" in an "authentic" turn-of-the-century decor, it also hosts musical soirées with traditional Parisian songs one evening per month.

Poquelin (Le) 🗷 ∇ 20 | 17 | 18 | 51
17, rue Molière, 1ᵉʳ (Palais Royal-Musée du Louvre/Pyramides), 01 42 96 22 19; fax 01 42 96 05 72
■ "Dark and cozy", with a "theatrically themed" interior that recalls the nearby Comédie Française, this "*petit*" place "off the beaten path" "is as charming as it gets" – thanks to its proprietors, a "delightfully attentive couple" who serve up "very good" Traditional French food and "specialties from the Auvergne."

Port Alma 🗷 20 | 15 | 19 | 73
10, av de New York, 16ᵉ (Alma-Marceau), 01 47 23 75 11; fax 01 47 20 42 92
🗷 "Fish and nothing but" "delicious" fish is featured at this "quiet", contemporary seafooder with a maritime-influenced decor on the quay near the Place de l'Alma; some scoff at the "pricey" menu and "slightly rigid" service typical of this "high-rent neighborhood", but all's "redeemed by the view of the Eiffel Tower" from a large picture window – and a signature "chocolate soufflé that's a sin."

Potager du Roy (Le) 🗷 21 | 18 | 21 | 56
1, rue du Maréchal-Joffre, Versailles (RER Versailles-Rive Gauche), 01 39 50 35 34; fax 01 30 21 69 30
🗷 Named for the nearby kitchen garden that once furnished France's royalty with fruit and vegetables, this "old-fashioned", "tiny place" in Versailles serves Traditional French food and a reasonable weekday lunch menu, "including a good glass of wine" admirers attest; but a few revolutionaries decree this "so-so" spot wouldn't measure up to the Sun King's standards.

Pouilly Reuilly 🗷 ∇ 23 | 19 | 17 | 38
68, rue André Joineau, Le Pré-St-Gervais (Hoche), 01 48 45 14 59; fax 01 48 45 93 93
■ It's easy to "feel like one of the locals" at this authentic, early-20th-century bistro, "certainly the best table" in the

get updates at zagat.com 155

| F | D | S | €C |

villagelike suburb of Pré-St-Gervais; the menu of "very-good cuisine" highlights down-to-earth classics such as blood sausage, sweetbreads and baba au rhum, delivered by "fast service."

Poule au Pot (La) ◐   -|-|-| M

9, rue Vauvilliers, 1er (Châtelet-Les Halles/Louvre-Rivoli), 01 42 36 32 96; fax 01 40 91 90 64; www.lapouleaupot.com
Night-owls who hanker for the "definitive" onion soup, eponymous chicken in a pot or "lots of" other Traditional French favorites flock to this "fun, relaxed Classic Bistro" (an institution since 1935) in Les Halles; it's a taste of "authentic Paris at its lusty, straight-ahead best", served up – along with prime "people-watching" – until 5 AM.

Pravda   -|-|-| M

49, rue Jean-Pierre Timbaud, 11^e (Parmentier), 01 48 06 19 76; www.lepravda.com
Youthful comrades of this "original" in the funky 11th commend its "trendy decor with a Slavic touch", including "a real *Pravda* newspaper on display", and "Russian-inspired cuisine that's not bad, accompanied by a large selection of vodkas", all at relatively proletarian prices.

PRÉ CATELAN (LE) ☒   26 | 27 | 24 | 125

Bois de Boulogne, route de Suresnes, 16e (Porte Dauphine), 01 44 14 41 14; fax 01 45 24 43 25; www.lenotre.fr
■ There's something "magical" about this "dreamlike" veteran in the Bois de Boulogne, "far from the noise of the city": "in the summer, the garden is the most beautiful spot in Paris to dine" (or better yet, lunch), while in the winter, a fireplace warms the 1900 interior; of course, all this, plus chef Frédéric Anton's "world-class" Haute Cuisine "creations", "comes with a high price", but the Tuesday–Saturday noontime "prix fixe is a true bargain", so "don't miss" the chance to "celebrate a special occasion" here.

Pressoir (Au) ☒   -|-|-| E

257, av Daumesnil, 12e (Michel Bizot), 01 43 44 38 21; fax 01 43 43 81 77
Year in, year out, chef Henri Séguin forges on as a standard-bearer of the tried-and-true classics (seasonal game and a warm seafood platter) at his refined table with leather armchairs and oak paneling deep in the 12th; both business folk and bourgeois couples come here for "Traditional French cuisine that's top quality", though – weight-watchers beware – "not light."

Pré Verre (Le) ☒   -|-|-| M

8, rue Thénard, 5e (Maubert-Mutualité), 01 43 54 59 47; fax 01 43 54 59 47
"Everything is tremendous" in this casual, bustling New French addition to the Latin Quarter (from the "charming people" behind Clos Morillons), which serves "highly

| F | D | S | €C |

ambitious" dishes made with "exotic spices" and an "imaginative list of cheap wines"; there are jazz album covers on the walls and jazz music on the sound system – just "don't get seated in the basement."

Procope (Le) ◐ 16 | 21 | 17 | 51

13, rue de l'Ancienne Comédie, 6ᵉ (Odéon), 01 40 46 79 00; fax 01 40 46 79 09; www.procope.com

◪ In the heart of Saint-Germain, the city's oldest cafe is a "history buff's delight", attracting those who come to "experience the ghosts" of Voltaire, Diderot and Robespierre in a "gorgeous" setting of salons and old portraits; but while traditionalists are "happily surprised" by the Classic French cuisine and "helpful" staff, modernists mutter "don't bother" with this "tired old" "tourist trap" ("should be made into a museum and put out of its misery").

Prosper – | – | – | M

89, rue du Rocher, 8ᵉ (Villiers), 01 43 87 55 03

Opened last year in the up-and-coming Les Batignolles area, this restaurant "à la mode" draws a prosper-ous business clientele with its "soigné decor" including "very comfortable armchairs" in red leather and picture windows that open wide in the summer; culinary director Guy Legay (ex Ritz) oversees a menu of inventive, "very New French cuisine", but some sniff prices, though relatively modest, seem "steep for what's on the plate."

P'tit Troquet (Le) ⌧ 22 | 18 | 23 | 36

28, rue de l'Exposition, 7ᵉ (Ecole Militaire), 01 47 05 80 39; fax 01 47 05 80 39

■ "What you envision a Paris neighborhood restaurant to be" profess fans of this "down-to-earth" family-run eatery near the Eiffel Tower – from the "well-prepared", "no-nonsense Classic Bistro grub" to the "authentic" 1930s decor and zinc bar; a "warm welcome" pervades an atmosphere that's "intimate", both figuratively and literally: the "tables are so close together they're almost communal."

Pure Café ⌧ – | – | – | I

14, rue Jean-Macé, 11ᵉ (Faidherbe-Chaligny), 01 43 71 47 22

This young Contemporary Bistro with its horseshoe-shaped bar on the corner of a tiny street in the 11th serves inexpensive, "inventive cuisine that's hit-or-miss depending on the day"; what's more dependable is the "warm welcome" and, in summer, a small but "charming patio" on the sidewalk.

Quai Ouest ◐ 15 | 17 | 13 | 38

1200, quai Marcel Dassault, St-Cloud (Pont-de-St-Cloud), 01 46 02 35 54; fax 01 46 02 33 02

■ "French TV stars", business-lunch types and cool courting couples hit the scene on the Seine in this "hip",

| F | D | S | €C |

"gigantesque" and "consistently fun" loftlike barge with a "superb terrace" overlooking the river in Saint-Cloud; it dishes up a "pretty diverse" array of Eclectic eats and, on Sundays, a popular "brunch and clown" ("to be avoided if you don't like kids"); just steer clear of this ship if you're "afraid of noise" or in a hurry, since "service is rather slow."

404 (Le) ☻ | 21 | 25 | 18 | 42 |
69, rue des Gravilliers, 3ᵉ (Arts et Métiers), 01 42 74 57 81; fax 01 42 74 03 41
■ As long as you're ready for the noise and "clowns-in-a-Volkswagen seating", you'll have "an absolutely transporting experience" at this "unique", "sexy Moroccan" in the "hard-to-find" Sentier; "delicious food" ("fabulous tagines", "terrific couscous and stuffed sardines"), plus a "festive" atmosphere created by "fashionably loud music", "friendly staff" and "super-funky" North African decor mean "reservations are necessary" if you want to join the crowd "dancing on the tables."

Quinson (Le) ⌧ | - | - | - | M |
5, pl Etienne Pernet, 15ᵉ (Commerce/Félix Faure), 01 45 32 48 54; fax 01 44 19 73 18
A taste of Marseille in the heart of the 15th, this circa-1945 bistro has earned a reputation for its "excellent bouillabaisse" and fish dishes ranging from salt cod brandade to sea bass; adorned with model boats, its simple bistro setting is "calm", if perhaps "a little sad."

R. ☻ | 11 | 19 | 13 | 49 |
6-8, rue de la Cavalerie, 15ᵉ (La Motte-Picquet-Grenelle), 01 45 67 06 85
■ Though "hard to find" – it's situated atop a "nondescript apartment building" in the 15th – it's "worth the effort" to visit this penthouse proffering a "sublime view" of the Eiffel Tower from designer Christophe Pillet's "totally 1970s-style" interior (or – "even more enjoyable – the 22-seat terrace in summer"); served by "slightly amateurish but sweet staffers", the "simple", "imaginative" New French cuisine matches the minimalist setting, except for the big-basin loos ("am I here to wash my hands or baptize a baby?").

R'Aliment ⌧ | - | - | - | I |
57, rue Charlot, 3ᵉ (Temple), 01 48 04 88 28; fax 01 48 04 88 28; www.resodesign.com
In the quiet end of the Marais, this New French from the local Reso Design firm is right in step with trends both culinary and decorative; the daily changing menu features light, healthy fare that's heavy on organic pasta and vegetarian dishes, served in a stainless-steel interior whose cool, minimalist whites are punctuated with long, tall lime-green tables.

| F | D | S | €C |

Ramulaud ⏺ ▽ 18 | 13 | 16 | 33
269, rue Faubourg-St-Antoine, 11ᵉ (Faidherbe-Chaligny/ Nation), 01 43 72 23 29
■ "Stylish, noisy and animated", this New Bistro is the kind of place where you might see agricultural activist "José Bové meeting with top Chirac advisors", a pretty strong recommendation for the "inventive", often organic food; the "knowledgeable staff" compounds the "guaranteed fun", even if some beef "there are so many supplements on the prix fixe that it doesn't make sense to have a prix fixe."

Ravi ⏺ 🖼 ▽ 23 | 21 | 18 | 56
50, rue de Verneuil, 7ᵉ (Rue du Bac), 01 42 61 17 28
🖼 Regulars rave this small spot in the 7th serves "the best Indian food in Paris" that's well worth the "fairly expensive" prices – especially considering the "warm welcome" and "lovely" traditional setting that accompany it; some do get ravi-nous waiting on the one "overtaxed" server (just "consider it an opportunity to enjoy every moment of an excellent meal").

Récamier (Le) 🖼 21 | 19 | 19 | 76
4, rue Récamier, 7ᵉ (Sèvres-Babylone), 01 45 48 86 58; fax 01 42 22 84 76
🖼 "Delightfully stuffy", this century-old hangout for the political and literary aristocracy of the chic 7th is a "classic" with "honest, well-prepared food" (including "probably the best boeuf bourguignon in Paris"), guaranteed to "transport you back to Burgundy"; it's "expensive" (some snipe "overpriced"), but when the warm weather hits, "the terrace in a cul-de-sac is pure pleasure."

Rech (Le) 🖼 ▽ 20 | 16 | 17 | 55
62, av des Ternes, 17ᵉ (Charles de Gaulle-Etoile/Ternes), 01 45 72 29 47; fax 01 45 72 41 60
■ Locals have been coming to this neighborhood brasserie near the Place des Ternes since 1925, knowing they can count on "delicious" "pre-nouvelle cuisine" classics: "fine fish", top-notch Gillardeau oysters and a house-ripened "Camembert to die for"; although the decor seemingly hasn't changed since its opening, the tables are "spaced well apart" and there's a sidewalk terrace that's a real "refuge in summer."

Réconfort (Le) ⏺ – | – | – | M
37, rue de Poitou, 3ᵉ (St-Sébastien Froissart), 01 49 96 09 60; fax 01 49 96 09 62
Housed in a 16th-century stone building on a "charming" street in the 3rd, this quaint table is decorated like a private home – one so chock-full of knickknacks it's almost "baroque"; however, dis-conforted critics come here "more for the ambiance" and "good-natured service" than the standard Provençal fare.

get updates at zagat.com 159

| F | D | S | €C |

RÉGALADE (LA) 🚫   25 | 14 | 17 | 43
49, av Jean Moulin, 14ᵉ (Alésia), 01 45 45 68 58; fax 01 45 40 96 74
🔲 It's "a schlep" to the "southern 14th", but it's "worth it" for what many deem "the best bistro in Paris, hands down"; chef-owner Yves Camdeborde, founder of "the bistro-gastro trend" of "gourmet food on a budget", has the enraptured reserving "weeks in advance" to eat his "rich, innovative" takes on Classic favorites, "particularly a decadent country pâté" "that starts every meal"; so who cares if the "room is loud and cramped" and the service "rushed", the food is "so good it makes everything else irrelevant."

RELAIS D'AUTEUIL   26 | 21 | 25 | 108
"PATRICK PIGNOL" 🚫
31, bd Murat, 16ᵉ (Michel Ange-Molitor/Porte d'Auteuil), 01 46 51 09 54; fax 01 40 71 05 03
■ In the high-end district near the Porte d'Auteuil, this "*grand petit* restaurant" may be "small" in size but it belongs in the big leagues insist enthusiasts enamored of chef-owner Patrick Pignol's "imaginatively prepared" Haute Cuisine and extensive wine list; completing the picture is a simple yet "beautiful dining room", all paneled and pastels, and "amicable service" overseen by Madame P.

Relais de l'Entrecôte (Le) ☾   23 | 14 | 17 | 35
20 bis, rue St-Benoit, 6ᵉ (St-Germain-des-Prés), 01 45 49 16 00; fax 01 45 49 29 75
15, rue Marbeuf, 8ᵉ (Franklin D. Roosevelt), 01 49 52 07 17; fax 01 47 23 34 98
■ Addicts of a "mythic entrecôte", "crisp, hot frites" and "secret-magic sauce" "stand in line" (no reservations taken) and sit "on top of each other" at this "outstanding" steakhouse "staple" near the Champs-Elysées and in Saint-Germain; when ordering from the "friendly but no-nonsense servers", "rare, medium or well done are the only words you need to know" because the "reasonably priced" beef's the only game in town here; but "when they have perfected this so well, why serve anything else?"

Relais de Venise (Le) ☾   20 | 13 | 17 | 36
271, bd Péreire, 17ᵉ (Porte Maillot), 01 45 74 27 97
🔲 "Rain or shine, there's always a line at the door" of this "simple, consistent" "food factory" close to Porte Maillot, where carnivores satisfy their craving with a one-choice menu: "exceptional entrecôte and inimitable fries" (plus the "best profiteroles"); you'll wait for a seat but not for your food, given the "sometimes too efficient" waitresses.

RELAIS LOUIS XIII 🚫   26 | 24 | 24 | 93
8, rue des Grands-Augustins, 6ᵉ (Odéon/St-Michel), 01 43 26 75 96; fax 01 44 07 07 80; www.relaislouis13.com
■ You "feel like you were just crowned king" at this Haute Cuisine table in the 6th owned by chef Manuel Martinez,

| F | D | S | €C |

who honed his "conservative but perfectly done cooking" at the Tour d'Argent; catered to by "courteous staffers", a "not very *nouvelle* crowd" comes for a "classic" "taste of Vieux Paris", from the "signature duck" to the "intimate" 16th-century interior complete with "spiral staircase" and "timbered walls."

Relais Plaza (Le) ◐ | 21 | 21 | 23 | 69 |
Hôtel Plaza-Athénée, 21, av Montaigne, 8ᵉ (Alma-Marceau/ Franklin D. Roosevelt), 01 53 67 64 00; fax 01 53 67 66 66; www.plaza-athenee-paris.com

■ That "Hermès scarf won't be out of place" in the "chic" "art deco" digs of this Plaza-Athénée site whose brasserie bites and "excellent" Eclectic eats are, like its more famous Haute Cuisine sibling, under the "influence of Ducasse"; an "international clientele" agrees that it's a "great place for lunch" as well as "after the opera or symphony."

Réminet | 24 | 15 | 21 | 48 |
3, rue des Grands Degrés, 5ᵉ (Maubert-Mutualité/St-Michel), 01 44 07 04 24; fax 01 44 07 17 37

■ Run by a "husband-and-wife duo", this "charming, little bistro" is having trouble remaining "happily undiscovered" in a Latin Quarter neighborhood better known for tourist traps; thanks to the "lovely, memorable" New French cuisine, candlelit, "quaint atmosphere" and the "highly personal service from Madame", the place is "getting more and more crowded" but respondents shrug "oh, well, can't keep it a secret forever."

Rendez-vous des Camionneurs (Au) 🚭🚬 | – | – | – | M |
34, rue des Plantes, 14ᵉ (Alésia/Plaisance), 01 45 40 43 36

A "throwback" to another era, this "real neighborhood bistro" in the unpretentious 14th near Place d'Alésia – whose name means 'truck drivers' hangout' – has long been a great place to fill up your tank with "simple but flavorful cooking", featuring robust Classics in an "easygoing" ambiance and at unbeatable prices.

Rendez-vous des Chauffeurs (Au) | – | – | – | I |
11, rue des Portes Blanches, 18ᵉ (Marcadet-Poissonniers), 01 42 64 04 17

"Like your dream of a neighborhood bistro" off the beaten track in the humble part of the 18th, this nearly 100-year-old standby is named for the cab drivers who once ate here between round-the-clock shifts; it still cooks copious amounts of dirt-cheap Traditional fare for local "regulars."

Repaire de Cartouche (Le) 🚭 | 20 | 13 | 17 | 40 |
99, rue Amelot, 11ᵉ (St-Sébastien Froissart), 01 47 00 25 86; fax 01 43 38 85 91

◪ Chef-owner Rodolphe Paquin has made a name for himself with his "great value" of a Classic Bistro in the

| F | D | S | €C |

increasingly gentrified 11th; but while converts cheer his "remarkable" "regional" cuisine and "inventive" take on earthy dishes, skeptics snipe the "service is scattered" and the country-inn interior both "dreary" and "dated."

Restaurant de la Tour ⊠ | – | – | – | M |
6, rue Desaix, 15ᵉ (Dupleix/La Motte-Picquet-Grenelle), 01 43 06 04 24; fax 01 44 49 05 06
Located just steps from the Eiffel Tower, this Classic French run by a "pleasant" couple attracts a (not surprisingly) "very touristy" clientele, which finds that "after a day of sightseeing, this is the perfect place to relax with a good bottle of wine and great food" in a contemporary yellow-and-rust-colored, Provençal-inspired decor.

Restaurant du Marché ⊠ | – | – | – | M |
59, rue de Dantzig, 15ᵉ (Porte de Versailles), 01 48 28 31 55; fax 01 48 28 18 31
This veteran 15th arrondissement Classic Bistro with red-leather benches and a pewter bar boasts a "new chef-owner", Francis Lévêque (ex the late Dame Jeanne), who cooks up an "excellent value" of a menu that includes duck hachis Parmentier (minced bird with mashed potatoes) and warm madeleine; disciples delight in it being "different every day", but detractors decree it "a bit disappointing."

Restaurant du Musée d'Orsay | 15 | 23 | 14 | 35 |
Musée d'Orsay, 1, rue de Légion d'Honneur, 7ᵉ (Solférino), 01 45 49 47 03; fax 01 42 22 34 12
☑ "After seeing the Impressionists", go and be impressed by the "spectacular setting" of this "elegant, old" Musée d'Orsay eatery, "a perfect respite from the bustling crowds" at "lunch or tea hour" with "gilding and chandeliers" throughout; as for the Classic French food, some describe it as "artful" while others say it's "so-so", sunk further by sometimes "surly service."

Restaurant du Palais Royal ⊠ | 19 | 22 | 19 | 65 |
110, Galerie de Valois, 1ᵉʳ (Bourse/Palais Royal-Musée du Louvre), 01 40 20 00 27; fax 01 40 20 00 82
■ When the warm weather hits, this "elegant" table is a royal "treat" for a "leisurely lunch" or "quiet dinner" thanks to its "exceptional terrace" "overlooking the Palais Royal" (while a "convivial" contemporary room welcomes cold-weather clients); Med-influenced, "trustworthy Classic French cuisine" and a "good wine list" mean this garden getaway "never disappoints"; "sure, you pay for eating [here] – but it's worth paying for."

Riad (Le) | – | – | – | E |
42, av Charles de Gaulle, Neuilly (Les Sablons/Porte Maillot), 01 46 24 42 61; fax 01 46 40 19 91
It's a quick jaunt from Neuilly to North Africa at this Moroccan establishment just west of Porte Maillot offering

F | **D** | **S** | **€C**

"delicious" couscous, tagines, pastillas and imported wines along with "pleasant service", all in an "exotic decor" composed of cozy nooks and cushioned banquettes.

River Café   17 | 20 | 14 | 46
146, quai de Stalingrad, Issy-les-Moulineaux (RER Issy-Val de Seine), 01 40 93 50 20; fax 01 41 46 19 45
◪ The river is the reason to dine on this houseboat in Issy-les-Moulineaux – but only if you "insist" on a table with a "pretty little view of the Seine" (as opposed to the industrial wharf on the other side); with such engaging surrounds, the "simple" New French eats and sometimes "absent" service tend to fade into the background.

Robe et le Palais (La) 🅢   – | – | – | M
13, rue des Lavandières-Ste-Opportune, 1ᵉʳ (Châtelet-Les Halles), 01 45 08 07 41; fax 01 45 08 07 41
Select one of the "mouthwatering" vintages, including 40 "by the glass" choices, and soak up the "jovial ambiance" in this little *bistrot à vins* just steps from the Place du Châtelet that features a changing blackboard menu of "sound" food, with roots in the Southwest and Corsica, and "convivial service."

Robert et Louise 🅢🍴   – | – | – | M
64, rue Vieille-du-Temple, 3ᵉ (Rambuteau), 01 42 78 55 89
Fancy yourself dining "in a couple's home" when you sit at the "long communal tables" at this Marais mainstay and partake of the "basic hearth-cooked" Classic Bistro food that's heavy on roasted meats but also includes such wild cards as "escargot thrown into the fire"; while it's nothing short of "atmospheric", some find the rustic setting a little "rundown."

Roi du Pot-au-Feu (Le) 🅢   ▽ 18 | 15 | 18 | 36
34, rue Vignon, 9ᵉ (Havre-Caumartin/Madeleine), 01 47 42 37 10
■ "Bring on the beef and marrow" say subjects of this meat-stew sovereign, a "good-humored" 1930s Classic Bistro that's a "perfect retreat" on a "cold wintery day" or "after shopping" at the nearby Grands Boulevards department stores; just be sure to also "bring an appetite, as the portions are large."

Romantica (La) 🅢   21 | 19 | 18 | 62
73, bd Jean Jaurès, Clichy (Mairie-de-Clichy), 01 47 37 29 71; fax 01 47 37 76 32
■ "An address to keep under wraps at all costs", this Clichy Italian lives up to its name thanks to a setting that encompasses an "idyllic" garden for warm-weather dining; the kitchen turns out "pastas with pizzazz", like those spectacularly "flambéed in a Parmesan wheel"; though tabs are a bit "pricey", most admit "the experience is worth it."

| | | | | F | D | S | €C |

Rosimar ⌫
▽ 23 | 8 | 21 | 41

26, rue Poussin, 16ᵉ (Michel Ange Auteuil/Porte d'Auteuil), 01 45 27 74 91; fax 01 45 20 75 05

◪ "You feel you're in Catalonia" at this "small, out-of-the-way" Spaniard near the Porte d'Auteuil; savvy surveyors say *sí* to "the best paella in France" (that must be ordered when you reserve) and the "very friendly" husband-and-wife owners; the kitchen and their service far outscores the "love-it-or-hate-it" multi-mirrored decor that sends some reaching for supplemental sangria.

RÔTISSERIE D'EN FACE (LA) ⌫
22 | 17 | 20 | 48

2, rue Christine, 6ᵉ (Odéon/St-Michel), 01 43 26 40 98; fax 01 43 54 22 71; www.jacques-cagna.com

■ "Comfortable as a favorite pair of shoes" say regulars of Jacques Cagna's "cheerful" "baby bistro" in the 6th; that it's more "Californian" than Classic French sits well with the crowds of Americans who "rely" on its "simple" roast meat–heavy menu that may lack a few "fireworks" but has "no duds either."

Rôtisserie du Beaujolais (La)
21 | 16 | 18 | 44

19, quai de la Tournelle, 5ᵉ (Jussieu/Pont-Marie), 01 43 54 17 47; fax 01 56 24 43 71

◪ This quai-side, casual and "less-expensive offshoot of the Tour d'Argent" fills up with tables of "gossiping neighbors" from the 5th and tourists who "depend" on it for "finger-licking", if "not very exciting", Classic Bistro and "Country French food"; the "cramped, noisy" room fades away if you "sit by the window" where "the only thing holier than the rotisserie chicken is a view of Notre Dame."

Rotonde ☾
13 | 15 | 15 | 43

105, bd du Montparnasse, 6ᵉ (Vavin), 01 43 26 48 26; fax 01 46 34 52 40

◪ Regulars find it "comforting" that this "Montparnasse old-time boulevardier" is "always the same": nothing "special" but a "good enough brasserie" that's "open late" everyday; if some complain it has become "overpriced", at least it's a treat for "a drink to watch the passing crowd."

Rouge Vif (Le) ⌫
▽ 15 | 12 | 15 | 35

48, rue de Verneuil, 7ᵉ (Musée d'Orsay/Solférino), 01 42 86 81 87

◪ The "charming" staff "provides the fun" at this "local haunt" "close to the Musée d'Orsay" that's not the place "for a romantic date but is excellent with loud friends"; if some are unimpressed by the "unpretentious" Southwestern–Classic Bistro food, they rave over the "reasonable" tabs.

Rubis (Le) ⌫
▽ 13 | 8 | 13 | 24

10, rue du Marché St Honoré, 1ᵉʳ (Tuileries), 01 42 61 03 34

◪ This 100-year-old Place du Marché Saint-Honoré–area wine bistro is postcard Paris, specializing in "respectably priced" Beaujolais by the glass and a simple Classic French lunch menu, though some confide "you can do better for the money in the neighborhood"; in the evening when the kitchen's closed, it's "ideal for a pre-dinner bottle of wine and charcuterie plate."

Rucola (La) ☒ — | — | — | M
198, bd Malesherbes, 17ᵉ (Wagram), 01 44 40 04 50; fax 01 44 40 04 50

Latin-lovers are trekking from afar to this "excellent" Italian trattoria near Place de Wagram that's painted in warm Mediterranean colors and run "by a young, attentive crew" under the direction of two former Sormani employees; "fresh products" and "truly al dente pasta" are two constants on a menu that changes regions every two weeks.

Rue Balzac ◐ — 18 | 19 | 19 | 59
3-5, rue Balzac, 8ᵉ (George V), 01 53 89 90 91; fax 01 53 89 90 94

■ Fans croon about this "à la mode" address off the Champs-Elysées, not just for the "chance to catch a glimpse of [rocker and part-owner] Johnny Hallyday", but also for "accommodating" service, "interesting" New French cuisine by a Michel Rostang protégé and modern decor that includes frescoes and red-velvet banquettes; it's unabashedly "pricey" and may "try too hard to be trendy", but that's show biz.

Rughetta (La) — 15 | 11 | 13 | 29
41, rue Lepic, 18ᵉ (Abbesses/Blanche), 01 42 23 41 70

◪ Perched on a winding Montmartre street, this "friendly" Italian gets "crowded" with a local "show-biz clientele" and tourists craving "quick" pastas and "Roman-style pizzas"; though decor and service won't win awards, it's nonetheless "difficult to get a table" on weekends and in the summer, when the small terrace is a treat.

Safran (Le) ☒ — | — | — | M
29, rue d'Argenteuil, 1ᵉʳ (Pyramides), 01 42 61 25 30; fax 01 42 61 25 30

Followers of chef Caroll Sinclair who formerly frequented her eponymous address at the Bastille have to seek out her latest venture, a "pretty" saffron-colored bistro, on a little-trafficked street in the 1st; but while some applaud her "good organic" Mediterranean-inspired cooking, the more stringent say it's "hit-or-miss", citing "small portions" and "long delays" in service.

Saint Vincent (Le) ☒ — | — | — | M
26, rue de la Croix-Nivert, 15ᵉ (Cambronne), 01 47 34 14 94; fax 01 45 66 46 58

It's "far from nouvelle" at this classic, family-run bistro in the 15th that serves "hearty traditional" Lyonnais fare – think coq au vin, andouillette – along with Beaujolais wines; though the regular crowd is quite international

| F | D | S | €C |

thanks to the nearby UNESCO headquarters, the ambiance is pure French.

Sale e Pepe ⌀ | – | – | – | I |
30, rue Ramey, 18ᵉ (Château Rouge/Jules Joffrin), 01 46 06 08 01
It's like dining "at home" – albeit a spirited Sicilian one – at this small, casual address in the 18th that's known for its "convivial" ambiance and family-style formula: "you can't choose your dish because there's only one kind of pizza and pasta" – but at these prices, nobody's complaining.

Salon d' Hélène ⌀ | 19 | 18 | 16 | 57 |
4, rue d' Assas, 6ᵉ (Sèvres-Babylone), 01 42 22 00 11; fax 01 42 22 25 40
▼ A "less-expensive alternative" to Hélène Darroze's "exquisite restaurant upstairs" in the 6th, this *salon* is the place to graze on "tapas"-size portions of her signature riffs on Southwestern cooking; the praise isn't universal, as some find her offerings a little too "strange", and the overall experience "a let-down after the high expectations" garnered by "such a well-known chef."

Sardegna a Tavola ⌀ | – | – | – | M |
1, rue de Cotte, 12ᵉ (Ledru-Rollin), 01 44 75 03 28; fax 01 44 75 03 28
Italophiles willingly traverse the town for the "generous" portions of "exceptional" "regional cuisine" at this unofficial "embassy of Sardegna" hidden away in the 12th; they come despite "uneven service" and the modest, even "cheap" decor, complete with vines hanging from the ceiling; P.S. "reservations obligatory."

Sarladais (Le) ⌀ | – | – | – | M |
2, rue de Vienne, 8ᵉ (St-Augustin), 01 45 22 23 62; fax 01 45 22 23 62
Bring an appetite to this "very-good Southwestern table", a "real sleeper off the beaten track" near the Gare Saint-Lazare, where the "hearty", "non–lean cuisine" specialties – lots of "duck-based dishes and a large variety of foie gras" – are a "fantastic value"; the region's warmth is reflected in the "friendly, unobtrusive service."

Sasso ⌀ | – | – | – | I |
36, rue Raymond Losserand, 14ᵉ (Pernety), 01 42 18 00 38
A sassy, "young crowd" packs this "noisy" neighborhood trattoria in the 14th (an offshoot of Les Cailloux) for "simple" pasta and risotto dishes from all over Italy that are "not too expensive"; "nice" service and light streaming through the picture windows creates "agreeable" ambiance.

Saudade ⌀ | – | – | – | M |
34, rue des Bourdonnais, 1ᵉʳ (Châtelet-Les Halles), 01 42 36 03 65; fax 01 42 36 27 77; www.restaurantsaudade.com
'Saudade' means nostalgia, and Lisbon lovers longing for authentic "Portuguese chic" find it at this table near

| F | D | S | €C |

Châtelet cooking up the country's classics, such as grilled cod and roast suckling pig, accompanied by a "fabulous wine list" that boasts a "good choice of Portos and Vinho Verde"; the service is "elegant" and so is the live fado music the first Tuesday of every month.

Sauvignon (Au) ▽ | 16 | 14 | 13 | 19 |
80, rue des Saints-Pères, 7ᵉ (Sèvres-Babylone), 01 45 48 49 02; fax 01 45 49 41 00

■ A "great place to go for lunch after shopping" if all you want is "a glass of inexpensive wine and an open-faced sandwich" on "famous Poîlane bread", this "quintessential Parisian wine bar" is an oasis in the 7th (a neighborhood not known for cheap and cheerful choices); in the summer "grab an outside table" and "watch *le tout* Paris pass by."

Saveurs de Claude (Aux) | – | – | – | M |
12, rue Stanislas, 6ᵉ (Notre-Dame-des-Champs/Vavin), 01 45 44 41 74; fax 01 45 44 41 95

After doing the rounds of Guy Savoy's bistros, chef Claude Lamain has recently opened his own place in Montparnasse, with a minimalist art deco decor and open kitchen where clients can watch him bring original touches to "delicious", affordably priced Traditional French dishes with lots of vegetables, "well presented" by "knowledgeable" servers.

Saveurs du Marché (Aux) | – | – | – | M |
4, rue de l'Eglise, Neuilly (Pont de Neuilly), 01 47 45 72 11; fax 01 46 37 72 13

An open market just steps away means that freshness is guaranteed at this new table in the well-heeled suburb of Neuilly, where the young chef-owner offers skillfully prepared Traditional French food and simple seasonal dishes to a local clientele.

Sawadee | 19 | 11 | 15 | 32 |
53, av Emile Zola, 15ᵉ (Charles Michels), 01 45 77 68 90; fax 01 45 77 57 78

■ Believers in Bangkok make a beeline for this site in the 15th, where the menu of "good westernized Thai is a gentle introduction" to Southeast Asian classics in an aquarium-dominated decor; some "disappointed" curry connoisseurs deem the cuisine bereft of "zest", but to many it's still the "best" Siamese in town.

Scheffer (Le) | 22 | 15 | 18 | 37 |
22, rue Scheffer, 16ᵉ (Trocadéro), 01 47 27 81 11

■ "You can't go wrong" at this "truly old-style bistro", the sort of "neighborhood eatery" "that is rare in the 16th"; its popularity means "you have to squeeze between all the other locals to get to your chair" (and be prepared for "too many smokers") before digging into the "ideal" "Classic French dishes" that are "excellent value", especially for this well-heeled neighborhood.

	F	D	S	€C

Sébillon ◐ | 16 | 16 | 16 | 52 |
66, rue Pierre Charron, 8ᵉ (George V), 01 43 59 28 15; fax 01 43 59 30 00
20, av Charles de Gaulle, Neuilly (Les Sablons/Porte Maillot), 01 46 24 71 31; fax 01 46 24 43 50

◪ "Known for its all-you-can-eat leg of lamb and beans" sliced at the table, this "classic" brasserie with one address in Neuilly and another just off the Champs-Elysées is "always a hit with out-of-towners who say 'how French!'"; alas, that "traditional" "*vieille* France" image also means it's "*sans* surprise" – and soul, some sneer.

16 Haussmann (Le) ◐ 🆉 | 15 | 16 | 15 | 48 |
Hôtel Ambassador, 16, bd Haussmann, 9ᵉ (Chaussée d'Antin/Richelieu-Drouot), 01 44 83 40 58; fax 01 44 83 40 57; www.hotelambassador-paris.com

◪ Just up the street from the Galeries Lafayette and Au Printemps, this hotel dining room with a colorfully "modern", "pleasantly cold" interior by Philippe Starck offers an "interesting formula", especially for lunch, with its "consistently good" combination of Classic French–Med fare fans feel; but foes profess the food's "without passion."

Senso ◐ | 17 | 20 | 17 | 56 |
Hôtel de la Trémoille, 14, rue de la Trémoille, 8ᵉ (Alma-Marceau/Franklin D. Roosevelt), 01 56 52 14 14; fax 01 56 52 14 13; www.hotel-tremoille.com

■ Terence Conran's "stylish" establishment in the 8th manages to be simultaneously "trendy" and "grown-up", "without ridiculous attributes like model waitresses and tiring lounge music"; the sober ivory-toned interior provides "agreeable and relaxing decor far from the tumult of the Champs" nearby, while the "simple", "tasty" New French cuisine never strays too far from the classics; P.S. the "excellent bar" offers a cheaper bite and "a chic drink."

Sept Quinze (Le) 🆉 | 22 | 14 | 20 | 35 |
29, av Lowendal, 15ᵉ (Cambronne/Ségur), 01 43 06 23 06; fax 01 45 67 14 11

■ Its name refers to its location straddling the 7th and 15th, and regulars from both arrondissements flock to this "lively neighborhood" eatery for its "inventive, even audacious cuisine" (Med-Provençal, with some California-like "tasty twists"), "cool ambiance", "young, charming staff" and "nifty wine selection"; the only drawback is the "noise" that comes from cramming "too many tables into the room."

7ème Sud Grenelle | 16 | 16 | 15 | 37 |
159, rue de Grenelle, 7ᵉ (La Tour-Maubourg), 01 44 18 30 30; fax 01 44 18 07 42 ◐
52 rue de Boulainvilliers, 16ᵉ (La Muette), 01 45 20 18 32

◪ A "young, trendy" crowd gets "noisy" over "good Mediterranean and North African food" ("solid, if not

| F | D | S | €C |

spectacular") at this rare outpost of hip in a quiet corner near the Ecole Militaire; some say the service can be "a little slow", but for "a little neighborhood place" it's "pleasant" and "original", especially for relatively moderate prices; P.S. "there's [a new] one in the 16th too."

Si ☒ ⎯ | ⎯ | ⎯ | M |
14, rue Charlot, 3ᵉ (Arts et Métiers/Filles-du-Calvaire), 01 42 78 02 31; fax 01 42 78 02 31
It's hard to say no to the "original" Med meals in this "convivial" corner near the Musée Picasso, where the 1970s-style "decor is minimalist but the cuisine is not" (e.g. raw red mullet with tapenade, or preserved duck with potatoes); a particularly inexpensive lunchtime menu is another reason for saying *sí*.

Sinago (Le) ☒ ⎯ | ⎯ | ⎯ | I |
17, rue de Maubeuge, 9ᵉ (Cadet/Notre-Dame-de-Lorette), 01 48 78 11 14
Asian-food aficionados in-the-know make tracks to this tiny place in the Gare du Nord neighborhood for "refined, traditional" Cambodian dishes such as pork-filled crêpes and fish with ginger; prices are as modest as the boatlike decor (the fixings, like the name, are from an actual ship).

6 New York ☒ 20 | 19 | 19 | 62 |
6, av de New York, 16ᵉ (Alma-Marceau), 01 40 70 03 30; fax 01 40 70 04 77
◪ Overlooking the Seine near the Place de l'Alma, with an "incredible view of the Eiffel Tower", this New French "aspires to being discreetly fashionable", but "unlike other trendy places, the cooking has real quality" (no surprise, since it's done by "a student of [chef/co-owner] Jean-Pierre Vigato"); however, dissenters deep-six the "noisy" digs and generically "chic" atmosphere – it could be "in New York or California, and I don't go to Paris for U.S. ambiance."

Sizin ☒ ⎯ | ⎯ | ⎯ | I |
47, rue St-Georges, 9ᵉ (St-Georges), 01 44 63 02 28
Ceramic tiles and old postcards of Istanbul help create an authentic ambiance at this family-run traditional Turkish table in the 9th, where the menu includes hummus, skewered lamb brochettes with tomatoes and homemade baklava – all helped down by native potables, such as Kavaklidere wine and strong anise-flavored raki.

Soleil (Le) ▽ 23 | 18 | 23 | 49 |
109, av Michelet, St-Ouen (Porte de Clignancourt), 01 40 10 08 08; fax 01 40 10 16 85
■ Antiques hunters with an appetite claim this Classic Bistro is "a great find", "a refuge from the fray of the flea market" at Saint-Ouen, where hitting upon a good meal used to be a bigger challenge than unearthing a Louis XVI commode; here, the "hospitable", "multilingual patron is

	F	D	S	€C

Sologne (La) 🛇
164, av Daumesnil, 12ᵉ (Daumesnil), 01 43 07 68 97;
fax 01 43 44 66 23

▬|▬|▬| M

When hunting season hits, locals are wild about the "very good game" on the menu at this pleasant bourgeois address with exposed stone walls in the 12th; the rest of the year, chef-owner Didier Maillet's affordable Traditional French "daily specials" are much appreciated.

Sora Lena 🛇
18, rue Bayen, 17ᵉ (Ternes), 01 45 74 73 73;
fax 01 45 74 73 52

▬|▬|▬| M

Sporting a restful taupe-colored decor accented by Japanese lanterns and Vietnamese light fixtures, as well as a '70s vintage disco soundtrack that animates the room without overwhelming it, this new spot near the Place des Ternes has immediately started pulling in a glamorous, young crowd, including a lot of recognizable film and show-biz folks; the young, Italy-reared Cambodian chef previously worked at Sormani, a pedigree that appears in his deft Mediterranean cooking, brought by men in black.

SORMANI 🛇
4, rue du Général Lanrezac, 17ᵉ (Charles de Gaulle-Etoile),
01 43 80 13 91; fax 01 40 55 07 37

25 | 18 | 22 | 85

■ Considered by many the "best Italian in Paris", this star near the Etoile "always offers a wonderful time", but pizza-lovers beware – pies have no place among the "cuisine de luxe" here ("the amount of truffles used is almost obscene"); if prices are a tad tough, the "service is gentle"; a recent renovation brings a "really red" touch to the "small" setting.

Soufflé (Le) 🛇
36, rue du Mont-Thabor, 1ᵉʳ (Concorde), 01 42 60 27 19;
fax 01 42 60 54 98

21 | 16 | 20 | 44

▱ "If you love" those rising egg whites, "this is the place" say surveyors who blow hot over this "old standby" in a "superb location" near the Place de la Concorde – a veritable "soufflé central" with an "incredible variety" of "cloudlike" sweet and savory versions served by "old-fashioned" waiters who seem part of the slightly "frayed-around-the-edges" decor; some are deflated by it being a "big American hangout", and the rest of the Classic French menu is pretty "narrow", but still, it's a "must, at least once."

Soupière (La) 🛇
154, av de Wagram, 17ᵉ (Wagram), 01 46 22 80 10;
fax 01 46 22 27 09

▬|▬|▬| M

A "local crowd" ignores the "dull" trompe l'oeil decor in favor of the forest floor – specifically, the wild mushrooms

| F | D | S | €C |

that chef-owner and fungi fanatic Christian Thuillart makes the centerpiece of his "satisfyingly good" Traditional French menu; regulars from the Place de Wagram neighborhood in the 17th arrondissement also appreciate this "genteel mom-and-pop kind of place" for its "very-nice service" and reasonable prix fixes.

Sousceyrac (A) 🖾   19 | 14 | 19 | 54
35, rue Faidherbe, 11ᵉ (Charonne/Faidherbe-Chaligny), 01 43 71 65 30; fax 01 40 09 79 75

◪ Fans of this "solidly down-home Southwestern" site in the 11th say it's "old-fashioned", and "that's a compliment", given the "delightful" traditional specialties, including "one of the best hares *à la royale* in Paris (in hunting season)" and "friendly" service; but grousers grumble it's got a "gloomy atmosphere", "waiters who should be in the retirement home" and "equally old food."

Spicy ⬤   18 | 17 | 17 | 38
8, av Franklin D. Roosevelt, 8ᵉ (Franklin D. Roosevelt/ St-Philippe-du-Roule), 01 56 59 62 59; fax 01 56 59 62 50; www.spicyrestaurant.com

■ White-collar types working in the 8th make this "casual" corner a convenient "canteen" for "business lunches" or "a quick meal before the movies"; the Asian-Med–influenced New French "food is good, though not extraordinary" ("tartare lovers take note" – this is a house specialty); still, the "warm" brick-and-wood "setting is agreeable" and a rise in the Service score confirms that the young staff's "welcoming" efforts have "improved."

Spoon, Food & Wine 🖾   22 | 20 | 19 | 72
Sofitel Hôtel Marignan, 14, rue de Marignan, 8ᵉ (Franklin D. Roosevelt), 01 40 76 34 44; www.spoon.tm.fr

◪ Alain Ducasse devotees adore his "sophisticated" world-food bistro off the Champs-Elysées with its "casual", tightly spaced "Zen decor", "incredible wine list" and "interesting menu concept" that allows you to mix and match the elements to create "fresh, imaginative and surprising" Eclectic dishes; but the worn-out wail "if I wanted to think that much about a meal, I'd cook for myself" and carp that the service at this "chichi money machine" is "good but not as efficient as you'd expect at these prices."

Square (Le) 🖾   10 | 14 | 11 | 37
31, rue St-Dominique, 7ᵉ (Invalides/Solférino), 01 45 51 09 03

◪ Squares abstain from this "lively", very "en vogue" site that's "good for a younger set" interested more in the scene than in the "mediocre" "Classic" French food (at least, it's a "good value" for the high-toned 7th); habitués head for the outside tables, which offer a view of a "nice little park" and respite when the place gets too "smoky and loud."

get updates at zagat.com   171

F	D	S	€C

Square Trousseau (Le) ◐ 🥄   17 | 17 | 13 | 39
1, rue Antoine Vollon, 12ᵉ (Bastille/Ledru-Rollin), 01 43 43 06 00; fax 01 43 43 00 66

🥄 A "chic clientele" says "it's worth the trip" east of the Bastille to this "timeless Classic" Bistro for its original "1900 decor", "creative take on Traditional fare" and eagerly sought tables overlooking a "lovely little square"; alas, the place's popularity means the service can be "poor", and some pessimists protest that it "takes itself a little too seriously."

Stella ◐   – | – | – | M
133, av Victor Hugo, 16ᵉ (Rue de la Pompe/Victor Hugo), 01 56 90 56 00; fax 01 56 90 56 01

This venerable brasserie with a winsome '50s-vintage interior has returned under new ownership, and is being frequented by almost exactly the same tweed-wearing, bourgeois 16th-arrondissement clientele it always had; its allure includes shellfish trays, solid Classic French favorites, swift service and reasonable prices for this expensive part of town.

Stella Maris 🥄   23 | 15 | 21 | 78
4, rue Arsène Houssaye, 8ᵉ (Charles de Gaulle-Etoile), 01 42 89 16 22; fax 01 42 89 16 01

■ "Wow" exclaim enthusiasts of this "hidden pearl" near the Etoile in the 8th, where chef Tateru Yoshino brings an "inventive" deft hand and Japanese perfectionism to "excellent" French Classic cuisine (including "very good game in season"); if some whisper the "art deco decor" is "hushed" and "a trifle soulless", "the service is fortunately warm and welcoming."

Stéphane Martin 🥄   ∇ 22 | 17 | 22 | 48
67, rue des Entrepreneurs, 15ᵉ (Charles Michels/Commerce), 01 45 79 03 31; fax 01 45 79 44 69

■ "As charming as can be" say supporters of this "out-of-the-way locale" in the 15th arrondissement, where the namesake chef-owner exhibits "perfect mastery" of "refined" dishes that are "inventive (but not wildly so) riffs on Traditional" French fare as well as an "excellent value"; his wife, Marie-Lucille, oversees both the "good wine list" and "attentive service."

Strapontins (Les)   – | – | – | M
16, av Richerand, 10ᵉ (Bonsergent/République), 01 42 41 94 79

Hipsters in the funky Canal Saint-Martin area rub elbows with hospital workers from down the street at this newly arrived "neo-bistro" with its long gray-and-white banquettes, saying it's "a decent place to grab a bite" of Classic French cuisine from an oft-changing menu without breaking the bank.

| F | D | S | €C |

Stresa (Le) 🗷 | 19 | 13 | 14 | 83 |
7, rue Chambiges, 8ᵉ (Alma-Marceau), 01 47 23 51 62
■ A "chic" clientele of stars and supermodels makes it "hard to get a table" at this gastronomic Italian, an 8th arrondissement institution that always attracts an 'in' crowd – not for the 1950s decor, but "for the fun, the atmosphere and the owners"; there's no denying "it is expensive" ("watch out for those wines") but "the whole scene is worth the pricey tag."

Studio (The) ● | ∇ 11 | 17 | 14 | 29 |
41, rue du Temple, 4ᵉ (Hôtel-de-Ville/Rambuteau), 01 42 74 10 38; fax 01 42 41 50 34; www.the-studio.fr
■ 'Salsa night' means both dipping and dancing at this Tex-Mex located in a "lovely big courtyard" with "a view of the classes at the Marais Dance Center"; it's an ideal destination on a "summer evening or for a drink" though nobody's bending over backward for the "mediocre food"; then again, "with a few margaritas, who cares?"

Sud (Le) 🗷 | 16 | 23 | 15 | 49 |
91, bd Gouvion-St-Cyr, 17ᵉ (Porte Maillot), 01 45 74 02 77; fax 01 45 74 35 36
■ "Escape to Provence without leaving Paris" profess patrons of this regional retreat – "just off the heavy traffic of Porte Maillot" – that's "guaranteed to transport you" with its "fabulous decor" including an interior patio, olive trees and "singing crickets" ("be sure to be seated upstairs"); the Mediterranean-Provençal cuisine ranges from "pretty good to passable", but the "warm ambiance" "makes it worthwhile."

Suite (La) | 14 | 18 | 11 | 66 |
40, av George V, 8ᵉ (George V), 01 53 57 49 49; fax 01 53 57 49 48
■ "Make sure to wear your new Gucci stilettos" to this "slightly decadent" restaurant/nightspot in the 8th run by the Guettas, king and queen of Paris nightlife; it's a "clublike" space with white "1960s-style" decor where "the most jet-set crowd in Paris" flocks "to see and be seen" despite the "average" New French food and "absolutely unprofessional service" provided by "hostesses who look and dress like models."

Table d'Anvers (La) 🗷 | 23 | 15 | 21 | 80 |
2, pl d'Anvers, 9ᵉ (Anvers), 01 48 78 35 21; fax 01 45 26 66 67
■ With "new owners" and a new chef, this "delightful" Traditional French at the foot of Montmartre wins praise as "an absolute treat in an out-of-the-way location" for its "sublime" cooking and "highly courteous service"; the only thing that gives wallet-watchers pause is the "somewhat pricey" check.

get updates at zagat.com

| F | D | S | €C |

Table de la Fontaine (La) ●☒ – | – | – | M
5, rue Henri Monnier, 9ᵉ (St-Georges), 01 45 26 26 30; fax 01 40 23 90 69
"One of the nicer, less touristy places in the area" around Pigalle, this table with its theatrical red-and-gold decor is "perfect for dinner with friends", serving "quite good" Med meals – veal kidneys *à l'orange,* chicken with olives and chile peppers – at "prices that can't be beat."

Table de Lucullus (La) ☒ – | – | – | E
129, rue Legendre, 17ᵉ (Brochant/La Fourche), 01 40 25 02 68; fax 01 40 25 02 68
One of the most intriguing catches of the day, though "still to be discovered", is this "funky", tiny table up in the 17th run by "young, talented" Nicolas Vagnon, a "brilliant culinary mad scientist" whose seafood menu (written on oversized blackboard menus) is "fresh-fresh-fresh", all wild, and remarkably "original"; P.S. "there is a nonsmoking policy."

Table du Baltimore (La) – | – | – | E
Sofitel Demeure Hôtel Baltimore, 88, bis av Kléber, 16ᵉ (Kléber), 01 44 34 54 34; fax 01 44 34 54 44; www.hotelbaltimore.com
"Wish more people would find this place" profess fans of chef Jean-Philippe Pérol, whose talent for "imaginative" Haute Cuisine – perfected during his tenure as second-in-command at Pré Catelan – remains "confidential" while he is hidden in this upscale hotel restaurant in the 16th; for now, it's primarily business folk who commandeer this "calm" space, perhaps to indulge in a seven-course champagne menu that includes a bottle of bubbly.

Table Oliviers & Co. (La) ☒ – | – | – | M
Oliviers & Co., 8, rue de Lévis, 17ᵉ (Villiers), 01 53 42 18 04; fax 01 53 42 18 15; www.oliviers-co.com
"It smells like the south" at this "warm" Mediterranean midday spot set in one of the French olive-oil chain's boutiques in a "charming out-of-the-way location" in the 17th; it serves mini-portions of "marvelous country fare", plus Provençal wines, to a bustling lunchtime crowd at a communal table d'hôte.

TAILLEVENT ☒ 28 | 27 | 28 | 150
15, rue Lamennais, 8ᵉ (Charles de Gaulle-Etoile/ George V), 01 44 95 15 01; fax 01 42 25 95 18; www.taillevent.com
■ "Reserve far ahead for your own slice of heaven" (minutes from l'Etoile) at "the grandest establishment on Earth" – the *Survey*'s perennial No. 1 for Food, Service and Popularity – serving "the epitome of Classic French" Haute Cuisine under "genius" chef Alain Solivérès; "come here to be cosseted" (for "the staff to be any better they'd have to spoon-feed you"), knowing that owner "Jean-Claude Vrinat sets

| F | D | S | €C |

the standard for elegance" in a "beautifully decorated townhouse" whose cellar "makes wine lovers drool."

Taïra ⊠
| – | – | – | E |

10, rue des Acacias, 17ᵉ (Argentine), 01 47 66 74 14; fax 01 47 66 74 14

East meets West in this small, modern room in the 17th, where chef-owner Taïra Kurihara's "unique Contemporary French–Japanese fusion cooking" results in "superb fish dishes" that seem "moderately priced", given their "inventive" nature (and also the three-course prix fixe at both lunch and dinner).

Taka ⊠
∇ | 24 | 14 | 21 | 34 |

1, rue Véron, 18ᵉ (Abbesses), 01 42 23 74 16

■ Open only at night, this "miniscule establishment" is a "haunt known by the locals" of Montmartre as a "real Japanese" (right down to "the bill, calculated on an abacus"); it was one of the first to provide Parisians with authentically "savory" dishes, including "super-fresh" sushi and what raw-fish fans call the "best sashimi in Paris"; if the Nipponese-style decor is a little "simple", the service is "personalized" and "sweet."

Tan Dinh ⊠⌿
| 22 | 13 | 21 | 60 |

60, rue de Verneuil, 7ᵉ (Rue du Bac/Solférino), 01 45 44 04 84; fax 01 45 44 36 93

■ The "best Vietnamese outside of Saigon" fawn fans of this family-run establishment behind the Musée d'Orsay, as renowned for its "fabulous", even "intimidating" wine list (including a spectacular selection of Pomerols) and "charming" staff as for the "subtle flavors and spices" of its cuisine; "forget the decor", which is "nothing to write home about", and bring along a wad of cash ("how can they get by without taking credit cards?") to cover a bill that some find "a tad excessive."

Tang ⊠
| 21 | 14 | 19 | 62 |

125, rue de la Tour, 16ᵉ (Rue de la Pompe), 01 45 04 35 35; fax 01 45 04 58 19

◾ If there's one point upon which all surveyors agree, it's that this 16th arrondissement Asian is "*cher*" – and though admirers argue the "well-prepared" Cantonese food and "professional service" are worth the price, skeptics snap this "pretentious" place has lost its tang, asking sarcastically "does it taste better if it's expensive?"

Tanjia ●⊠
| 13 | 19 | 12 | 53 |

23, rue de Ponthieu, 8ᵉ (Franklin D. Roosevelt), 01 42 25 95 00; fax 01 42 25 95 02

◾ A "young, cosmopolitan Euro crowd with money to spend" turns out for the "Marrakesh-in-Paris ambiance" of this address near the Champs-Elysées run by the ever-fashionable Guetta duo; but gourmands grouse the

get updates at zagat.com

| F | D | S | €C |

exotically "beautiful decor" and belly dancers on weekends don't make up for "good but not extraordinary", "vaguely Moroccan" cuisine and servers with a "tendency to forget you are there"; N.B. a post-*Survey* chef change may outdate the Food score.

Tante Jeanne 🚫 | – | – | – | E |

116, bd Péreire, 17ᵉ (Péreire), 01 43 80 88 68; fax 01 47 66 53 02; www.bernard-loiseau.com

"This is a place to recommend, even after the loss of Bernard Loiseau", the late, esteemed Burgundian chef; this address in the 17th, the last of his three Paris establishments to open, offers "delicious" Classic French, accompanied by an interesting selection of Burgundy wines, in an "agreeable" chandeliered-and-mirrored setting.

Tante Louise 🚫 | 22 | 16 | 21 | 60 |

41, rue Boissy-d'Anglas, 8ᵉ (Concorde/Madeleine), 01 42 65 06 85; fax 01 42 65 28 19; www.bernard-loiseau.com

■ "Long live the aunt" (*tante*) say faithful followers of "deceased chef Bernard Loiseau's" 8th arrondissement bistro, who continue to come for the "overall high quality" of the "simple" "Traditional" French dishes with a Burgundy accent, "cordial service" and an "elegant" '30s-style decor.

Tante Marguerite 🚫 | 21 | 16 | 22 | 58 |

5, rue de Bourgogne, 7ᵉ (Assemblée Nationale/Invalides), 01 45 51 79 42; fax 01 47 53 79 56; www.bernard-loiseau.com

■ "Go just to see the politicians" who lunch at the recently departed chef Bernard Loiseau's comfortable annex near the Assemblée Nationale on "good" Classic French "rural dishes" that "neither disappoint nor surprise"; the "sophisticated, smooth service" is just what one would expect in this bourgeois part of town.

Tastevin | 25 | 21 | 21 | 58 |

9, av Eglé, Maisons-Laffitte (RER Maisons-Laffitte), 01 39 62 11 67; fax 01 39 62 73 09

■ "The walk into the park, the rooms and the meal are all delightful" at this bucolic yet "chic" Classic French with "a Napoleon III–style atmosphere" in the gardens at Maisons-Laffitte; "pleasant", "traditional cooking" by chef-owner Michel Blanchet combines with the warm reception of his wife Amélia to make this country outing "a marvelous experience", especially if you sit outside in summer.

Taverne de Maître Kanter ● | ∇ 13 | 10 | 12 | 33 |

16, rue Coquillière, 1ᵉʳ (Châtelet-Les Halles/Louvre-Rivoli), 01 42 36 74 24; fax 01 43 42 19 75

◪ With its "beer-hall atmosphere and the convenience of being open 24/7", this "Alsatian venue" close to Les Halles is "practical for nighttime hunger pangs", and also offers "a safe bet for large appetites" in need of a choucroute or seafood platter anytime of the day; however, pickier

F | D | S | €C

palates would rather "run away" from what they deem "pedestrian" brasserie fare.

Taverne "L'Esprit Boulevard" ◐ ⎯|⎯|⎯| M
24, bd des Italiens, 9ᵉ (Opéra/Richelieu-Drouot), 01 55 33 10 00; fax 01 55 33 10 09
Ballet-goers who crave oysters and beer after the show can bound over to this immense, "upbeat", baroque-style restaurant near the Opéra Garnier; belonging to one of the city's brasserie dynasties, it's a "classic Blanc Brothers" joint, serving simple fare from choucroute to shellfish seven days a week and late into the night.

Télégraphe (Le) ◐   15 | 22 | 17 | 57
41, rue de Lille, 7ᵉ (Rue du Bac/Solférino), 01 42 92 03 04; fax 01 42 92 02 77
■ "You'll feel like you entered a Klimt painting" when you see the "gorgeous art nouveau decor" at this "cool space" with a courtyard garden near the Musée d'Orsay; a dormitory for telegraph operators a century ago, it now serves "good" kosher Classic French fare and, though not as "trendy" as in recent years, it is "still crowded and noisy", and "a good bet for first-time Paris visitors."

Temps des Cerises (Le) ◐ 🈲   ▽ 15 | 15 | 15 | 27
18, rue de la Butte-aux-Cailles, 13ᵉ (Place d'Italie), 01 45 89 69 48
■ Working-class stiffs appreciate the "proletarian meals at proletarian prices" at this "very-well-known Butte-aux-Cailles" classic run by an employees' cooperative, where "strangers" share "long communal tables" and tuck into "copious" portions of "basic grub in a laid-back fun atmosphere"; the whole experience is so "typically French" that the crowd even "breaks out into song sometimes."

Terminus Nord ◐   17 | 21 | 16 | 41
23, rue de Dunkerque, 10ᵉ (Gare du Nord), 01 42 85 05 15; fax 01 40 16 13 98; www.flobrasserie.com
■ A "perfect welcome to Paris after the Chunnel" (or conversely, the "last chance for a decent meal if you're using Eurostar"), this "big, bustling brasserie" "convenient to the Gare du Nord" "brings back *la belle époque*" with its "polished wood, beveled glass" and "acrobatic waiters carrying silver plates of shellfish"; the "reliable", "tasty" seafood is "typical of the Flo Group", its owner.

Terrasse (La)   ⎯|⎯|⎯| E
Hôtel Terrass, 12, rue Joseph de Maistre, 18ᵉ (Abbesses/ Place de Clichy), 01 44 92 34 00; fax 01 42 52 29 11; www.terrass-hotel.com
The name says it all, since most people come to "this secret hideaway" in a Montmartre hotel for (and, some say, "only for") the "beautiful view over all Paris" offered by the seventh-floor "terrace when the weather is fine"; surveyors

| F | D | S | €C |

are more mum when it comes to the Med-Provençal menu, but at least the prices, while elevated, aren't sky-high.

Terroir (Le) ⓢ | 18 | 11 | 18 | 53 |
11, bd Arago, 13ᵉ (Les Gobelins), 01 47 07 36 99;
fax 01 42 72 52 20

■ "A must when you're in the mood for *la France profonde*" rave reviewers of this "rustic" bistro in the 13th, where "huge portions" of "down-home" "Traditional French cuisine" are made from "ingredients that taste like they were in the garden this morning"; "the owner, Michel Chavanon, knows everyone and treats all his clients like friends."

Thanksgiving | ▽ 15 | 10 | 14 | 32 |
20, rue St-Paul, 4ᵉ (St-Paul), 01 42 77 68 28; fax 01 42 77 70 83;
www.thanksgivingparis.com

■ "Homesick Americans" get their fix of gumbo and pecan pie at this "quaint, small" restaurant in the Marais specializing in "big portions" (U.S.-style) of "surprisingly good" Cajun-Creole cuisine and a "copious brunch" on weekends at "moderate" prices; pining pilgrims "suffering from peanut-butter withdrawal" can stock up on such "much-needed staples" at the adjacent store.

Thierry Burlot ⓢ | – | – | – | E |
(aka Le Quinze)
8, rue Nicolas Charlet, 15ᵉ (Pasteur), 01 42 19 08 59;
fax 01 45 67 09 13

After knocking around several institutions, Crillon-trained chef and "rising star" Thierry Burlot is at last on his own, running this small table in the15th; his technical dexterity comes through in his "wonderfully creative", monthly changing New French menu, served in a "casually elegant", subdued-toned setting.

Thiou ⓢ | 22 | 21 | 17 | 52 |
49, quai d'Orsay, 7ᵉ (Invalides), 01 40 62 96 70; fax 01 40 62 97 30
3, rue Surcouf, 7ᵉ (Invalides), 01 40 62 96 50; fax 01 40 62 96 70
12, av George V, 8ᵉ (Alma-Marceau), 01 47 20 89 56

■ Mme. Thiou's fashionable fan club has considered her "a star" since her days cooking at the old Les Bains Douches, and they now trek happily to her "refined" establishment on the Quai d'Orsay for "authentic, flavorful" and "original Thai cuisine" "that's among the best in Paris"; the budget-conscious boogie to the nearby annex on the Rue Surcouf, which is "cheaper and as nice, though you won't be able to people-watch"; N.B. the branch in the 8th is unrated.

Thoumieux ☾ | 16 | 17 | 15 | 40 |
Hôtel Thoumieux, 79, rue St-Dominique, 7ᵉ (Invalides/
La Tour-Maubourg), 01 47 05 49 75; fax 01 47 05 36 96;
www.thoumieux.com

◪ Those wondering "what it must have been like in Paris 40 years ago" get a taste at this "quintessential" brasserie with "mirrored walls and crisp, white table linens" that's been open since 1923 near Les Invalides; tourists and "local regulars" crowd together "elbow to elbow" for "solid and consistent" "comfort" food from the Southwest that's "edible" if not excellent, served by authentically "arrogant waiters" seven days a week.

Timbre (Le) ▽ 18 | 11 | 19 | 35

3, rue St-Beuve, 6ᵉ (Vavin), 01 45 49 10 40

■ Barely bigger than the postage stamp it's named for, this "nice spot" with "no decor" is easy to miss, but those who discover it behind the Luxembourg gardens give their stamp of approval to the "tasty" Classic Bistro food, prepared without pretension", and the British cheese platter, at prices worth writing home about.

Timgad (Le) 23 | 23 | 18 | 50

21, rue Brunel, 17ᵉ (Argentine), 01 45 74 23 70; fax 01 40 68 76 46

■ Adventurers looking for a "transporting evening" are not disappointed by this "fabulous Moroccan", "the best in Paris", that's open every day in the 17th; the ornate Moorish interior (which has "nothing Parisian" about it) makes an exotic backdrop for "always-perfect" tagines and all-you-can-eat couscous, accompanied by North African wines.

Tire-Bouchon (Le) 22 | 13 | 22 | 37

62, rue des Entrepreneurs, 15ᵉ (Charles Michels), 01 40 59 09 27; fax 01 40 59 09 27

■ There's "all the charm of a mom and pop" at this "small", "convivial" corner in the 15th, where the "chef-owner and his wife know what the word welcome means"; the "original" New French cuisine is enhanced by a "good wine list" ('tire-bouchon' means corkscrew in French) and "interesting tasting menu", resulting in an experience that "verges on fine dining without the high prices."

Toi — | — | — | M

27, rue du Colisée, 8ᵉ (Franklin D. Roosevelt/St-Philippe-du-Roule), 01 42 56 56 58; fax 01 42 56 09 60

Admirers of Austin Powers will feel right at home at this hip, new lounge/eatery near the Champs-Elysées, whose "fun psychedelic decor" conjures up the swinging '70s; it's already a playground for Paris' golden youth, pre- or post-clubbing, with an "original" New French menu that ranges from sandwiches to more substantial eats.

Tokyo Eat — | — | — | M

Palais de Tokyo, 13, av du President Wilson, 16ᵉ (Iéna), 01 47 20 00 29; fax 01 47 20 05 62

Contemporary culture vultures with a taste for fusion food can sate their appetites at the cavernous Palais de Tokyo museum in the 16th, where this spacious newcomer offers a futuristic feast for the eyes; though officially New French,

| F | D | S | €C |

the offerings from the open kitchen at the Eat cafe are also "good for a sushi fix" between installations, while a quicker bite can be had downstairs at the Idem cafeteria.

Tong Yen ● | 21 | 9 | 17 | 58 |
1 bis, rue Jean Mermoz, 8ᵉ (Franklin D. Roosevelt), 01 42 25 04 23; fax 01 45 63 51 57

◪ For four decades, owner Thérèse Luong has greeted the town's movers and shakers at her 8th arrondissement institution for "remarkable" Chinese and Southeast Asian classics that some call "the best in Paris"; the "expensive" prices and "dusty", "dated" interior lead some to suggest she "spend a bit of money renewing the decor", but stalwart patrons profess "if the President of the Republic dines here, it's good enough for me."

Tonkinoise (La) ⌀ | – | – | – | I |
20, rue Philibert Lucot, 13ᵉ (Maison Blanche), 01 45 85 98 98

Aficionados of authentic Vietnamese food are willing to make the pilgrimage to this *petite* pay-no-mind address in the 13th for real family-style cooking, from shrimp cakes to "soups that are all worth trying"; and there's no reason not to when the prices are so low.

Tonnelle Saintongeaise (La) ⌧ | – | – | – | M |
32, bd Vital Bouhot, Neuilly (Pont-de-Levallois), 01 46 24 43 15; fax 01 46 24 36 33

Chic island dwellers make this homey restaurant on the Ile de la Jatte in Neuilly their weekday warm-weather hangout, noting it's "very nice in summer, especially with its covered courtyard for rainy weather"; when it turns cold outside they take refuge in a glass-enclosed winter garden, over plates of Classic French fare like steamed mussels and steak tartare.

Toque (La) ⌧ | – | – | – | E |
16, rue de Tocqueville, 17ᵉ (Villiers), 01 42 27 97 75; fax 01 47 63 97 69

Clients take their toques off to this "very small" (30 seats) site in the 17th with its "charming" painted trompe l'oeil sky, where chef-owner Jacky Joubert has offered an inventive and "excellent" take on Classic French cooking for the past 25 years; the "service is friendly and attentive", and the prices "attractive" for the quality of the cuisine.

Toupary (Le) ⌧ | 13 | 24 | 15 | 47 |
La Samaritaine, 2, quai du Louvre, 1ᵉʳ (Pont-Neuf), 01 40 41 29 29; fax 01 42 33 96 79

◪ "Tourists aren't the only ones blown away" by the "magnificent vista" this restaurant offers from its perch atop the Samaritaine department store ("reserve early for a window seat"); but Parisians and visitors alike grumble that "it's all about the view", since the "service is efficient if unfriendly" and the "disappointing" Traditional French cuisine falls flat.

TOUR D'ARGENT (LA) | 25 | 28 | 26 | 137 |
17, quai de la Tournelle, 5ᵉ (Cardinal Lemoine/ Pont Marie), 01 43 54 23 31; fax 01 44 07 12 04; www.latourdargent.com

◪ "The grande dame of Paris restaurants" is "a mythical place" "packed with" patrons who gasp at the "fairy-tale" view of Notre Dame and order the Haute Cuisine's "exquisite numbered duck" while gushing over "gracious service" and the "vertiginous" wine list ("500,000 bottles"); if critics knock down this tower as "a museum" "living on its glory" and hence "overpriced" ("am I paying for lighting of [the cathedral] by myself?"), it's still a "gotta-go-once" address (hint: at lunch "the prices are easier to handle").

Tourelle (La) ⌀ | - | - | - | I |
43, rue Croix des Petits Champs, 1ᵉʳ (Bourse/Louvre-Rivoli), 01 42 61 35 41

This cozy little *bistrot à vins* is a big hit with employees from the adjacent Banque de France as well as with boutique owners, antique dealers and shoppers drawn to the fashion stores lining the Place des Victoires nearby; one or two old-fashioned dishes are offered daily to complement a menu that runs to cheese, charcuterie, salads and excellent wines from the nearby Caves Augé.

Tournesol (Le) | 14 | 17 | 16 | 47 |
2, av de Lamballe, 16ᵉ (Passy), 01 45 25 95 94; fax 01 45 25 43 09

■ The "excellent ambiance" of this "cool" "neighborhood" hang means it's "always full" with Passy's "privileged youth", who crowd in for the "party" atmosphere created by "good", "basic Bistro cuisine", and summer terrace "facing the Seine."

TRAIN BLEU (LE) | 17 | 28 | 18 | 58 |
Gare de Lyon, 12ᵉ (Gare de Lyon), 01 43 43 09 06; fax 01 43 43 97 96; www.le-train-bleu.com

◪ "May the train never come" sigh fans of the "awesome belle-epoque interior" in this brasserie at the Gare de Lyon, where the "frescoed ceilings" and "fabulous murals" "take one back to days of yore"; "a new chef" has some convinced that the Classic French "food is improving", while others say it's simply "competent"; but "the real star" is the setting, "perfect for a glass of champagne" "even if you don't need" to travel anywhere.

Tricotin ☾ | - | - | - | I |
15, av de Choisy, 13ᵉ (Porte de Choisy), 01 45 84 74 44; fax 01 45 85 17 54

"Lines out the door" attest to the fact that "this large, loud, bustling restaurant is the real deal", a "reference" for "authentic Chinese food" and other Southeast Asian

| F | D | S | €C |

specialties in the 13th arrondissement's Chinatown; nobody's raving about the "canteen setting" or dour service, but the "extremely reasonable" prices make those easier to swallow.

Triporteur (Le) ☒   – | – | – | M

4, rue de Dantzig, 15ᵉ (Convention), 01 45 32 82 40
A loyal clientele of "regulars" brings a "joyous, noisy atmosphere" to this "charming" "neighborhood" address deep in the 15th, with its "young, dynamic staff" that "takes real pleasure in receiving" you; the "blackboard menu" proposes Basque-inspired cuisine that is "mouthwatering", "straightforward and unpretentious", but do note that "reservations are imperative."

TROIS MARCHES (LES) ☒   25 | 24 | 23 | 85

Hôtel Trianon Palace, 1, bd de la Reine, Versailles (RER Versailles-Rive Droite), 01 39 50 13 21; fax 01 30 21 01 25; www.trianonpalace.fr
■ "How charming" coo customers of this Haute Cuisine table, "only a five-minute walk to the Palais" of Versailles; the scene is all "elegance in a small-village environment", from the "exquisite food" to "multitiered cheese carts", from a "staff falling all over you" to a lovely "summer terrace" overlooking what were once Louis XIV's gardens; P.S. "don't deprive yourself of the Hôtel Trianon's charms" afterwards.

TROQUET (LE) ☒   25 | 15 | 19 | 37

21, rue François Bonvin, 15ᵉ (Sèvres-Lecourbe/Volontaire), 01 45 66 89 00; fax 01 45 66 89 83
■ An "enthusiastic welcome awaits" at this "neighborhood find" in the 15th, a "justly popular little bistro that packs them in for an extraordinary four-course prix fixe" of "always-fresh" New French fare ("throw in a few more euros and get a fifth course of cheese") "rich with creative flavors"; the menu may be "brief" but "the daily changes keep you coming back for more."

Trou Gascon (Au) ☒   24 | 17 | 22 | 68

40, rue Taine, 12ᵉ (Daumesnil), 01 43 44 34 26; fax 01 43 07 80 55
■ "Foie gras, confit, cassoulet": bring on the "great Gascon food" cry fans of this "longtime favorite" belonging to chef Alain Dutournier, a "homey", though contemporary, site with "cordial" "old-timey waiters" located a bit "off the beaten path" in the 12th; and while some huff it's "hugely expensive", most others call it a "bargain" for "the best Southwestern in Paris."

Truffe Noire (La) ☒   19 | 13 | 16 | 62

2, pl Parmentier, Neuilly (Les Sablons/Porte Maillot), 01 46 24 94 14; fax 01 46 24 94 60
■ Black-gold diggers strike it rich at this Neuilly address specializing in "truffles, elegantly prepared in a variety of

F | D | S | €C

forms"; although the "slightly formal" setting is "a bit old-fashioned", it remains a "charming" outpost for "consistently good quality" Classic French cuisine.

TRUFFIÈRE (LA) 25 | 22 | 24 | 68
4, rue Blainville, 5ᵉ (Cardinal Lemoine/Place Monge), 01 46 33 29 82; fax 01 46 33 64 74; www.latruffiere.com
■ "Time stops when you're seated by the fireplace" in the vaulted cellar of this "cozy, welcoming" 17th-century house in the 5th; the "refined" menu, a combo of New and Classic French dishes, is "laced with gorgeous truffles", "the wine list is phenomenal" and the "cheese cart is huge", so no one minds that "it's a bit of a tourist trap" where "your money disappears without even waving good-bye."

Trumilou (Le) 16 | 9 | 17 | 31
84, quai de l'Hôtel-de-Ville, 4ᵉ (Hôtel-de-Ville/Pont-Marie), 01 42 77 63 98; fax 01 48 04 91 89
■ "When you don't want to dress up", this "old-style" family-run bistro "steps from the Hôtel de Ville" is ideal for a "convenient and casual" Classic meal that "tastes like what your French mom would make"; the environs may look "a little worn around the edges", but all agree it's a "great value" nonetheless.

Tsé-Yang 18 | 20 | 19 | 67
25, av Pierre 1er de Serbie, 16ᵉ (Alma-Marceau/Iéna), 01 47 20 70 22; fax 01 49 52 03 68
■ Beijing goes bourgeois at this "classy" Chinese in the 16th that boasts a "classic" imperial setting, "attentive service" and "extensive" wine list; its "excellent" menu from all over the mainland omits the Vietnamese or Thai dishes found at other Sino sites in Paris; regulars tout the Peking duck as "the best" – but warn, "you pay for it."

Tsukizi ⌀ – | – | – | M
2 bis, rue des Ciseaux, 6ᵉ (Mabillon/St-Germain-des-Prés), 01 43 54 65 19
Nipponphiles note that "if you miss Tokyo" this "tiny place" "is closest to the real thing", bringing "Japanese charm" to Saint-Germain with an assortment of "delicate" sushis and sashimis served at the bar or a few tables; but your yen for raw fish should match the yen in your wallet, for while it's moderate overall, "expensive" extras mean it's easy to "inadvertently run up the tab."

Ty Coz ⌀ – | – | – | E
35, rue St-Georges, 9ᵉ (St-Georges), 01 48 78 42 95
Enthusiasts say it's "like being in Brittany" at this veteran address in the 9th, where the regional fare includes "nice fish" and "great crêpes and cider"; detractors disagree, calling the provincial-style decor with exposed beams "dark and sad", and the menu "overpriced" for the "exact same [thing] you can find at any little hole."

| | | | F | D | S | €C |

Va et Vient (Le) 🚫 — — — — M
8, rue des Batignolles, 17ᵉ (Place de Clichy/Rome), 01 45 22 54 22; www.vaetvient.fr
Clients come and come again to this family-run hole-in-the-wall bistro (formerly a cafe/bar) in the increasingly trendy Batignolles neighborhood; its "pleasant" ambiance, replete with copper pots hanging from the wall, is the backdrop for "huge, tasty portions" of Traditional French and Alsatian- style cooking (onion tart, pork shank) just like *grand-mère* used to make.

Vagenende ⓿ — 15 | 23 | 15 | 45
142, bd St-Germain, 6ᵉ (Odéon), 01 43 26 68 18; fax 01 40 51 73 38
▣ Serving late seven days a week, this "historic" Left Bank brasserie is "busy all the time", mainly with travelers who come to "feast the eyes" on the "great 1900-era decor"; while the setting's authentically "belle epoque, the food is less than belle" – though it remains "reliable" and "reasonably priced"; but even if the "old warhorse" seems "a little tired", it keeps charging – and that – like the "personnel, who have been around for ages" – is "part of the charm."

Vaudeville (Le) ⓿ — 16 | 21 | 17 | 48
29, rue Vivienne, 2ᵉ (Bourse), 01 40 20 04 62
▣ "Near the Bourse, drown your stock-market sorrows" at this "cheerful", "classic" brasserie that seems "less of a factory than others [owned by] the Flo Group" with its "pretty" "art deco surroundings" and raw bar that's "heaven for oyster and shellfish lovers"; if the rest of the traditional menu "can be uneven", this trouper still offers a "hustling" good show "for a Sunday night out."

Verre Bouteille (Le) ⓿ — — — — M
85, av des Ternes, 17ᵉ (Porte Maillot), 01 45 74 01 02; fax 01 47 63 07 02
5, bd Gouvion-St-Cyr, 17ᵉ (Porte de Champerret), 01 47 63 39 99; fax 01 47 63 07 02
www.leverrebouteille.com
A low-key bite and a tipple are on the menu at this pair of "agreeably" relaxed neighborhood wine bars in the 17th offering an identical selection of Classic Bistro "simple dishes" that are somewhat "inconsistant – good one day, bad the next" – and a couple of dozen wines by the glass; at the more casual Ternes location, night-owls can wet their beaks until 4:30 AM.

Verre Volé (Le) — — — — I
67, rue de Lancry, 10ᵉ (République), 01 48 03 17 34; fax 01 68 03 17 34
This "walk-in closet–size" wine bar/boutique is as offbeat as the Canal Saint-Martin neighborhood it calls home;

| F | D | S | €C |

Viaduc Café (Le) ☕   12 | 15 | 14 | 30
43, av Daumesnil, 12ᵉ (Bastille/Gare de Lyon), 01 44 74 70 70; fax 01 44 74 70 71; www.viaduc-cafe.fr

◪ Weekend strollers appreciate this "pit stop on the promenade" "under the arcades" of a renovated railway viaduct in the 12th for its "pretty", "airy" decor and "nice but noisy terrace"; but most mutter that the mixture of "basic" Classic and New French cuisine, delivered by "indifferent" servers, is "terribly uneven", so stick to "salads and fresh foods", "a drink with friends" or the "crowded" Sunday jazz brunch.

Vieille Fontaine Rôtisserie (La)   ∇ 20 | 22 | 19 | 46
8, av Grétry, Maisons-Laffitte (RER Poissy), 01 39 62 01 78; fax 01 39 62 13 43; www.lesbouchonsdefrancoisclerc.com

■ There's a "great feel" to this "sublime setting" in Maisons-Laffitte, a "beautiful house" with authentic Napoleon III decor offering "better-than-average" New and Classic French cuisine (especially rotisseried meats) at lower-than-average prices; its "summer terrace" overlooking a park makes it especially welcoming in warm weather.

Vieux Bistro (Le)   20 | 15 | 17 | 44
14, rue du Cloître Notre-Dame, 4ᵉ (Cité), 01 43 54 18 95; fax 01 44 07 35 63

◪ "The name fits to a 'T'" at this "old-time bistro in the shadow of Notre Dame", where the faithful feed on "solid French fare" that's "some of the most Classic and best Lyonnais cuisine" in the city; "it hasn't lost a step, despite" an influx of tourists (though visitors remark that "the back room seems to be reserved for English-speakers"), but natives and foreigners alike are struck by the offhand service "that lacks grace, even after Sunday mass."

Villa (La)   – | – | – | M
17-19, rue St-Blaise, 20ᵉ (Porte de Bagnolet), 01 30 09 92 36

In a quiet, almost rural, part of the 20th, this cozy, little bistro is making a reputation for itself with generous, high-quality Spanish-Argentinean cooking, including beef imported from the Pampas; the young clientele also enjoys the relaxed atmosphere, friendly service and good selection of Iberian and South American wines.

Villa Corse (La) ☕🖼   18 | 19 | 13 | 40
164, bd de Grenelle, 15ᵉ (Cambronne/La Motte-Picquet-Grenelle), 01 53 86 70 81; fax 01 53 86 90 73

■ Corsicans adrift in Paris seize an "invitation to travel" home without leaving the 15th at this "villa" where the

| F | D | S | €C |

"cozy" setting, complete with a library, is as "warm" as the climate on the actual Ile de Beauté; the "real regional products" include a tempting charcuterie platter and a "good wine cellar" featuring robust reds from the island.

Village d'Ung et Li Lam ❶ — — — M
10, rue Jean Mermoz, 8ᵉ (Franklin D. Roosevelt), 01 42 25 99 79; fax 01 42 25 12 06
Ung is in the glass-walled kitchen, Li Lam is at the door and there's a surprising six-ton aquarium on the ceiling at this "convivial space" steps from the Champs, where for two decades fans of Thai and Chinese cuisine have "satisfied their appetite" over plates of shrimp dumplings, Peking duck and chocolate nems (fried stuffed pastries).

Village Kabyle ⌧ — — — M
4, rue Aimé Lavy, 18ᵉ (Jules Joffrin), 01 42 55 03 34
The inimitable Wally le Saharien's second (smaller, plainer) address, in the northern reaches of the 18th, is an oasis for "out-of-the-ordinary couscous" (including one variety with tripe) and other Kabyle specialties from the Algerian desert, along with North African wines for parched palates.

Villa Mauresque (La) ⌧ — — — M
5-7, rue du Cdt-Rivière, 8ᵉ (St-Philippe-du-Roule), 01 42 25 16 69; fax 01 42 56 37 05; www.villamauresque.com
This North African table in the chic 8th "has a certain exoticism" with its three rooms replicating the different ambiances of Marrakesh, Fez and Casablanca; patrons praise the "refined presentation" but pan the "more good-looking than effective staff" and "small portions" of "trendy" Franco-Moroccan cuisine that have some diners asking for moor.

Villaret (Le) ❶⌧ 27 16 19 44
13, rue Ternaux, 11ᵉ (Oberkampf/Parmentier), 01 43 57 89 76; fax 01 43 57 89 69
■ Delighted diners say this "brick-and-stone-walled", "unpretentious setting" "off the beaten track" in the 11th is a "jewel" offering "one of best values in Paris": "abundant portions" of "incredible, true Classic French cuisine" with modern, "inventive" touches and "subtle combinations" of flavors, along with a list of "exceptional but affordable wines"; what's more, the "gastronomic adventure" changes with the menu every day.

Vinci (Le) ⌧ — — — E
23, rue Paul Valéry, 16ᵉ (Victor Hugo), 01 45 01 68 18; fax 01 45 01 60 37
This "chic" "neighborhood Italian" near the Place Victor Hugo may be "small" but it turns out *grande* cuisine" thanks to a chef who worked with Joël Robuchon and so brings fine French technique to "very-good" imported products, with "excellent service" to boot.

| F | D | S | €C |

Vinea Café (Le) ◐ — | — | — | M
26-28, Cour St-Emilion, 12ᵉ (Cour St-Emilion), 01 44 74 09 09; fax 01 44 74 06 66; www.vinea-cafe.fr
Shoppers browsing the "trendy Bercy district" and the Cour Saint-Emilion (old home to the city's wine storehouses) can stop for a bite of Med-influenced French cuisine at this wood-and-stone café with two terraces, open daily and for Sunday brunch, with a DJ spinning tunes weekend nights.

Vin et Marée — 16 | 11 | 15 | 43
165, rue St-Honoré, 1ᵉʳ (Palais Royal-Musée du Louvre), 01 42 86 06 96; fax 01 42 86 06 97 ⓢ
71, av de Suffren, 7ᵉ (La Motte-Picquet-Grenelle), 01 47 83 27 12; fax 01 43 06 62 35
276, bd Voltaire, 11ᵉ (Nation), 01 43 72 31 23; fax 01 40 09 05 24
108, av du Maine, 14ᵉ (Gaîté), 01 43 20 29 50; fax 01 43 27 84 11 ◐
183, bd Murat, 16ᵉ (Porte de St-Cloud), 01 46 47 91 39; fax 01 46 47 69 07
◪ Fin fanatics flock to this chain for seafood (and nothing but) that, while "simply prepared" ("you could do the same at home"), is "consistently good" and "always fresh", since the chalkboard menu follows the "offerings at Rungis market"; the "reasonable prices" make up for the "sad decor" and "a welcome that can be as cold as the fish" at some sites; but everywhere, sweet tooths swoon over the "famous baba au rhum" they say is "as big as your head."

20 de Bellechasse (Le) ⓢ — | — | — | M
20, rue de Bellechasse, 7ᵉ (Solférino), 01 47 05 11 11; fax 01 47 05 20 00
Just a few steps from the Musée d'Orsay in the stylish 7th, this casual, friendly Traditional Bistro offers generous portions, easy prices and cheerful young servers; very popular at noon with a crowd from the many government ministries in the area, it's quieter at night when frequented by a mix of locals and tourists; the decor is highlighted by the many framed caricatures of various celebrities.

Vin sur Vin ⓢ — 21 | 17 | 24 | 53
20, rue de Monttessuy, 7ᵉ (Alma-Marceau/Ecole Militaire), 01 47 05 14 20
■ Surveyors toast this "quiet", "intimate" place just a couple "blocks from the *Tour Eiffel*" for its "wonderful wine" cellar – 600 different vintages that constitute not a "list but a book" – complemented by "elegant", "inventive" New French cuisine and "exceptional, personalized service" by the oenophile owner and his wife.

VIOLON D'INGRES (LE) ⓢ — 24 | 19 | 22 | 101
135, rue St-Dominique, 7ᵉ (Ecole Militaire), 01 45 55 15 05; fax 01 45 55 48 42; www.leviolondingres.com
◪ "Like Ingres" himself, chef-owner Christian Constant is "technically impeccable" and his loyal supporters are

| | | | F | D | S | €C |

"never disappointed" by his "exquisite", "rather classic" Haute Cuisine and the "unobtrusive" service overseen by his wife, Catherine, in their narrowly proportioned and "conservatively decorated" establishment near the Eiffel Tower; the only constant regret for some is that it's been "taken over by tourists" – but hey, they have the right to "a harmonious indulgence" too.

Virgin Café ● ▽ 9 | 7 | 8 | 22

Virgin Megastore, 52-60, av Champs-Elysées, 8e (Franklin D. Roosevelt), 01 42 56 15 96; fax 01 49 53 03 76
■ "Music fans" hungry from trolling the aisles at the Virgin Megastore can grab a "basic" Classic French snack at this pit stop whose upper-level perch offers a "view over the Champs-Elysées"; it's hardly Haute Cuisine, but it's "cheap" and "handy for meeting up with friends."

Voltaire (Le) ☒ 23 | 20 | 21 | 64

27, quai Voltaire, 7e (Rue du Bac), 01 42 61 17 49
■ In the "same family for three generations", this clubby Classic Bistro facing the Louvre in Saint-Germain has a roster that's "just elaborate enough" to accommodate all tastes and remain "enjoyable from beginning to end"; service "in the grand tradition" and "classy ambiance" attract "wealthy Americans", "literary" bigwigs and the district's antique dealers, with "a bit expensive" prices helping to "keep out the riffraff."

Wadja ☒ 18 | 14 | 17 | 32

10, rue de la Grande Chaumière, 6e (Vavin), 01 46 33 02 02
■ Local artists won't be starving if they alight upon this "imaginative" Montparnasse bistro that's a "good value" for Classic "comfort food" (think "excellent leg of lamb cooked for seven hours"), an "impressive" wine list that includes some organic vintages and "lively" service.

Waknine ☒ ▽ 18 | 17 | 21 | 43

9, av Pierre-1er de Serbie, 16e (Iéna), 01 47 23 48 18; fax 01 47 23 87 33
■ Patrons settle into "comfy" brown velvet armchairs and order off a "solid" New French menu at this "noisy" but "inviting" address with a 1940s-inspired decor; additional pluses include a "kind" staff and its location in an area – the affluent 16th – short on "warm" "neighborhood places."

Wally Le Saharien ☒ – | – | – | M

36, rue Rodier, 9^e (Anvers/Notre-Dame-de-Lorette), 01 42 85 51 90; fax 01 42 85 81 90
Berber-cuisine buffs trek from all points to this atmospheric Algerian in a shabby part of the 9th for "superb" "classics" like an "airy" pigeon pastilla, "delicious" stuffed sardines and the signature desert-style "dry couscous", to be drunk with a "limited" North African wine selection; N.B dinner is exclusively a set menu.

	F	D	S	€C

Wepler ❶ | 16 | 17 | 17 | 42 |
14, pl Clichy, 18ᵉ (Place de Clichy), 01 45 22 53 24; fax 01 44 70 07 50; www.wepler.com

■ Oyster lovers find a pearl on the Place Clichy at this old-time (and still independently owned) "brasserie par excellence" where "everybody is having" "sparkling" "fresh, delicious seafood" platters (the other stuff's "just average") in a slightly "shabby" yet endearingly "nostalgic" 1930s setting that somehow feels more "cozy" when it's "crowded and noisy."

Willi's Wine Bar ⓢ | 19 | 16 | 19 | 43 |
13, rue des Petits-Champs, 1ᵉʳ (Palais Royal-Musée du Louvre/Pyramides), 01 42 61 05 09; fax 01 47 03 36 93; www.williswinebar.com

■ This "delightful watering hole" near the Palais Royal is "a must for wine geeks" who "squeeze" into the narrow space decorated with posters to sample "outstanding", "reasonably priced" international vintages along with "tasty" New Bistro food; owned by Brit Mark Williamson and staffed by "cheery" compatriots, it's a "second home" for "anglo"- and "oenophiles" who wish the kitchen didn't close "so early" (the bar beats on until midnight).

Wok Cooking ❶ | – | – | – | I |
25, rue des Taillandiers, 11ᵉ (Bastille), 01 55 28 88 77; fax 01 55 28 88 78

"Choose your ingredients" along with your preferred sauces "and they're stir-fried in front of you" at this Asian "concept" restaurant near the Bastille; it's "fun with a group", as the "antiseptic" setting provides little diversion for solo diners.

W, Restaurant | – | – | – | E |
Hôtel Warwick, 5, rue de Berri, 8ᵉ (George V), 01 45 61 82 08; fax 01 45 63 75 81; www.warwickparis.com

"Excellent" eats and "very nice service" are the draw at this "discreet" dining room in the Hôtel Warwick, steps from the Champs-Elysées; chef Franck Charpentier turns out "inventive" Haute Cuisine with a Provençal accent that possesses much more dash than the beige-colored, somewhat-"sterile environment"; however, sampling one of the 150 *eaux de vie* that they offer can ensure "a wonderful" time here.

Yen ⓢ | 20 | 22 | 19 | 45 |
22, rue St-Benoît, 6ᵉ (St-Germain-des-Prés), 01 45 44 11 18; fax 01 45 44 19 48

■ Soba and tempura, not sushi, are the stars at this "unpretentious", little Saint-Germain noodle house whose largely "Japanese" clientele and occasional "celebrities" are drawn by the "soothing" "Zen" ambiance, "pleasant" staff and "light, healthy" cuisine.

| | | | F | D | S | €C |

Yvan ●🆉 ▽ 17 | 14 | 18 | 66
*1 bis, rue Jean Mermoz, 8ᵉ (Franklin D. Roosevelt),
01 43 59 18 40; fax 01 42 89 30 95*
■ Although he "remains an absentee chef", owner Yvan Zaplatilek's "intimate and well-run" place near the Champs-Elysées reflects his Belgian roots with a "rustic menu" of "tasty" "classics such as waterzooi" (a creamy fish stew), served in a "snazzy" setting of red velvet and fresh flowers.

Yvan, Petit (Le) ●🆉 18 | 14 | 14 | 43
*1 bis, rue Jean Mermoz, 8ᵉ (Franklin D. Roosevelt),
01 42 89 49 65; fax 01 42 89 30 95*
■ A casual annex of its "big brother next door", this "fun little" bistro in the 8th reels in a "local crowd" with "good" Classic French food at a fine "value"; 'round "midnight", an "outing with friends" may lead to "dancing on the tables"; just be warned: "you might wait for your food while the waiters are busy" joining in the party.

Yves Quintard 🆉 19 | 19 | 16 | 49
99, rue Blomet, 15ᵉ (Convention/Vaugirard), 01 42 50 22 27; fax 01 42 50 22 27
■ Enthusiasts of this "small gem" run by a couple in the 15th praise Monsieur's "flavorful" updated interpretations of Classic French dishes and Madame's "genuinely warm welcome"; the beige room's "subdued lighting" provides just the right wattage for "a romantic dinner."

Zebra Square ● 11 | 16 | 11 | 48
*3, pl Clément-Ader, 16ᵉ (Mirabeau/RER Kennedy-Radio France),
01 44 14 91 91; fax 01 45 20 46 41; www.zebrasquare.com*
◪ On-air personalities from "the nearby Maison de la Radio" make this New French with a "zebra motif" their station of choice for breakfast or a "convenient" lunch despite merely "adequate" eats, "pricey" tabs and "servers too cool to actually do any serving"; it's more "fun for drinks" when a "loud" crowd heats up the sleekly "bohemian" room.

Ze Kitchen Galerie 🆉 23 | 20 | 21 | 53
4, rue des Grands-Augustins, 6ᵉ (St-Michel), 01 44 32 00 32; fax 01 44 32 00 33
◪ An open kitchen invites diners to watch chef-owner William Ledeuil (ex Les Bouquinistes) and his "young team" inject their culinary "verve" into the "exciting", "fusiony" Eclectic fare (like "soups that redefine the category") at this "snazzy", "art-filled" "piece of NY" in Saint-Germain; ze only main debate is over decor – "cool" "if you like the pared-down, minimalist look", "cold" if you don't.

Zéphyr (Le) ● 19 | 21 | 23 | 35
1, rue du Jourdain, 20ᵉ (Jourdain), 01 46 36 65 81; fax 01 46 36 65 81
■ The original "art deco" interior provides a "typically Parisian" setting for "refined" Contemporary Bistro cuisine

190   subscribe to zagat.com

| F | D | S | €C |

prepared by the "sure hand" of new chef-owner Ludovic Enne at this "animated" "real find" in the "out-of-the-way" 20th; open every day, it offers a prix fixe menu that's hard to beat.

Zeyer (Le) ☻   ▽ 17 | 15 | 17 | 36
62, rue d'Alésia, 14ᵉ (Alésia), 01 45 40 43 88; fax 01 45 40 64 51

■ This "authentic" brasserie "*à l'ancienne*" in the 14th uses fresh products as the basis for its "quality cuisine" like the "reputable fish dishes" and "good choucroute and tartare"; service is "amiable" and the "interestingly ugly" interior is the designer Slavik's 1970s update of the original 1930s decor.

Zinc-Zinc   – | – | – | E
209, av Charles de Gaulle, Neuilly (Pont de Neuilly), 01 40 88 36 06; fax 01 47 38 16 21

"Just what we need" quips the Neuilly party pack that's happy to find this "young and somewhat trendy" bistro with its "simple food" ranging from "tasty" tapas to such Classic French staples as farm-raised chicken; all's served in "light-filled", "lively surroundings" dominated by a central bar.

Zo ☻   ▽ 18 | 18 | 20 | 40
13, rue Montalivet, 8ᵉ (Champs-Elysées-Clémenceau), 01 42 65 18 18; fax 01 42 65 10 91; www.restaurantzo.com

■ Globally minded suits and style-mongers inhabiting the 8th call this "funky" address their local "canteen" thanks to an "interesting", "decently priced" menu that mingles Mediterranean and Japanese flavors; the most "daring" of them also wet their whistles with "homemade" fruit-flavored vodka shots.

Zygomates (Les) ⌀   ▽ 24 | 18 | 23 | 42
7, rue de Capri, 12ᵉ (Daumesnil/Michel Bizot), 01 40 19 93 04

■ "The name means the muscles that you grin with, and this friendly place indeed elicits smiles" for its "enjoyable", "excellent" Traditional French "cuisine with a flair" and its "youthful enthusiastic staff"; it's "well worth" going "off the beaten track" in the evolving 12th for this "miniscule" "treasure" set in a former butcher shop.

Indexes

FRENCH CUISINES
OTHER CUISINES
LOCATIONS
SPECIAL FEATURES

Indexes list the best of many within each category.

get updates at zagat.com

French Cuisine Index

FRENCH CUISINES

(Restaurant Names, Food Ratings and Arrondissements)

Belgian
Graindorge/21 (17e)
Yvan/17 (8e)

Bistros (Contemporary)
A et M Le Bistrot/15 (16e)
Affriolé/21 (7e)
Allobroges/– (20e)
Amognes/19 (11e)
Ardoise/22 (1er)
Astrance/26 (16e)
Astuce/– (15e)
Bath's/27 (8e)
Beurre Noisette/23 (15e)
Bistro de Gala/18 (9e)
Bistrot de l'Etoile Niel/21 (17e)
Bistrot du Cap/– (15e)
Bouche à Oreille (De)/– (14e)
Buisson Ardent/– (5e)
Butte Chaillot/20 (16e)
Café Burq/– (18e)
Café d'Angel/18 (17e)
Café de la Jatte/15 (Neuilly)
Café des Délices/21 (6e)
Café Moderne/– (2e)
Café Ruc/13 (1er)
Caïus/– (17e)
C'Amelot/21 (11e)
Cave Gourmande/25 (19e)
Comédiens/– (9e)
Contre-Allée/18 (14e)
Ebauchoir/– (12e)
Epi Dupin/24 (6e)
Gourmand/– (6e)
Maison du Jardin/24 (6e)
Manufacture/23 (Issy-les-Moul.)
Mon Vieil Ami/– (4e)
Pure Café/– (11e)
Ramulaud/18 (11e)
Troquet/25 (15e)
Zéphyr/19 (20e)

Bistros (Traditional)
Absinthe/19 (1er)
Affiche/– (8e)
Ami Pierre/– (11e)
AOC/– (5e)
Assiette/26 (14e)
Astier/21 (11e)
Atelier Maître Albert/– (5e)

Auberge Nicolas Flamel/16 (3e)
Babylone/– (7e)
Baracane/22 (4e)
Bar des Théâtres/14 (8e)
Benoît/23 (4e)
Bistro 121/– (15e)
Bistro du 17ème/16 (17e)
Bistro Melrose/– (17e)
Bistrot d'à Côté/21 (multi. loc.)
Bistrot d'Albert/– (17e)
Bistrot d'Alex/14 (6e)
Bistrot d'André/15 (15e)
Bistrot de Breteuil/14 (7e)
Bistrot de l'Université/– (7e)
Bistrot de Marius/17 (8e)
Bistrot de Paris/17 (7e)
Bistrot des Capucins/– (20e)
Bistrot des Dames/– (17e)
Bistrot des Vignes/17 (16e)
Bistrot d'Henri/20 (6e)
Bistrot du Dôme/19 (multi. loc.)
Bistrot du Peintre/15 (11e)
Bistrot du Sommelier/19 (8e)
Bistrot Papillon/20 (9e)
Bistrot Paul Bert/19 (11e)
Bistrot St. Ferdinand/15 (17e)
Bistrot Vivienne/17 (1er)
Bon Accueil/23 (7e)
Boulangerie/15 (20e)
Bourguignon du Marais/21 (4e)
Café Charbon/14 (11e)
Café Constant/– (7e)
Café de l'Industrie/11 (11e)
Café de Mars/17 (7e)
Café des Lettres/– (7e)
Café du Commerce/10 (15e)
Café Max/– (7e)
Café Ruc/13 (1er)
Camille/19 (3e)
Carpe Diem/– (Neuilly)
Cartet/– (11e)
Cave de l'Os à Moëlle/18 (15e)
Chardenoux/16 (11e)
Charpentiers/16 (6e)
Chez André/18 (8e)
Chez Catherine/21 (8e)
Chez Denise/22 (1er)
Chez Diane/19 (6e)
Chez Fred/18 (17e)
Chez Georges/23 (2e)

French Cuisine Index

Chez Gérard/*18* (Neuilly)
Chez Janou/*20* (3ᵉ)
Chez L'Ami Louis/*26* (3ᵉ)
Chez la Vieille/– (1ᵉʳ)
Chez Léon/– (17ᵉ)
Chez Maître Paul/*21* (6ᵉ)
Chez Marcel/– (6ᵉ)
Chez Nénesse/– (3ᵉ)
Chez Paul/*20* (11ᵉ)
Chez Paul/*21* (13ᵉ)
Chez René/*20* (5ᵉ)
Chez Savy/– (8ᵉ)
Chez Toutoune/*20* (5ᵉ)
Christine/*23* (6ᵉ)
Coconnas/*17* (4ᵉ)
. . . Comme Cochon/– (12ᵉ)
Contre-Allée/*18* (14ᵉ)
Crus de Bourgogne/– (2ᵉ)
D'Chez Eux/*21* (7ᵉ)
Dix Vins/*17* (15ᵉ)
Dos de la Baleine/*14* (4ᵉ)
Ebauchoir/– (12ᵉ)
Ecailler du Bistrot/– (11ᵉ)
Entracte/– (18ᵉ)
Entredgeu/– (17ᵉ)
Epi d'Or/*21* (1ᵉʳ)
Escargot Montorgueil/*18* (1ᵉʳ)
Ferme des Mathurins/– (8ᵉ)
Florimond/*22* (7ᵉ)
Fontaine de Mars/*19* (7ᵉ)
Fontaines/*20* (5ᵉ)
Fous d'en Face/*12* (4ᵉ)
Gauloise/*17* (15ᵉ)
Gavroche/*21* (2ᵉ)
Gourmets des Ternes/*21* (8ᵉ)
Grille/– (10ᵉ)
Grille St-Germain/*16* (6ᵉ)
Joséphine Ch. Dumonet/*19* (6ᵉ)
Languedoc/*17* (5ᵉ)
Lescure/*13* (1ᵉʳ)
Ma Bourgogne/*17* (4ᵉ)
Mascotte/– (8ᵉ)
Mesturet/– (2ᵉ)
Moissonnier/*21* (5ᵉ)
Moulin à Vent/*25* (5ᵉ)
Muscade/– (1ᵉʳ)
Noces de Jeannette/– (2ᵉ)
Oeillade/*16* (7ᵉ)
Papinou/– (Neuilly)
Petit Bofinger/*16* (multi. loc.)
Petite Cour/*20* (6ᵉ)
Petit Marguery/*23* (13ᵉ)
Petit Pontoise/– (8ᵉ)
Petit Rétro/*20* (16ᵉ)
Pharamond/*15* (1ᵉʳ)
Polidor/*14* (6ᵉ)
Pomponette/– (18ᵉ)

Pouilly Reuilly/*23* (Le Pré-St-Gervais)
Poule au Pot/– (1ᵉʳ)
P'tit Troquet/*22* (7ᵉ)
Quinson/– (15ᵉ)
Régalade/*25* (14ᵉ)
Rendez-vous/Camion./– (14ᵉ)
Rendez-vous/Chauff./– (18ᵉ)
Repaire de Cartouche/*20* (11ᵉ)
Rest. du Marché/– (15ᵉ)
Robert et Louise/– (3ᵉ)
Roi du Pot-au-Feu/*18* (9ᵉ)
Rôtisserie d'en Face/*22* (6ᵉ)
Rôtisserie du Beaujolais/*21* (5ᵉ)
Rouge Vif/*15* (7ᵉ)
Saint Vincent/– (15ᵉ)
Scheffer/*22* (16ᵉ)
Soleil/*23* (St-Ouen)
Square Trousseau/*17* (12ᵉ)
Terroir/*18* (13ᵉ)
Timbre/*18* (6ᵉ)
Tournesol/*14* (16ᵉ)
Trumilou/*16* (4ᵉ)
Va et Vient/– (17ᵉ)
Verre Bouteille/– (17ᵉ)
Verre Volé/– (10ᵉ)
Vieux Bistro/*20* (4ᵉ)
20 de Bellechasse/– (7ᵉ)
Voltaire/*23* (7ᵉ)
Zinc-Zinc/– (Neuilly)

Brasseries

Arbuci/*13* (6ᵉ)
Auberge Dab/*16* (16ᵉ)
Ballon des Ternes/*15* (17ᵉ)
Boeuf sur le Toit/*17* (8ᵉ)
Bofinger/*18* (4ᵉ)
Brasserie Balzar/*18* (5ᵉ)
Brasserie de la Poste/*14* (16ᵉ)
Brasserie de l'Ile St. L./*19* (4ᵉ)
Brasserie du Louvre/*20* (1ᵉʳ)
Brasserie Flo/*17* (10ᵉ)
Brasserie Julien/*18* (10ᵉ)
Brasserie Lipp/*17* (6ᵉ)
Brasserie Lorraine/*15* (8ᵉ)
Brasserie Lutétia/*15* (6ᵉ)
Brasserie Mollard/*18* (8ᵉ)
Café de Flore/*14* (6ᵉ)
Café de la Musique/*14* (19ᵉ)
Café Terminus/*19* (8ᵉ)
Charlot - Roi des Coq./*16* (9ᵉ)
Chez Francis/*15* (8ᵉ)
Chez Georges-Maillot/*18* (17ᵉ)
Chez Jenny/*18* (3ᵉ)
Chien qui Fume/*18* (1ᵉʳ)
Closerie des Lilas/*17* (6ᵉ)
Congrès Maillot/*12* (17ᵉ)

French Cuisine Index

Costes/*18* (1er)
Coupole/*17* (14e)
Editeurs/*13* (6e)
Flandrin/*13* (16e)
Garnier/*18* (8e)
Grand Café/*16* (9e)
Grand Colbert/*16* (2e)
Grandes Marches/*17* (12e)
Léon de Bruxelles/*13* (multi.)
Marty/*17* (5e)
Petit Lutétia/*14* (6e)
Petit Riche/*15* (9e)
Petit Zinc/*16* (6e)
Pichet de Paris/*18* (8e)
Pied de Cochon/*17* (1er)
Rech/*20* (17e)
Relais Plaza/*21* (8e)
Rotonde/*13* (6e)
Sébillon/*16* (multi. loc.)
Stella/– (16e)
Taverne Maître Kanter/*13* (1er)
Taverne L'Esprit Blvd./– (9e)
Terminus Nord/*17* (10e)
Thoumieux/*16* (7e)
Vagenende/*15* (6e)
Vaudeville/*16* (2e)
Wepler/*16* (18e)
Zeyer/*17* (14e)

Classic

Aiguière/– (11e)
Allard/*22* (6e)
Altitude 95/*15* (7e)
Ampère/*15* (17e)
Anacréon/*17* (13e)
Androuët/*20* (7e)
Apicius/*27* (17e)
Appart'/*14* (8e)
Aristide/– (17e)
Armand au Palais Royal/*21* (1er)
Auberge Bressane/*21* (7e)
Auberge d'Autrefois/– (16e)
Auberge Champ de Mars/*19* (7e)
Bacchantes/– (9e)
Bar des Théâtres/*14* (8e)
Bar Vendôme/*20* (1er)
Basilic/*13* (7e)
Beaujolais d'Auteuil/*17* (16e)
Beauvilliers/*23* (18e)
BE Boulangépicier/*19* (17e)
Bélier/– (6e)
Bermuda Onion/*13* (15e)
Beudant/– (17e)
Biche au Bois/*21* (12e)
Bistro des Deux Th./*16* (9e)
Bistrot d'à Côté/*21* (multi. loc.)
Bistrot d'André/*15* (15e)

Bistrot de Breteuil/*14* (7e)
Bistrot d'Henri/*20* (6e)
Bistrot du Sommelier/*19* (8e)
Bistrot St. Ferdinand/*15* (17e)
Boeuf Couronné/*23* (19e)
Bon Accueil/*23* (7e)
Bon Saint Pourçain/*19* (6e)
Café Beaubourg/*14* (4e)
Café de la Paix/*17* (9e)
Café de l'Esplanade/*14* (7e)
Café Faubourg/*18* (8e)
Café Flo/*14* (9e)
Café Les Deux Magots/*14* (6e)
Café Marly/*15* (1er)
Caméléon/*17* (6e)
Canard/– (17e)
Cap Seguin/*16* (Boulogne)
Caveau du Palais/*21* (1er)
Caves Pétrissans/*18* (17e)
Céladon/*22* (2e)
Chai 33/*13* (12e)
Chalet des Iles/*13* (16e)
Chartier/*12* (9e)
Chez Clément/*13* (multi.)
Chez Denise/*22* (1er)
Chez Françoise/*15* (7e)
Chez Gégène/*15* (Joinville)
Chez Georges/*23* (2e)
Chez L'Ami Louis/*26* (3e)
Chez la Vieille/– (1er)
Chez Nénesse/– (3e)
Chez Pauline/*18* (1er)
Chien qui Fume/*18* (1er)
Christine/*23* (6e)
Cinq/*28* (8e)
Closerie des Lilas/*17* (6e)
Clos Saint-Honoré/– (1er)
Coconnas/*17* (4e)
Côté Coulisses/– (2e)
Cou de la Girafe/*14* (8e)
Coupe-Chou/*21* (5e)
Crus de Bourgogne/– (2e)
Dagorno/– (19e)
Dame Tart./Café Very/*11* (1er)
Dauphin/*19* (1er)
De Lagarde/– (15e)
Deux Canards/*21* (10e)
Dôme du Marais/*18* (4e)
Drouant/*21* (2e)
Ecluse/*14* (multi. loc.)
Espadon/*25* (1er)
Etoile/*17* (8e)
Ferme des Mathurins/– (8e)
Ferme St-Simon/*23* (7e)
Fermette Marbeuf 1900/*17* (8e)
Flora Danica/*18* (8e)
Flore en l'Ile/*17* (4e)

196   **subscribe to zagat.com**

French Cuisine Index

Florimond/*22* (7ᵉ)
Fontaine Gaillon/*17* (2ᵉ)
Fouquet's/*16* (8ᵉ)
Gallopin/*15* (2ᵉ)
Gare/*13* (16ᵉ)
Gastroquet/– (15ᵉ)
Gérard Besson/*27* (1ᵉʳ)
Gitane/*18* (15ᵉ)
Gourmet de l'Isle/*23* (4ᵉ)
Grande Armée/*12* (16ᵉ)
Grande Rue/– (15ᵉ)
Grand Louvre/*16* (1ᵉʳ)
Grille/– (10ᵉ)
Guinguette/Neuilly/*12* (Neuilly)
Guirlande de Julie/*14* (4ᵉ)
Hangar/*21* (3ᵉ)
Huîtrier/*18* (17ᵉ)
Ile/*15* (Issy-les-Moulineaux)
Jardin des Cygnes/*20* (8ᵉ)
Jardins de Bagatelle/*18* (16ᵉ)
Joséphine Ch. Dumonet/*19* (6ᵉ)
Jules Verne/*24* (7ᵉ)
Kiosque/*17* (16ᵉ)
Languedoc/*17* (5ᵉ)
Lavinia/*15* (8ᵉ)
Léna et Mimile/*16* (5ᵉ)
Ma Bourgogne/*17* (4ᵉ)
Macéo/*19* (1ᵉʳ)
Maison de l'Amér. Lat./*14* (7ᵉ)
Marlotte/*17* (6ᵉ)
Martel/– (10ᵉ)
Mathusalem/*18* (16ᵉ)
Maupertu/*19* (7ᵉ)
Maxim's/*20* (multi. loc.)
Méditerranée/*20* (6ᵉ)
Monsieur Lapin/*21* (14ᵉ)
Moulin de la Galette/– (18ᵉ)
Murat/*13* (16ᵉ)
Natacha/*17* (14ᵉ)
Natachef/*16* (16ᵉ)
Obélisque/*23* (8ᵉ)
Orangerie/*22* (4ᵉ)
Orenoc/*21* (17ᵉ)
Os à Moëlle/*23* (15ᵉ)
Parc aux Cerfs/*15* (6ᵉ)
Park/– (2ᵉ)
Passiflore/*24* (16ᵉ)
Paul Chêne/*25* (16ᵉ)
Paul, Restaurant/*15* (1ᵉʳ)
Pavillon Montsouris/*20* (14ᵉ)
Pavillon Puebla/– (19ᵉ)
Père Claude/– (15ᵉ)
Pergolèse/*22* (16ᵉ)
Perraudin/– (5ᵉ)
Petit Colombier/*22* (17ᵉ)
Petite Chaise (A la)/*17* (7ᵉ)
Petite Tour/– (16ᵉ)

Petit Laurent/*21* (7ᵉ)
Petit Prince de Paris/*21* (5ᵉ)
Petit Rétro/*20* (16ᵉ)
Petit Riche/*15* (9ᵉ)
Petit St. Benoît/*16* (6ᵉ)
Petit Victor Hugo/*14* (16ᵉ)
Pierre au Palais Royal/*16* (1ᵉʳ)
Polidor/*14* (6ᵉ)
Poquelin/*20* (1ᵉʳ)
Potager du Roy/*21* (Versailles)
Pressoir/– (12ᵉ)
Procope (Le)/*16* (6ᵉ)
Récamier/*21* (7ᵉ)
Relais Louis XIII/*26* (6ᵉ)
Rest. de la Tour/– (15ᵉ)
Rest. du Musée d'Orsay/*15* (7ᵉ)
Rest. du Palais Royal/*19* (1ᵉʳ)
Rubis/*13* (1ᵉʳ)
Saveurs de Claude/– (6ᵉ)
Saveurs du Marché/– (Neuilly)
16 Haussmann/*15* (9ᵉ)
Sologne/– (12ᵉ)
Soufflé/*21* (1ᵉʳ)
Soupière/– (17ᵉ)
Square/*10* (7ᵉ)
Stella/– (16ᵉ)
Stella Maris/*23* (8ᵉ)
Stéphane Martin/*22* (15ᵉ)
Strapontins/– (10ᵉ)
Table d'Anvers/*23* (9ᵉ)
Taillevent/*28* (8ᵉ)
Tante Jeanne/– (17ᵉ)
Tante Louise/*22* (8ᵉ)
Tante Marguerite/*21* (7ᵉ)
Tastevin/*25* (Maisons-Laffitte)
Télégraphe/*15* (7ᵉ)
Temps des Cerises/*15* (13ᵉ)
Tonnelle Saintong./– (Neuilly)
Toque/– (17ᵉ)
Toupary/*13* (1ᵉʳ)
Tour d'Argent/*25* (5ᵉ)
Train Bleu/*17* (12ᵉ)
Triporteur/– (15ᵉ)
Truffe Noire/*19* (Neuilly)
Truffière/*25* (5ᵉ)
Viaduc Café/*12* (12ᵉ)
Vieille Fontaine Rôtiss./*20* (Maisons-Laffitte)
Villaret/*27* (11ᵉ)
Vinea Café/– (12ᵉ)
Virgin Café/*9* (8ᵉ)
Wadja/*18* (6ᵉ)
Yvan, Petit/*18* (8ᵉ)
Yves Quintard/*19* (15ᵉ)
Zebra Square/*11* (16ᵉ)
Zygomates/*24* (12ᵉ)

get updates at zagat.com

French Cuisine Index

Contemporary
Aiguière/– (11e)
Alcazar/16 (6e)
Ambassadeurs/26 (8e)
Amphyclès/24 (17e)
Amuse Bouche/17 (14e)
Angle du Faubourg/24 (8e)
Apicius/27 (17e)
Apollo/10 (14e)
Argenteuil/23 (1er)
Arpège/26 (7e)
Astor/22 (8e)
Astrance/26 (16e)
Atelier Berger/21 (1er)
Atelier Gourmand/– (17e)
Auberge du Clou/– (9e)
Avant Goût/22 (13e)
Avenue/16 (8e)
Bains/9 (3e)
Bamboche/22 (7e)
Baptiste/– (17e)
Béatilles/– (17e)
Berkeley/10 (8e)
Bistro d'Hubert/20 (15e)
Bistrot de l'Etoile Laur./20 (16e)
Bon 2/14 (2e)
Bouchons/Fr. Cl./17 (multi. loc.)
Bouquinistes/22 (6e)
Bourdonnais/Cantine/24 (7e)
Braisière/– (17e)
Bristol/27 (8e)
Café Beaubourg/14 (4e)
Café de l'Esplanade/14 (7e)
Café Lenôtre/19 (8e)
Café M/19 (8e)
Café Marly/15 (1er)
Caïus/– (17e)
Camélia/23 (Bougival)
Cap Vernet/16 (8e)
Carré des Feuillants/25 (1er)
Cartes Postales/20 (1er)
Cazaudehore La For./18 (St-Germain-en-Laye)
182 Rive Droite/– (16e)
Chamarré/21 (7e)
Chez Catherine/21 (8e)
Chez Jean/23 (9e)
Chez Michel/21 (10e)
Chiberta/24 (8e)
59 Poincaré/21 (16e)
Clos des Gourmets/22 (7e)
Clos Morillons/17 (15e)
Clovis/26 (8e)
Coin de la Rue/– (8e)
Colette/17 (1er)
Cottage Marcadet/24 (18e)
Cristal Room /– (16e)

Dédicace Café/– (6e)
1728/18 (8e)
Dôme du Marais/18 (4e)
Doobie's/11 (8e)
En Vue/– (8e)
Excuse/22 (4e)
Faucher/23 (17e)
Feuilles Libres/– (Neuilly)
Flora/23 (8e)
Fontaine d'Auteuil/– (16e)
Grande Rue/– (15e)
Hédiard/21 (8e)
Hélène Darroze/24 (6e)
Hiramatsu/28 (4e)
Ile/15 (Issy-les-Moulineaux)
Impatient/– (17e)
Jardin/21 (8e)
Jumeaux/– (11e)
Libre Sens/– (8e)
Lucas Carton/27 (8e)
Luna/24 (8e)
Macéo/19 (1er)
Magnolias/26 (Perreux-sur-Marne)
Maison du Jardin/24 (6e)
Maison Rouge/12 (4e)
Meurice/25 (1er)
Michel Rostang/27 (17e)
Montalembert/15 (7e)
O à la Bouche/18 (14e)
Pershing/12 (8e)
Petit Marché/– (3e)
Petit Pergolèse/– (16e)
Petit Poucet/17 (Levallois)
Pierre Gagnaire/28 (8e)
Pinxo/– (1er)
Plaza-Athénée/27 (8e)
Pré Verre/– (5e)
Prosper/– (8e)
R./11 (15e)
R'Aliment/– (3e)
Réminet/24 (5e)
River Café/17 (Issy-les-Moul.)
Rue Balzac/18 (8e)
Senso/17 (8e)
6 New York/20 (16e)
Spicy/18 (8e)
Spoon, Food/Wine/22 (8e)
Suite/14 (8e)
Thierry Burlot/– (15e)
Tire-Bouchon/22 (15e)
Toi/– (8e)
Tokyo Eat/– (16e)
Troquet/25 (15e)
Truffière/25 (5e)
Viaduc Café/12 (12e)
Vieille Fontaine Rôtiss./20 (Maisons-Laffitte)

198   subscribe to zagat.com

French Cuisine Index

Villa Mauresque/– (8e)
Vin sur Vin/21 (7e)
Waknine/18 (16e)
Zebra Square/11 (16e)

Haute Cuisine
Ambroisie/26 (4e)
Apicius/27 (17e)
Arpège/26 (7e)
Astor/22 (8e)
Atelier Joël Robuchon/26 (7e)
Bristol/27 (8e)
Carré des Feuillants/25 (1er)
Cazaudehore La For./18 (St-Germain-en-Laye)
Cinq/28 (8e)
Clovis/26 (8e)
Elysées du Vernet/26 (8e)
Espadon/25 (1er)
Etoile/17 (8e)
Grande Cascade/25 (16e)
Grand Véfour/28 (1er)
Guy Savoy/28 (17e)
Hiramatsu/28 (4e)
Jacques Cagna/25 (6e)
Jamin/25 (16e)
Jules Verne/24 (7e)
Lapérouse/21 (6e)
Lasserre/26 (8e)
Laurent/24 (8e)
Ledoyen/25 (8e)
Lucas Carton/27 (8e)
Maison Blanche/20 (8e)
Meurice/25 (1er)
Michel Rostang/27 (17e)
Montparnasse 25/23 (14e)
Muses/27 (9e)
Ormes/– (16e)
Paris/– (6e)
Pierre Gagnaire/28 (8e)
Plaza-Athénée/27 (8e)
Pré Catelan/26 (16e)
Relais d'Auteuil P. Pignol/26 (16e)
Relais Louis XIII/26 (6e)
Table du Baltimore/– (16e)
Taillevent/28 (8e)
Tour d'Argent/25 (5e)
Trois Marches/25 (Versailles)
Violon d'Ingres/24 (7e)
W, Restaurant/– (8e)

Regional
Alsace/Jura
Alsace/16 (8e)
Alsaco/18 (9e)
Bofinger/18 (4e)
Chez Jenny/18 (3e)
Mon Vieil Ami/– (4e)

Auvergne
Ambassade d'Auv./20 (3e)
Auvergne Gourmande/– (7e)
Bath's/27 (8e)
Bistrot à Vins Mélac/16 (11e)
Chantairelle/– (5e)
Chez Gérard/18 (Neuilly)
Lozère/21 (6e)
Mascotte/– (18e)
Nemrod/15 (6e)

Aveyron
Auberge Aveyron./– (12e)
Chez Savy/– (8e)

Basque
Bascou/20 (3e)
Bistro d'Hubert/20 (15e)
Pamphlet/21 (3e)

Brittany
Crêperie de Josselin/19 (14e)
Glénan/25 (7e)
Ty Coz/– (9e)

Corsican
Alivi/19 (4e)
Cafetière/19 (6e)
Cosi (Le)/– (5e)
Main d'Or/– (11e)
Villa Corse/18 (15e)

Gascony
Braisière/– (17e)
Comte de Gascogne/21 (Boulogne)

Jura
Chez Maître Paul/21 (6e)

Lyon
Assiette Lyonnaise/16 (8e)
Auberge Pyr. Cévennes/20 (11e)
Bellecour/24 (7e)
Benoît/23 (4e)
Bons Crus/– (1er)
Cartet/– (11e)
Chez Marcel/– (6e)
Chez René/20 (5e)
Lyonnais/22 (2e)
Moissonnier/21 (5e)
Opportun/– (14e)
Saint Vincent/– (15e)
Vieux Bistro/20 (4e)

Normandy
Fernandises/– (11e)

Provence
Aimant du Sud/– (13e)
Bastide Odéon/21 (6e)
Bistro de l'Olivier/20 (8e)
Bistrot d'Alex/14 (6e)

get updates at zagat.com   199

French Cuisine Index

Bon 2/*14* (2ᵉ)
B4/– (1ᵉʳ)
Casa Olympe/*19* (9ᵉ)
182 Rive Droite/– (16ᵉ)
Chez Janou/*20* (3ᵉ)
Chez Toutoune/*20* (5ᵉ)
Fish La Boissonnerie/*21* (6ᵉ)
Jardin/*21* (8ᵉ)
Olivades/*21* (7ᵉ)
Petit Niçois/*16* (7ᵉ)
Petits Marseillais/*15* (3ᵉ)
Réconfort/– (3ᵉ)
Safran/– (1ᵉʳ)
Sept Quinze/*22* (15ᵉ)
Si/– (3ᵉ)
Sud/*16* (17ᵉ)
Table de la Fontaine/– (9ᵉ)
Table Oliviers & Co./– (17ᵉ)
Terrasse/– (18ᵉ)

Southwest

Ambassade Sud-Ouest/*22* (7ᵉ)
Ami Pierre/– (11ᵉ)
Auberge Etchégorry/– (13ᵉ)
Auberge Pyr. Cévennes/*20* (11ᵉ)
Baracane/*22* (4ᵉ)
Bistrot des Capucins/– (20ᵉ)
Café Faubourg/*18* (8ᵉ)
Chez L'Ami Jean/*16* (7ᵉ)
Dauphin/*19* (1ᵉʳ)
D'Chez Eux/*21* (7ᵉ)
Domaine de Lintillac/*18* (9ᵉ)
Espace Sud-Ouest/*12* (multi.)
Fins Gourmets/*16* (7ᵉ)
Fontaine de Mars/*19* (7ᵉ)
Gamin de Paris/*19* (4ᵉ)
Gitane/*18* (15ᵉ)
Hélène Darroze/*24* (6ᵉ)
Il Etait une Oie/*15* (17ᵉ)
Maison Courtine/*22* (14ᵉ)
Mesturet/– (2ᵉ)
Oulette/*21* (12ᵉ)
Pinxo/– (1ᵉʳ)
Rouge Vif/*15* (7ᵉ)
Salon d' Hélène/*19* (6ᵉ)
Sarladais/– (8ᵉ)
Sousceyrac/*19* (11ᵉ)
Thoumieux/*16* (7ᵉ)
Triporteur/– (15ᵉ)
Trou Gascon/*24* (12ᵉ)

Seafood

Bar à Huîtres/*17* (multi. loc.)
Beudant/– (17ᵉ)
Bigorneau/– (16ᵉ)
Bistro de l'Olivier/*20* (8ᵉ)
Bistrot de Marius/*17* (8ᵉ)
Bistrot du Dôme/*19* (multi. loc.)
Brasserie Lutétia/*15* (6ᵉ)
Cagouille/*24* (14ᵉ)
Cap Vernet/*16* (8ᵉ)
Charlot - Roi des Coq./*16* (9ᵉ)
Comptoir/Saumon/– (multi.)
Dessirier/*22* (17ᵉ)
Divellec/*23* (7ᵉ)
Dôme/*22* (14ᵉ)
Duc/*25* (14ᵉ)
Ecailler du Bistrot/– (11ᵉ)
Espadon Bleu/*21* (6ᵉ)
Estaminet Gaya/– (1ᵉʳ)
Fables de La Fontaine/– (7ᵉ)
Fish La Boissonnerie/*21* (6ᵉ)
Garnier/*18* (8ᵉ)
Gaya Rive Gauche/*22* (7ᵉ)
Glénan/*25* (7ᵉ)
Goumard/*24* (1ᵉʳ)
Huîtrier/*18* (17ᵉ)
Luna/*24* (8ᵉ)
Maison Prunier/*22* (16ᵉ)
Marée/*24* (8ᵉ)
Marée de Versailles/*21*
  (Versailles)
Marius/*22* (16ᵉ)
Marius et Janette/*21* (8ᵉ)
Méditerranée/*20* (6ᵉ)
Petit Colombier Mer/– (17ᵉ)
Petrossian/*24* (7ᵉ)
Pichet de Paris/*18* (8ᵉ)
Port Alma/*20* (16ᵉ)
Quinson/– (15ᵉ)
Rech/*20* (17ᵉ)
Table de Lucullus/– (17ᵉ)
Ty Coz/– (9ᵉ)
Vin et Marée/*16* (multi. loc.)

Shellfish

Ballon des Ternes/*15* (17ᵉ)
Ballon et Coquillages/– (17ᵉ)
Bar à Huîtres/*17* (multi. loc.)
Bigorneau/– (16ᵉ)
Brasserie Lutétia/*15* (6ᵉ)
Brasserie Mollard/*18* (8ᵉ)
Charlot - Roi des Coq./*16* (9ᵉ)
Congrès Maillot/*12* (17ᵉ)
Coupole/*17* (14ᵉ)
Dessirier/*22* (17ᵉ)
Dôme/*22* (14ᵉ)
Ecailler du Bistrot/– (11ᵉ)
Garnier/*18* (8ᵉ)
Huîtrier/*18* (17ᵉ)
Maison Prunier/*22* (16ᵉ)
Marée de Versailles/*21*
  (Versailles)
Marius/*22* (16ᵉ)
Marius et Janette/*21* (8ᵉ)

French Cuisine Index

Petit Colombier Mer/– (17e)
Stella/– (16e)
Taverne L'Esprit Blvd./– (9e)
Terminus Nord/17 (10e)

Steakhouses

Boeuf Couronné/23 (19e)
Dagorno/– (19e)
Devez/12 (8e)
Gavroche/21 (2e)
Gourmets des Ternes/21 (8e)
Hippopotamus/10 (multi. loc.)
Louchebem/17 (1er)
Relais de l'Entrecôte/23 (multi.)
Relais de Venise/20 (17e)

Tearooms

Angelina/18 (1er)
A Priori Thé/17 (2e)
Dalloyau/22 (multi. loc.)
Deux Abeilles/14 (7e)
Fauchon/– (8e)
Jean-Paul Hévin/22 (1er)
Je Thé . . . Me/21 (15e)
Ladurée/21 (multi. loc.)
Loir dans la Théière/12 (4e)
Mariage Frères/19 (multi. loc.)
Muscade/– (1er)

Wine Bars/Bistros

Bacchantes/– (9e)
Baron Rouge/13 (12e)
Bar Rouge/– (9e)
Bistrot à Vins Mélac/16 (11e)
Bons Crus/– (1er)
Bouchons/Fr. Cl./17 (multi. loc.)
Bourguignon du Marais/21 (4e)
Café Burq/– (18e)
Café du Passage/– (11e)
Cave de l'Os à Moëlle/18 (15e)
Caves Legrand/– (2e)
Caves Pétrissans/18 (17e)
Cloche des Halles/– (1er)
Clown Bar/17 (11e)
. . . Comme Cochon/– (12e)
Coude Fou/16 (4e)
Couleurs de Vigne/– (15e)
Dix Vins/17 (15e)
Ecluse/14 (multi. loc.)
Enoteca/18 (4e)
Juvéniles/15 (1er)
Lavinia/15 (8e)
Mauzac/15 (5e)
Mesturet/– (2e)
Oenothèque/– (9e)
Robe et le Palais/– (1er)
Rubis/13 (1er)
Sauvignon/16 (7e)
Tourelle/– (1er)
Verre Bouteille/– (17e)
Verre Volé/– (10e)
Vin sur Vin/21 (7e)
Willi's Wine Bar/19 (1er)

get updates at zagat.com

Other Cuisine Index

OTHER CUISINES

(Restaurant Names, Food Ratings and Arrondissements)

American
Breakfast in America/– (5e)
Buffalo Grill/7 (multi. loc.)
Chicago Pizza/9 (8e)
Joe Allen/16 (1er)
Planet Hollywood/8 (8^e)

Argentinean
Anahï/19 (3^e)
El Palenque/18 (5^e)
Villa/– (20^e)

Armenian
Diamantaires/– (9^e)

Asian
Asian/14 (8^e)
Buddha Bar/16 (8^e)
Maoh Noodles Bar/13 (Neuilly)
Wok Cooking/– (11^e)

Belgian
Bouillon Racine/13 (6^e)

Cajun
Thanksgiving/15 (4^e)

Californian
Coffee Parisien/14 (multi. loc.)

Cambodian
Kambodgia/20 (16e)
Sinago/– (9e)

Caviar
Maison du Caviar/19 (8e)
Maison Prunier/22 (16e)
Petrossian/24 (7e)

Central European
Pitchi Poï/– (4e)

Chinese
(* dim sum specialist)
Chen Soleil d'Est/20 (15e)
Chez Ngo/19 (16e)
Chez Vong/21 (1er)*
China Club/17 (12e)
China Town Olymp./– (13e)
Davé/19 (1er)
Délices de Szechuen/18 (7e)
Diep/18 (8e)
Elysées Hong Kong/– (16e)
Lao Tseu/16 (7e)
Mandarin/Neuilly/– (Neuilly)
Mirama/20 (5e)
New Nioullaville/17 (11e)
Nouveau Village Tao/18 (13e)
Passy Mandarin/22 (16e)
Tang/21 (16e)
Tong Yen/21 (8e)
Tricotin/– (13e)
Tsé-Yang/18 (16e)
Village d'Ung et Li Lam/– (8e)

Creole
Thanksgiving/15 (4e)

Danish
Copenhague/21 (8e)
Flora Danica/18 (8e)
Petite Sirène Copenh./23 (9e)

Dessert
Angelina/18 (1er)
A Priori Thé/17 (2e)
Café Lenôtre/19 (8e)
Dalloyau/22 (multi. loc.)
Deux Abeilles/14 (7e)
Hédiard/21 (8e)
Je Thé … Me/21 (15e)
Ladurée/21 (multi. loc.)
Loir dans la Théière/12 (4e)
Mariage Frères/19 (multi. loc.)
Soufflé/21 (1er)

Eclectic
Ailleurs/11 (8e)
Auberge du Clou/– (9e)
B*fly/13 (8e)
Barramundi/– (9e)
Berkeley/10 (8e)
Café Fusion/– (13e)
Café Moderne/– (2e)
Chamarré/21 (7e)
Chez Prune/14 (10e)
Comptoir/Saumon/– (multi.)
Cosi/20 (6e)
Costes/18 (1er)
Doobie's/11 (8e)
Durand Dupont/9 (Neuilly)
Epicure 108/– (17e)

Other Cuisine Index

Etienne Marcel/17 (2ᵉ)
Famille/– (18ᵉ)
Fumoir/15 (1ᵉʳ)
Georges/17 (4ᵉ)
Juvéniles/16 (1ᵉʳ)
Kong/14 (1ᵉʳ)
Mandalay/– (Levallois)
Man Ray/15 (8ᵉ)
Maoh Noodles Bar/13 (Neuilly)
Market/22 (8ᵉ)
No Stress Café/– (9ᵉ)
Pershing/12 (8ᵉ)
Quai Ouest/15 (St-Cloud)
Relais Plaza/21 (8ᵉ)
Spoon, Food/Wine/22 (8ᵉ)
Taïra/– (17ᵉ)
Ze Kitchen Galerie/23 (6ᵉ)
Zo/18 (8ᵉ)

Ethiopian
Entoto/– (13ᵉ)

Greek
Délices d'Aphrodite/20 (5ᵉ)
Mavrommatis/19 (5ᵉ)

Hamburgers
Coffee Parisien/14 (multi. loc.)
Indiana Café/8 (multi. loc.)
Joe Allen/16 (1ᵉʳ)
Planet Hollywood/8 (8ᵉ)

Health Food
Bon/15 (16ᵉ)
R'Aliment/– (3ᵉ)

Indian
Annapurna/18 (8ᵉ)
Indra/21 (8ᵉ)
Maharajah/15 (5ᵉ)
New Jawad/17 (7ᵉ)
Ravi/23 (7ᵉ)

Indonesian
Djakarta Bali/– (1ᵉʳ)

Irish
Carr's/– (1ᵉʳ)

Italian
(N=Northern; S=Southern)
Al Caratello/– (18ᵉ)
Amici Mei/– (4ᵉ)
Appennino/– (13ᵉ) (N)
Bartolo/17 (6ᵉ)
Bauta/– (6ᵉ)
Beato/15 (7ᵉ)
Bel Canto/14 (multi. loc.)
Bellini/19 (16ᵉ)
Bocconi/– (8ᵉ)
Ca d'Oro/16 (1ᵉʳ) (N)
Caffé Toscano/– (7ᵉ)
Cailloux/– (13ᵉ)
Carpaccio/– (8ᵉ)
Casa Bini/20 (6ᵉ) (N)
Casa Vigata/– (11ᵉ)
Cherche Midi/18 (6ᵉ)
Chez Gildo/18 (7ᵉ)
Chez Livio/12 (Neuilly)
Chez Vincent/22 (19ᵉ)
Colette/17 (1ᵉʳ)
Conti/19 (16ᵉ)
Da Mimmo/19 (10ᵉ)
Dell Orto/– (9ᵉ)
Emporio Armani/19 (6ᵉ)
Enoteca/18 (4ᵉ)
Fellini/21 (multi. loc.)
Findi/17 (8ᵉ)
Finzi/16 (8ᵉ)
Fontanarosa/21 (15ᵉ)
Giulio Rebellato/20 (16ᵉ)
Gli Angeli/17 (3ᵉ)
Grand Venise/24 (15ᵉ)
I Golosi/18 (9ᵉ)
Il Baccello/20 (17ᵉ)
Il Barone/19 (14ᵉ)
Il Cortile/23 (1ᵉʳ)
Il Viccolo/17 (6ᵉ)
Lei/– (7ᵉ)
Ostéria/23 (4ᵉ)
Osteria Ascolani/– (18ᵉ)
Paolo Petrini/20 (17ᵉ)
Paris Seize/15 (16ᵉ)
Perron/21 (7ᵉ) (S)
Petit Marguery/20 (16ᵉ)
Romantica/21 (Clichy)
Rucola/– (17ᵉ)
Rughetta/15 (18ᵉ)
Sale e Pepe/– (18ᵉ)
Sardegna a Tavola/– (12ᵉ)
Sasso/– (14ᵉ)
Sormani/25 (17ᵉ)
Stresa/19 (8ᵉ)
Vinci/– (16ᵉ)

Japanese
(* sushi specialist)
Azabu/– (6ᵉ)
Benkay/23 (15ᵉ)
Foujita/16 (1ᵉʳ)*
Higuma/16 (1ᵉʳ)
Inagiku/17 (5ᵉ)
Isami/24 (4ᵉ)
Isse/25 (2ᵉ)
Kaïten/– (8ᵉ)

Other Cuisine Index

Kinugawa/*22* (multi. loc.)
Lô Sushi/*17* (multi. loc.)
Matsuri/*15* (multi. loc.)
Oïshi/– (2e)
Orient-Extrême/*19* (6e)
Taka/*24* (18e)
Tsukizi/– (6e)
Yen/*20* (6e)

Jewish
Jo Goldenberg/*13* (4e)
Patrick Goldenberg/– (17e)
Pitchi Poï/– (4e)

Kosher
Patrick Goldenberg/– (17e)
Télégraphe/*15* (7e)

Lebanese
Al Dar/*20* (multi. loc.)
Al Diwan/*20* (8e)
Byblos Café/*21* (16e)
Fakhr el Dine/*16* (multi. loc.)
Mont Liban/– (17e)
Noura/*19* (multi. loc.)

Mediterranean
Il Baccello/*20* (17e)
16 Haussmann/*15* (9e)
7ème Sud Grenelle/*16* (7e)
Sora Lena/– (17e)

Mexican
Anahuacalli/*24* (5e)

Middle Eastern
Chez Marianne/*15* (4e)

Moroccan
Al Mounia/*19* (16e)
Andy Whaloo/– (3e)
Atlas/*21* (5e)
Chez Omar/*20* (3e)
Comptoir Paris-Marrak./*15* (1er)
El Mansour/*21* (8e)
Etoile Marocaine/*21* (8e)
Mansouria/*22* (11e)
Martel/– (10e)
Oum el Banine/– (16e)
Pied de Chameau/*15* (4e)
404/*21* (3e)
Riad/– (Neuilly)
Tanjia/*13* (8e)
Timgad/*23* (17e)
Villa Mauresque/– (8e)

North African
7ème Sud Grenelle/*16* (multi.)
Village Kabyle/– (18e)
Wally Le Saharien/– (9e)

Nuevo Latino
Barroco/– (6e)

Pan-Latin
Barrio Latino/*8* (12e)

Pizza
Amici Mei/– (4e)
Bartolo/*17* (6e)
Chicago Pizza/*9* (8e)
Da Mimmo/*19* (10e)

Portuguese
Chez Albert/– (6e)
Saudade/– (1er)

Russian
Cantine Russe/*15* (16e)
Caviar Kaspia/*22* (8e)
Daru/– (8e)
Dominique/– (6e)
Pravda/– (11e)

Sandwiches
BE Boulangépicier/*19* (17e)
Cosi/*20* (6e)
Dame Tart./Café Very/*11* (multi.)
Ferme/– (1er)
Lina's/*13* (multi. loc.)
Sauvignon/*16* (7e)

Seychelles
Coco de Mer/– (5e)

Southeast Asian
Tong Yen/*21* (8e)
Tricotin/– (13e)

Spanish
(* tapas specialist)
Bar Rouge/– (9e)*
Bellotta-Bellotta/– (7e)
Bistrot La Catalogne/*13* (6e)
Casa Alcalde/*16* (15e)
Casa Hidalgo/– (11e)
Casa Tina/*12* (16e)
Fogón Saint Julien/*23* (5e)
Rosimar/*23* (16e)
Villa/– (20e)

Swedish
Café des Lettres/– (7e)

Other Cuisine Index

Tex-Mex
Indiana Café/*8* (multi. loc.)
Studio/*11* (4ᵉ)

Thai
Baan-Boran/*20* (1ᵉʳ)
Bains/*9* (3ᵉ)
Banyan/– (15ᵉ)
Blue Elephant/*20* (11ᵉ)
Chez Ngo/*19* (16ᵉ)
Chieng Mai/*18* (5ᵉ)
Erawan/*21* (15ᵉ)
Khun Akorn/*18* (11ᵉ)
Lao Siam/– (19ᵉ)
Paradis Thai/– (13ᵉ)
Sawadee/*19* (15ᵉ)
Thiou/*22* (multi. loc.)
Village d'Ung et Li Lam/– (8ᵉ)

Turkish
Sizin/– (9ᵉ)

Vegetarian
Bon/*15* (16ᵉ)
R'Aliment/– (3ᵉ)

Vietnamese
Baie d'Ha Long/– (16ᵉ)
Coin des Gourmets/*24* (5ᵉ)
Davé/*19* (1ᵉʳ)
Diep/*18* (8ᵉ)
Kambodgia/*20* (16ᵉ)
Kim Anh/*23* (15ᵉ)
Lac-Hong/*21* (16ᵉ)
Palanquin/*13* (6ᵉ)
Tan Dinh/*22* (7ᵉ)
Tonkinoise/– (13ᵉ)

Location Index

LOCATIONS

PARIS

1st arrondissement
Absinthe
Angelina
Ardoise
Argenteuil
Armand au Palais Royal
Atelier Berger
Baan-Boran
Bar Vendôme
Bistrot Vivienne
Bons Crus
B4
Brasserie du Louvre
Ca d'Oro
Café Marly
Café Ruc
Carré des Feuillants
Carr's
Cartes Postales
Caveau du Palais
Chez Denise
Chez la Vieille
Chez Pauline
Chez Vong
Chien qui Fume
Cloche des Halles
Clos Saint-Honoré
Colette
Comptoir Paris-Marrak.
Costes
Dame Tart./Café Very
Dauphin
Davé
Djakarta Bali
Ecluse
Epi d'Or
Escargot Montorgueil
Espadon
Estaminet Gaya
Fellini
Ferme
Foujita
Fumoir
Gérard Besson
Goumard
Grand Louvre
Grand Véfour
Higuma
Hippopotamus
Il Cortile
Jean-Paul Hévin
Joe Allen
Juvéniles
Kinugawa
Kong
Léon de Bruxelles
Lescure
Lô Sushi
Louchebem
Macéo
Matsuri
Meurice
Muscade
Paul, Restaurant
Pharamond
Pied de Cochon
Pierre au Palais Royal
Pinxo
Poquelin
Poule au Pot
Rest. du Palais Royal
Robe et le Palais
Rubis
Safran
Saudade
Soufflé
Taverne Maître Kanter
Toupary
Tourelle
Vin et Marée
Willi's Wine Bar

2nd arrondissement
A Priori Thé
Bon 2
Café Moderne
Caves Legrand
Céladon
Chez Clément
Chez Georges
Côté Coulisses
Crus de Bourgogne
Drouant
Etienne Marcel
Fontaine Gaillon
Gallopin
Gavroche
Grand Colbert
Hippopotamus
Indiana Café
Isse
Lina's
Lyonnais
Mesturet

Location Index

Noces de Jeannette
Noura
Oïshi
Park
Vaudeville

3rd arrondissement
Ambassade d'Auv.
Anahï
Andy Whaloo
Auberge Nicolas Flamel
Bains
Bar à Huîtres
Bascou
Buffalo Grill
Camille
Chez Janou
Chez Jenny
Chez L'Ami Louis
Chez Nénesse
Chez Omar
Gli Angeli
Hangar
Indiana Café
Pamphlet
Petit Marché
Petits Marseillais
404
R'Aliment
Réconfort
Robert et Louise
Si

4th arrondissement
Alivi
Ambroisie
Amici Mei
Baracane
Bel Canto
Benoît
Bistrot du Dôme
Bofinger
Bourguignon du Marais
Brasserie de l'Ile St. L.
Café Beaubourg
Chez Clément
Chez Marianne
Coconnas
Comptoir/Saumon
Coude Fou
Dalloyau
Dame Tart./Café Very
Dôme du Marais
Dos de la Baleine
Enoteca
Excuse
Flore en l'Ile
Fous d'en Face
Gamin de Paris
Georges
Gourmet de l'Isle
Guirlande de Julie
Hippopotamus
Hiramatsu
Isami
Jo Goldenberg
Léon de Bruxelles
Lina's
Loir dans la Théière
Ma Bourgogne
Maison Rouge
Mariage Frères
Mon Vieil Ami
Orangerie
Ostéria
Petit Bofinger
Pied de Chameau
Pitchi Poï
Studio
Thanksgiving
Trumilou
Vieux Bistro

5th arrondissement
Al Dar
Anahuacalli
AOC
Atelier Maître Albert
Atlas
Bar à Huîtres
Bouchons/Fr. Cl.
Brasserie Balzar
Breakfast in America
Buffalo Grill
Buisson Ardent
Chantairelle
Chez René
Chez Toutoune
Chieng Mai
Coco de Mer
Coin des Gourmets
Cosi (Le)
Coupe-Chou
Délices d'Aphrodite
El Palenque
Fogón Saint Julien
Fontaines
Hippopotamus
Inagiku
Languedoc
Léna et Mimile
Maharajah
Marty
Mauzac

get updates at zagat.com

Location Index

Mavrommatis
Mirama
Moissonnier
Moulin à Vent
Perraudin
Petit Prince de Paris
Pré Verre
Réminet
Rôtisserie du Beaujolais
Tour d'Argent
Truffière

6th arrondissement
Alcazar
Allard
Arbuci
Azabu
Barroco
Bartolo
Bastide Odéon
Bauta
Bélier
Bistrot d'Alex
Bistrot d'Henri
Bistrot La Catalogne
Bon Saint Pourçain
Bouillon Racine
Bouquinistes
Brasserie Lipp
Brasserie Lutétia
Café de Flore
Café des Délices
Café Les Deux Magots
Cafetière
Caméléon
Casa Bini
Charpentiers
Cherche Midi
Chez Albert
Chez Clément
Chez Diane
Chez Maître Paul
Chez Marcel
Christine
Closerie des Lilas
Coffee Parisien
Cosi
Dalloyau
Dédicace Café
Dominique
Editeurs
Emporio Armani
Epi Dupin
Espadon Bleu
Fish La Boissonnerie
Gourmand
Grille St-Germain

Hélène Darroze
Hippopotamus
Il Viccolo
Indiana Café
Jacques Cagna
Joséphine Ch. Dumonet
Ladurée
Lapérouse
Léon de Bruxelles
Lozère
Maison du Jardin
Mariage Frères
Marlotte
Méditerranée
Nemrod
Noura
Orient-Extrême
Palanquin
Parc aux Cerfs
Paris
Petite Cour
Petit Lutétia
Petit St. Benoît
Petit Zinc
Polidor
Procope (Le)
Relais de l'Entrecôte
Relais Louis XIII
Rôtisserie d'en Face
Rotonde
Salon d' Hélène
Saveurs de Claude
Timbre
Tsukizi
Vagenende
Wadja
Yen
Ze Kitchen Galerie

7th arrondissement
Affriolé
Altitude 95
Ambassade Sud-Ouest
Androuët
Arpège
Atelier Joël Robuchon
Auberge Bressane
Auberge Champ de Mars
Auvergne Gourmande
Babylone
Bamboche
Basilic
Beato
Bellecour
Bellotta-Bellotta
Bistrot de Breteuil
Bistrot de l'Université

Location Index

Bistrot de Paris
Bon Accueil
Bourdonnais/Cantine
Café Constant
Café de l'Esplanade
Café de Mars
Café des Lettres
Café Max
Caffé Toscano
Chamarré
Chez Françoise
Chez Gildo
Chez L'Ami Jean
Clos des Gourmets
Dalloyau
D'Chez Eux
Délices de Szechuen
Deux Abeilles
Divellec
Fables de La Fontaine
Ferme St-Simon
Fins Gourmets
Florimond
Fontaine de Mars
Gaya Rive Gauche
Glénan
Jules Verne
Lao Tseu
Lei
Lina's
Maison de l'Amér. Lat.
Maupertu
Montalembert
New Jawad
Oeillade
Olivades
Perron
Petite Chaise (A la)
Petit Laurent
Petit Niçois
Petrossian
P'tit Troquet
Ravi
Récamier
Rest. du Musée d'Orsay
Rouge Vif
Sauvignon
7ème Sud Grenelle
Square
Tan Dinh
Tante Marguerite
Télégraphe
Thiou
Thoumieux
Vin et Marée
20 de Bellechasse
Vin sur Vin
Violon d'Ingres
Voltaire

8th arrondissement

Affiche
Ailleurs
Al Diwan
Alsace
Ambassadeurs
Angle du Faubourg
Annapurna
Appart'
Asian
Assiette Lyonnaise
Astor
Avenue
B*fly
Bar des Théâtres
Bath's
Berkeley
Bistro de l'Olivier
Bistrot de Marius
Bistrot du Sommelier
Bocconi
Boeuf sur le Toit
Bouchons/Fr. Cl.
Brasserie Lorraine
Brasserie Mollard
Bristol
Buddha Bar
Café Faubourg
Café Lenôtre
Café M
Café Terminus
Cap Vernet
Carpaccio
Caviar Kaspia
Chez André
Chez Catherine
Chez Clément
Chez Francis
Chez Savy
Chiberta
Chicago Pizza
Cinq
Clovis
Coin de la Rue
Comptoir/Saumon
Copenhague
Cou de la Girafe
Dalloyau
Daru
Devez
Diep
1728
Doobie's
Ecluse

Location Index

El Mansour
Elysées du Vernet
En Vue
Espace Sud-Ouest
Etoile
Etoile Marocaine
Fakhr el Dine
Fauchon
Ferme des Mathurins
Fermette Marbeuf 1900
Findi
Finzi
Flora
Flora Danica
Fouquet's
Garnier
Gourmets des Ternes
Hédiard
Hippopotamus
Indiana Café
Indra
Jardin
Jardin des Cygnes
Kaïten
Kinugawa
Ladurée
Lasserre
Laurent
Lavinia
Ledoyen
Léon de Bruxelles
Libre Sens
Lina's
Lô Sushi
Lucas Carton
Luna
Maison Blanche
Maison du Caviar
Man Ray
Marée
Mariage Frères
Marius et Janette
Market
Mascotte
Maxim's
Obélisque
Pershing
Petit Pontoise
Pichet de Paris
Pierre Gagnaire
Planet Hollywood
Plaza-Athénée
Prosper
Relais de l'Entrecôte
Relais Plaza
Rue Balzac
Sarladais
Sébillon
Senso
Spicy
Spoon, Food/Wine
Stella Maris
Stresa
Suite
Taillevent
Tanjia
Tante Louise
Thiou
Toi
Tong Yen
Village d'Ung et Li Lam
Villa Mauresque
Virgin Café
W, Restaurant
Yvan
Yvan, Petit
Zo

9th arrondissement
Alsaco
Auberge du Clou
Bacchantes
Barramundi
Bar Rouge
Bistro de Gala
Bistro des Deux Th.
Bistrot Papillon
Buffalo Grill
Café de la Paix
Café Flo
Casa Olympe
Charlot - Roi des Coq.
Chartier
Chez Jean
Comédiens
Dell Orto
Diamantaires
Domaine de Lintillac
Grand Café
I Golosi
Indiana Café
Ladurée
Léon de Bruxelles
Lina's
Muses
No Stress Café
Oenothèque
Petit Bofinger
Petite Sirène Copenh.
Petit Riche
Roi du Pot-au-Feu
16 Haussmann
Sinago

Location Index

Sizin
Table d'Anvers
Table de la Fontaine
Taverne L'Esprit Blvd.
Ty Coz
Wally Le Saharien

10th arrondissement
Brasserie Flo
Brasserie Julien
Buffalo Grill
Chez Michel
Chez Prune
Da Mimmo
Deux Canards
Espace Sud-Ouest
Grille
Hippopotamus
Martel
Strapontins
Terminus Nord
Verre Volé

11th arrondissement
Aiguière
Ami Pierre
Amognes
Astier
Auberge Pyr. Cévennes
Bistrot à Vins Mélac
Bistrot du Peintre
Bistrot Paul Bert
Blue Elephant
Café Charbon
Café de l'Industrie
Café du Passage
C'Amelot
Cartet
Casa Hidalgo
Casa Vigata
Chardenoux
Chez Paul
Clown Bar
Ecailler du Bistrot
Ecluse
Fernandises
Indiana Café
Jumeaux
Khun Akorn
Léon de Bruxelles
Main d'Or
Mansouria
New Nioullaville
Pravda
Pure Café
Ramulaud
Repaire de Cartouche
Sousceyrac
Villaret
Vin et Marée
Wok Cooking

12th arrondissement
Auberge Aveyron.
Baron Rouge
Barrio Latino
Biche au Bois
Chai 33
China Club
... Comme Cochon
Ebauchoir
Grandes Marches
Lina's
Oulette
Pressoir
Sardegna a Tavola
Sologne
Square Trousseau
Train Bleu
Trou Gascon
Viaduc Café
Vinea Café
Zygomates

13th arrondissement
Aimant du Sud
Anacréon
Appennino
Auberge Etchégorry
Avant Goût
Buffalo Grill
Café Fusion
Cailloux
Chez Paul
China Town Olymp.
Entoto
Léon de Bruxelles
Nouveau Village Tao
Paradis Thai
Petit Marguery
Temps des Cerises
Terroir
Tonkinoise
Tricotin

14th arrondissement
Amuse Bouche
Apollo
Assiette
Bar à Huîtres
Bel Canto
Bistrot du Dôme
Bouche à Oreille (De)
Buffalo Grill

get updates at zagat.com 211

Location Index

Cagouille
Chez Clément
Contre-Allée
Coupole
Crêperie de Josselin
Dôme
Duc
Espace Sud-Ouest
Hippopotamus
Il Barone
Indiana Café
Léon de Bruxelles
Maison Courtine
Monsieur Lapin
Montparnasse 25
Natacha
O à la Bouche
Opportun
Pavillon Montsouris
Petit Bofinger
Régalade
Rendez-vous/Camion.
Sasso
Vin et Marée
Zeyer

15th arrondissement
Astuce
Banyan
Benkay
Bermuda Onion
Beurre Noisette
Bistro 121
Bistro d'Hubert
Bistrot d'André
Bistrot du Cap
Bouchons/Fr. Cl.
Buffalo Grill
Café du Commerce
Casa Alcalde
Cave de l'Os à Moëlle
Chen Soleil d'Est
Chez Clément
Clos Morillons
Comptoir/Saumon
Couleurs de Vigne
Dalloyau
De Lagarde
Dix Vins
Erawan
Espace Sud-Ouest
Fellini
Fontanarosa
Gastroquet
Gauloise
Gitane
Grande Rue

Grand Venise
Je Thé . . . Me
Kim Anh
Léon de Bruxelles
Os à Moëlle
Père Claude
Quinson
R.
Rest. de la Tour
Rest. du Marché
Saint Vincent
Sawadee
Sept Quinze
Stéphane Martin
Thierry Burlot
Tire-Bouchon
Triporteur
Troquet
Villa Corse
Yves Quintard

16th arrondissement
A et M Le Bistrot
Al Dar
Al Mounia
Astrance
Auberge Dab
Auberge d'Autrefois
Baie d'Ha Long
Beaujolais d'Auteuil
Bellini
Bigorneau
Bistrot de l'Etoile Laur.
Bistrot des Vignes
Bon
Brasserie de la Poste
Butte Chaillot
Byblos Café
Cantine Russe
Casa Tina
182 Rive Droite
Chalet des Iles
Chez Ngo
59 Poincaré
Coffee Parisien
Conti
Cristal Room
Elysées Hong Kong
Fakhr el Dine
Flandrin
Fontaine d'Auteuil
Gare
Giulio Rebellato
Grande Armée
Grande Cascade
Jamin
Jardins de Bagatelle

Location Index

Kambodgia
Kiosque
Lac-Hong
Maison Prunier
Marius
Mathusalem
Matsuri
Murat
Natachef
Noura
Ormes
Oum el Banine
Paris Seize
Passiflore
Passy Mandarin
Paul Chêne
Pergolèse
Petite Tour
Petit Marguery
Petit Pergolèse
Petit Rétro
Petit Victor Hugo
Port Alma
Pré Catelan
Relais d'Auteuil P. Pignol
Rosimar
Scheffer
7ème Sud Grenelle
6 New York
Stella
Table du Baltimore
Tang
Tokyo Eat
Tournesol
Tsé-Yang
Vinci
Vin et Marée
Waknine
Zebra Square

17th arrondissement

Ampère
Amphyclès
Apicius
Aristide
Atelier Gourmand
Ballon des Ternes
Ballon et Coquillages
Baptiste
Béatilles
BE Boulangépicier
Beudant
Bistro du 17ème
Bistro Melrose
Bistrot d'à Côté
Bistrot d'Albert
Bistrot de l'Etoile Niel
Bistrot des Dames
Bistrot St. Ferdinand
Bouchons/Fr. Cl.
Braisière
Buffalo Grill
Café d'Angel
Caïus
Canard
Caves Pétrissans
Chez Clément
Chez Fred
Chez Georges-Maillot
Chez Léon
Comptoir/Saumon
Congrès Maillot
Dessirier
Ecluse
Entredgeu
Epicure 108
Faucher
Graindorge
Guy Savoy
Huîtrier
Il Baccello
Il Etait une Oie
Impatient
Léon de Bruxelles
Lina's
Michel Rostang
Mont Liban
Orenoc
Paolo Petrini
Patrick Goldenberg
Petit Bofinger
Petit Colombier
Petit Colombier Mer
Rech
Relais de Venise
Rucola
Sora Lena
Sormani
Soupière
Sud
Table de Lucullus
Table Oliviers & Co.
Taïra
Tante Jeanne
Timgad
Toque
Va et Vient
Verre Bouteille

18th arrondissement

Al Caratello
Beauvilliers
Café Burq
Cottage Marcadet
Entracte
Famille

get updates at zagat.com 213

Location Index

Mascotte
Moulin de la Galette
Osteria Ascolani
Pomponette
Rendez-vous/Chauff.
Rughetta
Sale e Pepe
Taka
Terrasse
Village Kabyle
Wepler

19th arrondissement
Boeuf Couronné
Buffalo Grill

Café de la Musique
Cave Gourmande
Chez Vincent
Dagorno
Lao Siam
Pavillon Puebla

20th arrondissement
Allobroges
Bistrot des Capucins
Boulangerie
Villa
Zéphyr

OUTLYING AREAS

Bougival
Camélia

Boulogne-Billancourt
Cap Seguin
Chez Clément
Comte de Gascogne
Dalloyau

Clichy
Romantica

Issy-les-Moulineaux
Ile
Manufacture
River Café

Joinville-le-Pont
Chez Gégène

Le Pré-St-Gervais
Pouilly Reuilly

Levallois-Perret
Mandalay
Petit Poucet

Maisons-Laffitte
Tastevin
Vieille Fontaine Rôtiss.

Neuilly-sur-Seine
Bistrot d'à Côté
Café de la Jatte
Carpe Diem
Chez Gérard
Chez Livio

Coffee Parisien
Durand Dupont
Feuilles Libres
Guinguette/Neuilly
Lina's
Mandarin/Neuilly
Maoh Noodles Bar
Papinou
Riad
Saveurs du Marché
Sébillon
Tonnelle Saintong.
Truffe Noire
Zinc-Zinc

Orly
Maxim's

Perreux-sur-Marne
Magnolias

Puteaux
Hippopotamus

Saint-Cloud
Quai Ouest

Saint-Germain-en-Laye
Cazaudehore La For.

Saint-Ouen
Soleil

Versailles
Marée de Versailles
Potager du Roy
Trois Marches

214   subscribe to zagat.com

Special Feature Index

SPECIAL FEATURES

(Indexes list the best of many within each category. For multi-location restaurants, the availability of index features may vary by location.)

Breakfast
(See also Hotel Dining)
Alsace (8ᵉ)
Angelina (1ᵉʳ)
A Priori Thé (2ᵉ)
Avenue (8ᵉ)
Bar des Théâtres (8ᵉ)
Berkeley (8ᵉ)
Bon 2 (2ᵉ)
Brasserie Balzar (5ᵉ)
Brasserie Lorraine (8ᵉ)
Brasserie Mollard (8ᵉ)
Breakfast in America (5ᵉ)
Café Beaubourg (4ᵉ)
Café de Flore (6ᵉ)
Café de la Musique (19ᵉ)
Café de l'Esplanade (7ᵉ)
Café de l'Industrie (11ᵉ)
Café Flo (9ᵉ)
Café Lenôtre (8ᵉ)
Café Les Deux Magots (6ᵉ)
Café Marly (1ᵉʳ)
Café Ruc (1ᵉʳ)
Camille (3ᵉ)
Cazaudehore La For. (St-Germain-en-Laye)
Chalet des Iles (16ᵉ)
Chez Clément (multi.)
Chien qui Fume (1ᵉʳ)
Cloche des Halles (1ᵉʳ)
Closerie des Lilas (6ᵉ)
Congrès Maillot (17ᵉ)
Coupole (14ᵉ)
Cristal Room (16ᵉ)
Dalloyau (multi. loc.)
Dôme (14ᵉ)
Editeurs (6ᵉ)
En Vue (8ᵉ)
Fauchon (8ᵉ)
Ferme (1ᵉʳ)
Flandrin (16ᵉ)
Flore en l'Ile (4ᵉ)
Fontaines (5ᵉ)
Fouquet's (8ᵉ)
Gavroche (2ᵉ)
Grand Café (9ᵉ)
Grande Armée (16ᵉ)
Hédiard (8ᵉ)
Jardins de Bagatelle (16ᵉ)
Jo Goldenberg (4ᵉ)
Ladurée (multi. loc.)
Lina's (multi. loc.)
Loir dans la Théière (4ᵉ)
Ma Bourgogne (4ᵉ)
Main d'Or (11ᵉ)
Mascotte (8ᵉ)
Mascotte (18ᵉ)
Murat (16ᵉ)
Nemrod (6ᵉ)
Procope (Le) (6ᵉ)
R'Aliment (3ᵉ)
Rotonde (6ᵉ)
Stella (16ᵉ)
Taverne Maître Kanter (1ᵉʳ)
Taverne L'Esprit Blvd. (9ᵉ)
Terminus Nord (10ᵉ)
Tricotin (13ᵉ)
Vaudeville (2ᵉ)
Viaduc Café (12ᵉ)
Wepler (18ᵉ)
Zebra Square (16ᵉ)
Zeyer (14ᵉ)
Zinc-Zinc (Neuilly)

Brunch
Alcazar (6ᵉ)
Angelina (1ᵉʳ)
Appart' (8ᵉ)
A Priori Thé (2ᵉ)
Asian (8ᵉ)
B*fly (8ᵉ)
Barrio Latino (12ᵉ)
Barroco (6ᵉ)
Berkeley (8ᵉ)
Bermuda Onion (15ᵉ)
Boulangerie (20ᵉ)
B4 (1ᵉʳ)
Brasserie Lutétia (6ᵉ)
Breakfast in America (5ᵉ)
Café Beaubourg (4ᵉ)
Café Charbon (11ᵉ)
Café de Flore (6ᵉ)
Café de la Jatte (Neuilly)
Café de la Musique (19ᵉ)
Café de l'Esplanade (7ᵉ)

Special Feature Index

Café de l'Industrie (11e)
Café de Mars (7e)
Café des Lettres (7e)
Carr's (1er)
Chai 33 (12e)
Chez Prune (10e)
Comptoir Paris-Marrak. (1er)
Dalloyau (multi. loc.)
Doobie's (8e)
Durand Dupont (Neuilly)
Ferme (1er)
Findi (8e)
Flore en l'Ile (4e)
Fouquet's (8e)
Fumoir (1er)
Jardin des Cygnes (8e)
Joe Allen (1er)
Jo Goldenberg (4e)
Kiosque (16e)
Ladurée (multi. loc.)
Libre Sens (8e)
Lina's (7e)
Loir dans la Théière (4e)
Maison Rouge (4e)
Mariage Frères (multi. loc.)
Market (8e)
Moulin de la Galette (18e)
Nemrod (6e)
No Stress Café (9e)
Pershing (8e)
Pied de Chameau (4e)
Pitchi Poï (4e)
Quai Ouest (St-Cloud)
404 (3e)
R. (15e)
Senso (8e)
7ème Sud Grenelle (multi.)
Spicy (8e)
Studio (4e)
Télégraphe (7e)
Thanksgiving (4e)
Toi (8e)
Viaduc Café (12e)
Vinea Café (12e)
Wepler (18e)
W, Restaurant (8e)
Zebra Square (16e)

Business Dining

Affiche (8e)
Amphyclès (17e)
Angle du Faubourg (8e)
Argenteuil (1er)
Armand au Palais Royal (1er)
Astrance (16e)
Bistrot de l'Etoile Laur. (16e)
Bistrot de l'Etoile Niel (17e)
Bistrot St. Ferdinand (17e)
Boeuf Couronné (19e)
Boeuf sur le Toit (8e)
Bon 2 (2e)
Bourdonnais/Cantine (7e)
Buisson Ardent (5e)
Café de l'Esplanade (7e)
Café Faubourg (8e)
Cap Vernet (8e)
Caves Pétrissans (17e)
Céladon (2e)
Chez André (8e)
Chez L'Ami Louis (3e)
Chez Pauline (1er)
Chez Savy (8e)
Chiberta (8e)
Clos des Gourmets (7e)
Copenhague (8e)
Costes (1er)
Dessirier (17e)
Divellec (7e)
Dôme (14e)
Dôme du Marais (4e)
Drouant (2e)
Duc (14e)
Estaminet Gaya (1er)
Flora (8e)
Flora Danica (8e)
Fontaine d'Auteuil (16e)
Fouquet's (8e)
Gaya Rive Gauche (7e)
Gérard Besson (1er)
Glénan (7e)
Goumard (1er)
Graindorge (17e)
Grandes Marches (12e)
Guy Savoy (17e)
Hélène Darroze (6e)
Il Baccello (17e)
Il Cortile (1er)
Jules Verne (7e)
Lapérouse (6e)
Macéo (1er)
Maison Blanche (8e)
Mansouria (11e)
Marée (8e)
Marius (16e)
Marty (5e)
Maxim's (Orly)
Meurice (1er)
Montalembert (7e)
Paris (6e)
Paris Seize (16e)
Park (2e)
Petit Bofinger (4e)
Petit Marguery (13e)
Petit Pergolèse (16e)

Special Feature Index

Petrossian (7ᵉ)
Pichet de Paris (8ᵉ)
Pierre au Palais Royal (1ᵉʳ)
Pierre Gagnaire (8ᵉ)
Récamier (7ᵉ)
Relais Louis XIII (6ᵉ)
Salon d' Hélène (6ᵉ)
Sébillon (multi. loc.)
16 Haussmann (9ᵉ)
Senso (8ᵉ)
Sormani (17ᵉ)
Stella Maris (8ᵉ)
Stresa (8ᵉ)
Tan Dinh (7ᵉ)
Tante Louise (8ᵉ)
Thierry Burlot (15ᵉ)
Train Bleu (12ᵉ)
Trou Gascon (12ᵉ)
Vagenende (6ᵉ)
Vaudeville (2ᵉ)
Vin et Marée (multi. loc.)
Voltaire (7ᵉ)
W, Restaurant (8ᵉ)

Catering

Al Dar (16ᵉ)
Al Diwan (8ᵉ)
Astuce (15ᵉ)
Atelier Gourmand (17ᵉ)
Atlas (5ᵉ)
Avant Goût (13ᵉ)
Baan-Boran (1ᵉʳ)
Baie d'Ha Long (16ᵉ)
Banyan (15ᵉ)
BE Boulangépicier (17ᵉ)
Bellotta-Bellotta (7ᵉ)
Blue Elephant (11ᵉ)
Byblos Café (16ᵉ)
Caffé Toscano (7ᵉ)
Caïus (17ᵉ)
Cantine Russe (16ᵉ)
Casa Tina (16ᵉ)
Chez Fred (17ᵉ)
Chez Livio (Neuilly)
Chez Marianne (4ᵉ)
Chez Vong (1ᵉʳ)
China Town Olymp. (13ᵉ)
Coco de Mer (5ᵉ)
Comptoir/Saumon (multi.)
Cosi (6ᵉ)
Dalloyau (multi. loc.)
Daru (8ᵉ)
Dédicace Café (6ᵉ)
Délices d'Aphrodite (5ᵉ)
Deux Abeilles (7ᵉ)
Dominique (6ᵉ)
Etoile Marocaine (8ᵉ)

Fakhr el Dine (multi. loc.)
Fauchon (8ᵉ)
Feuilles Libres (Neuilly)
Findi (8ᵉ)
Flora Danica (8ᵉ)
Hédiard (8ᵉ)
Higuma (1ᵉʳ)
Inagiku (5ᵉ)
Jo Goldenberg (4ᵉ)
Khun Akorn (11ᵉ)
Kim Anh (15ᵉ)
Kinugawa (multi. loc.)
Lac-Hong (16ᵉ)
Lao Siam (19ᵉ)
Lao Tseu (7ᵉ)
Lina's (multi. loc.)
Maison du Caviar (8ᵉ)
Matsuri (multi. loc.)
Mavrommatis (5ᵉ)
New Jawad (7ᵉ)
New Nioullaville (11ᵉ)
Noura (multi. loc.)
Oum el Banine (16ᵉ)
Pamphlet (3ᵉ)
Passy Mandarin (16ᵉ)
Patrick Goldenberg (17ᵉ)
Petrossian (7ᵉ)
Pitchi Poï (4ᵉ)
404 (3ᵉ)
Riad (Neuilly)
Roi du Pot-au-Feu (9ᵉ)
Rosimar (16ᵉ)
Sauvignon (7ᵉ)
Timgad (17ᵉ)
Tong Yen (8ᵉ)
Tsé-Yang (16ᵉ)
Villa (20ᵉ)
Village d'Ung et Li Lam (8ᵉ)
Village Kabyle (18ᵉ)
Wally Le Saharien (9ᵉ)

Celebrity Chefs

Ambroisie (4ᵉ), *Bernard Pacaud*
Apicius (17ᵉ), *Jean Pierre Vigato*
Asian (8ᵉ), *Alain Passard*
Astrance (16ᵉ), *Pascal Barbot*
Atelier Joël Robuchon (7ᵉ),
    Joël Robuchon
Bistrot d'à Côté (multi. loc.),
    Michel Rostang
Bouquinistes (6ᵉ), *Guy Savoy*
Bristol (8ᵉ), *Eric Fréchon*
Butte Chaillot (16ᵉ), *Guy Savoy*
Carré des Feuillants (1ᵉʳ),
    Alain Dutournier
Cinq (8ᵉ), *Philippe Legendre*
Elysées/Vernet (8ᵉ), *Eric Briffard*

Special Feature Index

Espadon (1er), *Michel Roth*
Fables de La Fontaine (7e),
   Christian Constant
Grand Véfour (1er), *Guy Martin*
Guy Savoy (17e), *Guy Savoy*
Hélène Darroze (6e), *Hélène Darroze*
Hiramatsu (4e), *Hiroyuki Hiramatsu*
Jacques Cagna (6e),
   Jacques Cagna
Jamin (16e), *Benoît Guichard*
Lasserre (8e), *Jean-Louis Nomicos*
Ledoyen (8e), *Christian Le Squer*
Lucas Carton (8e), *Alain Senderens*
Lyonnais (2e), *Alain Ducasse*
Market (8e),
   Jean-Georges Vongerichten
Michel Rostang (17e),
   Michel Rostang
Mon Vieil Ami (4e),
   Antoine Westermann
Pierre Gagnaire (8e),
   Pierre Gagnaire
Pinxo (1er), *Alain Dutournier*
Plaza-Athénée (8e), *Alain Ducasse*
Régalade (14e),
   Yves Camdeborde
Salon d' Hélène (6e),
   Hélène Darroze
Spoon, Food/Wine (8e),
   Alain Ducasse
Taillevent (8e), *Alain Solivérès*
Trou Gascon (12e),
   Alain Dutournier
Violon d'Ingres (7e),
   Christian Constant
Ze Kitchen Galerie (6e),
   William Ledeuil

Cheese Trays

Ambroisie (4e)
Ampère (17e)
Amphyclès (17e)
Androuët (7e)
Arpège (7e)
Astier (11e)
Astor (8e)
Atelier Joël Robuchon (7e)
Atelier Gourmand (17e)
Béatilles (17e)
Beauvilliers (18e)
Benoît (4e)
Bistro de Gala (9e)
Bistrot à Vins Mélac (11e)
Bistrot du Sommelier (8e)
Boeuf Couronné (19e)
Bon Accueil (7e)
Bouchons/Fr. Cl. (multi. loc.)
Bourguignon du Marais (4e)
Braisière (17e)
Café Constant (7e)
Café de Flore (6e)
Camélia (Bougival)
Carré des Feuillants (1er)
Céladon (2e)
Chardenoux (11e)
Chez Catherine (8e)
Chez Fred (17e)
Chez Gildo (7e)
Chez Jean (9e)
Chez Maître Paul (6e)
Chez René (5e)
Cloche des Halles (1er)
Divellec (7e)
Dôme (14e)
Dôme du Marais (4e)
Elysées du Vernet (8e)
Epicure 108 (17e)
Epi d'Or (1er)
Espadon (1er)
Estaminet Gaya (1er)
Faucher (17e)
Ferme St-Simon (7e)
Fernandises (11e)
Fins Gourmets (7e)
Flora (8e)
Fontaine Gaillon (2e)
Fontaines (5e)
Fouquet's (8e)
Garnier (8e)
Goumard (1er)
Graindorge (17e)
Grande Cascade (16e)
Grand Véfour (1er)
Guy Savoy (17e)
Hélène Darroze (6e)
Jamin (16e)
Jules Verne (7e)
Lasserre (8e)
Laurent (8e)
Lavinia (8e)
Ledoyen (8e)
Maison Courtine (14e)
Marée (8e)
Mesturet (2e)
Meurice (1er)
Michel Rostang (17e)
Moissonnier (5e)
Montparnasse 25 (14e)
Oenothèque (9e)
Papinou (Neuilly)
Paris (6e)
Passiflore (16e)
Pergolèse (16e)
Petit Colombier (17e)

Special Feature Index

Petit Laurent (7e)
Pierre Gagnaire (8e)
Plaza-Athénée (8e)
Port Alma (16e)
Pressoir (12e)
Relais d'Auteuil P. Pignol (16e)
Relais Louis XIII (6e)
Rôtisserie du Beaujolais (5e)
Sébillon (multi. loc.)
Soufflé (1er)
Stella (16e)
Table du Baltimore (16e)
Tante Jeanne (17e)
Tante Louise (8e)
Terrasse (18e)
Terroir (13e)
Thoumieux (7e)
Tour d'Argent (5e)
Train Bleu (12e)
Trois Marches (Versailles)
Trou Gascon (12e)
Truffe Noire (Neuilly)
Truffière (5e)
Vaudeville (2e)
Villaret (11e)
Violon d'Ingres (7e)
W, Restaurant (8e)
Yves Quintard (15e)

Child-Friendly

Affiche (8e)
Aiguière (11e)
Alcazar (6e)
Altitude 95 (7e)
Ampère (17e)
Amuse Bouche (14e)
Anahuacalli (5e)
A Priori Thé (2e)
Asian (8e)
Atelier Joël Robuchon (7e)
Atlas (5e)
Auberge Dab (16e)
Bar à Huîtres (multi. loc.)
Bar Vendôme (1er)
BE Boulangépicier (17e)
Bistro 121 (15e)
Bistro d'Hubert (15e)
Bistrot d'André (15e)
Bistrot de Breteuil (7e)
Bistrot du Dôme (4e)
Boeuf sur le Toit (8e)
Bofinger (4e)
Bouillon Racine (6e)
Brasserie de la Poste (16e)
Brasserie du Louvre (1er)
Brasserie Julien (10e)
Brasserie Lutétia (6e)
Brasserie Mollard (8e)
Buffalo Grill (multi. loc.)
Café de la Musique (19e)
Café de la Paix (9e)
Chai 33 (12e)
Chalet des Iles (16e)
Chez Clément (multi.)
Chez Jenny (3e)
Chez Livio (Neuilly)
Chez Toutoune (5e)
Chicago Pizza (8e)
Comptoir/Saumon (15e)
Congrès Maillot (17e)
Coupole (14e)
Dame Tart./Café Very (multi.)
Fouquet's (8e)
Gare (16e)
Gauloise (15e)
Gitane (15e)
Gourmet de l'Isle (4e)
Grandes Marches (12e)
Hippopotamus (multi. loc.)
Indiana Café (multi. loc.)
Kiosque (16e)
Ladurée (8e)
Languedoc (5e)
Léon de Bruxelles (multi.)
Monsieur Lapin (14e)
Noura (6e)
Orenoc (17e)
Pavillon Montsouris (14e)
Pavillon Puebla (19e)
Petit Bofinger (multi. loc.)
Petite Cour (6e)
Petite Sirène Copenh. (9e)
Petite Tour (16e)
Petit Lutétia (6e)
Petit Poucet (Levallois)
Pied de Cochon (1er)
Planet Hollywood (8e)
Port Alma (16e)
Procope (Le) (6e)
Quai Ouest (St-Cloud)
Relais de l'Entrecôte (multi.)
Rendez-vous/Camion. (14e)
Rest. du Musée d'Orsay (7e)
Rest. du Palais Royal (1er)
River Café (Issy-les-Moul.)
Rôtisserie d'en Face (6e)
Rôtisserie du Beaujolais (5e)
Rotonde (6e)
Saint Vincent (15e)
Sardegna a Tavola (12e)
Sébillon (multi. loc.)
Spicy (8e)
Studio (4e)
Tang (16e)

get updates at zagat.com

Special Feature Index

Taverne Maître Kanter (1er)
Terminus Nord (10e)
Terrasse (18e)
Terroir (13e)
Toupary (1er)
Train Bleu (12e)
Trumilou (4e)
Vagenende (6e)
Vaudeville (2e)
Viaduc Café (12e)
Vieux Bistro (4e)
Village d'Ung et Li Lam (8e)
Virgin Café (8e)
Wepler (18e)

Closed in August
(Call ahead to confirm)
Absinthe (1er)
A et M Le Bistrot (16e)
Affriolé (7e)
Ailleurs (8e)
Aimant du Sud (13e)
Allard (6e)
Allobroges (20e)
Alsaco (9e)
Ambassade Sud-Ouest (7e)
Ambroisie (4e)
Amici Mei (4e)
Amognes (11e)
Ampère (17e)
Amphyclès (17e)
Amuse Bouche (14e)
Anacréon (13e)
Androuët (7e)
Angle du Faubourg (8e)
Apicius (17e)
Ardoise (1er)
Armand au Palais Royal (1er)
Assiette (14e)
Astier (11e)
Astor (8e)
Astrance (16e)
Atelier Gourmand (17e)
Auberge Champ de Mars (7e)
Auberge Etchégorry (13e)
Auberge Pyr. Cévennes (11e)
Auvergne Gourmande (7e)
Avant Goût (13e)
Azabu (6e)
Babylone (7e)
Baie d'Ha Long (16e)
Ballon des Ternes (17e)
Bamboche (7e)
Baptiste (17e)
Barroco (6e)
Bartolo (6e)
Bascou (3e)

Bath's (8e)
Béatilles (17e)
BE Boulangépicier (17e)
Bel Canto (multi. loc.)
Bélier (6e)
Bellecour (7e)
Bellini (16e)
Bellotta-Bellotta (7e)
Benoît (4e)
Beudant (17e)
Beurre Noisette (15e)
Biche au Bois (12e)
Bistrot à Vins Mélac (11e)
Bistrot de l'Université (7e)
Bistrot de Paris (7e)
Bistrot des Capucins (20e)
Bistrot du Sommelier (8e)
Bistrot La Catalogne (6e)
Bistrot Papillon (9e)
Bistrot Paul Bert (11e)
Braisière (17e)
Brasserie de l'Ile St. L. (4e)
Buisson Ardent (5e)
Butte Chaillot (16e)
Café d'Angel (17e)
Café de Mars (7e)
Café des Délices (6e)
Café Lenôtre (8e)
Café Max (7e)
Cafetière (6e)
Cailloux (13e)
Caméléon (6e)
Camélia (Bougival)
C'Amelot (11e)
Canard (17e)
Cantine Russe (16e)
Carpaccio (8e)
Carré des Feuillants (1er)
Cartet (11e)
Casa Olympe (9e)
Cave de l'Os à Moëlle (15e)
Cave Gourmande (19e)
Caves Pétrissans (17e)
Céladon (2e)
Chen Soleil d'Est (15e)
Chez Albert (6e)
Chez Catherine (8e)
Chez Diane (6e)
Chez Georges (2e)
Chez Gildo (7e)
Chez Jean (9e)
Chez L'Ami Jean (7e)
Chez L'Ami Louis (3e)
Chez la Vieille (1er)
Chez Léon (17e)
Chez Marcel (6e)
Chez Nénesse (3e)

Special Feature Index

Chez René (5e)
Chez Savy (8e)
Chiberta (8e)
Cloche des Halles (1er)
Clos Morillons (15e)
Clovis (8e)
Coco de Mer (5e)
Conti (16e)
Copenhague (8e)
Cosi (Le) (5e)
Cottage Marcadet (18e)
Da Mimmo (10e)
Daru (8e)
D'Chez Eux (7e)
De Lagarde (15e)
Délices de Szechuen (7e)
Dell Orto (9e)
Deux Canards (10e)
Dix Vins (15e)
Domaine de Lintillac (9e)
Dôme du Marais (4e)
Dominique (6e)
Doobie's (8e)
Drouant (2e)
Duc (14e)
Ecailler du Bistrot (11e)
Elysées du Vernet (8e)
Entoto (13e)
Entracte (18e)
Entredgeu (17e)
Epi d'Or (1er)
Epi Dupin (6e)
Espadon Bleu (6e)
Estaminet Gaya (1er)
Excuse (4e)
Fellini (15e)
Ferme des Mathurins (8e)
Fernandises (11e)
Fins Gourmets (7e)
Florimond (7e)
Fontaine d'Auteuil (16e)
Garnier (8e)
Gavroche (2e)
Gaya Rive Gauche (7e)
Gérard Besson (1er)
Giulio Rebellato (16e)
Glénan (7e)
Gli Angeli (3e)
Gourmets des Ternes (8e)
Grande Rue (15e)
Grandes Marches (12e)
Grand Véfour (1er)
Grand Venise (15e)
Grille (10e)
Hangar (3e)
Hédiard (8e)
Hiramatsu (4e)
Huîtrier (17e)
Il Viccolo (6e)
Impatient (17e)
Inagiku (5e)
Isami (4e)
Isse (2e)
Jacques Cagna (6e)
Jamin (16e)
Je Thé ... Me (15e)
Joe Allen (1er)
Joséphine Ch. Dumonet (6e)
Jumeaux (11e)
Kambodgia (16e)
Lac-Hong (16e)
Languedoc (5e)
Lapérouse (6e)
Lasserre (8e)
Ledoyen (8e)
Lescure (1er)
Lucas Carton (8e)
Luna (8e)
Lyonnais (2e)
Magnolias (Perreux-sur-Marne)
Maison Courtine (14e)
Maison du Jardin (6e)
Mandarin/Neuilly (Neuilly)
Marée (8e)
Marius (16e)
Marlotte (6e)
Mascotte (8e)
Mavrommatis (5e)
Meurice (1er)
Michel Rostang (17e)
Moissonnier (5e)
Monsieur Lapin (14e)
Montparnasse 25 (14e)
Moulin à Vent (5e)
Muses (9e)
Natachef (16e)
O à la Bouche (14e)
Obélisque (8e)
Oenothèque (9e)
Olivades (7e)
Orangerie (4e)
Orenoc (17e)
Orient-Extrême (6e)
Ormes (16e)
Os à Moëlle (15e)
Ostéria (4e)
Pamphlet (3e)
Paolo Petrini (17e)
Parc aux Cerfs (6e)
Paris (6e)
Park (2e)
Passiflore (16e)
Passy Mandarin (16e)
Paul Chêne (16e)

get updates at zagat.com

Special Feature Index

Pergolèse (16ᵉ)
Perraudin (5ᵉ)
Perron (7ᵉ)
Petite Sirène Copenh. (9ᵉ)
Petite Tour (16ᵉ)
Petit Laurent (7ᵉ)
Petit Marguery (13ᵉ)
Petit Niçois (7ᵉ)
Petit Pergolèse (16ᵉ)
Petrossian (7ᵉ)
Pharamond (1ᵉʳ)
Pierre au Palais Royal (1ᵉʳ)
Pomponette (18ᵉ)
Poquelin (1ᵉʳ)
Port Alma (16ᵉ)
Pressoir (12ᵉ)
P'tit Troquet (7ᵉ)
Quinson (15ᵉ)
R'Aliment (3ᵉ)
Régalade (14ᵉ)
Relais d'Auteuil P. Pignol (16ᵉ)
Relais de l'Entrecôte (8ᵉ)
Relais Louis XIII (6ᵉ)
Relais Plaza (8ᵉ)
Réminet (5ᵉ)
Rendez-vous/Camion. (14ᵉ)
Repaire de Cartouche (11ᵉ)
Rest. de la Tour (15ᵉ)
Rest. du Marché (15ᵉ)
Riad (Neuilly)
Robert et Louise (3ᵉ)
Rosimar (16ᵉ)
Rouge Vif (7ᵉ)
Rucola (17ᵉ)
Sardegna a Tavola (12ᵉ)
Sarladais (8ᵉ)
Sauvignon (7ᵉ)
16 Haussmann (9ᵉ)
Sept Quinze (15ᵉ)
7ème Sud Grenelle (multi.)
Sinago (9ᵉ)
6 New York (16ᵉ)
Sormani (17ᵉ)
Soufflé (1ᵉʳ)
Soupière (17ᵉ)
Sousceyrac (11ᵉ)
Spoon, Food/Wine (8ᵉ)
Square Trousseau (12ᵉ)
Stéphane Martin (15ᵉ)
Stresa (8ᵉ)
Sud (17ᵉ)
Table de Lucullus (17ᵉ)
Table du Baltimore (16ᵉ)
Table Oliviers & Co. (17ᵉ)
Taillevent (8ᵉ)
Tan Dinh (7ᵉ)
Tang (16ᵉ)

Tante Jeanne (17ᵉ)
Tante Louise (8ᵉ)
Tante Marguerite (7ᵉ)
Tastevin (Maisons-Laffitte)
Terroir (13ᵉ)
Thiou (multi. loc.)
Timbre (6ᵉ)
Tire-Bouchon (15ᵉ)
Tong Yen (8ᵉ)
Tonkinoise (13ᵉ)
Tonnelle Saintong. (Neuilly)
Toque (17ᵉ)
Trois Marches (Versailles)
Troquet (15ᵉ)
Trou Gascon (12ᵉ)
Truffe Noire (Neuilly)
Vagenende (6ᵉ)
Villa Mauresque (8ᵉ)
Villaret (11ᵉ)
Vinci (16ᵉ)
Vin sur Vin (7ᵉ)
Wally Le Saharien (9ᵉ)
Zygomates (12ᵉ)

Critic-Proof
(Get lots of business despite so-so food)
Café Marly (1ᵉʳ)
Chez Clément (multi.)
Hippopotamus (multi. loc.)
Léon de Bruxelles (multi.)

Dancing
Arbuci (6ᵉ)
Bˣfly (8ᵉ)
Bains (3ᵉ)
Barramundi (9ᵉ)
Barrio Latino (12ᵉ)
Brasserie de la Poste (16ᵉ)
Café de Mars (7ᵉ)
Chez Clément (17ᵉ)
Chez Gégène (Joinville)
Coupole (14ᵉ)
Etoile (8ᵉ)
Planet Hollywood (8ᵉ)
Suite (8ᵉ)
Tanjia (8ᵉ)
Vinea Café (12ᵉ)
Yvan, Petit (8ᵉ)

Dining Alone
(Other than hotels and places with counter service)
Affiche (8ᵉ)
Aimant du Sud (13ᵉ)
Alcazar (6ᵉ)
Alsace (8ᵉ)

Special Feature Index

Ampère (17e)
Amuse Bouche (14e)
Ballon des Ternes (17e)
Bar des Théâtres (8e)
Bar Rouge (9e)
Bistrot à Vins Mélac (11e)
Bistrot d'Alex (6e)
Bistrot de Marius (8e)
Bistrot du Peintre (11e)
Boeuf sur le Toit (8e)
Bouchons/Fr. Cl. (multi. loc.)
Bouillon Racine (6e)
Bourguignon du Marais (4e)
Brasserie de l'Ile St. L. (4e)
Breakfast in America (5e)
Buffalo Grill (multi. loc.)
Buisson Ardent (5e)
Café Beaubourg (4e)
Café de Flore (6e)
Café des Lettres (7e)
Café du Commerce (15e)
Café du Passage (11e)
Café Lenôtre (8e)
Café Les Deux Magots (6e)
Café Marly (1er)
Carr's (1er)
Caves Legrand (2e)
Charlot - Roi des Coq. (9e)
Chez Jenny (3e)
Chez Marcel (6e)
Chez Marianne (4e)
Closerie des Lilas (6e)
Congrès Maillot (17e)
Coupole (14e)
Ecluse (multi. loc.)
Ferme des Mathurins (8e)
Fernandises (11e)
Fins Gourmets (7e)
Fish La Boissonnerie (6e)
Fumoir (1er)
Gauloise (15e)
Hippopotamus (multi. loc.)
Indiana Café (multi. loc.)
Isami (4e)
Isse (2e)
Je Thé . . . Me (15e)
Joe Allen (1er)
Joséphine Ch. Dumonet (6e)
Ladurée (multi. loc.)
Languedoc (5e)
Lina's (multi. loc.)
Marty (5e)
Natachef (16e)
Nemrod (6e)
Oenothèque (9e)
Paradis Thai (13e)
Petit Colombier (17e)
Petite Chaise (A la) (7e)
Petite Sirène Copenh. (9e)
Petit Lutétia (6e)
Petit Marguery (13e)
Petit Pergolèse (16e)
Petit Rétro (16e)
Petit Riche (9e)
Polidor (6e)
Poule au Pot (1er)
Rubis (1er)
Sologne (12e)
Terminus Nord (10e)
Vagenende (6e)
Viaduc Café (12e)
Vin et Marée (multi. loc.)
Virgin Café (8e)
Wepler (18e)
Wok Cooking (11e)
Zéphyr (20e)

Entertainment

(Call for days and times of performances)
Alivi (4e) (Corsican)
Annapurna (8e) (sitar)
Asian (8e) (DJ)
B*fly (8e) (DJ)
Bains (3e) (DJ)
Barrio Latino (12e) (salsa)
Barroco (6e) (Brazilian orchestra)
Bar Vendôme (1er) (piano)
Bel Canto (multi. loc.) (opera)
Berkeley (8e) (DJ)
Ca d'Oro (1er) (Italian)
Café Charbon (11e) (concerts)
Café de la Mus. (19e) (jazz/world)
Café Faubourg (8e) (piano)
Carr's (1er) (Irish)
Chez Françoise (7e) (piano)
Chicago Pizza (8e) (DJ/dancers)
China Club (12e) (concerts)
China Town Olymp. (13e) (karaoke)
Diamantaires (9e) (orchestra)
Djakarta (1er) (Balinese dancing)
Jardin (8e) (harp)
Jardin des Cygnes (8e) (piano)
Jo Goldenberg (4e) (Yiddish)
Jules Verne (7e) (piano)
Lasserre (8e) (piano)
Man Ray (8e) (DJ)
Maxim's (8e) (piano)
Petit Riche (9e) (theater)
Pied de Chameau (4e) (varies)
Quai Ouest (St-Cloud) (clown)
Réconfort (3e) (jazz)
Relais Plaza (8e) (jazz)
Saudade (1er) (fado music)

get updates at zagat.com

Special Feature Index

Spicy (8e) (musicians)
Tanjia (8e) (DJ/dancers)
Viaduc Café (12e) (jazz)
Vinea Café (12e) (DJ)
Zebra Square (16e) (DJ)
Zo (8e) (DJ)

Family-Style
Aimant du Sud (13e)
Allard (6e)
Allobroges (20e)
Ampère (17e)
Ardoise (1er)
Aristide (17e)
Babylone (7e)
Bartolo (6e)
Bistrot d'Alex (6e)
Bon Accueil (7e)
Cafetière (6e)
Closerie des Lilas (6e)
Espace Sud-Ouest (multi.)
Flore en l'Ile (4e)
Fontaine de Mars (7e)
Marty (5e)
Mon Vieil Ami (4e)
Repaire de Cartouche (11e)
Toupary (1er)
Wok Cooking (11e)

Fireplaces
Atelier Maître Albert (5e)
Auberge du Clou (9e)
Bon (16e)
Carr's (1er)
Cazaudehore La For.
   (St-Germain-en-Laye)
Chalet des Iles (16e)
China Club (12e)
Coin de la Rue (8e)
Costes (1er)
Coupe-Chou (5e)
Cristal Room (16e)
Diamantaires (9e)
1728 (8e)
Fontaine Gaillon (2e)
Grande Cascade (16e)
Je Thé... Me (15e)
Montalembert (7e)
Orangerie (4e)
Paradis Thai (13e)
Pavillon Montsouris (14e)
Petit Colombier (17e)
Petit Poucet (Levallois)
Petit Victor Hugo (16e)
Pré Catelan (16e)
Quai Ouest (St-Cloud)
River Café (Issy-les-Moul.)

Robert et Louise (3e)
Romantica (Clichy)
Sud (17e)
Tastevin (Maisons-Laffitte)
Truffière (5e)

Historic Places
(Year opened; * building)
1582 Tour d'Argent (5e)
1650 Aiguière (11e)*
1680 Petite Chaise (A la) (7e)
1686 Procope (Le) (6e)
1728 1728 (8e)*
1758 Ambassadeurs (8e)*
1760 Grand Véfour (1er)
1766 Lapérouse (6e)
1800 Andy Whaloo (3e)*
1823 A Priori Thé (2e)*
1832 Escargot Montorgueil (1er)
1845 Polidor (6e)
1855 Brasserie du Louvre (1er)
1856 Charpentiers (6e)
1862 Café de la Paix (9e)
1864 Bofinger (4e)
1865 Dagorno (19e)
1867 Brasserie Mollard (8e)
1868 Ladurée (rue Royale)
1870 Boeuf Couronné (19e)
1872 Goumard (1er)
1876 Gallopin (2e)
1880 Auberge du Clou (9e)*
1880 Brasserie Lipp (6e)
1880 Drouant (2e)
1880 Petit Riche (9e)
1881 Café Terminus (8e)
1885 Café Les Deux Magots (6e)
1886 Brasserie Balzar (5e)
1890 Amphyclès (17e)*
1890 Brasserie Julien (10e)
1892 Wepler (18e)
1893 Aristide (17e)
1893 Maxim's (8e)
1895 Caves Pétrissans (17e)
1896 Chartier (9e)
1898 Espadon (1er)
1899 Fouquet's (8e)
1900 Brasserie de l'Ile St. L. (4e)
1900 Café Lenôtre (8e)*
1900 Chez Gégène (Joinville)
1900 Chez Pauline (1er)
1900 Gauloise (15e)
1900 Grande Cascade (16e)
1900 Ledoyen (8e)
1900 Noces de Jeannette (2e)
1900 Paul, Restaurant (1er)
1900 Pré Catelan (16e)
1901 Petit St. Benoît (6e)

Special Feature Index

1901 Train Bleu (12e)
1903 Angelina (1er)
1903 Bistrot de Paris (7e)
1903 Perraudin (5e)
1904 Vagenende (6e)
1905 Bons Crus (1er)
1906 Rendez-vous/Chauff. (18e)
1908 Chardenoux (11e)
1909 Bistrot d'André (15e)
1909 Pomponette (18e)
1910 Brasserie Lutétia (6e)
1910 Fontaine de Mars (7e)
1910 Pouilly Reuilly (Le Pré-St-Gervais)
1912 Benoît (4e)
1913 Marty (5e)
1913 Zeyer (14e)
1914 Sébillon (Neuilly)
1918 Daru (8e)
1919 Chez Marcel (6e)
1919 Lescure (1er)
1920 Closerie des Lilas (6e)
1920 59 Poincaré (16e)*
1920 Jo Goldenberg (4e)
1922 Café du Commerce (15e)
1923 Cantine Russe (16e)
1923 Sousceyrac (11e)
1923 Thoumieux (7e)
1924 Bristol (8e)
1924 Chez L'Ami Louis (3e)
1925 Biche au Bois (12e)
1925 Grand Venise (15e)
1925 Guinguette/Neuilly (Neuilly)
1925 Rech (17e)
1925 Terminus Nord (10e)
1926 Chez Georges-Maillot (17e)
1927 Brasserie Lorraine (8e)
1927 Caviar Kaspia (8e)
1927 Coupole (14e)
1928 Cazaudehore La For. (St-Germain-en-Laye)
1928 Dominique (6e)
1929 Diamantaires (9e)
1929 Jardin des Cygnes (8e)
1929 Petit Colombier (17e)
1929 Tante Louise (8e)
1929 Zéphyr (20e)
1930 Allard (6e)
1930 Garnier (8e)
1930 Trumilou (4e)
1931 Chez L'Ami Jean (7e)
1932 Chiberta (8e)
1932 Crus de Bourgogne (2e)
1935 Epi d'Or (1er)
1935 Poule au Pot (1er)
1936 Cartet (11e)
1936 Relais Plaza (8e)

1937 Chez André (8e)
1937 Léna et Mimile (5e)
1939 Voltaire (7e)
1940 Flandrin (16e)
1942 Lasserre (8e)
1942 Méditerranée (6e)
1945 Auberge Bressane (7e)
1945 Chez Fred (17e)
1945 Ferme des Mathurins (8e)
1945 Pied de Cochon (1er)
1945 Quinson (15e)
1946 Chez Maître Paul (6e)
1946 Taillevent (8e)
1947 Moulin à Vent (5e)
1948 Rubis (1er)
1949 Chez Françoise (7e)
1950 Conti (16e)
1950 Terrasse (18e)
1950 Va et Vient (17e)
1951 Bartolo (6e)
1951 Deux Canards (10e)
1952 Bistro 121 (15e)
1954 Coconnas (4e)
1954 Sauvignon (7e)

Holiday Meals

(Special prix fixe meals offered at major holidays)
Ambassadeurs (8e)
Ambroisie (4e)
Amognes (11e)
Amphyclès (17e)
Apicius (17e)
Arpège (7e)
Astor (8e)
Atelier Joël Robuchon (7e)
Benoît (4e)
Bristol (8e)
Café Les Deux Magots (6e)
Chen Soleil d'Est (15e)
Chiberta (8e)
Cinq (8e)
Coupole (14e)
Daru (8e)
Divellec (7e)
Espadon (1er)
Faucher (17e)
Goumard (1er)
Grande Cascade (16e)
Guy Savoy (17e)
Huîtrier (17e)
Jardins de Bagatelle (16e)
Jules Verne (7e)
Lapérouse (6e)
Lasserre (8e)
Ledoyen (8e)
Lucas Carton (8e)

get updates at zagat.com

Special Feature Index

Marée (8e)
Maxim's (8e)
Montparnasse 25 (14e)
Paris (6e)
Petrossian (7e)
Pierre Gagnaire (8e)
Potager du Roy (Versailles)
Pré Catelan (16e)
Relais Louis XIII (6e)
Romantica (Clichy)
Rue Balzac (8e)
Salon d' Hélène (6e)
Sormani (17e)
Table d'Anvers (9e)
Taillevent (8e)
Tan Dinh (7e)
Terrasse (18e)
Tour d'Argent (5e)
Trou Gascon (12e)
Wally Le Saharien (9e)

Hotel Dining

Four Seasons George V
   Cinq (8e)
Grand Hôtel Inter-Continental
   Café de la Paix (9e)
Hôtel Ambassador
   16 Haussmann (9e)
Hôtel Astor
   Astor (8e)
Hôtel Balzac
   Pierre Gagnaire (8e)
Hôtel Bristol
   Bristol (8e)
Hôtel Castille
   Il Cortile (1er)
Hôtel Concorde St-Lazare
   Café Terminus (8e)
Hôtel Costes
   Costes (1er)
Hôtel de Crillon
   Ambassadeurs (8e)
   Obélisque (8e)
Hôtel de La Bourdonnais
   Bourdonnais/Cantine (7e)
Hôtel de la Trémoille
   Senso (8e)
Hôtel du Louvre
   Brasserie du Louvre (1er)
Hôtel El Dorado
   Bistrot des Dames (17e)
Hôtel Hyatt
   Café M (8e)
Hôtel Le Parc
   59 Poincaré (16e)

Hôtel Lutétia
   Brasserie Lutétia (6e)
   Paris (6e)
Hôtel Meurice
   Meurice (1er)
Hôtel Montalembert
   Montalembert (7e)
Hôtel Novotel Tour Eiffel
   Benkay (15e)
Hotel Pershing Hall
   Pershing (8e)
Hôtel Plaza-Athénée
   Plaza-Athénée (8e)
   Relais Plaza (8e)
Hôtel Prince de Galles
   Jardin des Cygnes (8e)
Hôtel Ritz
   Bar Vendôme (1er)
   Espadon (1er)
Hôtel Royal Monceau
   Carpaccio (8e)
   Jardin (8e)
Hôtel Scribe
   Muses (9e)
Hôtel Terrass
   Terrasse (18e)
Hôtel Thoumieux
   Thoumieux (7e)
Hôtel Trianon Palace
   Trois Marches (Versailles)
Hôtel Vernet
   Elysées du Vernet (8e)
Hôtel Warwick
   W, Restaurant (8e)
Hôtel Westminster
   Céladon (2e)
Hyatt Paris Vendôme
   Park (2e)
Le Méridien Etoile
   Orenoc (17e)
Le Méridien-Montparnasse
   Montparnasse 25 (14e)
L'Hôtel
   Bélier (6e)
Sofitel Arc de Triomphe
   Clovis (8e)
Sofitel Demeure Hôtel
   Table du Baltimore (16e)
Sofitel Hôtel Marignan
   Spoon, Food/Wine (8e)
Sofitel Le Faubourg
   Café Faubourg (8e)

Special Feature Index

"In" Places
Alcazar (6e)
Anahï (3e)
Andy Whaloo (3e)
Apollo (14e)
Astrance (16e)
Atelier Joël Robuchon (7e)
Avant Goût (13e)
Avenue (8e)
B*fly (8e)
Bains (3e)
Bar des Théâtres (8e)
Bélier (6e)
Bon (16e)
Bouquinistes (6e)
B4 (1er)
Buddha Bar (8e)
Café Beaubourg (4e)
Café Burq (18e)
Café Charbon (11e)
Café d'Angel (17e)
Café de Flore (6e)
Café de la Jatte (Neuilly)
Café de l'Esplanade (7e)
Café Marly (1er)
Café Ruc (1er)
Cailloux (13e)
Chez Omar (3e)
Chez Prune (10e)
China Club (12e)
Coin de la Rue (8e)
Colette (1er)
Costes (1er)
Cristal Room (16e)
Emporio Armani (6e)
Etienne Marcel (2e)
Famille (18e)
Fouquet's (8e)
Fumoir (1er)
Georges (4e)
Guy Savoy (17e)
Kong (1er)
Man Ray (8e)
Market (8e)
404 (3e)
Régalade (14e)
Relais Plaza (8e)
Salon d' Hélène (6e)
Spoon, Food/Wine (8e)
Stresa (8e)
Thiou (7e)
Ze Kitchen Galerie (6e)

Jacket Required
(* Tie also required)
Ambroisie (4e)*
Arpège (7e)
Astrance (16e)
Carré des Feuillants (1er)*
Cinq (8e)
Espadon (1er)*
Grande Cascade (16e)*
Grand Véfour (1er)
Jules Verne (7e)*
Lasserre (8e)*
Ledoyen (8e)*
Lucas Carton (8e)*
Maxim's (8e)*
Meurice (1er)*
Michel Rostang (17e)*
Orangerie (4e)
Plaza-Athénée (8e)*
Pré Catelan (16e)*
Relais Plaza (8e)
Salon d' Hélène (6e)
Sarladais (8e)
Taillevent (8e)
Tour d'Argent (5e)*

Late Dining
(Weekday closing hour)
Alcazar (6e) (1 AM)
Al Diwan (8e) (1 AM)
Alsace (8e) (24 hrs.)
Andy Whaloo (3e) (1 AM)
Arbuci (6e) (1 AM)
Auberge Dab (16e) (2 AM)
B*fly (8e) (1 AM)
Bar à Huîtres (multi. loc.) (2 AM)
Bar des Théâtres (8e) (1 AM)
Berkeley (8e) (1 AM)
Bistro Melrose (17e) (1 AM)
Boeuf sur le Toit (8e) (1 AM)
Bofinger (4e) (1 AM)
B4 (1er) (1 AM)
Brasserie Julien (10e) (1 AM)
Brasserie Lipp (6e) (1 AM)
Café de Flore (6e) (1:30 AM)
Café du Passage (11e) (1 AM)
Café Les Deux Magots (6e) (1 AM)
Café Marly (1er) (1 AM)
Café Ruc (1er) (1 AM)
Caviar Kaspia (8e) (1 AM)
Charlot - Roi des Coq. (9e) (1 AM)
Chez André (8e) (1 AM)
Chez Clément (multi.) (1 AM)
Chien qui Fume (1er) (1 AM)
China Town Olymp. (13e) (1 AM)
Congrès Maillot (17e) (2 AM)
Costes (1er) (24 hrs.)
Coupe-Chou (5e) (1 AM)
Coupole (14e) (1:30 AM)
Dominique (6e) (1 AM)

get updates at zagat.com

Special Feature Index

Ecluse (multi. loc.) (1 AM)
Editeurs (6e) (2 AM)
Espace Sud-Ouest (multi.) (1 AM)
Etoile (8e) (1 AM)
Flore en l'Ile (4e) (2 AM)
Gamin de Paris (4e) (2 AM)
Gavroche (2e) (2 AM)
Georges (4e) (2 AM)
Grand Café (9e) (24 hrs.)
Grand Colbert (2e) (1 AM)
Grande Armée (16e) (2 AM)
Indiana Café (multi. loc.) (1 AM)
Léon de Bruxelles (multi.) (varies)
Ma Bourgogne (4e) (1 AM)
Maison du Caviar (8e) (1 AM)
Maison Rouge (4e) (2 AM)
Osteria Ascolani (18e) (2 AM)
Pied de Chameau (4e) (1 AM)
Pied de Cochon (1er) (24 hrs.)
Planet Hollywood (8e) (1 AM)
Poule au Pot (1er) (5 AM)
Procope (Le) (6e) (1 AM)
Rotonde (6e) (1 AM)
Senso (8e) (2 AM)
Tanjia (8e) (1 AM)
Tav. Maître Kanter (1er) (24 hrs.)
Tav. L'Esprit Blvd. (9e) (1 AM)
Terminus Nord (10e) (1 AM)
Toi (8e) (2 AM)
Vagenende (6e) (1 AM)
Vaudeville (2e) (1 AM)
Verre Bouteille (17e) (4:30 AM)
Viaduc Café (12e) (3 AM)
Vinea Café (12e) (2 AM)
Wepler (18e) (1 AM)

Meet for a Drink

Alcazar (6e)
B*fly (8e)
Bains (3e)
Bar des Théâtres (8e)
Baron Rouge (12e)
Bistrot à Vins Mélac (11e)
Bistrot du Peintre (11e)
Bons Crus (1er)
Bourguignon du Marais (4e)
Café Beaubourg (4e)
Café Burq (18e)
Café Charbon (11e)
Café de Flore (6e)
Café de la Musique (19e)
Café de l'Esplanade (7e)
Café de l'Industrie (11e)
Café Les Deux Magots (6e)
Café Marly (1er)
Café Ruc (1er)
Carr's (1er)

Cloche des Halles (1er)
Closerie des Lilas (6e)
Coin de la Rue (8e)
Comptoir Paris-Marrak. (1er)
Coude Fou (4e)
Coupole (14e)
Dame Tart./Café Very (1er)
Dôme (14e)
Ecluse (multi. loc.)
Enoteca (4e)
Etoile (8e)
Excuse (4e)
Ferme (1er)
Fish La Boissonnerie (6e)
Fontaines (5e)
Fouquet's (8e)
Fumoir (1er)
Gavroche (2e)
Grande Armée (16e)
Loir dans la Théière (4e)
Ma Bourgogne (4e)
Man Ray (8e)
Nemrod (6e)
No Stress Café (9e)
River Café (Issy-les-Moul.)
Rubis (1er)
Sauvignon (7e)
Viaduc Café (12e)
Vinea Café (12e)
Willi's Wine Bar (1er)
Zebra Square (16e)

No Air-Conditioning

A et M Le Bistrot (16e)
Aimant du Sud (13e)
Alivi (4e)
Alsaco (9e)
Ambassade Sud-Ouest (7e)
Amici Mei (4e)
Ami Pierre (11e)
Amognes (11e)
Amuse Bouche (14e)
Anahï (3e)
Anahuacalli (5e)
Angelina (1er)
AOC (5e)
Apollo (14e)
Appennino (13e)
A Priori Thé (2e)
Argenteuil (1er)
Aristide (17e)
Assiette (14e)
Atelier Berger (1er)
Auberge Champ de Mars (7e)
Auberge Nicolas Flamel (3e)
Auvergne Gourmande (7e)
Babylone (7e)

228 subscribe to zagat.com

Special Feature Index

Ballon des Ternes (17e)
Bamboche (7e)
Baracane (4e)
Bascou (3e)
Bermuda Onion (15e)
Biche au Bois (12e)
Bistro d'Hubert (15e)
Bistrot d'à Côté (multi. loc.)
Bistrot d'André (15e)
Bistrot de l'Université (7e)
Bistrot de Marius (8e)
Bistrot de Paris (7e)
Bistrot des Capucins (20e)
Bistrot des Dames (17e)
Bistrot d'Henri (6e)
Bistrot du Dôme (4e)
Bistrot La Catalogne (6e)
Bistrot Vivienne (1er)
Bon Saint Pourçain (6e)
Brasserie Balzar (5e)
Brasserie de l'Ile St. L. (4e)
Breakfast in America (5e)
Buisson Ardent (5e)
Ca d'Oro (1er)
Café Beaubourg (4e)
Café Burq (18e)
Café Charbon (11e)
Café d'Angel (17e)
Café de Mars (7e)
Café des Lettres (7e)
Café du Commerce (15e)
Café Max (7e)
Cagouille (14e)
Cailloux (13e)
Caméléon (6e)
C'Amelot (11e)
Canard (17e)
Cantine Russe (16e)
Cap Seguin (Boulogne)
Carr's (1er)
Cartes Postales (1er)
Cartet (11e)
Caveau du Palais (1er)
Caves Pétrissans (17e)
182 Rive Droite (16e)
Chalet des Iles (16e)
Chantairelle (5e)
Chardenoux (11e)
Charpentiers (6e)
Chartier (9e)
Cherche Midi (6e)
Chez Albert (6e)
Chez Clément (multi.)
Chez Denise (1er)
Chez Diane (6e)
Chez Francis (8e)
Chez Françoise (7e)
Chez Fred (17e)
Chez Gérard (Neuilly)
Chez Jean (9e)
Chez L'Ami Louis (3e)
Chez la Vieille (1er)
Chez Léon (17e)
Chez Marcel (6e)
Chez Marianne (4e)
Chez Michel (10e)
Chez Nénesse (3e)
Chez Omar (3e)
Chez Paul (11e)
Chez Paul (13e)
Chez Pauline (1er)
Chez Prune (10e)
Chez René (5e)
Chez Toutoune (5e)
Cloche des Halles (1er)
Closerie des Lilas (6e)
Clown Bar (11e)
Coco de Mer (5e)
Coconnas (4e)
Coin des Gourmets (5e)
. . . Comme Cochon (12e)
Comptoir/Saumon (15e)
Comte de Gascogne (Boulogne)
Contre-Allée (14e)
Cosi (Le) (5e)
Crus de Bourgogne (2e)
Dame Tart./Café Very (multi.)
Dauphin (1er)
Dell Orto (9e)
Deux Abeilles (7e)
Devez (8e)
Dix Vins (15e)
Djakarta Bali (1er)
Dôme du Marais (4e)
Durand Dupont (Neuilly)
Ecluse (multi. loc.)
El Palenque (5e)
Enoteca (4e)
Entoto (13e)
Entracte (18e)
Entredgeu (17e)
Epi d'Or (1er)
Epi Dupin (6e)
Famille (18e)
Faucher (17e)
Fernandises (11e)
Fins Gourmets (7e)
Flandrin (16e)
Flore en l'Ile (4e)
Florimond (7e)
Fontaines (5e)
Foujita (1er)
Fouquet's (8e)
Gastroquet (15e)

get updates at zagat.com 229

Special Feature Index

Gli Angeli (3^e)
Gourmet de l'Isle (4^e)
Gourmets des Ternes (8^e)
Graindorge (17^e)
Grande Cascade (16e)
Guinguette/Neuilly (Neuilly)
Il Barone (14e)
Impatient (17e)
Jardins de Bagatelle (16e)
Jumeaux (11e)
Khun Akorn (11e)
Louchebem (1er)
Lyonnais (2e)
Ma Bourgogne (4e)
Marius (16e)
Martel (10e)
Mascotte (8e)
Mascotte (18e)
Maupertu (7e)
Mauzac (5e)
Moissonnier (5e)
Moulin à Vent (5e)
Muscade (1er)
Natacha (14e)
Natachef (16e)
No Stress Café (9e)
Os à Moëlle (15e)
Papinou (Neuilly)
Patrick Goldenberg (17e)
Pavillon Puebla (19e)
Perraudin (5e)
Petit Bofinger (17e)
Petite Sirène Copenh. (9e)
Petit Laurent (7e)
Petit Lutétia (6e)
Petit Marché (3e)
Petit Marguery (13e)
Petit Niçois (7e)
Petit Poucet (Levallois)
Petits Marseillais (3e)
Pharamond (1er)
Pitchi Poï (4e)
Pomponette (18e)
Poquelin (1er)
Potager du Roy (Versailles)
Poule au Pot (1er)
Pravda (11e)
Pré Catelan (16e)
Procope (Le) (6e)
Prosper (8e)
P'tit Troquet (7e)
Pure Café (11e)
R'Aliment (3e)
Réconfort (3e)
Relais de l'Entrecôte (8e)
Relais de Venise (17e)
Rendez-vous/Camion. (14e)
Rendez-vous/Chauff. (18e)
Repaire de Cartouche (11e)
Rest. du Marché (15e)
Rest. du Palais Royal (1er)
River Café (Issy-les-Moul.)
Robe et le Palais (1er)
Robert et Louise (3e)
Roi du Pot-au-Feu (9e)
Romantica (Clichy)
Rughetta (18e)
Sale e Pepe (18e)
Sauvignon (7e)
Saveurs de Claude (6e)
Saveurs du Marché (Neuilly)
Scheffer (16e)
Sept Quinze (15e)
Si (3e)
Sinago (9e)
Soleil (St-Ouen)
Square Trousseau (12e)
Table de Lucullus (17e)
Taka (18e)
Tastevin (Maisons-Laffitte)
Temps des Cerises (13e)
Terroir (13e)
Thanksgiving (4e)
Timbre (6e)
Tokyo Eat (16e)
Tonnelle Saintong. (Neuilly)
Tournesol (16e)
Train Bleu (12e)
Triporteur (15e)
Troquet (15e)
Truffe Noire (Neuilly)
Tsukizi (6°)
Vaudeville (2e)
Viaduc Café (12e)
Villa Mauresque (8e)
Vin et Marée (16e)
Waknine (16e)
Willi's Wine Bar (1er)
Zéphyr (20e)
Zygomates (12e)

Nonsmoking Sections
A et M Le Bistrot (16e)
Affiche (8e)
Affriolé (7e)
Alcazar (6e)
Al Dar (multi. loc.)
Al Diwan (8e)
Al Mounia (16e)
Altitude 95 (7e)
Ambassade Sud-Ouest (7e)
Ambassadeurs (8e)
Ambroisie (4e)
Ampère (17e)

Special Feature Index

Amphyclès (17e)
Anacréon (13e)
Annapurna (8e)
AOC (5e)
Appart' (8e)
Appennino (13e)
A Priori Thé (2e)
Arbuci (6e)
Aristide (17e)
Astor (8e)
Astuce (15e)
Atelier Berger (1er)
Atelier Maître Albert (5e)
Atlas (5e)
Auberge Aveyron. (12e)
Auberge Dab (16e)
Auberge Etchégorry (13e)
Auberge Pyr. Cévennes (11e)
Avenue (8e)
B*fly (8e)
Baan-Boran (1er)
Baie d'Ha Long (16e)
Ballon des Ternes (17e)
Banyan (15e)
Baracane (4e)
Barramundi (9e)
Barrio Latino (12e)
Bar Vendôme (1er)
Basilic (7e)
Bath's (8e)
Bauta (6e)
Beato (7e)
Beudant (17e)
Benkay (15e)
Bigorneau (16e)
Bistro 121 (15e)
Bistro du 17ème (17e)
Bistrot à Vins Mélac (11e)
Bistrot d'Alex (6e)
Bistrot d'André (15e)
Bistrot de Breteuil (7e)
Bistrot de l'Etoile Niel (17e)
Bistrot de l'Université (7e)
Bistrot des Capucins (20e)
Bistrot des Vignes (16e)
Bistrot du Dôme (multi. loc.)
Bistrot du Sommelier (8e)
Bistrot La Catalogne (6e)
Bistrot Papillon (9e)
Bistrot St. Ferdinand (17e)
Blue Elephant (11e)
Bocconi (8e)
Boeuf sur le Toit (8e)
Bon Accueil (7e)
Bon Saint Pourçain (6e)
Bons Crus (1er)
Bouchons/Fr. Cl. (multi. loc.)
Boulangerie (20e)
Bourdonnais/Cantine (7e)
Bourguignon du Marais (4e)
Braisière (17e)
Brasserie Balzar (5e)
Brasserie de la Poste (16e)
Brasserie de l'Ile St. L. (4e)
Brasserie du Louvre (1er)
Brasserie Flo (10e)
Brasserie Lutétia (6e)
Brasserie Mollard (8e)
Buddha Bar (8e)
Buffalo Grill (multi. loc.)
Buisson Ardent (5e)
Butte Chaillot (16e)
Ca d'Oro (1er)
Café Beaubourg (4e)
Café Burq (18e)
Café Charbon (11e)
Café de Flore (6e)
Café de la Jatte (Neuilly)
Café de la Musique (19e)
Café de la Paix (9e)
Café de l'Esplanade (7e)
Café de l'Industrie (11e)
Café du Passage (11e)
Café Faubourg (8e)
Café Flo (9e)
Café Fusion (13e)
Café M (8e)
Café Marly (1er)
Café Moderne (2e)
Caffé Toscano (7e)
Cagouille (14e)
Caïus (17e)
Caméléon (6e)
Camélia (Bougival)
Camille (3e)
Cantine Russe (16e)
Cap Seguin (Boulogne)
Cap Vernet (8e)
Carré des Feuillants (1er)
Carr's (1er)
Casa Alcalde (15e)
Casa Hidalgo (11e)
Caveau du Palais (1er)
Cave de l'Os à Moëlle (15e)
Caves Pétrissans (17e)
Caviar Kaspia (8e)
Cazaudehore La For. (St-Germain-en-Laye)
Céladon (2e)
Chai 33 (12e)
Chantairelle (5e)
Charlot - Roi des Coq. (9e)
Chartier (9e)
Chen Soleil d'Est (15e)

get updates at zagat.com 231

Special Feature Index

Cherche Midi (6e)
Chez Albert (6e)
Chez André (8e)
Chez Catherine (8e)
Chez Clément (multi.)
Chez Denise (1er)
Chez Francis (8e)
Chez Françoise (7e)
Chez Fred (17e)
Chez Georges-Maillot (17e)
Chez Gérard (Neuilly)
Chez Gildo (7e)
Chez Janou (3e)
Chez Jean (9e)
Chez Jenny (3e)
Chez L'Ami Louis (3e)
Chez Léon (17e)
Chez Livio (Neuilly)
Chez Marianne (4e)
Chez Michel (10e)
Chez Nénesse (3e)
Chez Omar (3e)
Chez Pauline (1er)
Chez René (5e)
Chez Vong (1er)
Chiberta (8e)
Chicago Pizza (8e)
Chieng Mai (5e)
Chien qui Fume (1er)
China Town Olymp. (13e)
Christine (6e)
Cinq (8e)
Clos Saint-Honoré (1er)
Clovis (8e)
Coin des Gourmets (5e)
Comédiens (9e)
Congrès Maillot (17e)
Contre-Allée (14e)
Copenhague (8e)
Cosi (6e)
Cosi (Le) (5e)
Costes (1er)
Côté Coulisses (2e)
Coupole (14e)
Crêperie de Josselin (14e)
Cristal Room (16e)
Dalloyau (multi. loc.)
Dame Tart./Café Very (multi.)
Da Mimmo (10e)
Dauphin (1er)
Dédicace Café (6e)
Délices de Szechuen (7e)
Dell Orto (9e)
Dessirier (17e)
Deux Abeilles (7e)
Devez (8e)
Diamantaires (9e)

Diep (8e)
1728 (8e)
Djakarta Bali (1er)
Dôme (14e)
Dôme du Marais (4e)
Dos de la Baleine (4e)
Drouant (2e)
Durand Dupont (Neuilly)
Ebauchoir (12e)
Ecailler du Bistrot (11e)
Ecluse (multi. loc.)
El Mansour (8e)
El Palenque (5e)
Elysées du Vernet (8e)
Elysées Hong Kong (16e)
Emporio Armani (6e)
Entoto (13e)
Epicure 108 (17e)
Epi Dupin (6e)
Erawan (15e)
Espace Sud-Ouest (multi.)
Espadon (1er)
Etienne Marcel (2e)
Etoile Marocaine (8e)
Excuse (4e)
Fakhr el Dine (16e)
Fauchon (8e)
Ferme (1er)
Ferme des Mathurins (8e)
Ferme St-Simon (7e)
Fermette Marbeuf 1900 (8^e)
Feuilles Libres (Neuilly)
Findi (8^e)
Finzi (8e)
Flora Danica (8e)
Fontaine de Mars (7e)
Fontaine Gaillon (2e)
Fouquet's (8e)
Fous d'en Face (4e)
Fumoir (1er)
Gallopin (2e)
Gare (16e)
Garnier (8e)
Gastroquet (15e)
Georges (4e)
Gitane (15e)
Goumard (1er)
Gourmand (6e)
Gourmet de l'Isle (4e)
Graindorge (17e)
Grand Café (9e)
Grand Colbert (2e)
Grande Armée (16e)
Grande Rue (15e)
Grandes Marches (12e)
Grand Véfour (1er)
Grand Venise (15e)

Special Feature Index

Guirlande de Julie (4e)
Hédiard (8e)
Hélène Darroze (6e)
Higuma (1er)
Huîtrier (17e)
Il Cortile (1er)
Ile (Issy-les-Moulineaux)
Impatient (17e)
Jardins de Bagatelle (16e)
Joséphine Ch. Dumonet (6e)
Kong (1er)
Lac-Hong (16e)
Ladurée (8e)
Lao Siam (19e)
Lasserre (8e)
Léon de Bruxelles (multi.)
Lescure (1er)
Loir dans la Théière (4e)
Lô Sushi (multi. loc.)
Louchebem (1er)
Macéo (1er)
Magnolias (Perreux-sur-Marne)
Maharajah (5e)
Main d'Or (11e)
Maison Courtine (14e)
Mandalay (Levallois)
Mandarin/Neuilly (Neuilly)
Mansouria (11e)
Market (8e)
Marlotte (6e)
Maupertu (7e)
Maxim's (Orly)
Mesturet (2e)
Murat (16e)
Muses (9e)
Natacha (14e)
Nemrod (6e)
New Nioullaville (11e)
Noces de Jeannette (2e)
Noura (multi. loc.)
Nouveau Village Tao (13e)
O à la Bouche (14e)
Oeillade (7e)
Oïshi (2e)
Olivades (7e)
Opportun (14e)
Orenoc (17e)
Orient-Extrême (6e)
Ormes (16e)
Os à Moëlle (15e)
Palanquin (6e)
Pamphlet (3e)
Paolo Petrini (17e)
Paradis Thai (13e)
Parc aux Cerfs (6e)
Paris Seize (16e)
Park (2e)
Passy Mandarin (16e)
Paul Chêne (16e)
Paul, Restaurant (1er)
Pavillon Montsouris (14e)
Pavillon Puebla (19e)
Père Claude (15e)
Perraudin (5e)
Perron (7e)
Petit Bofinger (4e)
Petit Colombier (17e)
Petit Laurent (7e)
Petit Lutétia (6e)
Petit Marché (3e)
Petit Marguery (13e)
Petit Marguery (16e)
Petit Niçois (7e)
Pied de Chameau (4e)
Pied de Cochon (1er)
Pierre au Palais Royal (1er)
Pinxo (1er)
Pitchi Poï (4e)
Pomponette (18e)
Port Alma (16e)
Procope (Le) (6e)
P'tit Troquet (7e)
404 (3e)
Rech (17e)
Relais de l'Entrecôte (6e)
Relais de Venise (17e)
Relais Louis XIII (6e)
Rest. du Palais Royal (1er)
Riad (Neuilly)
Romantica (Clichy)
Rughetta (18e)
Saveurs de Claude (6e)
Saveurs du Marché (Neuilly)
Sébillon (multi. loc.)
16 Haussmann (9e)
Senso (8e)
6 New York (16e)
Sizin (9e)
Sologne (12e)
Sormani (17e)
Soufflé (1er)
Sousceyrac (11e)
Spoon, Food/Wine (8e)
Stella (16e)
Stéphane Martin (15e)
Stresa (8e)
Sud (17e)
Table d'Anvers (9e)
Table du Baltimore (16e)
Taillevent (8e)
Tang (16e)
Tante Louise (8e)
Tastevin (Maisons-Laffitte)
Taverne Maître Kanter (1er)

get updates at zagat.com 233

Special Feature Index

Taverne L'Esprit Blvd. (9e)
Temps des Cerises (13e)
Terrasse (18e)
Thanksgiving (4e)
Thoumieux (7e)
Toque (17e)
Toupary (1er)
Tourelle (1er)
Train Bleu (12e)
Tricotin (13e)
Trois Marches (Versailles)
Troquet (15e)
Truffière (5e)
Tsé-Yang (16e)
Ty Coz (9e)
Vagenende (6e)
Vaudeville (2e)
Vieille Fontaine Rôtiss. (Maisons-Laffitte)
Village d'Ung et Li Lam (8e)
Vinci (16e)
Vinea Café (12e)
Vin et Marée (14e)
20 de Bellechasse (7e)
Violon d'Ingres (7e)
Virgin Café (8e)
Wally Le Saharien (9e)
Wepler (18e)
Yvan (8e)
Zeyer (14e)
Zo (8e)
Zygomates (12e)

Noteworthy Newcomers

Affiche (8e)
Al Caratello (18e)
Apollo (14e)
Appennino (13e)
Astuce (15e)
Atelier Joël Robuchon (7e)
Auberge d'Autrefois (16e)
Auvergne Gourmande (7e)
Ballon et Coquillages (17e)
Banyan (15e)
Bar Rouge (9e)
Bigorneau (16e)
Bistrot des Vignes (16e)
Bistrot du Cap (15e)
Bocconi (8e)
Bouche à Oreille (De) (14e)
Breakfast in America (5e)
Buisson Ardent (5e)
Café Burq (18e)
Café Constant (7e)
Café Fusion (13e)
Café Lenôtre (8e)
Café Moderne (2e)
Caïus (17e)
Casa Hidalgo (11e)
Caves Legrand (2e)
182 Rive Droite (16e)
Coin de la Rue (8e)
Côté Coulisses (2e)
Couleurs de Vigne (15e)
Cristal Room (16e)
1728 (8e)
Ecailler du Bistrot (11e)
Entredgeu (17e)
Estaminet Gaya (1er)
Famille (18e)
Fauchon (8e)
Gourmand (6e)
Jean-Paul Hévin (1er)
Kong (1er)
Lei (7e)
Libre Sens (8e)
Louchebem (1er)
Mandalay (Levallois)
Mesturet (2e)
Mont Liban (17e)
Mon Vieil Ami (4e)
No Stress Café (9e)
Opportun (14e)
Osteria Ascolani (18e)
Papinou (Neuilly)
Paradis Thai (13e)
Pershing (8e)
Petit Colombier Mer (17e)
Petit Pergolèse (16e)
Petit Pontoise (8e)
Pinxo (1er)
Pré Verre (5e)
Prosper (8e)
Ramulaud (11e)
Sale e Pepe (18e)
Saveurs de Claude (6e)
Saveurs du Marché (Neuilly)
Sora Lena (17e)
Square (7e)
Strapontins (10e)
Suite (8e)
Table de la Fontaine (9e)
Toi (8e)
Tokyo Eat (16e)
Tourelle (1er)
Va et Vient (17e)
Villa (20e)
Village Kabyle (18e)
20 de Bellechasse (7e)

Special Feature Index

Outdoor Dining
(G=garden; P=patio;
S=sidewalk; T=terrace)
Absinthe (1er) (S, T)
Aimant du Sud (13e) (S, T)
Al Dar (multi. loc.) (S, T)
Alivi (4e) (T)
Al Mounia (16e) (S)
Ampère (17e) (S)
AOC (5e) (T)
Apollo (14e) (T)
A Priori Thé (2e) (P)
Astuce (15e) (S)
Atlas (5e) (S)
Auberge Aveyron. (12e) (S, T)
Auberge du Clou (9e) (S, T)
Auvergne Gourmande (7e) (S)
Avenue (8e) (T)
Baie d'Ha Long (16e) (T)
Ballon des Ternes (17e) (S, T)
Bartolo (6e) (S, T)
Bar Vendôme (1er) (P)
Basilic (7e) (G, T)
Beauvilliers (18e) (S, T)
BE Boulangépicier (17e) (S)
Bel Canto (14e) (T)
Bélier (6e) (P)
Berkeley (8e) (T)
Bermuda Onion (15e) (T)
Bistro d'Hubert (15e) (T)
Bistro du 17ème (17e) (S)
Bistrot d'à Côté (multi.) (S, T)
Bistrot d'André (15e) (S, T)
Bistrot de Breteuil (7e) (T)
Bistrot de l'Etoile Niel (17e) (S, T)
Bistrot de Marius (8e) (S)
Bistrot des Dames (17e) (G)
Bistrot du Cap (15e) (T)
Bistrot La Catalogne (6e) (S)
Bistrot St. Ferdinand (17e) (T)
Bistrot Vivienne (1er) (T)
Bon 2 (2e) (S, T)
Bon Saint Pourçain (6e) (S)
Bouchons/Fr. Cl. (multi. loc.) (S, T)
Bourguignon du Marais (4e) (T)
Brasserie de la Poste (16e) (S)
Brasserie du Louvre (1er) (T)
Bristol (8e) (G)
Buisson Ardent (5e) (S)
Butte Chaillot (16e) (S)
Ca d'Oro (1er) (S)
Café Beaubourg (4e) (T)
Café de Flore (6e) (S, T)
Café de la Jatte (Neuilly) (G, T)
Café de la Musique (19e) (T)
Café de l'Esplanade (7e) (S)

Café de l'Industrie (11e) (S)
Café de Mars (7e) (S)
Café des Lettres (7e) (P)
Café Lenôtre (8e) (G, P)
Café Les Deux Magots (6e) (G, T)
Café Marly (1er) (T)
Café Max (7e) (S, T)
Cagouille (14e) (T)
Cantine Russe (16e) (G)
Cap Seguin (Boulogne) (T)
Cap Vernet (8e) (T)
Caveau du Palais (1er) (S, T)
Cazaudehore La For. (St-
 Germain-en-Laye) (G, T)
182 Rive Droite (16e) (T)
Chai 33 (12e) (T)
Chalet des Iles (16e) (G, T)
Chantairelle (5e) (G)
Cherche Midi (6e) (S)
Chez Clément (multi.) (S, T)
Chez Francis (8e) (S)
Chez Françoise (7e) (T)
Chez Gégène (Joinville) (S, T)
Chez Georges-Maillot (17e) (S, T)
Chez Janou (3e) (T)
Chez Livio (Neuilly) (T)
Chez Marcel (6e) (S)
Chez Omar (3e)
Chez Paul (13e) (S)
Chez Prune (10e) (S)
Chez René (5e) (T)
Chez Vong (1er) (T)
Chien qui Fume (1er) (S, T)
Cinq (8e) (T)
59 Poincaré (16e) (P)
Cloche des Halles (1er) (S, T)
Clos des Gourmets (7e) (T)
Closerie des Lilas (6e) (T)
Coconnas (4e) (T)
Comptoir/Saumon (multi.) (S, T)
Congrès Maillot (17e) (S, T)
Contre-Allée (14e) (S)
Copenhague (8e) (T)
Costes (1er) (G, P)
Cou de la Girafe (8e) (S, T)
Coupe-Chou (5e) (T)
Dalloyau (multi. loc.) (S, T)
Dame Tart./Café Very (multi.) (T)
Dédicace Café (6e)
Délices d'Aphrodite (5e) (S)
Délices de Szechuen (7e) (S, T)
Dessirier (17e) (S, T)
Deux Abeilles (7e) (S)
Devez (8e) (S)
Diamantaires (9e)
Djakarta Bali (1er) (S)
Dominique (6e) (S)

get updates at zagat.com 235

Special Feature Index

Drouant (2e) (S)
Durand Dupont (Neuilly) (G)
Ecluse (multi. loc.) (S, T)
Entracte (18^e) (T)
Espadon (1er) (G, T)
Faucher (17^e) (S, T)
Feuilles Libres (Neuilly) (S)
Flandrin (16^e) (S, T)
Flora Danica (8^e) (G, T)
Flore en l'Ile (4^e) (S, T)
Fontaine de Mars (7^e) (S, T)
Fontaine Gaillon (2e) (T)
Fontaines (5e) (S, T)
Fontanarosa (15e) (T)
Fouquet's (8e) (S, T)
Fous d'en Face (4e) (S)
Gallopin (2e) (S)
Gare (16e) (G, T)
Gauloise (15e) (S, T)
Gaya Rive Gauche (7e) (S)
Georges (4e) (T)
Gitane (15e) (S)
Giulio Rebellato (16e) (S)
Gourmets des Ternes (8e) (S)
Grand Café (9e) (S)
Grande Armée (16e) (S)
Grande Cascade (16e) (T)
Grille St-Germain (6e) (S)
Guinguette/Neuilly (Neuilly) (T)
Guirlande de Julie (4e) (S)
Hangar (3e) (S)
Hippopotamus (multi. loc.) (S, T)
Il Cortile (1er) (P)
Ile (Issy-les-Moulineaux) (G, T)
Jardin (8e) (S, T)
Jardin des Cygnes (8e) (T)
Jardins de Bagatelle (16e) (G, T)
Je Thé … Me (15e) (S, T)
Khun Akorn (11e) (T)
Kim Anh (15e) (T)
Kiosque (16e) (T)
Ladurée (multi. loc.) (S, T)
Lao Tseu (7e) (T)
Laurent (8e) (G, T)
Léna et Mimile (5e) (T)
Lescure (1er) (S, T)
Lina's (multi. loc.) (S, T)
Ma Bourgogne (4e) (T)
Maison Blanche (8e) (T)
Maison de l'Amér. Lat. (7e) (G)
Mandarin/Neuilly (Neuilly) (T)
Manufacture (Issy-les-Moul.) (T)
Marée de Versailles (Versailles) (T)
Marius (16e) (S, T)
Marius et Janette (8e) (S, T)
Market (8e) (S)
Marlotte (6e) (S, T)

Marty (5e) (S, T)
Mascotte (8e) (S, T)
Mascotte (18e) (S, T)
Mathusalem (16e) (S, T)
Maupertu (7e) (S, T)
Mavrommatis (5e) (S, T)
Méditerranée (6e) (S, T)
Montalembert (7e) (S, T)
Mont Liban (17e) (S, T)
Moulin à Vent (5e) (S, T)
Moulin de la Galette (18e) (P)
Murat (16e) (S)
Muscade (1er) (G)
Nemrod (6e) (S, T)
New Nioullaville (11e) (S)
No Stress Café (9e) (S, T)
Noura (multi. loc.) (G, T)
Oulette (12e) (S, T)
Parc aux Cerfs (6e) (P)
Park (2e) (T)
Patrick Goldenberg (17e) (S, T)
Paul, Restaurant (1er) (S, T)
Pavillon Montsouris (14e) (G, T)
Pavillon Puebla (19e) (T)
Pershing (8e) (P)
Petite Chaise (A la) (7e) (S)
Petite Cour (6e) (T)
Petit Marguery (13e) (T)
Petit Marguery (16e) (S)
Petit Poucet (Levallois) (G, P, T)
Petit Victor Hugo (16e) (S, T)
Petit Zinc (6e) (P, S, T)
Pied de Chameau (4e) (T)
Pied de Cochon (1er) (S, T)
Pitchi Poï (4e) (T)
Plaza-Athénée (8e) (P)
Pomponette (18e) (S, T)
Poule au Pot (1er) (T)
Pré Catelan (16e) (G, T)
Pure Café (11e) (S, T)
Quai Ouest (St-Cloud) (T)
R. (15e) (T)
Ramulaud (11e) (S)
Récamier (7e) (T)
Rech (17e) (S, T)
Relais de l'Entrecôte (multi.) (S, T)
Relais de Venise (17e) (S, T)
Réminet (5e) (S)
Rest. du Marché (15e) (S, T)
Rest. du Palais Royal (1er) (G)
River Café (Issy-les-Moul.) (G, T)
Robe et le Palais (1er) (S)
Roi du Pot-au-Feu (9e) (S)
Romantica (Clichy) (P, T)
Rotonde (6e) (S, T)
Rughetta (18e) (T)
Sauvignon (7e) (S)

236 subscribe to zagat.com

Special Feature Index

Saveurs de Claude (6e) (S)
Sawadee (15e) (S, T)
Senso (8e) (S)
Sept Quinze (15e) (S, T)
7ème Sud Grenelle (7e) (S)
Sologne (12e) (S, T)
Soupière (17e) (S, T)
Square (7e) (S)
Square Trousseau (12e) (S)
Strapontins (10e) (S, T)
Studio (4e) (P)
Sud (17e) (P)
Table d'Anvers (9e) (S, T)
Tastevin (Maisons-Laffitte) (G)
Taverne L'Esprit Blvd. (9e) (S, T)
Télégraphe (7e) (T)
Terrasse (18e) (T)
Thiou (7e) (S)
Tonnelle Saintong. (Neuilly) (G)
Toupary (1er) (T)
Trois Marches (Versailles) (G)
Vagenende (6e) (S, T)
Viaduc Café (12e) (S, T)
Vieille Fontaine Rôtiss.
  (Maisons-Laffitte) (G)
Villa Corse (15e) (T)
Vinea Café (12e) (T)
Vin et Marée (multi. loc.) (S)
20 de Bellechasse (7e) (S)
Zebra Square (16e) (S, T)
Zéphyr (20e) (T)

Parking

A et M Le Bistrot (16e)
Ailleurs (8e)
Al Diwan (8e)
Ambassadeurs (8e)
Ambroisie (4e)
Amphyclès (17e)
Apollo (14e)
Arpège (7e)
Auberge Bressane (7e)
B*fly (8e)
Bains (3e)
Bar Vendôme (1er)
Bath's (8e)
Beato (7e)
Beaujolais d'Auteuil (16e)
Bel Canto (14e)
Benkay (15e)
Bigorneau (16e)
Bistro 121 (15e)
Bistrot d'à Côté (17e)
Bistrot de l'Etoile Niel (17e)
Bistrot de Marius (8e)
Bistrot de Paris (7e)
Bocconi (8e)

Boeuf Couronné (19e)
Boeuf sur le Toit (8e)
Bon (16e)
Bouquinistes (6e)
Brasserie du Louvre (1er)
Brasserie Flo (10e)
Brasserie Julien (10e)
Brasserie Lorraine (8e)
Bristol (8e)
Café de la Jatte (Neuilly)
Café de la Paix (9e)
Café Faubourg (8e)
Café Lenôtre (8e)
Café Terminus (8e)
Cap Seguin (Boulogne)
Carpaccio (8e)
Carré des Feuillants (1er)
Caviar Kaspia (8e)
Céladon (2e)
Chalet des Iles (16e)
Chen Soleil d'Est (15e)
Chez Françoise (7e)
Chez Jenny (3e)
Chez Livio (Neuilly)
Chez Vong (1er)
Chiberta (8e)
59 Poincaré (16e)
Closerie des Lilas (6e)
Clovis (8e)
Comte de Gascogne (Boulogne)
Congrès Maillot (17e)
Copenhague (8e)
Costes (1er)
Coupole (14e)
Cristal Room (16e)
Dagorno (19e)
Da Mimmo (10e)
Dessirier (17e)
Diep (8e)
Divellec (7e)
1728 (8e)
Doobie's (8e)
Drouant (2e)
Duc (14e)
El Mansour (8e)
Elysées du Vernet (8e)
Espadon (1er)
Etoile (8e)
Faucher (17e)
Feuilles Libres (Neuilly)
Findi (8e)
Flandrin (16e)
Flora Danica (8e)
Fontaine Gaillon (2e)
Fouquet's (8e)
Gare (16e)
Georges (4e)

get updates at zagat.com 237

Special Feature Index

Goumard (1er)
Grand Café (9e)
Grand Colbert (2e)
Grande Armée (16e)
Grande Cascade (16e)
Grandes Marches (12e)
Grand Véfour (1er)
Grand Venise (15e)
Guy Savoy (17e)
Hédiard (8e)
Hélène Darroze (6e)
Huîtrier (17e)
Il Cortile (1er)
Ile (Issy-les-Moulineaux)
Jacques Cagna (6e)
Jardin (8e)
Jardin des Cygnes (8e)
Jules Verne (7e)
Kong (1er)
Lapérouse (6e)
Lasserre (8e)
Lucas Carton (8e)
Maison Blanche (8e)
Maison du Caviar (8e)
Man Ray (8e)
Marée (8e)
Marius (16e)
Marius et Janette (8e)
Market (8e)
Marty (5e)
Maxim's (8e)
Méditerranée (6e)
Meurice (1er)
Michel Rostang (17e)
Montalembert (7e)
Montparnasse 25 (14e)
Murat (16e)
Muses (9e)
Obélisque (8e)
Orangerie (4e)
Orenoc (17e)
Paris (6e)
Park (2e)
Passiflore (16e)
Paul Chêne (16e)
Pavillon Montsouris (14e)
Pergolèse (16e)
Pershing (8e)
Petit Pergolèse (16e)
Petit Poucet (Levallois)
Petrossian (7e)
Pierre Gagnaire (8e)
Pinxo (1er)
Plaza-Athénée (8e)
Pré Catelan (16e)
Pressoir (12e)
Quai Ouest (St-Cloud)

R. (15e)
Relais d'Auteuil P. Pignol (16e)
Relais Plaza (8e)
River Café (Issy-les-Moul.)
Romantica (Clichy)
Rôtisserie d'en Face (6e)
Rue Balzac (8e)
Salon d' Hélène (6e)
Sébillon (Neuilly)
Senso (8e)
6 New York (16e)
Sora Lena (17e)
Spicy (8e)
Spoon, Food/Wine (8e)
Stella (16e)
Sud (17e)
Suite (8e)
Table du Baltimore (16e)
Taillevent (8e)
Tanjia (8e)
Télégraphe (7e)
Thiou (7e)
Thoumieux (7e)
Timgad (17e)
Toi (8e)
Tong Yen (8e)
Toupary (1er)
Tour d'Argent (5e)
Trois Marches (Versailles)
Truffe Noire (Neuilly)
Villa Corse (15e)
Village d'Ung et Li Lam (8e)
Vin et Marée (multi. loc.)
W, Restaurant (8e)
Yvan, Petit (8e)
Zebra Square (16e)
Zo (8e)

People-Watching

Absinthe (1er)
Anahï (3e)
Angle du Faubourg (8e)
Arpège (7e)
Astor (8e)
Astrance (16e)
Atelier Joël Robuchon (7e)
Avenue (8e)
Bains (3e)
Beauvilliers (18e)
Bélier (6e)
Benoît (4e)
Berkeley (8e)
Brasserie Balzar (5e)
Brasserie Lipp (6e)
Bristol (8e)
Café de Flore (6e)
Café de l'Esplanade (7e)

Special Feature Index

Café Les Deux Magots (6e)
Chez L'Ami Louis (3e)
Chez Omar (3e)
Cinq (8e)
Coin de la Rue (8e)
Colette (1er)
Copenhague (8e)
Costes (1er)
Divellec (7e)
Dôme (14e)
Drouant (2e)
Duc (14e)
Elysées du Vernet (8e)
Epi Dupin (6e)
Espadon (1er)
Etienne Marcel (2e)
Famille (18e)
Faucher (17e)
Ferme St-Simon (7e)
Flandrin (16e)
Fouquet's (8e)
Gare (16e)
Gauloise (15e)
Georges (4e)
Grande Armée (16e)
Grand Véfour (1er)
Guy Savoy (17e)
Hélène Darroze (6e)
Il Cortile (1er)
Isse (2e)
Joséphine Ch. Dumonet (6e)
Kong (1er)
Ladurée (multi. loc.)
Lasserre (8e)
Ledoyen (8e)
Lucas Carton (8e)
Maison Blanche (8e)
Maison de l'Amér. Lat. (7e)
Maison Prunier (16e)
Maison Rouge (4e)
Man Ray (8e)
Market (8e)
Méditerranée (6e)
Natacha (14e)
Orangerie (4e)
Petrossian (7e)
Pierre Gagnaire (8e)
Plaza-Athénée (8e)
Pravda (11e)
Pré Catelan (16e)
Récamier (7e)
Relais Plaza (8e)
Salon d' Hélène (6e)
Senso (8e)
6 New York (16e)
Sormani (17e)
Spoon, Food/Wine (8e)
Square Trousseau (12e)
Stresa (8e)
Taillevent (8e)
Tan Dinh (7e)
Tanjia (8e)
Thiou (7e)
Tong Yen (8e)
Tour d'Argent (5e)
Voltaire (7e)

Power Scenes

Ambassadeurs (8e)
Apicius (17e)
Arpège (7e)
Assiette (14e)
Astor (8e)
Atelier Joël Robuchon (7e)
Benoît (4e)
Brasserie Balzar (5e)
Brasserie Lipp (6e)
Bristol (8e)
Café de Flore (6e)
Café Marly (1er)
Carré des Feuillants (1er)
Caviar Kaspia (8e)
Cazaudehore La For. (St-Germain-en-Laye)
Céladon (2e)
Closerie des Lilas (6e)
Copenhague (8e)
Costes (1er)
Cristal Room (16e)
Divellec (7e)
Dôme (14e)
Duc (14e)
Elysées du Vernet (8e)
Espadon (1er)
Etoile (8e)
Faucher (17e)
Ferme St-Simon (7e)
Fouquet's (8e)
Gare (16e)
Georges (4e)
Grande Armée (16e)
Grande Cascade (16e)
Grand Véfour (1er)
Guy Savoy (17e)
Hiramatsu (4e)
Jamin (16e)
Jardin (8e)
Jules Verne (7e)
Lasserre (8e)
Laurent (8e)
Ledoyen (8e)
Lucas Carton (8e)
Maison Blanche (8e)
Marée (8e)

get updates at zagat.com 239

Special Feature Index

Marius (16e)
Marius et Janette (8e)
Market (8e)
Meurice (1er)
Michel Rostang (17e)
Montalembert (7e)
Montparnasse 25 (14e)
Natacha (14e)
Paris (6e)
Pavillon Montsouris (14e)
Pichet de Paris (8e)
Pierre Gagnaire (8e)
Plaza-Athénée (8e)
Port Alma (16e)
Pré Catelan (16e)
Relais d'Auteuil P. Pignol (16e)
Relais Plaza (8e)
Stresa (8e)
Taillevent (8e)
Tan Dinh (7e)
Tong Yen (8e)
Tonnelle Saintong. (Neuilly)
Tour d'Argent (5e)
Violon d'Ingres (7e)
Voltaire (7e)

Quick Bites

Altitude 95 (7e)
Angelina (1er)
A Priori Thé (2e)
Bar des Théâtres (8e)
Baron Rouge (12e)
Barrio Latino (12e)
Bar Rouge (9e)
BE Boulangépicier (17e)
Bistrot à Vins Mélac (11e)
Bons Crus (1er)
Breakfast in America (5e)
Buddha Bar (8e)
Buffalo Grill (multi. loc.)
Café Beaubourg (4e)
Café de Flore (6e)
Café des Lettres (7e)
Café du Commerce (15e)
Café Flo (9e)
Café Les Deux Magots (6e)
Café Marly (1er)
Cave de l'Os à Moëlle (15e)
Chez Marianne (4e)
Cloche des Halles (1er)
Clown Bar (11e)
Coffee Parisien (multi. loc.)
Coin de la Rue (8e)
Congrès Maillot (17e)
Cosi (6e)
Crêperie de Josselin (14e)
Dalloyau (multi. loc.)
Dame Tart./Café Very (multi.)
Ecluse (multi. loc.)
Emporio Armani (6e)
Espace Sud-Ouest (multi.)
Ferme (1er)
Fous d'en Face (4e)
Fumoir (1er)
Garnier (8e)
Hédiard (8e)
Indiana Café (multi. loc.)
Je Thé . . . Me (15e)
Joe Allen (1er)
Juvéniles (1er)
Léon de Bruxelles (multi.)
Lina's (multi. loc.)
Loir dans la Théière (4e)
Lô Sushi (multi. loc.)
Ma Bourgogne (4e)
Maison du Caviar (8e)
Mariage Frères (multi. loc.)
Mauzac (5e)
Maxim's (Orly)
Mesturet (2e)
Mirama (5e)
Murat (16e)
Nemrod (6e)
Noura (multi. loc.)
Petite Sirène Copenh. (9e)
Pinxo (1er)
Rest. du Musée d'Orsay (7e)
Rubis (1er)
Sauvignon (7e)
Tsukizi (6e)
Viaduc Café (12e)
Vinea Café (12e)
Vin sur Vin (7e)
Virgin Café (8e)
Wok Cooking (11e)

Quiet Conversation

Affiche (8e)
Aiguière (11e)
Alivi (4e)
Allard (6e)
Allobroges (20e)
Ambassade d'Auv. (3e)
Ampère (17e)
Amuse Bouche (14e)
Anacréon (13e)
Angelina (1er)
A Priori Thé (2e)
Argenteuil (1er)
Aristide (17e)
Armand au Palais Royal (1er)
Assiette (14e)
Astrance (16e)
Atelier Berger (1er)

240 subscribe to zagat.com

Special Feature Index

Auberge du Clou (9e)
Auberge Pyr. Cévennes (11e)
Auvergne Gourmande (7e)
Bamboche (7e)
Basilic (7e)
Béatilles (17e)
Beauvilliers (18e)
Bélier (6e)
Bellini (16e)
Beudant (17e)
Bistro de Gala (9e)
Bistrot du Peintre (11e)
Boeuf Couronné (19e)
Boeuf sur le Toit (8e)
Bouillon Racine (6e)
Bourdonnais/Cantine (7e)
Buisson Ardent (5e)
Butte Chaillot (16e)
Ca d'Oro (1er)
Café de Flore (6e)
Café des Lettres (7e)
Café Faubourg (8e)
Café Lenôtre (8e)
Café Les Deux Magots (6e)
Café M (8e)
Café Marly (1er)
Camélia (Bougival)
Carpaccio (8e)
Cartes Postales (1er)
Cartet (11e)
Cave Gourmande (19e)
Caves Legrand (2e)
Caviar Kaspia (8e)
Chardenoux (11e)
Charpentiers (6e)
Chez Georges (2e)
Chez Jean (9e)
Chez Maître Paul (6e)
Chez Pauline (1er)
Chez René (5e)
Chiberta (8e)
Conti (16e)
Copenhague (8e)
Coupe-Chou (5e)
Crus de Bourgogne (2e)
Daru (8e)
Dauphin (1er)
Dessirier (17e)
Djakarta Bali (1er)
Ecluse (multi. loc.)
El Mansour (8e)
Entoto (13e)
Entracte (18e)
Epi d'Or (1er)
Erawan (15e)
Escargot Montorgueil (1er)
Estaminet Gaya (1er)
Excuse (4e)
Faucher (17e)
Fins Gourmets (7e)
Fontanarosa (15e)
Gamin de Paris (4e)
Garnier (8e)
Gaya Rive Gauche (7e)
Gérard Besson (1er)
Glénan (7e)
Goumard (1er)
Graindorge (17e)
Huîtrier (17e)
Il Cortile (1er)
Joséphine Ch. Dumonet (6e)
Jules Verne (7e)
Jumeaux (11e)
Kiosque (16e)
Ladurée (multi. loc.)
Lapérouse (6e)
Macéo (1er)
Magnolias (Perreux-sur-Marne)
Maison Blanche (8e)
Marée (8e)
Mariage Frères (multi. loc.)
Marlotte (6e)
Marty (5e)
Maupertu (7e)
Méditerranée (6e)
Montalembert (7e)
No Stress Café (9e)
Obélisque (8e)
Orenoc (17e)
Ormes (16e)
Oulette (12e)
Pamphlet (3e)
Petite Sirène Copenh. (9e)
Petrossian (7e)
Pierre au Palais Royal (1er)
Pierre Gagnaire (8e)
Potager du Roy (Versailles)
Récamier (7e)
Rest. du Marché (15e)
Sarladais (8e)
Saudade (1er)
16 Haussmann (9e)
Sologne (12e)
Stella Maris (8e)
Taïra (17e)
Tan Dinh (7e)
Tanjia (8e)
Terrasse (18e)
Toupary (1er)
Trou Gascon (12e)
Tsé-Yang (16e)
Vieux Bistro (4e)
Vin sur Vin (7e)

get updates at zagat.com

Special Feature Index

Romantic Places
Allard (6e)
Ambassadeurs (8e)
Ambroisie (4e)
Amphyclès (17e)
Arpège (7e)
Astor (8e)
Astrance (16e)
Bamboche (7e)
Beauvilliers (18e)
Bélier (6e)
Blue Elephant (11e)
Bouillon Racine (6e)
Bouquinistes (6e)
Brasserie Flo (10e)
Brasserie Julien (10e)
Bristol (8e)
Buisson Ardent (5e)
Café Les Deux Magots (6e)
Café Marly (1er)
Casa Olympe (9e)
Caviar Kaspia (8e)
Chalet des Iles (16e)
Chardenoux (11e)
Chez Catherine (8e)
Chez Diane (6e)
Chez Pauline (1er)
China Club (12e)
Closerie des Lilas (6e)
Coconnas (4e)
Copenhague (8e)
Costes (1er)
Coupe-Chou (5e)
Coupole (14e)
Cristal Room (16e)
Délices d'Aphrodite (5e)
Dôme (14e)
El Mansour (8e)
Elysées du Vernet (8e)
Epi d'Or (1er)
Espadon (1er)
Flora Danica (8e)
Fontaine de Mars (7e)
Gavroche (2e)
Georges (4e)
Gourmet de l'Isle (4e)
Grande Cascade (16e)
Grand Véfour (1er)
Guirlande de Julie (4e)
Guy Savoy (17e)
Il Cortile (1er)
Jacques Cagna (6e)
Jardin (8e)
Jardins de Bagatelle (16e)
Joséphine Ch. Dumonet (6e)
Jules Verne (7e)
Ladurée (multi. loc.)
Lapérouse (6e)
Lasserre (8e)
Laurent (8e)
Ledoyen (8e)
Macéo (1er)
Maison Blanche (8e)
Maison de l'Amér. Lat. (7e)
Man Ray (8e)
Maxim's (8e)
Meurice (1er)
Moulin de la Galette (18e)
Muscade (1er)
Orangerie (4e)
Paul, Restaurant (1er)
Pavillon Montsouris (14e)
Pavillon Puebla (19e)
Petit Prince de Paris (5e)
Petrossian (7e)
Plaza-Athénée (8e)
Potager du Roy (Versailles)
Pré Catelan (16e)
Relais Louis XIII (6e)
Romantica (Clichy)
Rughetta (18e)
Sormani (17e)
Sousceyrac (11e)
Stella Maris (8e)
Tan Dinh (7e)
Tanjia (8e)
Timgad (17e)
Toupary (1er)
Tour d'Argent (5e)
Train Bleu (12e)
Trois Marches (Versailles)
Trou Gascon (12e)

Singles Scenes
Absinthe (1er)
A et M Le Bistrot (16e)
Ailleurs (8e)
Alsace (8e)
Alsaco (9e)
Amici Mei (4e)
Angle du Faubourg (8e)
Apollo (14e)
Astor (8e)
Auberge du Clou (9e)
B*fly (8e)
Bains (3e)
Bar des Théâtres (8e)
Baron Rouge (12e)
Barramundi (9e)
Barrio Latino (12e)
Bélier (6e)
Berkeley (8e)
Bistro des Deux Th. (9e)
Bistrot à Vins Mélac (11e)

Special Feature Index

Bistrot d'à Côté (17e)
Bistrot d'Alex (6e)
Bon (16e)
Brasserie Balzar (5e)
Brasserie de la Poste (16e)
Buddha Bar (8e)
Café Beaubourg (4e)
Café Burq (18e)
Café de Flore (6e)
Café de la Jatte (Neuilly)
Café de la Paix (9e)
Café de l'Esplanade (7e)
Café du Passage (11e)
Café Lenôtre (8e)
Café Les Deux Magots (6e)
Café M (8e)
Café Marly (1er)
Café Ruc (1er)
Carr's (1er)
Cave de l'Os à Moëlle (15e)
182 Rive Droite (16e)
Cherche Midi (6e)
Chez Gégène (Joinville)
China Club (12e)
Closerie des Lilas (6e)
Clown Bar (11e)
Coin de la Rue (8e)
Comédiens (9e)
Costes (1er)
Emporio Armani (6e)
Enoteca (4e)
Etienne Marcel (2e)
Etoile (8e)
Fumoir (1er)
Grille St-Germain (6e)
Joe Allen (1er)
Kiosque (16e)
Kong (1er)
Loir dans la Théière (4e)
Lô Sushi (multi. loc.)
Maison Rouge (4e)
Man Ray (8e)
Maxim's (Orly)
Murat (16e)
Natacha (14e)
Pinxo (1er)
R'Aliment (3e)
Rubis (1er)
Sauvignon (7e)
Vinea Café (12e)
Zo (8e)

Sleepers

(Good to excellent food, but little known)
Ambassade Sud-Ouest (7e)
Beurre Noisette (15e)
Boeuf Couronné (19e)
Camélia (Bougival)
Cartes Postales (1er)
Caveau du Palais (1er)
Cave Gourmande (19e)
Chez Jean (9e)
Chez Vincent (19e)
Clovis (8e)
Coin des Gourmets (5e)
Cottage Marcadet (18e)
Epi d'Or (1er)
Etoile Marocaine (8e)
Fogón Saint Julien (5e)
Fontanarosa (15e)
Giulio Rebellato (16e)
Glénan (7e)
Graindorge (17e)
Grand Venise (15e)
Hangar (3e)
Indra (8e)
Isami (4e)
Isse (2e)
Jardin (8e)
Je Thé . . . Me (15e)
Kambodgia (16e)
Kim Anh (15e)
Lozère (6e)
Luna (8e)
Maison Courtine (14e)
Maison du Jardin (6e)
Manufacture (Issy-les-Moul.)
Marius (16e)
Monsieur Lapin (14e)
Montparnasse 25 (14e)
Paolo Petrini (17e)
Paul Chêne (16e)
Pergolèse (16e)
Perron (7e)
Petit Colombier (17e)
Petite Sirène Copenh. (9e)
Petit Laurent (7e)
Petit Marguery (16e)
Poquelin (1er)
Pouilly Reuilly (Le Pré-St-Gervais)
Ravi (7e)
Rech (17e)
Rosimar (16e)
Soleil (St-Ouen)
Stéphane Martin (15e)
Taka (18e)
Vieille Fontaine Rôtiss. (Maisons-Laffitte)
Villaret (11e)
Zygomates (12e)

get updates at zagat.com

Special Feature Index

Sunday Dining
(B=brunch; L=lunch;
D=dinner)
Al Caratello (18e) (L, D)
Alcazar (6e) (B, L, D)
Al Dar (multi. loc.) (L, D)
Al Diwan (8e) (L, D)
Alivi (4^e) (L, D)
Al Mounia (16^e) (L, D)
Alsace (8^e) (L, D)
Altitude 95 (7^e) (L, D)
Ambassade d'Auv. (3^e) (L, D)
Ambassadeurs (8^e) (L, D)
Anahuacalli (5^e) (L, D)
Apollo (14^e) (L, D)
Arbuci (6^e) (L, D)
Ardoise (1er) (L, D)
Asian (8^e) (B, L, D)
Assiette (14^e) (L, D)
Assiette Lyonnaise (8^e) (L, D)
Astrance (16^e) (L, D)
Atelier Joël Robuchon (7^e) (L, D)
Atlas (5e) (L, D)
Auberge Aveyron. (12e) (L)
Auberge Bressane (7e) (L, D)
Auberge Dab (16e) (L, D)
Auberge d'Autrefois (16e) (L)
Auberge du Clou (9e) (L, D)
Avenue (8e) (L, D)
Azabu (6e) (D)
B*fly (8e) (B, L, D)
Ballon des Ternes (17e) (L, D)
Ballon et Coquillages (17e) (L, D)
Bar à Huîtres (multi. loc.) (L, D)
Bar des Théâtres (8e) (L, D)
Bar Vendôme (1er) (L, D)
Basilic (7e) (L, D)
Beaujolais d'Auteuil (16e) (L, D)
Benkay (15e) (L, D)
Benoît (4e) (L, D)
Berkeley (8e) (B, L, D)
Bigorneau (16e) (L, D)
Bistro 121 (15e) (L, D)
Bistro de l'Olivier (8e) (L, D)
Bistro des Deux Th. (9e) (L, D)
Bistro d'Hubert (15e) (L, D)
Bistro du 17ème (17e) (L, D)
Bistrot d'à Côté (17e) (L, D)
Bistrot de Breteuil (7e) (L, D)
Bistrot de l'Etoile Laur. (16e) (D)
Bistrot de Marius (8e) (L, D)
Bistrot de Paris (7e) (L, D)
Bistrot des Dames (17e) (L, D)
Bistrot du Dôme (multi. loc.) (L, D)
Bistrot du Peintre (11e) (L, D)
Bistrot St. Ferdinand (17e) (L, D)

Blue Elephant (11^e) (L, D)
Boeuf sur le Toit (8^e) (L, D)
Bouillon Racine (6^e) (L, D)
Boulangerie (20^e) (B, L, D)
Bourdonnais/Cantine (7e) (L, D)
B4 (1er) (B, L, D)
Brasserie Balzar (5e) (L, D)
Brasserie de l'Ile St. L. (4e) (L, D)
Brasserie du Louvre (1er) (L, D)
Brasserie Flo (10e) (L, D)
Brasserie Julien (10e) (L, D)
Brasserie Lipp (6e) (L, D)
Brasserie Lorraine (8e) (L, D)
Brasserie Lutétia (6e) (B, L, D)
Brasserie Mollard (8e) (L, D)
Bristol (8e) (L, D)
Buddha Bar (8e) (D)
Butte Chaillot (16e) (L, D)
Byblos Café (16e) (L, D)
Café Beaubourg (4e) (B, L, D)
Café Charbon (11e) (B, L, D)
Café de Flore (6e) (B, L, D)
Café de la Jatte (Neuilly) (B, L, D)
Café de la Mus. (19e) (B, L, D)
Café de l'Esplanade (7e) (B, L, D)
Café de l'Industrie (11e) (B, L, D)
Café de Mars (7e) (B)
Café des Lettres (7e) (B)
Café du Commerce (15e) (L, D)
Café du Passage (11e) (D)
Café Faubourg (8e) (L, D)
Café Lenôtre (8e) (L, D)
Café Les Deux Magots (6e) (L, D)
Café Marly (1er) (L, D)
Café Ruc (1er) (L, D)
Café Terminus (8e) (L, D)
Caffé Toscano (7e) (L, D)
Cagouille (14e) (L, D)
Camille (3e) (L, D)
Carpaccio (8e) (L, D)
Casa Alcalde (15e) (L, D)
Casa Bini (6e) (D)
Casa Tina (16e) (L, D)
Casa Vigata (11e) (L, D)
Caveau du Palais (1er) (L, D)
Cave de l'Os à Moëlle (15e) (L)
Cazaudehore La For. (St-
  Germain-en-Laye) (L, D)
Chai 33 (12e) (B, D)
Chalet des Iles (16e) (L, D)
Charlot - Roi des Coq. (9e) (L, D)
Charpentiers (6e) (L, D)
Chartier (9e) (L, D)
Cherche Midi (6e) (L, D)
Chez André (8e) (L, D)
Chez Clément (multi.) (L, D)
Chez Francis (8e) (L, D)

Special Feature Index

Chez Françoise (7e) (L, D)
Chez Gégène (Joinville) (L, D)
Chez Georges-Maillot (17e) (L, D)
Chez Janou (3e) (L, D)
Chez Jenny (3e) (L, D)
Chez L'Ami Louis (3e) (L, D)
Chez Livio (Neuilly) (L, D)
Chez Maître Paul (6e) (L, D)
Chez Marianne (4e) (L, D)
Chez Ngo (16e) (L, D)
Chez Paul (11e) (L, D)
Chez Paul (13e) (L, D)
Chez Toutoune (5^e) (L, D)
Chieng Mai (5^e) (L, D)
Chien qui Fume (1er) (L, D)
China Club (12e) (D)
China Town Olymp. (13e) (L, D)
Cinq (8e) (L, D)
Closerie des Lilas (6e) (L, D)
Coin des Gourmets (5e) (L, D)
Comptoir Paris-Marrak. (1er)(B, L, D)
Costes (1er) (L, D)
Coude Fou (4e) (L, D)
Coupe-Chou (5e) (D)
Coupole (14e) (L, D)
Dagorno (19e) (L, D)
Dame Tart./Café Very (multi.) (L, D)
Dauphin (1er) (L, D)
Dédicace Café (6e) (L, D)
Délices de Szechuen (7e) (L, D)
Dessirier (17e) (L, D)
Devez (8e) (L, D)
Diamantaires (9e) (L, D)
Diep (8e) (L, D)
Dôme (14e) (L, D)
Durand Dupont (Neuilly) (B, L, D)
Ecluse (multi. loc.) (L, D)
Editeurs (6e) (L, D)
Elysées Hong Kong (16e) (L, D)
Enoteca (4e) (L, D)
Espace Sud-Ouest (multi.) (L, D)
Espadon (1er) (L, D)
Etienne Marcel (2e) (L, D)
Etoile Marocaine (8e) (L, D)
Fakhr el Dine (multi. loc.) (L, D)
Fellini (1er) (L, D)
Fermette Marbeuf 1900 (8e) (L, D)
Findi (8e) (B, L)
Fish La Boissonnerie (6e) (L, D)
Flandrin (16^e) (L, D)
Flora Danica (8^e) (L, D)
Flore en l'Ile (4^e) (B, L, D)
Fogón Saint Julien (5^e) (L, D)
Fontaine de Mars (7^e) (L, D)
Fontanarosa (15^e) (L, D)
Foujita (1er) (L, D)
Fouquet's (8e) (B, L, D)

Fumoir (1er) (B, L, D)
Gamin de Paris (4e) (L, D)
Gare (16e) (L, D)
Garnier (8e) (L, D)
Gauloise (15e) (L, D)
Georges (4e) (L, D)
Giulio Rebellato (16e) (L, D)
Gli Angeli (3e) (L, D)
Goumard (1er) (L, D)
Gourmet de l'Isle (4e) (L, D)
Grand Café (9e) (L, D)
Grand Colbert (2e) (L, D)
Grande Armée (16e) (L, D)
Grande Cascade (16e) (L, D)
Grand Louvre (1er) (L, D)
Grille St-Germain (6e) (L, D)
Guinguette/Neuilly (Neuilly) (L, D)
Guirlande de Julie (4e) (L, D)
Higuma (1er) (L, D)
Huîtrier (17e) (L, D)
Ile (Issy-les-Moulineaux) (L, D)
Isami (4e) (D)
Jardin des Cygnes (8e) (B)
Jardins de Bagatelle (16e) (L, D)
Joe Allen (1er) (B, L, D)
Jo Goldenberg (4e) (B, L, D)
Jules Verne (7e) (L, D)
Khun Akorn (11e) (L, D)
Kim Anh (15e) (D)
Kiosque (16e) (B, L, D)
Kong (1er) (L, D)
Ladurée (multi. loc.) (B, L, D)
Languedoc (5e) (L, D)
Lao Siam (19e) (L, D)
Lao Tseu (7e) (L, D)
Libre Sens (8e) (B, L, D)
Lô Sushi (multi. loc.) (L, D)
Ma Bourgogne (4e) (L, D)
Maharajah (5e) (L, D)
Maison du Caviar (8e) (L, D)
Maison Rouge (4e) (B, L, D)
Marius et Janette (8e) (L, D)
Market (8e) (B, L, D)
Martel (10e) (D)
Marty (5e) (L, D)
Mascotte (18e) (L, D)
Mavrommatis (5e) (L, D)
Méditerranée (6e) (L, D)
Meurice (1er) (L, D)
Mirama (5e) (L, D)
Monsieur Lapin (14e) (L, D)
Mont Liban (17e) (L, D)
Mon Vieil Ami (4e) (L, D)
Moulin de la Galette (18e) (B, L)
Murat (16e) (L, D)
New Jawad (7e) (L, D)
New Nioullaville (11e) (L, D)

get updates at zagat.com 245

Special Feature Index

Nouveau Village Tao (13e) (L, D)
Obélisque (8e) (L, D)
Oïshi (2e) (L, D)
Orangerie (4e) (D)
Orenoc (17e) (L, D)
Paradis Thai (13e) (L, D)
Parc aux Cerfs (6e) (L, D)
Passy Mandarin (16e) (L, D)
Patrick Goldenberg (17e) (L, D)
Paul, Restaurant (1er) (L, D)
Pavillon Montsouris (14e) (L, D)
Père Claude (15e) (L, D)
Petite Chaise (A la) (7e) (L, D)
Petite Cour (6e) (L, D)
Petite Tour (16e) (L, D)
Petit Lutétia (6e) (L, D)
Petit Marché (3e) (L, D)
Petit Marguery (16e) (L, D)
Petit Niçois (7e) (L, D)
Petit Poucet (Levallois) (L, D)
Petits Marseillais (3e) (L, D)
Petit St. Benoît (6e) (L, D)
Petit Zinc (6e) (L, D)
Pied de Chameau (4e) (B, D)
Pied de Cochon (1er) (L, D)
Pierre Gagnaire (8e) (D)
Pinxo (1er) (L, D)
Pitchi Poï (4e) (B, L, D)
Planet Hollywood (8e) (L, D)
Polidor (6e) (L, D)
Quai Ouest (St-Cloud) (B, L, D)
404 (3e) (B, L, D)
Ramulaud (11e) (L, D)
Relais de l'Entrecôte (multi.) (L, D)
Relais de Venise (17e) (L, D)
Relais Plaza (8e) (L, D)
Réminet (5e) (L, D)
Rendez-vous/Chauff. (18e) (L, D)
Riad (Neuilly) (L, D)
River Café (Issy-les-Moul.) (L, D)
Rôtisserie du Beaujolais (5e) (L, D)
Rotonde (6e) (L, D)
Rughetta (18e) (L, D)
Sébillon (multi. loc.) (L, D)
Senso (8e) (B, L, D)
7ème Sud Grenelle (multi.) (B, L, D)
Spicy (8e) (B, L, D)
Stella (16e) (L, D)
Studio (4e) (B, D)
Terminus Nord (10e) (L, D)
Terrasse (18e) (L, D)
Thoumieux (7e) (L, D)
Timgad (17e) (L, D)
Toi (8e) (B, L, D)
Tong Yen (8e) (L, D)
Tonkinoise (13e) (L, D)
Tour d'Argent (5e) (L, D)
Tournesol (16e) (D)
Train Bleu (12e) (L, D)
Tricotin (13e) (L, D)
Truffière (5e) (L, D)
Trumilou (4e) (L, D)
Tsé-Yang (16e) (L, D)
Vagenende (6e) (L, D)
Vaudeville (2e) (L, D)
Verre Bouteille (17e) (L, D)
Verre Volé (10e) (L, D)
Viaduc Café (12e) (B, L, D)
Vieille Fontaine Rôtiss.
   (Maisons-Laffitte) (L)
Vieux Bistro (4e) (L, D)
Village d'Ung et Li Lam (8e) (D)
Vinea Café (12e) (B, L, D)
Wepler (18e) (B, L, D)
Zebra Square (16e) (B, L, D)
Zéphyr (20e) (L, D)
Zinc-Zinc (Neuilly) (L, D)

Tasting Menus
Allobroges (20e)
Al Mounia (16e)
Amphyclès (17e)
Androuët (7e)
Apicius (17e)
Arpège (7e)
Astor (8e)
Astrance (16e)
Atelier Berger (1er)
Auberge Nicolas Flamel (3e)
Avant Goût (13e)
Baie d'Ha Long (16e)
Bambocho (7e)
Bath's (8e)
Béatilles (17e)
Bistro de Gala (9e)
Bistrot du Sommelier (8e)
Bourdonnais/Cantine (7e)
Braisière (17e)
Bristol (8e)
Carré des Feuillants (1er)
Cartes Postales (1er)
Casa Tina (16e)
Chamarré (7e)
Chez Jean (9e)
Chez Michel (10e)
Chez Vincent (19e)
Chiberta (8e)
Cinq (8e)
Clos Morillons (15e)
Clos Saint-Honoré (1er)
Clovis (8e)
Comte de Gascogne (Boulogne)
Copenhague (8e)
Elysées du Vernet (8e)

Special Feature Index

Epicure 108 (17e)
Espadon (1er)
Faucher (17e)
Flora (8e)
Florimond (7e)
Fogón Saint Julien (5e)
Gérard Besson (1er)
Glénan (7e)
Goumard (1er)
Grande Cascade (16e)
Grand Véfour (1er)
Guy Savoy (17e)
Hélène Darroze (6e)
Jacques Cagna (6e)
Jamin (16e)
Jardin (8e)
Jules Verne (7e)
Lapérouse (6e)
Lasserre (8e)
Laurent (8e)
Ledoyen (8e)
Lucas Carton (8e)
Magnolias (Perreux-sur-Marne)
Mavrommatis (5e)
Maxim's (8e)
Meurice (1er)
Michel Rostang (17e)
Montparnasse 25 (14e)
Muses (9e)
O à la Bouche (14e)
Olivades (7e)
Os à Moëlle (15e)
Paolo Petrini (17e)
Paris (6e)
Pergolèse (16e)
Pierre Gagnaire (8e)
Plaza-Athénée (8e)
Potager du Roy (Versailles)
Pré Catelan (16e)
Pressoir (12e)
Relais d'Auteuil P. Pignol (16e)
Relais Louis XIII (6e)
Réminet (5e)
Romantica (Clichy)
Sawadee (15e)
Sologne (12e)
Sormani (17e)
Stella Maris (8e)
Table d'Anvers (9e)
Taillevent (8e)
Tang (16e)
Thierry Burlot (15e)
Tire-Bouchon (15e)
Trois Marches (Versailles)
Troquet (15e)
Violon d'Ingres (7e)
W, Restaurant (8e)
Yves Quintard (15e)

Teen Appeal

Alcazar (6e)
Altitude 95 (7e)
Anahuacalli (5e)
Apollo (14e)
Appart' (8e)
Appennino (13e)
Asian (8e)
Avenue (8e)
B*fly (8e)
Barrio Latino (12e)
Bartolo (6e)
Bermuda Onion (15e)
Blue Elephant (11e)
Bon (16e)
Breakfast in America (5e)
Buddha Bar (8e)
Café Beaubourg (4e)
Café Burq (18e)
Café Charbon (11e)
Café de la Jatte (Neuilly)
Café de la Musique (19e)
Café de l'Esplanade (7e)
Café de l'Industrie (11e)
Café de Mars (7e)
Café du Commerce (15e)
Café Lenôtre (8e)
Café Marly (1er)
Café Max (7e)
Café Ruc (1er)
Cailloux (13e)
C'Amelot (11e)
Carr's (1er)
Cave Gourmande (19e)
Chartier (9e)
Chez Clément (multi.)
Chez Marianne (4e)
Chez Omar (3e)
Chez Prune (10e)
Chez Vong (1er)
Chicago Pizza (8e)
China Club (12e)
Coco de Mer (5e)
Coffee Parisien (multi. loc.)
Coin des Gourmets (5e)
Comptoir Paris-Marrak. (1er)
Cosi (6e)
Coude Fou (4e)
Coupole (14e)
Crêperie de Josselin (14e)
Dame Tart./Café Very (1er)
Délices d'Aphrodite (5e)

get updates at zagat.com 247

Special Feature Index

Enoteca (4e)
Entoto (13e)
Espace Sud-Ouest (multi.)
Etoile (8e)
Ferme (1er)
Fish La Boissonnerie (6e)
Fogón Saint Julien (5e)
Fous d'en Face (4e)
Fumoir (1er)
Gamin de Paris (4e)
Georges (4e)
Gli Angeli (3e)
Gourmet de l'Isle (4e)
Hangar (3e)
Hippopotamus (multi. loc.)
Ile (Issy-les-Moulineaux)
Indiana Café (multi. loc.)
Isami (4e)
Joe Allen (1er)
Kiosque (16e)
Kong (1er)
Lao Siam (19e)
Léon de Bruxelles (multi.)
Lina's (multi. loc.)
Loir dans la Théière (4e)
Lô Sushi (multi. loc.)
Ma Bourgogne (4e)
Man Ray (8e)
Mirama (5e)
Natachef (16e)
No Stress Café (9e)
Paradis Thaï (13e)
Petite Sirène Copenh. (9e)
Petits Marseillais (3e)
Pied de Cochon (1er)
Planet Hollywood (8e)
Polidor (6e)
Quai Ouest (St-Cloud)
404 (3e)
Rendez-vous/Camion. (14e)
Rendez-vous/Chauff. (18e)
River Café (Issy-les-Moul.)
Sept Quinze (15e)
Spicy (8e)
Spoon, Food/Wine (8e)
Square Trousseau (12e)
Tricotin (13e)
Trumilou (4e)
Vaudeville (2e)
Viaduc Café (12e)
Vinea Café (12e)
Virgin Café (8e)
Wok Cooking (11e)
Yen (6e)
Zebra Square (16e)
Zéphyr (20e)

Theme Restaurants

Auberge Nicolas Flamel (3e)
Bar à Huîtres (multi. loc.)
Barrio Latino (12e)
Bel Canto (multi. loc.)
Bellotta-Bellotta (7e)
Bistrot d'André (15e)
Breakfast in America (5e)
Buddha Bar (8e)
Café de la Musique (19e)
Chez Clément (multi.)
Chicago Pizza (8e)
Coco de Mer (5e)
Léon de Bruxelles (multi.)
Lina's (multi. loc.)
Monsieur Lapin (14e)
Planet Hollywood (8e)
Virgin Café (8e)
Wok Cooking (11e)

Transporting Experiences

Alsaco (9e)
Anahï (3e)
Annapurna (8e)
Asian (8e)
Atlas (5e)
Baie d'Ha Long (16e)
Benkay (15e)
Blue Elephant (11e)
Buddha Bar (8e)
Café de la Jatte (Neuilly)
Chalet des Iles (16e)
Chen Soleil d'Est (15e)
Chez Gégène (Joinville)
Chez Vong (1er)
China Club (12e)
Coco de Mer (5e)
Délices d'Aphrodite (5e)
Djakarta Bali (1er)
Enoteca (4e)
Entoto (13e)
Erawan (15e)
Etoile Marocaine (8e)
Fakhr el Dine (multi. loc.)
Fogón Saint Julien (5e)
Isami (4e)
Isse (2e)
Jardins de Bagatelle (16e)
Man Ray (8e)
Mansouria (11e)
Mavrommatis (5e)
Monsieur Lapin (14e)
Saudade (1er)
Soufflé (1er)
Stella Maris (8e)
Taïra (17e)
Tan Dinh (7e)

248   subscribe to zagat.com

Special Feature Index

Tanjia (8e)
Timgad (17e)
Tricotin (13e)
Tsé-Yang (16e)
Wally Le Saharien (9e)
Yen (6e)

Views

Alsace (8e)
Altitude 95 (7e)
Avenue (8e)
Bar Vendôme (1er)
Benkay (15e)
Bermuda Onion (15e)
Bistrot de Breteuil (7e)
Bistrot du Cap (15e)
Bouquinistes (6e)
Brasserie de l'Ile St. L. (4e)
Café Beaubourg (4e)
Café de Flore (6e)
Café de la Jatte (Neuilly)
Café de la Musique (19e)
Café de l'Esplanade (7e)
Café Lenôtre (8e)
Café Marly (1er)
Cap Seguin (Boulogne)
Cap Vernet (8e)
Caviar Kaspia (8e)
Cazaudehore La For. (St-Germain-en-Laye)
Chalet des Iles (16e)
Chantairelle (5e)
Charlot - Roi des Coq. (9e)
Chez Francis (8e)
Chez Gégène (Joinville)
Chez Paul (13e)
Chez Prune (10e)
Clos des Gourmets (7e)
Coconnas (4e)
Copenhague (8e)
Cosi (Le) (5e)
D'Chez Eux (7e)
Délices de Szechuen (7e)
Durand Dupont (Neuilly)
Emporio Armani (6e)
Etoile (8e)
Flora Danica (8e)
Flore en l'Ile (4e)
Fontaine de Mars (7e)
Fouquet's (8e)
Fumoir (1er)
Georges (4e)
Grande Armée (16e)
Grande Cascade (16e)
Grandes Marches (12e)
Grand Véfour (1er)
Guirlande de Julie (4e)

Hédiard (8e)
Isami (4e)
Jardin des Cygnes (8e)
Jardins de Bagatelle (16e)
Jules Verne (7e)
Kong (1er)
Lapérouse (6e)
Lasserre (8e)
Ledoyen (8e)
Maison Blanche (8e)
Maison de l'Amér. Lat. (7e)
Méditerranée (6e)
Paul, Restaurant (1er)
Pavillon Puebla (19e)
Pershing (8e)
Petit Poucet (Levallois)
Petits Marseillais (3e)
Pitchi Poï (4e)
Port Alma (16e)
Quai Ouest (St-Cloud)
R. (15e)
Relais de l'Entrecôte (6e)
Relais de Venise (17e)
Relais Plaza (8e)
Réminet (5e)
Rest. de la Tour (15e)
Rest. du Musée d'Orsay (7e)
Rest. du Palais Royal (1er)
River Café (Issy-les-Moul.)
Romantica (Clichy)
Rotonde (6e)
Square Trousseau (12e)
Terrasse (18e)
Tonnelle Saintong. (Neuilly)
Toupary (1er)
Tour d'Argent (5e)
Vaudeville (2e)
Voltaire (7e)

Visitors on Expense Account

Ambroisie (4e)
Amphyclès (17e)
Arpège (7e)
Assiette (14e)
Atelier Joël Robuchon (7e)
Bath's (8e)
Béatilles (17e)
Beauvilliers (18e)
Benoît (4e)
Bourdonnais/Cantine (7e)
Café Faubourg (8e)
Carpaccio (8e)
Carré des Feuillants (1er)
Caviar Kaspia (8e)
Chen Soleil d'Est (15e)
Chez L'Ami Louis (3e)

get updates at zagat.com

Special Feature Index

Chez Pauline (1er)
Chiberta (8e)
Clovis (8e)
Copenhague (8e)
Dessirier (17e)
Divellec (7e)
Dôme (14e)
Drouant (2e)
Duc (14e)
Estaminet Gaya (1er)
Faucher (17e)
Ferme St-Simon (7e)
Flora Danica (8e)
Fouquet's (8e)
Garnier (8e)
Gaya Rive Gauche (7e)
Gérard Besson (1er)
Goumard (1er)
Grand Véfour (1er)
Guy Savoy (17e)
Hélène Darroze (6e)
Il Cortile (1er)
Isse (2e)
Jacques Cagna (6e)
Jamin (16e)
Joséphine Ch. Dumonet (6e)
Jules Verne (7e)
Lasserre (8e)
Laurent (8e)
Ledoyen (8e)
Lucas Carton (8e)
Maison Blanche (8e)
Mansouria (11e)
Marée (8e)
Marius (16e)
Maxim's (multi. loc.)
Michel Rostang (17e)
Muses (9e)
Natacha (14e)
Obélisque (8e)
Orangerie (4e)
Orenoc (17e)
Oulette (12e)
Petit Colombier (17e)
Pierre au Palais Royal (1er)
Pierre Gagnaire (8e)
Pré Catelan (16e)
Pressoir (12e)
Relais Louis XIII (6e)
Relais Plaza (8e)
Sousceyrac (11e)
Stella Maris (8e)
Table d'Anvers (9e)
Taillevent (8e)
Taïra (17e)
Tante Jeanne (17e)
Tante Marguerite (7e)
Tour d'Argent (5e)
Trois Marches (Versailles)
Trou Gascon (12e)
W, Restaurant (8e)

Waterside

Brasserie de l'Ile St. L. (4e)
Buffalo Grill (13e)
Cap Seguin (Boulogne)
Chalet des Iles (16e)
Chez Gégène (Joinville)
Chez Prune (10e)
Guinguette/Neuilly (Neuilly)
Petit Poucet (Levallois)
Quai Ouest (St-Cloud)
River Café (Issy-les-Moul.)

Winning Wine Lists

Ambassadeurs (8e)
Ambroisie (4e)
Amphyclès (17e)
Atelier Joël Robuchon (7e)
Bar Rouge (9e)
Bistrot du Sommelier (8e)
Bistrot Paul Bert (11e)
Bouchons/Fr. Cl. (multi. loc.)
Bourguignon du Marais (4e)
Bristol (8e)
Café Burq (18e)
Café Lenôtre (8e)
Cagouille (14e)
Carré des Feuillants (1er)
Cave de l'Os à Moëlle (15e)
Caves Legrand (2e)
Caves Pétrissans (17e)
Chai 33 (12e)
Cinq (8e)
Dessirier (17e)
Divellec (7e)
Drouant (2e)
Ecluse (multi. loc.)
Elysées du Vernet (8e)
Enoteca (4e)
Excuse (4e)
Faucher (17e)
Ferme St-Simon (7e)
Fish La Boissonnerie (6e)
Fogón Saint Julien (5e)
Gérard Besson (1er)
Grande Cascade (16e)
Grand Véfour (1er)
Guy Savoy (17e)
Hélène Darroze (6e)
Il Cortile (1er)
Jacques Cagna (6e)
Jamin (16e)
Jardin (8e)

Special Feature Index

Joséphine Ch. Dumonet (6e)
Jules Verne (7e)
Lasserre (8e)
Laurent (8e)
Lavinia (8e)
Ledoyen (8e)
Lucas Carton (8e)
Macéo (1er)
Marée (8e)
Maxim's (multi. loc.)
Meurice (1er)
Michel Rostang (17e)
Montparnasse 25 (14e)
Muses (9e)
Oenothèque (9e)
Oulette (12e)
Paris (6e)
Petit Marguery (13e)
Petrossian (7e)
Pierre au Palais Royal (1er)
Pierre Gagnaire (8e)
Plaza-Athénée (8e)
Pressoir (12e)
Récamier (7e)
Relais Louis XIII (6e)
Saudade (1er)
Sousceyrac (11e)
Spoon, Food/Wine (8e)
Stella Maris (8e)
Table d'Anvers (9e)
Taillevent (8e)
Tante Marguerite (7e)
Tour d'Argent (5e)
Trois Marches (Versailles)
Trou Gascon (12e)
Vin sur Vin (7e)

Wine Vintage Chart

This chart is designed to help you select wine to go with your meal. It is based on the same 0 to 30 scale used throughout this *Survey*. The ratings (prepared by our friend **Howard Stravitz**, a law professor at the University of South Carolina) reflect both the quality of the vintage and the wine's readiness for present consumption. Thus, if a wine is not fully mature or is over the hill, its rating has been reduced. We do not include 1987, 1991–1993 vintages because they are not especially recommended for most areas. A dash indicates that a wine is either past its peak or too young to rate.

	'85	'86	'88	'89	'90	'94	'95	'96	'97	'98	'99	'00	'01	'02
WHITES														
French:														
Alsace	24	18	22	28	28	26	25	24	24	26	24	26	27	–
Burgundy	26	25	–	24	22	–	29	28	24	23	25	24	21	–
Loire Valley	–	–	–	–	24	–	20	23	22	–	24	25	23	–
Champagne	28	25	24	26	29	–	26	27	24	24	25	25	26	–
Sauternes	21	28	29	25	27	–	21	23	26	24	24	24	28	–
California (Napa, Sonoma, Mendocino):														
Chardonnay	–	–	–	–	–	–	25	21	25	24	24	22	26	–
Sauvignon Blanc/Semillon	–	–	–	–	–	–	–	–	–	25	25	23	27	–
REDS														
French:														
Bordeaux	24	25	24	26	29	22	26	25	23	25	24	27	24	–
Burgundy	23	–	21	24	27	–	26	28	25	22	28	22	20	24
Rhône	25	19	27	29	29	24	25	23	24	28	27	26	25	–
Beaujolais	–	–	–	–	–	–	–	–	22	21	24	25	18	20
California (Napa, Sonoma, Mendocino):														
Cab./Merlot	26	26	–	21	28	29	27	25	28	23	26	23	26	–
Pinot Noir	–	–	–	–	–	26	23	23	25	24	26	25	27	–
Zinfandel	–	–	–	–	25	22	23	21	22	24	–	25	–	
Italian:														
Tuscany	26	–	24	–	26	22	25	20	29	24	28	26	25	–
Piedmont	26	–	26	28	29	–	23	27	27	25	25	26	23	–

20,000+ restaurants. One location.

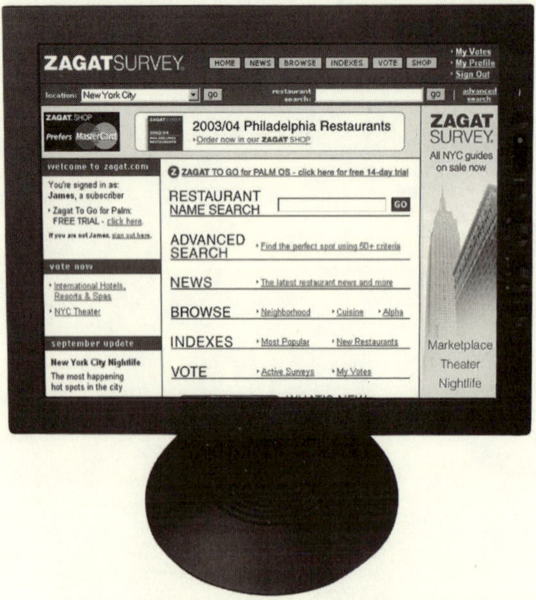

zagat.com

As a zagat.com subscriber you'll:

- Receive the ZagatWire newsletter with the latest restaurant industry news.

- Keep up on restaurant openings and closings.

- Enjoy full access to over 20,000 restaurant ratings and reviews for 70 major cities worldwide.

- Use our Advanced Search Tools to find the perfect spot every time.

- Enjoy savings of up to 25% at our online Shop.

Subscribe at www.zagat.com